YET SAINTS THEIR WATCH ARE KEEPING

The Church's one foundation
Is Jesus Christ her Lord;
She is his new creation
By water and the word.
From heav'n he came and sought her
To be his holy bride;
With his own blood he bought,
And her life he died.

Tho' with a scornful wonder
Men see her sore opprest,
By schisms rent asunder,
By heresies distressed,
Yet saints their watch are keeping,
Their cry goes up, "How long?"
And soon the night of weeping
Shall be the morn of song.

—Samuel John Stone, hymn

Yet Saints Their Watch Are Keeping

FUNDAMENTALISTS, MODERNISTS, AND THE DEVELOPMENT OF EVANGELICAL ECCLESIOLOGY, 1887–1937

J. Michael Utzinger

MERCER UNIVERSITY PRESS
MACON, GEORGIA

ISBN 978-0-86554-902-9
MUP/H665

First Edition.

Library of Congress Cataloging-in-Publication Data

Utzinger, J. Michael.
Yet saints their watch are keeping : fundamentalists, modernists,
and the development of evangelical ecclesiology, 1887/1937 / J.
Michael Utzinger. --
1st ed.
Stinger. cm.
Includes bibliographical references and index.
ISBN-13: 978-0-86554-902-9 (hardback : Stinger. paper)
ISBN-10: 0-86554-902-8 (hardback : Stinger. paper)
1. Evangelicalism—United States—History.
2. Evangelicalism—United States—Case studies. 3. Modernist-
fundamentalist controversy. 4. United
States—Church history. I. Title.
BR1642.U5U89 2006
262.00973—d22
2006022103

For Joy

O God, we pray for thy church, which is set to-day amid the perplexities of a changing order, and face to face with a great new task. We remember with love the nurture she gave to our spiritual life in its infancy, the tasks she set for our growing strength, the influence of devoted hearts she gathers, the steadfast power of good she has exerted. When we compare her with all other human institutions, we rejoice, for there is none like her. But when we judge her by the mind of her Master, we bow in pity and in contrition. Oh, baptize her afresh in the life-giving spirit of Jesus! Grant her a new birth, though it be with the travail of repentance and humiliation. Bestow upon her a more imperious responsiveness to duty, a swifter compassion with suffering, and an utter loyalty to the will of God. Put on her lips the ancient gospel of her Lord. Help her to proclaim boldly the coming of the Kingdom of God and the doom of all who resist it. Fill her with the prophets' scorn for tyranny, and with a Christ-like tenderness for the heavy-laden and down-trodden. Give her faith to espouse the cause of the people, and their hands that grope after freedom and light to recognize the bleeding hands of Christ. Bid her cease from seeking her own life, lest she lose it. Make her valiant to give up her life to humanity that, like her crucified Lord, she may mount by the path of the cross to a higher glory.

"Prayer for the Church"
—Walter Rauschenbusch
For God and the People, Prayers for the Social Awakening (1909)

CONTENTS

ACKNOWLEDGMENTS

This manuscript would not have been possible but for the support and input of many different friends, colleagues, and organizations. Heather A. Warren supported my project from the beginning. Her patience, kindness, and insight certainly made this a better book than might otherwise have been. This manuscript, from its inception to now, has also benefited from the thoughtful comments, advice, and support of James D. Hunter, Gerald P. Fogarty, William M. Wilson, Carlos M. N. Eire, Daniel Westberg, Andrew E. Tickle, Pamela D. H. Cochran, Joel A. Carpenter, Darryl Hart, Robert Benne, and members of the Southeastern Colloquium of American Religious Studies. This is not to suggest that they agree with my conclusions, only that my work is better for their input. Hampden-Sydney students who took my Christian Apocalypticism class in the spring of 2003 read and discussed large portions of chapter 5. Their candid questions made that chapter stronger and clearer than it would otherwise have been.

All thoughtful academicians understand that librarians and archivists "rule the world" by helping students and scholars, often with little thanks. I wish to thank Carol Ann Harris of the Conwellana-Templana collection of Temple University, Rita Erskine who helped me with the Lutzweiler collection of fundamentalist and evangelical magazines at the University of Notre Dame, Bob Shuster at the Billy Graham Center archives at Wheaton College, and William C. Kostlevy, Du Plessis Center archivist at Fuller Seminary, who at the time served in the B. L. Fisher Library at Asbury Theological Seminary. I also used select documents in the special collections at the Cincinnati Bible College and Seminary, the Presbyterian Historical Society (Philadelphia), Dallas Theological Seminary, the New York Public Library, Lynchburg College, Union Theological Seminary (Richmond), and the Wisconsin Historical Society at the University of Wisconsin in Madison.

I am pleased to single out Gerry Randall at the Eggleston Library of Hampden-Sydney College. She always seemed able to pull a rabbit out of her ILL hat, while I had the honor of being the highest volume user of interlibrary loan on campus for several years in a row. Thank you!

This manuscript was also financially supported by three summer research grants awarded by the Hampden-Sydney Dean of Faculty's office and the Committee on Professional Development in 2001, 2003, and 2004. Hampden-Sydney College also graciously awarded me a subvention for publication.

Several of my colleagues at Hampden-Sydney deserve special mention. Jim Arieti took time to teach me how to create an index. Saranna Thornton helped me negotiate the maze of institutional support. Richard McClintock computerized my diagrams in chapters 1, 7, 8, and 9. Jerry Carney provided unqualified support as my department chair, mentor, and friend. Bob Hall not only read several chapters of the book but engaged me in lively and useful discussion. John David Ramsey also read and commented on several portions of the manuscript and rightfully encouraged me to embrace my "inner theologian."

I also appreciate the editorial staff at Mercer University Press. Marc Jolley and Marsha Luttrell showed much patience and kindness. Kevin Manus always had the answers for the questions I asked.

Finally, I am thankful for the support of family and friends. John and Jill Dehne, Daniel and Sandrine Utzinger, and Jon and Diane Davis provided room, board, and good company on various research trips. My parents, John and Rita Utzinger, gave me constant support on all levels. Indeed my father read most of what I wrote with keen interest, insight, and criticism. My father-in-law, David N. Boettcher, read the entire manuscript with an editor's eye and a theologian's heart. But most of all I am grateful to the women in my life: Claire, Eve, and Joy. Claire and Eve showed more patience than young girls ought to have; perhaps one day they will find this book was worthy of their time and mine. Finally, I dedicate this book to Joy, my dearest love: I am profoundly moved by your patience, intelligence, advice, and sense of humor.

In luce tua videmus lucem.

—JMU

PREFACE

During the summer of 1997, I had breakfast with Nicholas Wolterstorff at a seminar sponsored by the Pew Younger Scholars Program and Intervarsity Christian Fellowship at the University of Notre Dame. He asked me what my dissertation topic was, to which I replied "evangelical ecclesiology." Wolterstorff looked puzzled and then wryly asked, "Evangelical ecclesiology? Is there such a thing?" This exchange represents well the way modern evangelicals have recently approached the doctrine of the church. In 2002 Regent College in Vancouver hosted a conference, the published papers of which were subsequently titled *Evangelical Ecclesiology: Illusion or Reality?*[1] Although the subtitle of the volume of the conference proceedings reiterates Wolterstorff's initial reaction, the fact that this conference occurred (followed by another at Wheaton College in 2004) suggests a growing interest by many evangelicals to explore and articulate theologically their vision of the church's identity and mission in the world.[2]

Robert E. Webber, in his recent volume on the proclivities of post-boomer evangelicals, devoted two chapters to ecclesiology.[3] He observed that these younger evangelicals are drawn to a vision of the church that is incarnational and, therefore, "visible." A key component of this engagement with and attraction to the visible church is their attempt to reconnect with the history of their churches and thereby the true church.[4] Indeed, these younger evangelicals have a cadre of historians, notably Timothy Smith, Donald Dayton, George Marsden, Mark Noll, and Grant Wacker, who concretely placed their forebears in time and space. Such historical studies not only satisfied their craving to know their own history (in an American

---

[1] John G. Stackhouse, Jr., *Evangelical Ecclesiology: Reality or Illusion?* (Grand Rapids: Baker Academic, 2003).

[2] The 13th Annual Wheaton Theology Conference, "The Community of the Word: Toward an Evangelical Ecclesiology," took place at Wheaton College from 15–17 April 2004.

[3] Robert E. Webber, *The Younger Evangelicals: Facing the Challenges of the New World* (Grand Rapids: Baker Books, 2002) 107–123, 131–46.

[4] Ibid., 71–82.

culture obsessed with hyphenated monikers of identity), but also helped question the assumption that the church was simply a spiritual entity of believers. The origin of my study is informed by this ethos of younger evangelicals drawn to understand the church as part of what Roman Catholic theologian Edward Schillebeeckx called "the human story of God."[5] The ideas explored in this book are driven by the theological conviction that evangelicals, liberal and conservative, insofar as they are Christian, do and must have an ecclesiology. While I am willing to admit with John G. Stackhouse, Jr. that often evangelicals have implied a church-idea more than they have articulated one, limited reflection hardly suggests that their ecclesiology is illusory.[6] The floor on which we walk still holds us up whether we notice it or not.

What follows, therefore, is an investigation of historical theology. I primarily consider the development of ecclesiology within the Northern evangelical Protestant establishment in the United States before and during the time of the so-called fundamentalist-modernist controversies during the 1920s and 1930s.[7] I have chosen this period because American evangelicals today perceive this time as a turning point in their relationship with their denominations and culture. Many modern conservative evangelicals understand themselves to be the heirs of the fundamentalists during this period. Others see themselves the heirs of more liberal or moderate evangelicals and have thrived in the more open atmosphere of the Protestant "mainline." Some abandoned distinctly evangelical churches and united with the very denominations their spiritual forebears believed infected by

---

[5] Edward Schillebeeckx, *Church: The Human Story of God* (New York: Crossroad Publishing Company, 1993).

[6] Stackhouse, *Evangelical Ecclesiology*, 9.

[7] My use of the term "establishment" follows William R. Hutchison, who suggested that it was an intra-Protestant entity made up of a group of denominations (including the Protestant Episcopal Church, Congregationalists, Northern Baptists, the Methodist Episcopal Church, the Disciples of Christ, and the Presbyterian Church in the U.S.A.) and a network of leaders within the wider association of American Protestantism. See "Protestantism as Establishment," in *Between the Times: The Travail of the Protestant Establishment in America, 1900–1960*, ed. William R. Hutchison (New York: Cambridge University Press, 1989) 3–18. This term is similarly used in Robert T. Handy, *Undermined Establishment: Church-State Relations in America, 1880–1920* (Princeton: Princeton University Press, 1991) 7–29; Sydney Ahlstrom, *A Religious History of the American People* (New Haven: Yale University Press, 1972) 842–48; and Martin E. Marty, *Modern American Religion Volume 2: The Noise of Conflict, 1919–1941* (Chicago: University of Chicago Press, 1991) 9–14.

modernism. Many raised in the "liberal mainline" have found solace and stability among conservatives. All of these evangelicals, whether liberal or conservative, have today experienced in their denominations debates and struggles over hot-button issues that dominate American headlines: abortion, stem-cell research, the "war on terror," the role of women, homosexuality, and the like. Within denominations these debates have caused evangelicals to raise questions about how one can be the Church of Christ in American culture today. Can believers in a denomination be yoked with those with whom they theologically or socially disagree? Can one remain evangelical if the ethos of the movement seems so narrow, conservative, and closed to the movement of the Holy Spirit? Have "mainline" denominations forsaken the faith once delivered? How can one witness to the gospel of Christ in such a manner that it influences culture in a positive way?

While it is not my intent to answer these present questions, I wish to point out that the time of the fundamentalist-modernist controversies in the United States shows that such ecclesiological questions are not new. Although the historical circumstances were different, evangelicals worried about how to be the church concretely within the cultural milieu in which they lived. Because the basic ecclesiological questions of past evangelicals were similar, I wish to suggest that an exploration into this subject will provide insight into the nature of evangelicalism generally. Specifically, evangelicals, liberal and conservative, can be characterized by a denominational ambivalence. This ambivalence lends itself not only to participation in trans-denominational religious movements, like fundamentalism and modernism, but also an attraction to denominational organizations and structures. In other words, evangelicals tenaciously cling to their denominational affiliations, while they have no compunction to work outside of them. Bruce Hindmarsh has called this the "oxymoron" of evangelical ecclesiology: "that while celebrating the spiritual union of all the truly regenerate, the movement itself was dogged by separatism."[8] Evangelicals, like other American Christians, practically maintain the scandal of their divisions in concrete denominational institutions; nonetheless, they recognize that those who compose the church transcend denominational affiliation. Further, this ecclesiological ambivalence among

---

[8] Bruce Hindmarsh, "Is Evangelical Ecclesiology an Oxymoron? A Historical Perspective," in Stackhouse, *Evangelical Ecclesiology*, 34–36.

evangelicals lends itself to change, disturbance, and revitalization within their home denominations.

An investigation into the development of their ecclesiology will also add texture to the current historiography of evangelicals during this period. The given historical narrative suggests that the disputes between fundamentalists and modernists fragmented Northern evangelical denominations. Fundamentalists, following a sectarian and separatist impulse, left their denominational affiliations, allowing modernists to shape the mainline denominations unimpeded.[9] Another closely related narrative suggests that fundamentalists lost public respectability after the Scopes trial in 1925; hence, they withdrew from the public sphere to build their own institutions apart from denominational affiliations.[10] In both cases the controversy symbolized the decline of Protestantism and denominationalism in America.

Much in these stories is correct. Indeed, many fundamentalists began to create educational and missionary organizations to compete with what they perceived to be modernist-controlled denominational machinery. Modernists did typically maintain their denominational affiliations and continue to influence the shape of mainline denominations. Nonetheless, this picture does not acknowledge that very few fundamentalist leaders and churches actually left their denominational affiliations. The given story also ignores the fact that modernist and liberal evangelicals often entertained separation from their denominational homes. In one instance, Presbyterian liberals not fundamentalists threatened schism. By looking into the ecclesiological change of Northern evangelical denominations I intend to develop and add clarity to the narrative of the fundamentalist-modernist controversies of the 1920s and 1930s. To this end, my study will look at the effects of both fundamentalism and modernism on the developing ecclesiologies of their respective denominations, particularly among Northern Presbyterians, Northern Baptists, and the Disciples of Christ. By

---

[9] Marty, *Modern American Religion Volume 2*; Ferenc Morton Szasz, *The Divided Mind of Protestant America, 1880–1930* (University: University of Alabama Press, 1982).

[10] George M. Marsden, *Fundamentalism and American Culture: The Shaping of Twentieth-Century Evangelicalism, 1870–1925* (New York: Oxford University Press, 1980); William R. Hutchison, *The Modernist Impulse in American Protestantism* (Cambridge: Harvard University Press, 1976; reprint, Durham NC: Duke University Press, 1992).

xiv

telling the stories of these two movements together, one sees the remarkable persistence of denominational institutions in the face of serious conflict rather than a portent of Protestant decline. In the end, evangelicals valued their denominational institutions and believed they were worth saving through compromise.

Because this is an investigation into the developing ecclesiologies of these communions, I have necessarily focused more time on the way evangelicals have related to particular denominational institutions. Therefore, I did not imagine this to be a comprehensive study of all aspects of fundamentalism or modernism. Some parts of this story are familiar, but I have added historical characters and incidences that have not been told in other histories. Some dramatic stories, like the Scopes trial, are tangential to this study and, by and large, are ignored. It is my hope that this analysis might illuminate that evangelicals, both liberal and conservative, have revitalized their denominations as much as they have divided them, valued them as much as criticized them, compromised for the sake of Christ's gospel as much as contended for the faith once delivered.

—JMU
Hampden-Sydney, Virginia
Feast Day of St. James, the Apostle 2005

CHAPTER 1

Introduction
Toward a Historical Ecclesiology

Ecclesiology is not simply a thing observed but a method of observation. It is a branch of theology that attempts to understand and articulate the identity and mission of the church. Because the church as a community exists in time and space, it can be observed in the past. Theologian Joseph Komonchak has argued that the object of ecclesiology is "the whole set (or sets) of experiences, understandings, symbols, words, judgments, statements, decisions, actions, relations, and institutions which distinguish the group of people called 'the Church.'"[1] I believe this definition can be simplified into the cognitive (understandings, symbols, words, judgments, and statements) and behavioral (experiences, decisions, actions, relations, and institutions) dimensions of a Christian community. This does not mean that everything is ecclesiology. Rather, those cognitive and behavioral dimensions of the church that *function* to create a Christian community's identity and mission constitute that group's embodied and lived ecclesiology.

Komanchak's definition moves away from what Roger Haight has labeled an "ecclesiology from above." An ecclesiology from above attempts to define the essential nature of the church. This attempt, Haight argues, is typically ahistorical and christocentric, focuses upon a specific community of faith as its object and principle of interpretation, and has its foundation in the authority structure of a particular community of faith.[2] Many factors

---

[1] Joseph A. Komonchak, "Ecclesiology and Social Theory: a Methodological Essay," *Thomist* 45/2 (April 1981): 274.

[2] Roger Haight, *Historical Ecclesiology*, vol. 1 of *Christian Community in History* (New York: Continuum Press, 2004) 18–23.

make such a model of ecclesiology less useful to understand evangelicalism in the late nineteenth and early twentieth centuries. First, this study looks at the effect of two trans-denominational movements on several Northern evangelical denominations in the United States; therefore, it does not focus on particular communities of faith. Furthermore, the ecclesiology within particular communions was disputed by individuals from within denominational boundaries. An ecclesiology from above, insofar as it attempts to identify a normative vision of the church, will lend itself to a theological reductionism that attempts to assert who was in fact the true church. It will miss or ignore the fact that contending parties during this period attempted to influence and change that vision of the church. These were, in fact, communions in contention.

The alternative to an ecclesiology from above is what Haight calls an "ecclesiology from below," or historical ecclesiology. "The primary object of ecclesiology," he argues, "is the historical organization [of the church] that has a historical life."[3] Ecclesiology from below takes seriously the modern conditions of pluralism and historical consciousness that not only exists now but shaped the worldview of evangelicals in the late nineteenth and early twentieth centuries as well. In other words, an ecclesiology from below does not assume that particular Christian communions have immutable characters that define who is inside or outside the group. In this sense, I assume that what the church is and how it manifests its mission can be contested. With more or less success, individuals, groups, or movements contend with one another within their religious communions to faithfully shape the identity and mission of the church as they understand it. Because the church is a social reality that exists in history, the historical theologian must admit that the ecclesiology of evangelicals can and often does change as new contexts and circumstances arise in history. An ecclesiology from below also suggests that even if a Christian community did not make specific declarations or have a developed doctrinal tradition concerning the true church, the historian can observe the "implicit ecclesiology" of that group by gaining an understanding of what the members of a particular community think and do, and how what they think and do makes them the true church.[4]

More important for this discussion, Komanchak and Haight point to the notion that ecclesiology informs a church about the way it relates its

---

[3] Ibid., 4.
[4] Komonchak, "Ecclesiology and Social Theory," 274.

own identity to that of other social realities. In other words, ecclesiology is apologetic in nature; it defends and interprets the church's identity and message. Similarly, theologian James Gustafson described the church as a community in which "the world is interpreted in the light of that which binds Christians together," while "the Church influences the world by the interpretation of its message."[5] According to Gustafson, theologians, teachers, ministers, preachers, and evangelists act as brokers between the church and the wider culture. This also means that studying these types of figures is crucial for determining the ecclesiology of any historical period. Ecclesiology, therefore, is an interpretive enterprise and a negotiation between Christian communities and other social realities. In this sense, one should expect that ecclesiological discourse, whether expressed theologically or socially, not only indicates the existence of a relatively cohesive interpretive community but defends one. The church, however, is also attempting to interpret God's will in current circumstances; therefore, ecclesiology from below will typically be pneumatological rather than christological. In other words, discerning the voice of the Holy Spirit, who reveals God's will to the church since Christ's ascension, will be a primary focus of the church in the modern day. Also, the purpose of the church is relative to one's understanding of the consummation of the divine plan on earth (or heaven), or eschatology. For these reasons, I look carefully at the sources of evangelical pneumatology and eschatology and their influence on the development of evangelical ecclesiology in the late nineteenth and early twentieth centuries.

Finally, there exists a symbiotic relationship between the ecclesiology expressed by a community and that group's encounter with other social realities. In other words, the ecclesiology of a group will *develop* as the church interacts with new social realities or new versions of them. This leads the historical theologian to consider what facilitates ecclesiological change. Returning to our working definition, any person or group of persons that has the ability to mobilize a church's resources can influence the way a Christian community thinks and acts—its cognitive and behavioral dimensions. The historical theologian tracing ecclesiological development, therefore, examines those persons or groups that intend to change a group's ecclesiology.

---

[5] James M. Gustafson, *Treasure in Earthen Vessels: The Church as a Human Community* (New York: Harper & Row Publishers, 1961) 56.

First, Christian communities use the contents of divine revelation as a means by which to distinguish themselves theologically and socially as the people of God. Therefore, Christians themselves have naturally claimed that God has been (and continues to be) the primary means by which ecclesiology develops. For example, the earliest Christian communities claimed that God uniquely revealed himself in the person of Jesus of Nazareth; therefore, early Christian communities claimed on the basis of this divine revelation that Jesus was the Messiah (Christ) and the risen Lord. On one level, these proclamations of the church were propositional in character: they made historical claims about God in the person of Jesus. On another level, however, these very dogmas functionally served the community by distinguishing insiders (believers) from outsiders (non-believers); as Wayne Meeks has observed, these dogmatic statements helped create social boundaries and a unique identity.[6] Revelation and dogma, therefore, can function as a means of forming what Komonchak called a "common consciousness" among the members of a church.[7] However, in the modern age, Christians understand that interpreting the will of the Holy Spirit is crucial for comprehending the modern mission of the church. One of the most obvious differences between different stripes of evangelicals (whether modernist, fundamentalist, Pentecostal, reformed, or holiness) is their interpretation of the role of the Holy Spirit in the church today and how the Spirit reveals the will of God in the present. Therefore, pneumatology provides an important window into ecclesiological development.

A second factor in ecclesiological change is the power exercised by a person or group with ecclesiastical authority. Max Weber suggested that a

---

[6] Wayne A. Meeks, *The First Urban Christians: The Social World of the Apostle Paul* (New Haven: Yale University Press, 1983) 84. The very word *ekklesia*, translated from Greek as "church," comes from the verb "to call out" and intimates a differentiation between those inside the Christian community and everyone else. As George Lindbeck has suggested, dogma always (though not exclusively) has a functional character as a means by which a church community creates it own social reality and perceives social realities outside of itself. Lindbeck compared a religion to a cultural-linguistic system. A religion's "doctrines, cosmic stories, or myths, and ethical directives are integrally related to the rituals it practices, the sentiments or experiences it evokes, the actions it recommends, and the institutional forms it develops." See *The Nature of Doctrine: Religion and Theology in a Postliberal Age* (Philadelphia: Westminster Press, 1984) 33.

[7] Komonchak, "Ecclesiology and Social Theory," 274.

social relationship is oriented around legitimate authority if its conduct "enjoys the prestige of being exemplary or binding." [8] He went on to explain that convention and law guarantee the legitimacy of an authority, while tradition, faith, or law serves to validate (or invalidate) it.[9] In the case of evangelicals in this study, the legitimacy of denominational (i.e., constitutional) authority is the very issue under contention. Different parties argued about whether they provided the most authentic interpretation of the denominational structures that defined the group and its mission. Such interpretive statements would be considered valid, according to Weber's theory, insofar as denominational constituents believed in the absolute value of the interpretation on the basis of tradition, faith, reason, or accepted legality. However, evangelicals in Northern denominations in the late nineteenth and twentieth centuries enjoyed no such consensus. Therefore, the anatomy of their debates must be carefully explored.

Finally, religious movements constitute a key means of ecclesiological development for this study. Sociologist William S. Bainbridge has defined a religious movement as "a relatively organized attempt by a number a people to cause or prevent change in a religious organization or in religious aspects of life."[10] In the early twentieth century, fundamentalism and modernism existed as trans-denominational movements within a broader evangelical Protestantism attempting to affect ecclesiological change within their respective religious communities. Clustering around particular intellectual currents of the time, these movements sought to help their denominations change in the face of a perceived cultural crisis. These movements were not discreet groups but rather they centered on or clustered around particular theological presuppositions, including ecclesiology. These movements gained theological sustenance outside the circumscribed boundaries of denominational affiliation, while attempting to shape the mission and identity of their denominations to their ecclesiological vision.

---

[8] Max Weber, *Basic Concepts in Sociology*, trans. H. P. Secher (London: Peter Owen, 1962) 72.

[9] Ibid., 75–83.

[10] William Sims Bainbridge, *The Sociology of Religious Movements* (New York: Routledge, 1997) 3.

The Shape of the Disputes

Although the definitions of fundamentalism, modernism, and evangelicalism have been exhaustively debated, Roger E. Olson provides a useful device for describing the nature of these trans-denominational movements: bounded sets versus centered sets.[11] On the one hand, the denominations this study considers are examples of what Olson describes as "bounded sets." In other words, there is rarely little ambiguity about whether one is part of a particular denomination. Membership is determined on a constitutional level. Further, one is not "sort of" a member. If contested, membership can be determined "legally" by interpreting the constitution of the denomination through official channels. Although interpretation allows for change in denominational boundaries, ultimately one is granted the privileges of membership or not. On the other hand, movements like evangelicalism, fundamentalism, and modernism are better described as "centered sets," which have "a clear and definite center of gravity but no unambiguous boundaries."[12] William Hutchison, for example, argued that modernism surrounded "a cluster of beliefs" including "adaptation, cultural immanentism, and a religious-based progressivism."[13] An individual, organization, or group can, therefore, be more or less "modernist" depending upon the relative proximity of his or its beliefs to the core beliefs of modernism. Likewise, fundamentalism is a cluster of beliefs centered on personal immanentism (holiness of life), scriptural authority, individual conversion, and emphasis on evangelism. Not surprisingly, therefore, the generally use of the terms "fundamentalism" and "modernism" during the early twentieth century was neither neat nor precise. My use of these terms is also loose, reflecting the centered set character of the movements rather than circumscribed definitions. Furthermore, these movements should not be understood as polar opposites either. Both groups shared certain American evangelical presuppositions: the importance of religious experience, opposition to state-supported church institutions (including the

---

[11] Roger E. Olson, "Free Church Ecclesiology and Evangelical Spirituality: A Unique Compatibility," in John G. Stackhouse, Jr., *Evangelical Ecclesiology: Reality or Illusion?* (Grand Rapids: Baker Academic, 2003) 163. Olson credits Paul G. Hiebert for these categories. See "Conversion, Culture, and Categories," *Gospel in Context* 1/4 (October 1978): 24–29.

[12] Ibid.

[13] Hutchison, *Modernist Impulse* (Cambridge: Harvard University Press, 1976; reprint, Durham NC: Duke University Press, 1992) 2.

preservation of individual religious liberty of conscience), the intent to sustain democratic institutions through a religious engagement with American culture, and a denominational ambivalence caused, in part, by a trans-denominational character.

The fundamentalist-modernist controversies that took place in several denominations require that these two set models be overlapped. The centered set movements of fundamentalism and modernism attempted to shape the way a particular denomination understood its identity and mission. However, by attempting to change their churches' mission, they questioned the boundaries of their denominations. It could no longer be taken for granted what a good Presbyterian, Baptist, or Disciple was, and this caused an ecclesiological crisis within these denominations. The disputes were attempts to resolve this denominational disequilibrium. In the Northern Baptist Convention, the Presbyterian Church in the U.S.A., and the Disciples of Christ, the resolution eventually came by compromise.

The shape of the ecclesiological disputes, however, can not be simply described in linear terms, such as fundamentalism versus modernism (see model 1.1). Many recent scholars have convincingly argued against such "bipolar" models of Protestantism.[14] However, while they claimed to find the voice of moderate or middle majority, they have not so much replaced a linear, bipolar model of Protestantism as suggested that observers look at a different place on the line. Of greater concern, they often imply that the centrists represent "real" evangelicalism. This study of ecclesiology suggests another model to understand the denominational controversies during the 1920s and 1930s (see model 1.2). In this model competing groups, or parties, attempt to define the denominational identity and mission of the organization. However, as the model suggests, fundamentalism and modernism are not opposites. The controversies were primarily an ecclesiological dispute within denominational boundaries rather than the result of two sides of a culture war. In other words, theologically liberal and conservative evangelicals both saw the same cultural crisis that they believed must be addressed. Social challenges, such as non-Protestant immigration, urbanization, and dwindling church attendance, threatened their sense of vocation and mission within American culture. In the late nineteenth

---

[14] David Edwin Harrell, "Bipolar Protestantism: The Straight and Narrow Ways," in *Re-forming the Center: American Protestantism, 1900 to the Present*, ed. Douglas Jacobsen and William Vance Trollinger (Grand Rapids: William B. Eerdmans Publishing Company, 1998) 15–30.

century Northern, urban evangelicals among the Episcopalians, Congregationalists, Baptists, Methodists, Disciples, and Presbyterians sought to regain their influence within the wider culture by creating more effective strategies of engagement, in essence redefining their ideas of church mission. In this Northern "establishment," competing visions of church mission and identity were able to exist side by side under the broad canopies of denominational structures.

Model 1.1

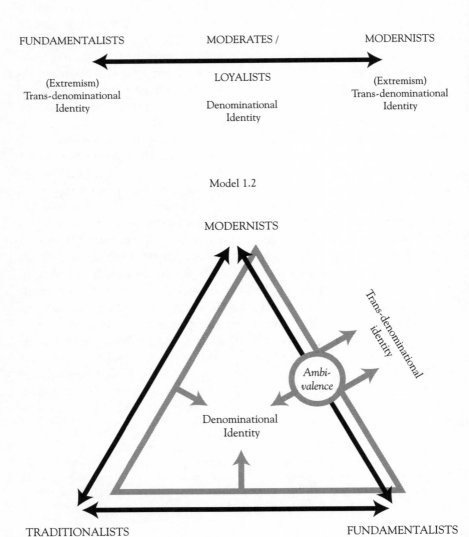

FUNDAMENTALISTS   MODERATES /   MODERNISTS

(Extremism)   LOYALISTS   (Extremism)
Trans-denominational   Trans-denominational
Identity   Denominational   Identity
                                  Identity

Model 1.2

MODERNISTS

Trans-denominational
identity

Ambi-
valence

Denominational
Identity

TRADITIONALISTS   FUNDAMENTALISTS

A generation later, fundamentalism and modernism developed within denominational tents as movements that coalesced around different views of the church. Evangelicals' optimistic belief following the First World War that they would rebuild the world in the image of Christ was crushed by the collapse of the Interchurch World Movement and an economic depression. With strained denominational resources, conflict emerged within establishment churches caused by competing movements' attempts to shape the church. Further, the denominations of the Protestant establishment had gradually centralized and consolidated their denominational machinery, allowing the potential disenfranchisement of many groups who represented different ecclesiological visions. Because ecclesiology becomes embodied in concrete structures that need resources for their implementation, the centralized denominational structures coupled with constrained resources became a recipe for contention (particularly among the Baptists, Presbyterians, and Disciples). Those who believed that they had been pushed outside of the new denominational power structures revolted, and the resulting controversy shook the foundations of their church communities. Fundamentalists and modernists represented distinct but related ecclesial visions, which had coexisted in the past but were forced to compete with one another in newly constructed denominations that seemed to accommodate only one ecclesiological vision.

This study will be divided into two major parts. The first looks at the sources of ecclesiological change within the Northern evangelical Protestant establishment. In chapter two, I will look at the growing sense of cultural crisis articulated by evangelical leaders in the late nineteenth century. Josiah Strong, in his best-selling book *Our Country* (1885), became the voice of the cultural crisis concerning members of the Protestant "establishment." Strong and other evangelical leaders acknowledged what can be called an ecclesiological .crisis among the establishment churches in the context of American democracy. These evangelicals, looking to Alexis de Tocqueville, believed that democracy had its limitations when not tempered by "true" religion. The "dilemma of democracy" created by growing religious pluralism caused them to rethink the role of their churches in American culture. The mobilization of the fundamentalist and modernist movements occurred within existing social networks and associations created by these strategists and their followers. As the leaders of evangelical Protestantism perceived that their influence among average citizen was waning, they seriously questioned how to regain their cultural ascendancy in order to carry out their cultural vocation as they understood it. Nonetheless, they optimistically looked forward to a "new era," a revitalized Christian America, if only this influence could be reasserted.

Next, I will examine how the crisis perceived by evangelical leaders led to different ecclesiological (vocational) strategies to obviate the "dilemma of democracy." In chapter three I will examine the two overlapping strategies of cultural engagement within the Protestant establishment: social Christianity and soul-saving revivalism. These versions of ecclesiological vocation purported by social Christian and soul-saving revivalism, because they implicitly questioned the authority of the old orthodoxy within the establishment, required theological justification. Chapters four and five then look at how these two different understandings of church vocation by evangelicals were intimately linked to their understanding of pneumatology and eschatology. The pneumatology (advocated especially by progressive orthodoxy and Keswick Holiness) and the eschatology (promoted by postmillennialism and dispensationalism) not only provided such a theological justification for evangelicals' vocational understandings of the church, but specifically influenced the way they began to understand who and what constituted the church's identity. The alignment of the advocates of revivalism and Keswick Holiness tended toward a more populist ecclesiology, while proponents of social Christianity and progressive orthodoxy tended to favor an institutionally centralized ecclesiology. The eschatological dimension created a denominational ambivalence that lent itself to participation in trans-denominational movements.

The second section examines the dynamics of ecclesiological change within three denominations that experienced major disturbances during the two decades following the First World War. In chapter six, I will explain how the different ecclesiological visions gave rise to new alignments within the Protestant establishment, namely fundamentalism and modernism. As the churches of the Protestant establishment began to consolidate their denominational machinery and limit their resources, the ability of these two ecclesiological visions to coexist was greatly strained. Their disputes, catalyzed by denominational centralization and the collapse of the Interchurch World Movement, resulted in controversies shaped by the particular ecclesiologies of their home denominations. Therefore, in chapters seven, eight, and nine, I will examine the unfolding conflict in the Northern Baptist Convention, the Presbyterian Church in the U.S.A., and the Disciples of Christ, respectively.

PART 1

1887–1920

The question then becomes this: Will the church enlarge her conceptions and activities to the wide measure of her mission and apply the principles of the Gospel to the entire life of each community? Here is the opportunity of the ages for her to gain a commanding influence over the lives of the multitude and fashion the unfolding civilization of the future.
—Josiah Strong, *The New Era* (1893)

Even the purest theological issue, however, will in the long run have cultural consequences...And, for the most part, it is inevitable that we should, when we defend our religion, be defending at the same time our culture, and vice versa: we are obeying the fundamental instinct to preserve our existence.
—T. S. Eliot, *Notes toward the Definition of Culture* (1948)

CHAPTER 2

The New Era:
American Evangelicals and the Dilemma of Democracy

As suggested by Joseph Komonchak and Robert Haight, any determination of evangelical ecclesiology must necessarily consider the cultural and historical context in which it exists and evolves. Evangelicals believed they had a specific mission to American culture but perceived that their denominations teetered on a precipice of failure. Josiah Strong represented the views of most Northern evangelical Protestants in the late nineteenth century. He became famous for writing the book *Our Country: Its Possible Future and Its Present Crisis*, which in 1885 became an American best-seller second only to Harriet Beecher Stowe's *Uncle Tom's Cabin* (1841). In *Our Country*, Strong asserted that American society faced eight great perils: immigration, Romanism, non-evangelical religion in the public schools, Mormonism, intemperance, socialism, wealth, and urbanization.[1] Nonetheless, he believed that diligent Anglo-Saxon Protestant influence could overcome these perils and lead the United States toward fulfilling her divine destiny, the institution of the kingdom of God on earth.[2] Eight years later Strong wrote, "We are entering a new era of which the twentieth century will be the beginning and for which the nineteenth century has been

---

[1] Josiah Strong, *Our Country: Its Possible Future and Its Present Crisis* (New York: The Baker & Taylor Co., 1891) viii–x.
[2] Ibid., 208–27.

a preparation."[3] Although his observation bubbled with optimism, he believed that evangelical Protestants stood at a crucial crossroads in history. He noted that great social challenges awaited the church and thought its response to them would determine the course of American society.

In Strong's book *The New Era or Coming Kingdom* (1893), the eight perils of *Our Country* collapsed into one great problem: the city, a topic that occupied him for the remainder of his life.[4] With the exception of the Latter Day Saints in Utah, all of the eight perils thrived in the cities of the Northern and Eastern United States during the late nineteenth century. The population of urban America more than tripled between 1880 and 1920 to around 50 million, making one in every two Americans a city dweller.[5] During this same period a massive wave of European immigrants flocked to American ports and cities, the majority of whom were poor and came from dominantly Roman Catholic nations (although Judaism and Eastern Orthodoxy had notable constituencies as well). The debate over religion in public schools continued to spark controversy, as Protestants primarily looked toward establishing "common," or state-run, school systems. Catholics had sought, since the Third Plenary Council of Baltimore (1884), to institute a parochial school in each territorial parish and objected to the use of their tax dollars to support an education system that seemed to equate the word "public" with "Protestant." The disparity of wealth between poor workers and wealthy business owners, exacerbated by an economic depression that began in 1893, also manifested itself most blatantly in the

[3] Josiah Strong, *The New Era or the Coming Kingdom* (New York: The Baker & Taylor Co., 1893) 1.

[4] Strong actually reckoned that there existed two great problems, the country and the city. However, the substance of his concern about the country consisted in the exodus of Americans from a rural to an urban setting. For example, he wrote: "Vast movements of population are of profound significance both in their cause and effect.... I refer to the tide of population which is setting out so strongly from country to city, and which is depleting one and congesting the other, to the detriment of both." Ibid., 164. Cf. Josiah Strong, *The Challenge of the City* (New York: The Young People's Missionary Movement of the United States and Canada, 1907) and Strong, *The New World Life* (New York: Doubleday, Page & Company, 1913) 228–84. See also Dorthea R. Muller, "Josiah Strong and the Social Gospel: A Christian's Response to the City," *Journal of Presbyterian History* 39 (Summer 1961): 150–75.

[5] United States Bureau of the Census, *Historical Statistics of the United States, Colonial Times to 1970* (Washington: U. S. Dept. of Commerce, 1975) 11.

cities, giving rise to a variety of labor unions, radical political parties, and, too often, violence.

Middle-class Americans in the late nineteenth century had a strong ambivalence toward the city. Strong noted that the city was superlative; it had the best of America and the worst. He admitted that exciting technology and convenience, heroic determination, and Christian virtue all existed in urban America. However, what made the city a problem for him and other Americans included its rapidly increasing population of foreign-born constituents, who lived isolated in an environment that encouraged moral bankruptcy, social radicalism, violence, government corruption, and irreligion.[6] Strong was not alone. Frederick Jackson Turner, in his celebrated essay presented to the American Historical Society in 1893, proclaimed that "the frontier has gone, and with it has closed the first period of American history."[7] Believing that the frontier had the most decisive influence on the American ethos, he believed the close of the frontier had serious implications for the future of the increasingly urban and industrial United States. In fact, Turner reflected two decades later that the social and economic changes of the nation had meant nothing less than the birth of a new nation.[8] "Pulp fiction" from the 1880s and 1890s also increasingly depicted the horrors of the city and how innocent men and women became the victims of its saloons, brothels, and organized crime syndicates.[9] During the same period, the public devoured sensationalized news coverage of urban unrest surrounding labor strikes, ethnic conflict, and mob violence in Chicago, New York, Boston, Philadelphia, Cincinnati, Milwaukee, Pittsburgh, and St. Louis.[10]

Along these same lines, authors of the naturalist literary movement in the United States saw the city as one of the places where they could uncover the brutal and dehumanizing aspects of American life. Stephen Crane's first novella, *Maggie: A Girl of the Streets* (1893), depicted the harsh, cruel, and violent life and death of a young woman growing up in a New York City

---

[6] Ibid., 179–202.

[7] Frederick Jackson Turner, "The Significance of the Frontier in American History," in *The Frontier in American History* (Tucson: University of Arizona Press, 1920, 1986) 38.

[8] Turner, "Social Forces in American History," in *Frontier*, 311. The essay was presented to the National Historical Association on 28 December 1910.

[9] Paul Boyer, *Urban Masses and Moral Order in America, 1820–1920* (Cambridge: Harvard University Press, 1978, 1997) 127–31.

[10] Ibid., 125–26.

tenement. Crane's story so shocked potential publishers that he eventually had to finance the book himself.[11] Theodore Dreiser's *Sister Carrie* (1900) presented the story of a young woman from a rural Wisconsin town who is seduced by the perils of urban Chicago. Although the heroine became an actress, she exchanged her innocence and purity for her success.[12] In both these stories religion played a negligible role for the characters dwelling in the city. Describing a rescue mission in *Maggie*, Crane wrote of the preacher, "While they got warm at the stove, he told his hearers just where he calculated they stood with the Lord. Many of the sinners were impatient over the pictured depths of their degradation. They were waiting for soup-tickets…. 'You are damned,' said the preacher. And the reader of sounds might have seen the reply go forth from the ragged people, 'Where's our soup?'"[13] The characters in *Maggie* went so far as to question the relevance of religion to the poor workers of the city. One nameless character at the mission, whom Crane surely saw as a representative New Yorker, asserted that upon meeting God "he would ask for a million dollars and a beer."[14] Crane left his readers wondering whether it was possible to reconcile what preachers and average city folk believed the urban masses needed most.

Despite the attempts of evangelical Protestants to tame urban America, Strong wrote that "the fact of a separation between the masses and the church has thus been generally assumed."[15] Many prominent religious figures of the day echoed Strong's concerns. The great urban revivalist Dwight L. Moody admitted that "the gulf between the church and the masses is growing deeper, wider, and darker every hour."[16] Popular preacher and social Christianity advocate Washington Gladden recalled in his autobiography that "the city, from the first day, was a thing stupendous and overpowering, a mighty monster, with portentous energies; the sense of its power to absorb human personalities and to shape human destinies was often vivid and painful."[17] The city concerned such evangelicals as Moody, Gladden, and Strong because they believed that it constituted a microcosm

---

[11] Stephen Crane, *Maggie: A Girl of the Streets and Other Short Fiction* (New York: Bantam Classics, 1986) xii–xiii.

[12] Theodore Dreiser, *Sister Carrie* (New York: Bantam Books, 1982).

[13] Crane, *Maggie*, 13.

[14] Ibid., 14.

[15] Strong, *New Era*, 203.

[16] Cited in Strong, *New Era*, 204.

[17] Washington Gladden, *Recollections* (Boston: Houghton Mifflin Company, 1909) 90.

of American civilization. To suggest that the evangelical Protestant churches would ultimately fail in the cities was tantamount to admitting they would not succeed in their mission to Christianize the nation and the world.[18] More important, as demographic changes pointed to the fact that the United States was fast becoming an urban and industrial nation, waning influence in the cities presented a gloomy specter of things to come for evangelical churches.

Strong did not offer a new critical study of churches and their relationship to American culture and its cities; rather, he presented, in popular form, what most evangelicals had already begun to suspect: the influence of their religion slowly seemed to be eroding. Worse, the churches did not seem to have a clear strategy to reestablish themselves as the standard-bearers of Christianity and American culture. Strong also represented an evangelical Protestantism that had not yet heard of fundamentalism or modernism. When he spoke of the church, he assumed a general unity of Northern (and, more rarely, Southern) evangelical Baptists, Methodists, Congregationalists, Presbyterians, Episcopalians, and Disciples. The "rope of sand" that unified these communities consisted neither of polity nor confession but a popular mission to influence and propel Americans toward their God-given destiny to preserve the gospel and preach it to all nations. He felt no need to define the church beyond traditional biblical metaphors depicting it as the body of Christ.[19] In the New Era, Strong quoted without intellectual dissonance thinkers such as premillennial revivalist Dwight L. Moody, postmillennial liberal theologian Lyman Abbott, and economist and social Christianity advocate Richard T. Ely. Strong's melding of many lines of tradition did not reflect an uncritical mind; rather, he represented the complex mosaic that was the evangelicalism of the late nineteenth century.

The church stood at the center of Strong's thinking between the extremes of the individual and society. Notably, his discussion of the church almost exclusively focused upon its mission and vocation rather than its identity. The ecclesiological questions Strong asked, typical of other evangelicals at this time, took for granted that the churches of the Protestant establishment constituted the true church in one fashion or another. His

---

[18] In 1907 Strong clearly articulated this line of thinking, writing that "the city is the microcosm of the new industrial world. To solve its problems for America is to solve them for mankind." See Challenge of the City, 85.

[19] Strong, New Era, 239.

concern, therefore, centered on the failure of evangelical churches to carry
out their true vocation among the masses. Commenting on Jesus'
summation of the Mosaic Law, love of God and love of neighbor, he
proclaimed that Christ constituted "the Saviour of *man* as well as *men*."[20]
According to Strong, Christians who carefully considered the teachings of
Jesus himself would draw the inescapable conclusion that the church had a
dual mission to transform the individual and society. The evangelical
churches, he noted, did a fine job teaching individuals that they should love
God because he first loved them having sent Jesus as the expiation of their
sins. Strong claimed, however, that these same churches had focused almost
exclusively upon the salvation of individuals to the detriment of the second
part of their mission. Having ignored this social side of its mission, the
church essentially allowed the bifurcation of American life into the sacred
and the secular.[21]

Strong believed that such a distinction between the sacred and the
secular allowed by the church was a remnant of a medieval, monastic
Manicheanism, which persisted within modern evangelical Protestantism.
Making a distinction between the sphere and the function of the church, he
argued that "it is as great a mistake to limit the sphere of the church as not
to limit its functions. The sphere of the church includes that of the state and
much more. It is as broad as the sphere of human consciousness, which is as
far-reaching as all human activity."[22] He also asserted that God's vocation
for the church not only included educating the individual to live morally but
functioning as the very conscience of society as a whole.[23] For this reason he
considered notions to exclude the church from any sphere of human activity
as "wrong and dangerous."[24]

This perceived cultural separation between the sacred and secular
invited grave concern among evangelical Protestants such as Strong. "With
a narrow conception of her mission," he wrote, the church "has sat with
folded hands while a thousand organizations have sprung up at her side to
do her proper work. No benevolent work or reform inspired by a Christian
spirit should have ever been forced to go outside the Christian church for

---

[20] Ibid., 113. Emphasis in the original.
[21] Ibid., 123–24.
[22] Ibid., 234.
[23] Ibid., 235. Cf. Samuel Zane Batten, "The Church as the Maker of
Conscience," *American Journal of Sociology* 7/5 (March 1902): 611–28.
[24] Strong, *New Era*, 234, 313.

organization."[25] Therefore, reclaiming the rightful role of the church in society included reappropriating areas the church itself relinquished. While never doubting the importance or goodness done by charitable organizations such as the Red Cross, the YMCA/YWCA, and the Women's Christian Temperance Union (WCTU), Strong suggested that the need for such extra-ecclesial organizations was a symptom of evangelical church communities' inability to adapt to the peculiar needs of the age. He asserted that "the skepticism which is most dangerous to Christianity to-day is not doubt as to age or authenticity or genuineness of its sacred books or dis-trust of timed-honored doctrines, but loss of faith in its vitality."[26] If only the church would fully accept the gospel and enlarge her mission to include the individual and society, he claimed, she would "gain a commanding influence over the lives of the multitude and fashion the unfolding civilization of the future."[27]

The Dilemma of Democracy

Despite their optimistic tone, evangelicals nonetheless sensed that they found themselves in a predicament in their relationship with American culture. The majority of them believed that their brand of religion best embodied the gospel of Christ and that these truths provided the moral bedrock upon which American democracy and individual liberty could best be maintained. The wish of evangelicals, therefore, to fashion the coming American society simultaneously hearkened back to the past and looked forward to the future. First, evangelicals supported the legal separation of church and state, which they believed protected religion from the corruption of government interference. Further, they believed American history confirmed that evangelical Protestantism in its diverse forms had maintained the republic from its inauguration through the most horrible of calamities, the Civil War. In other words, American history proved to them that their religion had provided (and would continue to provide), in the words of George Washington, "all the dispositions and habits which lead to political prosperity."[28] However, the American populace, which increasingly

---

[25] Ibid., 238.

[26] Ibid., 240.

[27] Ibid.

[28] George Washington, "Farewell Address," in *American Historical Masterpieces*, vol. 9 of *Modern Eloquence*, ed. Ashley H. Thorndike (New York: Modern Eloquence Corporation, 1928) 40. For an example of an evangelical making such a claim at the

appeared alienated from the influence of their churches, threatened, in their estimation, the very fabric of American democracy and, therefore, freedom of religion. Evangelicals feared that without freedom of religion their churches might be thwarted from carrying out their vocation to preach the gospel to all persons and nations.

Therefore, in the context of a legal separation of church and state, a dilemma arose for evangelicals: while they thought their influence was waning among average American citizens, they also believed the propagating of their brand of Christianity constituted a necessary element in the maintenance of American democracy. William Reed Huntington, a prominent New York City Episcopal priest and ecumenist, articulated well this dilemma of democracy evangelicals faced in their relationship with the wider American culture:

> The task set before the Christian Church in America is her familiar one of conquest; but open-eyed observers have to acknowledge that the conditions of the welfare are, in many respects, unparalleled. What we are witnessing is not the hopeful approach of a new religion to minds wholly unfamiliar with its message, but rather the painful endeavor of an old religion to maintain its hold upon a mixed multitude, already nominally under its sway, but so situated as to be peculiarly open to revolt. The suggestion that America may not continue permanently Christian is undoubtedly a painful one whether to make or to receive; but honest students of the signs of the times cannot with a clear conscience, refuse to take into account.[29]

Robert Handy noted that the combination of the ideals of voluntary religious association and the importance for Protestants to maintain their "cultural pre-eminence" for the sake of the republic required broad-based American support.[30] Evangelicals considered the masses or the "common man" to be more influential in purveying American culture than the intellectual elite. Indeed, one can imagine that Strong would have readily conceded the assertion made by historian Nathan Hatch that the driving

---

1887 Evangelical Alliance Conference, see James King, "The Christian Resources of Our Country," in *National Perils and Opportunities: The Discussion of the General Christian Conference held in Washington, D. C. December 7th, 8th, and 9th, 1887 under the Auspices and Direction of the Evangelical Alliance for the United States* (New York: The Baker & Taylor Co., 1887) 259–76.

[29] William Reed Huntington, *The Peace of the Church* (New York: Charles Scribner's Sons, 1893) xi.

[30] Robert T. Handy, *A Christian America: Protestant Hopes and Historical Realities*, 2d ed. (New York: Oxford University Press, 1984) 65.

force behind American Christianity has been its "democratic or populist orientation."[31]

Furthermore, evangelicals' perceived dilemma of democracy shows the importance that the preservation of a Christian America played in their ecclesiology. The possibility of losing the masses went to the core of American evangelical identity and even its existence. "If religion is to prove itself thoroughly adapted to human nature and destined to be final," argued Strong, "it must show itself equal to the great emergencies of the race, and able to meet the peculiar demands of every age."[32] The questions and concerns of evangelicals were not primarily the reconciliation of science and history with religion; rather, they surrounded the relationship of the evangelical churches' identity and mission in the face of a rapidly changing mission field.

In order to gain insight into how evangelicals understood the role of religion in American society, it is helpful to recall Alexis de Tocqueville, whose observations of American democracy were most often cited by their leaders at the end of the nineteenth century. With a worried eye the French aristocrat penned in his celebrated *Democracy in America* (1835–1840) that "the great problem of our time is the organization and establishment of democracies in Christian lands."[33] The French Revolution a fresh memory, he believed that republican institutions, democratic government, and liberty did not necessarily mean that truth, justice, and goodness would prevail in a society. Why did democracy in America work, when in France it degenerated into a reign of terror? Finding an answer to this question was imperative to de Tocqueville, who believed that the inevitable progress of history suggested that democracy would replace the governments of Europe.[34] In particular, the young Frenchman worried about the inherent potential of democracies to yield to the tyranny of the majority. "My greatest complaint" he wrote, "against democratic government as organized in the United States is not, as many Europeans make out, its weakness, but rather its irresistible strength. What I find most repulsive in America is not

[31] Nathan O. Hatch, *The Democratization of American Christianity* (New Haven: Yale University Press, 1989) 213.

[32] Strong, *New Era*, 240.

[33] Alexis de Tocqueville, *Democracy in America*, trans. George Lawrence (New York: Harper Perennial, 1969) 311.

[34] François Furet, *In the Workshop of History* (*L'Atelier de l'historie*) trans. Jonathan Mandelbaum (Chicago: University of Chicago Press, 1984) 171.

the extreme freedom reigning there but the shortage of guarantees against tyranny."[35] Practically speaking, de Tocqueville argued that there existed some social power that is superior to all others, and in a democracy this was the majority. He equally believed, however, that the freedom afforded by democratic governance would become a casualty in a society in which the majority's "power finds no obstacle that can restrain its course and give it time to moderate itself."[36]

It is in this context de Tocqueville understood that, for Americans, religion "should be considered as the first of their political institutions, for although it did not give them the taste for liberty, it singularly facilitates their use thereof."[37] Religion, more than anything else in American democratic government, restrained the social power of the majority and thereby preserved the individual liberties of citizens. "While the law allows the American people to do everything," observed the Frenchman, "there are things which religion prevents them from imagining and forbids them to dare."[38] De Tocqueville thought that the irreligious European counterexample stood as a stern warning for Americans: "Religion having lost its sway over men's souls, the clearest line of dividing good from ill has been obliterated; everything in the moral world seems doubtful and uncertain; kings and nations go forward at random, and none can say where are the natural limits of despotism and the bounds of license."[39] In fact, he surmised that without religion democracy would be undermined by the individualism, materialism, and social disorder it naturally spawned. He believed that ultimately citizens who had lost their moral stability "want the material order at least to be firm and stable, and as they cannot accept their ancient beliefs again, they hand themselves over to a master."[40] Liberty, therefore, is maintained by religion and threatened by license. "I am led to think," asserted de Tocqueville, "if he [a democratic citizen] has no faith he must obey, and if he is free he must believe."[41]

The majority of American evangelicals in the late nineteenth century took for granted classical interpretations of political liberalism, in particular

---

[35] de Tocqueville, *Democracy in America*, 252.
[36] Ibid.
[37] Ibid., 292.
[38] Ibid.
[39] Ibid., 312.
[40] Ibid., 444.
[41] Ibid.

de Tocqueville's reasoning that religion is necessary for the maintenance of democracy in the United States. As early as 1887, James King, an honorary corresponding secretary for the Evangelical Alliance, proclaimed (after extensively quoting de Tocqueville) that "almost everything worth possessing in our institutions was secured for us by our Christian ancestors. Let us hesitate before we surrender the fortresses that are the foundations and defense of our institutions."[42] Eight years later, the idea that religion preserved the republic had not died. Sounding much like de Tocqueville, the well-known Congregationalist preacher and editor of the *Christian Union* (later the *Outlook*), Lyman Abbott, wrote that "the first condition of self-government is the ability to recognize an invisible law, and subject one's self to its restraint...Jesus Christ not only prophesied democracy, but laid the foundations and furnished the inspiration essential for it."[43]

The proceedings of the 1887 conference of the Evangelical Alliance stand as an excellent bellwether for the Protestant establishment's opinion concerning this dilemma of democracy. For one thing, the participants in the conference reflected a broad evangelical constituency. Furthermore, the symposium's influence among them can be measured by the extensive national coverage it received in secular and religious newspapers as well as the numerous times evangelical leaders quoted the proceedings in their books, periodicals, sermons, and addresses.[44] The Alliance had existed in the United States since 1867 to promote worldwide trans-denominational cooperation and unity. Initially, this group had little influence because it did not have the involvement of ranking representatives of various Protestant denominations. However, by 1873 the group had convened its first national conference in New York City. Subsequent gatherings took place in Pittsburgh (1875), Detroit (1877), St. Louis (1879), Washington (1887), Boston (1889), and Chicago (1893). Between 1883 and 1886, the Alliance went through a process of reorganization that expanded its influence. The executive committee, rather than being run by interested clergy, became administered by active laity with business experience. Most important, the

---

[42] King, "Christian Resources," in *Perils and Opportunities*, 260.

[43] Lyman Abbott, *Christianity and Social Problems* (Boston: Houghton, Mifflin and Company, 1897) 55–56.

[44] Philip D. Jordan, *The Evangelical Alliance for the United States of America, 1847–1900: Ecumenism, Identity and the Religion of the Republic* (New York: The Edwin Mellen Press, 1982) 174–75.

Alliance gained an impressive facelift with the appointment of the now well-known Josiah Strong as its secretary general.[45]

By the time of the Washington conference in 1887, Alliance leadership had moved the focus of the group from earlier international ecumenism to concerns surrounding American social problems and Christian solutions to them. In characteristic graciousness, internationalists such as Philip Schaff yielded to the nationalist currents of a new generation of leadership led by William Dodge, Jr., James King, John Jay, and Josiah Strong.[46] Dodge used his extensive personal contacts to ensure that influential and respected members representing all the major American evangelical denominations attended the 1887 meeting.[47] Northern, urban constituents made up the majority of the participants, but Southern evangelicals attended, too. Among the representatives at the conference were eight Methodist bishops, four Episcopal bishops, two Moravian bishops, an African Methodist Episcopal bishop, and the moderators of the National Congregationalist Council and Southern Presbyterian Assembly. The conference, however, did not only include denominational leadership. Also present were two U.S. senators, a former state governor, a U.S. Army general, three editors of influential religious periodicals, and eleven college and university presidents. This is not to mention that President Grover Cleveland addressed the Alliance members at a White House reception.[48]

William Dodge, Jr., as president of the Evangelical Alliance, sounded the clarion call of the 1887 conference, announcing that "the American ideas of morality, frugal living, education, home life, and respect for law are changing rapidly, and it is the duty of the Christian Church to lead the new thought of the times, or certain disaster and punishment must come."[49] John Jay, a past Alliance president himself, immediately followed Dodge's opening address by soberly reminding the participants that "The future of the Christian civilization, which has come to us from our true-hearted and sturdy ancestors, on the preservation of which, in its purity and beauty, depend the character of our countrymen and the destiny of our country, rest

---

[45] Ibid., 152–53.

[46] Jordan, *Evangelical Alliance*, 152.

[47] Ibid., 153.

[48] Untitled transcription and list of names, in *Perils and Opportunities*, vii–ix, 341–42.

[49] William E. Dodge, "Opening Address," in *Perils and Opportunities*, 4.

upon the generation of to-day."[50] Further, the preponderance of papers delivered surrounding perils to the republic, such as the city, immigration, the misuse of wealth, Roman Catholic ultramontanism, labor/capital disputation, and social vices, clearly reflected the influence of the Evangelical Alliance's secretary general, Josiah Strong.

Two addresses at the Washington conference concerned the heart of the dilemma of democracy: the estrangement of the masses from the church. John F. Hurst, Methodist bishop of Buffalo, asserted that "no optimist, with the chimes of a dozen bells in his ears at once, dares to deny that throughout Christendom, where one individual pauses and enters the sanctuary on the Sabbath day, at least two others pass by, and go upon errands of indifference, work, or downright sin."[51] He listed, among the causes of the alienation, too few church buildings, insufficient work among immigrants, Sabbath desecration, and the influence of saloons. The bishop called for more church work among the urban poor and increased lay initiative, including the participation of women.[52] In another address on the same topic, Presbyterian minister and evangelist Arthur Tappen Pierson expressed the urgent need to attend to "the condition of the common people, for the condition of the common people is the condition of the commonwealth."[53] He lamented that "the church of Jesus Christ is, in the eyes of the working classes, inseparably linked with the aristocracy."[54] Pierson suggested that churches need to be more cordial to those in need by inculcating the gospel spirit of equality. In particular, practices like pew rents and the flight of churches from poor neighborhoods to wealthy ones needed to be abandoned.[55]

On the positive side, Alliance speakers emphasized that church cooperation provided the key to reaching the unchurched masses. In fact, the entire last day of the three-day meeting was dedicated to this topic. The lecture by the Episcopal bishop of Michigan, Samuel Harris, managed to arouse applause from his audience when he proclaimed that "it is felt that if our American civilization is much longer to endure as we prize it, then

[50] John Jay, "Address by Hon. John Jay," in *Perils and Opportunities*, 9.
[51] John F. Hurst, "Estrangement of the Masses from the Church," in *Perils and Opportunities*, 100.
[52] Ibid., 101–109.
[53] Arthur Tappan Pierson, "Estrangement of the Masses from the Church," in *Perils and Opportunities*, 116.
[54] Ibid., 117.
[55] Ibid., 121–22.

combination must take the place of division, and co-operation must take the place of competition, among the evangelical Christians of this land."[56] He went so far as to blame Protestant division for the eroding religious and moral influence over Americans.[57]

A more restrained, if not more well-thought-out, address by Congregationalist Washington Gladden considered how such cooperation might be inculcated among different evangelical denominations. While noting that "liturgical uniformity and consolidated government are impracticable," he argued that conference participants could "all agree that those who are seeking the Kingdom of God and its righteousness should not hinder or obstruct one another; that they should seek to combine their efforts for the establishment of the kingdom."[58] Echoing Gladden's plea for practical church cooperation, Josiah Strong's call for Alliance members to usher in "the era of applied Christianity" on a local level sounded like a nineteenth-century version of "think globally, act locally."[59] The Alliance secretary general envisioned local, federated networks of Christian activists organizing and coordinating the social and political activities of individual congregations.[60]

Despite the overwhelming sense of optimism that pervaded the meeting, however, some divisions had already become evident beneath the platitudes of cooperation. While it was one thing to agree that the dilemma of democracy existed and that they must work together to reach the unchurched, evangelicals did not necessarily agree on why their churches must combine their efforts; therefore, they often differed on the means of cooperation. Washington Gladden, for instance, claimed that "wholesale evangelization is not, according to my observation, profitable business; the hand-to-hand work of the churches is far more productive in the long run."[61] Behind his reasoning lay the notion that the church's vocation and mission was this-worldly; therefore, churches had a better opportunity to nurture an individual's moral development and character needed for his or

---

[56] Samuel Harris, "The Necessity of Co-operation in Christian Work," in *Perils and Opportunities*, 304.

[57] Ibid., 311.

[58] Washington Gladden, "Necessity of Co-operation in Christian Work," in *Perils and Opportunities*, 317.

[59] Josiah Strong, "Methods of Co-operation in Christian Work," in *Perils and Opportunities*, 347–48.

[60] Ibid., 349–53.

[61] Gladden, "Necessity of Co-operation," in *Perils and Opportunities*, 317–18.

her earthly work in the kingdom of God. Gladden proclaimed, "It is safe to say that a man converted in a church is worth to the kingdom of heaven here on earth more than a man converted in a[n athletic] rink."[62] Furthermore, Gladden believed that, because divisive doctrinal creeds and liturgical practices impeded churches from cooperative effort aimed at reaching the masses, these needed to be left out of any evangelical strategies to recapture culture. In the end, Gladden claimed, "the Christian co-operation which the times demand will follow the hearty recognition of one simple principle—that of the equality of all Christian churches."[63]

Not all evangelicals at the Washington conference found Gladden's postmillennial view of the kingdom of God congenial. It is hard not to imagine that the final address of the conference, presented by Baptist minister A. J. Gordon, did not have speakers like Gladden in mind when it asserted that "what we need is not a revival of ethics, as some are saying, but a revival of vital piety. For men will not recognize their stewardship to Christ until they recognize Christ's lordship over them."[64] Gordon no less than Gladden believed that the Christian had a duty to the poor and the unchurched. He insisted, however, that Christians misunderstood the present age when they assumed that reaching the masses essentially meant making the gospel conform to current intellectual trends. Instead, he boldly proclaimed that "it is not an orthodox creed which repels the masses, but an orthodox greed."[65] Gordon contended that the very fact the evangelicals hoarded wealth that subsequently repelled the masses proved that they failed to preach the transforming knowledge of Jesus Christ. The church, he proclaimed, could not be satisfied with spiritual destitution any more than physical poverty: "Reason and faith are like two compartments of an hour glass; when one is full the other is empty. Those who have been determined to *know* all things, revealed and unrevealed, have often thereby reduced their faith to the minimum, and in doing so they have contracted the very faculty by which we are to apprehend God."[66] This was a serious charge, according to Gordon, because the present-day perils had "their remedy in the eternal

---

[62] Ibid., 318.

[63] Ibid., 319.

[64] A. J. Gordon, "Individual Responsibility Growing Out of Our Perils and Opportunities," in *Perils and Opportunities*, 379.

[65] Ibid., 382.

[66] Ibid., 386.

provisions which we carry in the New Testament."[67] If Christ did not redeem and the Holy Spirit did not dwell within the Christian, any reform of society became a fruitless endeavor.

The 1887 Alliance meeting clearly presented both the "perils and opportunities" that evangelicals perceived they faced. The dilemma of democracy meant that they had to reach the masses. The issue, therefore, that consumed evangelicals in the Northern establishment was reaching the unchurched. "Why do not the people go to church? Is the question most frequently asked in these days," noted Everett D. Burr. His answer: "It is a question of method."[68] Although most establishment evangelicals had a commitment to mold positively American society, they had no agreed-upon nor intellectually consistent method to meet the challenge they perceived. The next chapter explores how evangelicals answered the most famous question of the day, "What would Jesus do?" and how the various answers affected ecclesiology in the Protestant establishment.

---

[67] Ibid., 380.

[68] Everett D. Burr, "The Methods of an Open and Institutional Church," *Open Church* 1/2 (April 1897): 99.

CHAPTER 3

What Would Jesus Do?
Evangelicals' Methods to Implement Their
Mission to American Culture

As they entered "the new era," many evangelicals worried that their denominations were not prepared to handle the great task before them. They became fixated with uncovering the best method for engaging American culture. This focus upon methods had important ecclesiological consequences within establishment denominations. Theologian Jürgen Moltmann rightfully observed that churches always face an identity-involvement crisis. On the one hand, he argued, the more Christian communities seek to become relevant by addressing the problems and questions of the wider culture, the more they find themselves faced with a crisis of identity. On the other hand, the more churches assert their identity in dogmatic formulas, rites, or peculiar codes of morality, "the more irrelevant and unbelievable they become."[1] In an effort to become culturally relevant, evangelicals in the Northern Protestant establishment ultimately weakened their denominational identities.

Evangelicals approached the dilemma of democracy asking a deceptively simple question: What would Jesus do? Charles Sheldon's novel *In His Steps, or What Would Jesus Do?* (1896) made the question in its title part of the evangelical consciousness of the late nineteenth and early

---

[1] One might easily add ethnic, linguistic, or national heritage. Jürgen Moltmann, *The Crucified God: The Cross of Christ as the Foundation and Criticism of Christian Theology* (New York: Harper & Row Publishers, 1974) 7.

twentieth centuries.[2] Sheldon's main protagonist, the Reverend Henry Maxwell, pricked by his conscience over having done nothing for a tramp who later died during his church service, preached a sermon in which he proposed that volunteers from the First Church of Raymond should "pledge themselves, earnestly and honestly, for an entire year, not to do anything without first asking the question, 'What would Jesus do?'"[3] The obvious rejoinder to such an invitation, one that did not escape Maxwell's potential volunteers, was, what if two persons or churches, trying to do what Jesus would do, should come to different conclusions? The minister responded with a cautious idealism. While admitting that he did not know whether the group could expect that all their actions would be uniformly Christ-like, he asserted that "when it comes to a genuine, honest, enlightened following of Jesus' steps, I cannot believe there will be any confusion either in our own minds or in the judgments of others."[4]

Had Maxwell been speaking about evangelicals of the late nineteenth and early twentieth centuries, he would have been wrong on both counts. In the pages of *The Independent*, Edward N. Packard represented many evangelicals as he ruminated about the difficulty of constructing and deploying a clear and consistent strategy to allow the church to accomplish its mission in American culture. "The familiar question, What would Jesus do? is more difficult to answer because he came into the world with a most definite work to perform, in which we can imitate him only in spirit.... For Christ gives us, not a program, but a law of the Spirit of Life. Jesus laid down principles, but left few rules."[5] Indeed, a multiplicity of methods to allow churches to perform their mission to American culture emerged. Following the 1887 Evangelical Alliance conference, many evangelical

---

[2] The actual circulation of this novel (which is still in print as of 2006) is difficult to calculate; however, the authorized version first published by the Chicago-based Advance Publishing Company in 1897 reportedly sold 113,000 copies by 31 March 1898. By 1900 many unauthorized editions began to be published in the United States, Canada, and Great Britain because Sheldon had not secured the proper copyright before he printed it four years earlier in the Congregationalist weekly the *Advance*. By the 1950s reasonable estimates had the novel's publication between 2 and 8 million. See John W. Ripley, "The Strange Story of Charles M. Sheldon's *In His Steps*," *Kansas Historical Quarterly* 34/3 (Autumn 1968): 241, 251.

[3] Charles M. Sheldon, *In His Steps* (Springdale PA: Whitaker House, 1979) 19.

[4] Ibid., 22.

[5] Edward N. Packard, "Can We Know What Jesus Would Do?" *Independent* 52/2671 (8 February 1900): 393–94.

leaders began a national conversation and debate over why and how they should reach the unchurched masses and overcome the dilemma of democracy. The Alliance, at its height, presented a relatively unified call for its constituent churches to regain cultural influence.[6] However, Josiah Strong's resignation as secretary general in 1898 because of his frustration that the Alliance could neither agree upon nor implement practical reforms was a portent of its rapid decline.[7]

Faced with what they saw as the impending erosion of their cultural influence, evangelicals began to put into practice various strategies to regain the populace, which the majority of them believed comprised the culture-forming component of the United States. Logically, if the churches positively influenced the masses, the dilemma of democracy would be obviated. Therefore, in order to recapture American culture, evangelicals needed to reconsider the exact nature of their churches' mission to and their relationship with unchurched, urban America. Further, denominations acted much like the Evangelical Alliance, having no univocal strategy to engage the problems they perceived. As a result, many evangelicals began to network with evangelicals outside of their denominational institutions who shared their cultural strategies. These networks not only formed the foundations of future trans-denominational movements (such as fundamentalism and modernism) but helped create a further feeling of denominational ambivalence among many evangelicals.

Generally, the intellectual sources of the strategies of cultural engagement in the Protestant establishment can be divided into two dominant camps, often described as "nurture" and "nature." Evangelicals advocating the importance of Christian nurture believed that the church could reclaim society by influencing individuals and expecting them to conform to an outwardly Christian America. They further supported a religious form of moral environmentalism, suggesting that by replacing the social surroundings in which sinful behavior thrived with those aligned with Christian ideals, individuals would develop a moral character and civilized habits. The church's primary religious function in the cities, therefore, was

---

[6] Josiah Strong, *The New World-Religion* (Garden City NJ: Doubleday, Page & Company, 1915) 463. Strong noted his frustration that the Alliance leaders primarily wanted to save the church and not society.

[7] Philip D. Jordan, *The Evangelical Alliance for the United States of America, 1847–1900: Ecumenism, Identity and the Religion of the Republic* (New York: The Edwin Mellen Press, 1982) 185–86.

to encourage moral order by reforming or eradicating American social institutions, such as big business, civil government, or saloons, which invited immorality among the masses. Many other evangelicals asserted that any reform of society depended upon the collective action of converted individuals, who practiced a subsequent life of holiness. In other words, the sinful nature of a human being must be overcome by a conversion to a godly life as a prerequisite to any social reform. These advocates of the age-old revivalistic traditions asserted that the church's function was to evangelize and convert individuals, who in turn would naturally make society more Christian.

It is important to remember that, while the intellectual forebears of nature and nurture often attacked one another's positions, no such intellectual clarity existed within establishment denominations. While leaders and theologians often demanded intellectual consistency, most evangelicals drew upon both of these traditions (often indiscriminately) as they attempted to devise strategies to influence American culture. Indeed, because denominations typically could not uphold consensus, many leaders sought camaraderie outside of their particular denominational umbrellas. Also important, evangelicals generally sought the salvation of individuals and the shaping of American culture within Christian principle. However, they often disagreed whether society better shaped individual souls or vice versa.

The idea of the malleability of human nature provided the intellectual bedrock for evangelicals promoting the reform of society and preservation of democracy based on Christian principles. Although Darwin's ideas could have been read in such a way as to lend credence to this anthropology, his *Origin of Species* did not spawn this widespread notion among evangelicals.[8] Timothy Smith argued that in the middle nineteenth century there existed an essential link between Christian perfectionism, millennialism, and social reform.[9] Indeed, well before Asa Gray began to popularize Darwin's work in the United States, revivalists and proponents of the Holiness movement had claimed that after conversion, the Christian should expect that his or her

---

[8] For many evangelicals, however, strategically applied evolutionary thought bolstered their arguments and gave them a modern and scientific appearance. See David N. Livingstone, *Darwin's Forgotten Defenders: The Encounter Between Evangelical Theology and Evolutionary Thought* (Grand Rapids: William B. Eerdmans Publishing Company, 1987).

[9] Timothy Smith, *Revivalism and Social Reform* (Baltimore: Johns Hopkins University Press, 1980) 148–62.

sinful human nature would be gradually transformed and molded to a godly and holy life. The dominant strains of Northern, urban evangelicalism, according to Smith, understood social reform as a logical extension of conversion and Christian perfection.[10]

Seeing the continuity between the revivalistic-holiness tradition and the rise of Protestant social reform in the United States provides an important clue to most late-nineteenth-century evangelicals' disapproval of the "social Darwinism" of the likes of Herbert Spencer, Benjamin Kidd, and William Graham Sumner.[11] These popularizers of social Darwinism stressed the almost imperceptible advance of evolution on a societal level coupled with a hands-off ethical attitude of survival of the fittest in regard to America's poor and underprivileged. The evangelical heirs of Christian perfectionism, whether revivalists or advocates of social Christianity, generally tended to be highly critical of such a *laissez-faire* ethical attitude toward the improvement of the masses.[12] Christ's kingdom, according to them, was not just for society's "fittest." They maintained the principle that the gospel message had the power to transform in the present all individuals regardless of moral state, class, sex, or race. This egalitarian, democratic gospel also meant that the church had a message that could, at least in theory, reach any person and uplift society as a whole.

Despite some common commitments to social betterment, however, evangelical Protestants did not agree upon the presuppositions and guiding principles of the reform process. Old disputes about human nature found a new audience in those attempting to reach the unchurched with the gospel. The debate surrounded the notion of nature versus nurture. One can trace this debate to Horace Bushnell and his *Christian Nurture* (1846). *Christian Nurture* was an attack against the American revivalistic tradition, which emphasized the conversion experience of individuals from their sinful nature

---

[10] Ibid., 151.

[11] A notable exception was Henry Ward Beecher, who advocated a Christianized form of social Darwinism. The classic work on social Darwinism in the United States remains Richard Hofstadter, *Social Darwinism in American Thought, 1860–1915* (Philadelphia: University of Pennsylvania Press, 1944); see especially chapter six, "The Dissenters," 86–102. Cf. Mike Hawkins, *Social Darwinism in European and American Thought: Nature as Model and Nature as Threat* (New York: Cambridge University Press, 1997).

[12] Hoftstadter, *Social Darwinism*, 86–91; see also Norris Magnuson, *Salvation in the Slums: Evangelical Social Work, 1865–1920*, paperback ed. (Grand Rapids: Baker Book House, 1990) 165–78.

to a new life in Christ. Advocates of revivalism (which we will turn to next), such as Charles Finney, saw churches as the locus of social change through the saving of souls. Finney wrote in 1835 that "when the Churches are thus awakened and reformed, the reformation and salvation of sinners will follow.... Harlots, and drunkards, and infidels, and all sorts of abandoned characters, are awakened and converted."[13] Bushnell retorted that rather than having a conversion experience, a "child is to grow up a Christian, and never know himself as being otherwise."[14] Specifically, the New England divine argued that the Christian family provided the best environment to train the individual in faith and morality. Sin, rather than being an innate prison from which one must be freed with divine intervention, was a natural disposition that could be gradually overcome with the help of divinely ordained institutions such as the family, church, and state.

The Nurturing Church: The Institutional Church Movement and the Social Gospel

Among evangelicals who advocated what was usually called "social Christianity," no initial consensus existed on what constituted the appropriate environment for Christian nurture. Bushnell, drawing upon his Puritan heritage, had suggested that the family was best suited to mold individuals at an early age. Reinforced by the belief that women were inherently more religious than men, mothers provided the conspicuous role of nurturing children in the ideals of the faith. A generation later no one doubted the importance of the family in religious nurture, but evangelicals became concerned that too many families had little or no association with the appropriate Protestant churches. Those participating within the institutional church movement most conspicuously promoted the nurturing church as a solution for reaching the masses. For all intents and purposes, the vocation of the church they envisaged was Bushnell's family writ large on a corporate scale.

Edward Judson, pastor of Judson Memorial Baptist Church in New York City, defined the institutional church as "an organized body of Christian believers, who, finding themselves in a hard and uncongenial

---

[13] Charles G. Finney, *Lectures on Revivals of Religion* (Chicago: Fleming H. Revell Company, n.d.) 8.

[14] Horace Bushnell, *Christian Nurture* (New Haven CT: Yale University Press, 1960) 4.

social environment, supplement the ordinary methods of the Gospel...by a system of organized kindness, a congeries of institutions, which, by touching people on physical, social, and intellectual sides, will conciliate them and draw them within the reach of the Gospel. The local church under the pressure of adverse environments tends to institutionalize."[15] His definition aptly captured both the motivation and style of the institutional church movement in which he participated. Everett D. Burr agreed, noting that "the church cannot minister to the needs of men until it ascertains exactly what the need is." The key, he suggested, was studying thoroughly the environs in which the church finds itself and subsequently devising particular strategies to meet particular needs.[16]

During the nineteenth century, urban evangelical churches commonly maintained their financial stability through the practice of charging pew rents and considered their function primarily to provide worship services on Sundays. As these church communities gradually succumbed to demographic changes, however, their membership and financial resources began to dwindle. St. George's Episcopal Church on the East Side of New York City was typical. By January of 1883 the congregation had only twenty families of worshippers, retained only two of the thirty or so lots of property deeded to it by its wealthy sister Trinity Church on Wall Street, and could not even scrape together the minimal funds to relocate the parish uptown.[17] Urban churches such as St. George's needed a strategy to reach out to their surrounding communities and make themselves spiritually and financially viable.

Leaders of the institutional church movement articulated three primary objectives: that a church should be *free*, *open*, and *institutional* in nature.[18] In other words, churches ought to abolish pew rents, keep their doors open during the week as well as on Sunday, and offer neighborhood services that could benefit its children, unemployed, and poor as well as its irreligious. A parish triumvirate of the Protestant Episcopal Church in the diocese of New

---

[15] Edward Judson, *The Institutional Church: A Primer in Pastoral Theology* (New York: Lentilhon & Company, 1899) 30–31.

[16] Everett D. Burr, "The Methods of an Open and Institutional Church," *Open Church* 1/2 (April 1897): 97.

[17] Elizabeth Moulton, *St. George's Church, New York* (New York: The Rector, Church Wardens, and Vestrymen of St. George's Church, 1964) 62.

[18] A nice summary of the movement's principles can be found in Charles L. Thompson, "Symposium on the Institutional Church," *Homiletic Review* 35/6 (December 1896): 560–64.

York provided the most celebrated models for this nationwide urban movement. St. George's, St. Bartholomew's, and Grace Episcopal Churches had three things in common: they were located within the swell of new working-class immigrant communities on the East Side of Manhattan; their members believed that they needed new tactics to survive in this changing environment; and each community called indefatigable, arguably brilliant rectors to meet these challenges.

William S. Rainsford, a noted architect of the movement, recalled that "in order to reach the great people of a great city the church must be absolutely free and open...People say I am a crank on the free church. Well, perhaps I am; but then I intend to live and die a crank."[19] After abolishing pew rents, he instituted a voluntary envelope tithing system, but the task was far from simple. Besides resistance from the few remaining parish families who donned brass plaques with surnames engraved upon them, St. George's rector had to take legal action to release pews owned by estates in England. Luckily, the senior warden J. P. Morgan agreed to buy out all the pews himself, and subsequently the church began to advertise in the *New York Times* that "ALL SEATS were now FREE."[20] Next, he opened the doors of the church on the weekdays and hung a sign on the porch that read, "COME IN, REST AND PRAY."[21] William Reed Huntington, pioneer ecumenist and rector of Grace Episcopal Church, followed Rainsford's example. He made the parish "open on week-days for the benefit of passers-by" beginning 1 May 1887.[22] The custodian recorded that 27,209 weekly visitors entered the church between May and November of that year.[23] Not quite as progressive as Rainsford, Huntington began offering free evensong on Sundays with the consent of the pew owners in the parish.[24]

The auxiliary institutions of these churches, however, provided the movement with its name and its most visible outreach. Rainsford not only instituted Sunday schools and made church services more "user friendly" but also opened a men's gymnasium, a cadet battalion, dancing classes, and a

---

[19] William Rainsford, *A Preacher's Story of His Work* (New York: The Outlook Company, 1904) 128–29.

[20] Moulton, 74, 68. Cf. Rainsford, *Preacher's Story*, 131.

[21] Moulton, 78.

[22] William Rhinelander Stewart, *Grace Church and Old New York* (New York: E. P. Dutton & Company, 1924) 183.

[23] Ibid.

[24] Stewart, *Grace Church*, 189–90, 218.

literary and drama society for community outreach.[25] Huntington's Grace
Church became known for its settlement work, complete with an industrial
training school, cooking and sewing classes, an employment society, a
history club, and a deaconess program.[26] David H. Greer's St.
Bartholomew's Church had even more varied institutions than St. George's
or Grace. Greer, who eventually became the bishop of the diocese of New
York, added a loan bureau, English classes for those of Asian descent, a
grocery selling supplies at cost to patrons, a surgical clinic, and a farm near
Bridgeport, Connecticut to give city children a summer vacation spot.[27]

While advocates of the institutional church believed that ignorance of
evangelicals toward the social conditions of the masses drove away the
working classes, they also argued that preaching impractical religious
platitudes and outdated theology drove away the educated middle classes.[28]
Rainsford acknowledged that "men are hungry for the Gospel of Jesus
Christ," but evangelicals "must give it to them in some form that does not
outrage their common sense."[29] He likened the old revivalistic tactics and
evangelistic tools used by many evangelicals to "a fisherman accustomed to
earn his bread at catching herrings; presently the run of herrings goes from
that section of the sea; in their place comes a tremendous run of smelts. If
the fisherman could change his nets, he would be a richer man than
before...but he starves because he cannot change the size of his meshes.
...that is about the idiotic policy that the Protestant Church has followed."[30]
Leaders of the institutional church movement asserted that the times
demanded that evangelicals change their nets to reach new types of
Americans. Similarly, Charles Dickinson, pastor of Berkeley Temple in
Boston, agreed, claiming that institutional churches followed the example of

---

[25] Ibid., 160–67. For a history of Rainsford's tenure of St. George's Church see
Henry Anstice, *The History of St. George's Church in the City of New York,
1752–1811–1911* (New York: Harper & Brothers, 1911) 292–369. For Jacob Riis's
journalistic contemporary depiction of St. George's, see his "Religion by Human
Touch," *World's Work* 1/5 (March 1901): 495–505.

[26] Florence E. Winslow, "The Settlement Work of Grace Church," *Charities
Review* 8/8 (October 1892): 418–25.

[27] Rufus Rockwell Wilson, "The Institutional Church and Its Work," *Outlook*
54/9 (29 August 1896): 385.

[28] William Rainsford, *The Story of a Varied Life: An Autobiography* (New York:
Doubleday, Page & Company, 1922). See especially chapters 16 and 18.

[29] Rainsford, *Preacher's Story*, 242.

[30] Ibid., 125–26.

Christ and, therefore, understood their mission as "ministration through adaptation."[31]

Accordingly, St. George's rector especially worked to get and keep educated, middle- and upper-classed men in the church in order to reach other men and young boys in the neighborhood. "There is a great danger" warned Rainsford, "that the public worship may be left to women, clergymen, and the uneducated." He devised a plan to appoint St. George's men as volunteer social lay workers. This, he believed, would keep them active parishioners by making them involved in the community surrounding the church. "The best way to keep lay-helpers is to give them work to do for their fellowmen—not always religious work—some men you cannot reach on that point at all—but sociological work: a class of boys to train, a battalion to organize, something that makes them feel they are giving service to those who have less than they—money, time, or skill. In that way you can hold the men as well as the women."[32] Finally, the rector asked the vestry to pay for three to five additional young clergy to aid in the parish work; these clergymen were usually seminarians or newly ordained graduates from General Theological Seminary in New York City. He convinced the young priests (whom he affectionately called "his boys") that in exchange for their work he would apprentice them and they would benefit from his practical experience and personal mentoring.[33] Through good preaching and social outreach, institutional leaders intended to reach the unchurched of all the urban classes.

While many religious leaders worried that the institutional church undermined spiritual growth, advocates responded that the real proof of the methods was in the pudding of numerical conversions. William Cross Merrill argued that Charles Dickinson's methods proved not only innovative but sound. Providing statistics of conversions at Berkley Temple, he showed that membership gains (by confession and letter) rose more than 68 percent after the church applied "institutional" changes. He further showed that

---

[31] Charles Dickinson, in *The Open or Institutional Church League Preliminary Conference Held in Madison Avenue Presbyterian Church, New York City, March 27, 1894* (Boston: Everett Press Company, 1894) 27.

[32] Rainsford, *A Preacher's Story*, 157.

[33] The duties of these clergymen included preaching, parishioner visitation, institutional work, and teaching Sunday school. See George Hodges and John Reichert, *The Administration of an Institutional Church: A Detailed Account of the Operation of St. George's Parish in the City of New York* (New York: Harper & Brothers, 1906) 3–6.

these gains outstripped other local churches in Boston and the nation as a whole. He also showed that between 1887 and 1892 institutional churches among Congregationalists in Worcester, Hartford, Jersey City, and Milwaukee had conversion rates superior to those of Congregationalism as a whole.[34] With such results it was no surprise that other evangelical churches in urban areas began to imitate the institutional church model. Institutional churches sprang up in cities throughout the country including but not limited to Brooklyn, Boston, Philadelphia, Buffalo, Los Angeles, Chicago, Jersey City, Hartford, Cleveland, Milwaukee, Kansas City, Worchester, Massachusetts, and Kalamazoo, Michigan.[35]

The institutional church model unleashed a wave of creative outreach to meet the needs of particular urban contexts. However, most of the churches did not make wholesale change; rather, church leaders added new methods to tried ones. Ruggles Street Baptist Church in Boston, Massachusetts, added to the church a "working man's" Bible class, a relief storeroom, and a dispensary. They also offered services such as milk sterilization for babies and classes in sewing, carpentry, housekeeping, woodcarving, and drawing.[36] Bethany Presbyterian Church in Philadelphia, pastored by evangelist J. Wilbur Chapman, was not as sour about traditional street missions and revivals as Rainsford. Bethany ran two missions, promoted an extensive children's and adult Sunday school program, and voted to allow their pastor to spend up to six months of the year

---

[34] Dickinson quoted in William Cross Merrill, "Spirituality and the Institutional Church," *Open or Institutional Church League Preliminary Conference*, 42–45.

[35] These churches include, among others, Jersey City Tabernacle (also called the People's Palace); Forth Church of Hartford; Pilgrim Church of Worcester; Berkeley Temple and Ruggles Street Baptist in Boston; Pilgrim Church, Cleveland; Plymouth Church, Milwaukee; First Christian Church, Kansas City; Lincoln Park Baptist Church, Cincinnati; Westminster Church, Buffalo; Bethlehem Institutional Church, Los Angeles; and Grace Baptist and Bethany Tabernacle in Philadelphia. See Wilson, "Institutional Work," 384–87; John L. Scudder, "The People's Palace of Jersey City," *Charities Review* 1/2 (December 1891): 90–92; Mary Brownson Hartt, "Westminster House" *Open Church* 2/3 (July 1898): 309–316; "A Californian Institutional Church" *Open Church* 2/3 (October 1898): 263–64; "A Cincinnati Institutional Church" *Open Church* 2/2 (April 1898) 279–81; James E. Davis, "Kansas City to Have Institutional Church," *Christian Standard* 53/18 (9 February 1918): 607; and Caroline Bartlett Crane, "The Story of an Institutional Church in a Small City," *Charities and the Commons* 14/6 (May 1905): 723–31.

[36] William T. Ellis, "New Era of Church Work: Ruggles St. Baptist Church, Boston," *Open Church* 2/1 (January 1898): 205–213.

evangelizing in revival meetings. Chapman constructed an intricate lay ministry in the church, choosing a 100-man "Pastor's League." Each man was placed in charge of five pews in the church "to watch strangers and see that no one gets away without recognition."[37] To these more traditional ministries, Bethany founded Deaconess Home, run by Mary B. Wharton, which provided a dispensary and a kitchen for sick neighborhood residents. Local entrepreneur John Wanamaker helped found Bethany College, which taught evening classes in traditional liberal arts subjects as well as practical subjects such as bookkeeping, stenography, penmanship, business forms, arithmetic, and typewriting. The college's industrial department provided courses in dressmaking, garment cutting, millinery, sewing, needlework, embroidery, woodworking, and electricity. The college cost $1–2 for the winter term and opened its doors to persons "of every color, age, condition, sex, and creed." In the eyes of one observer, the college allowed people "to better their condition, earn a more generous livelihood, and learn the fine art of noble and successful living."[38] Russell H. Conwell, pastor of Grace Baptist Church (known as "The Temple") in Philadelphia, instituted an orphanage, a hospital, and Temple College. The mission of Temple College was to provide a free education to working-class men and women who wished it.[39]

The culmination of the movement came in 1894 with the founding of the Open and Institutional Church League (OICL).[40] The platform of the league stated that it stood for "open church doors for every day and all the day, free seats, a plurality of Christian workers, the personal activity of all church members, a ministry to all the community through educational, reformatory and philanthropic channels, to the end that men may be won to Christ."[41] While the slight majority of its officers resided in New York and Philadelphia, its many vice presidents represented virtually all the regions of the urban North and West and included many well-known religious figures

---

[37] Mosley H. Williams, "The New Era of Church Work in Philadelphia" *Open Church* 1/2 (April 1897): 66–73.

[38] Ibid., 70.

[39] Albert Hatcher Smith, *The Life of Russell H. Conwell: Preacher, Lecturer, Philanthropist* (Boston: Silver, Burdette, and Co., 1899) 193, 203.

[40] The organization often labeled itself the Open or Institutional Church League. I have for the sake of consistency used the conjunction "and" unless copying a citation.

[41] *Officers, Constitution, and Platform of the Open and Institutional Church League* (New York: 83 Bible House, n.d.) 1.

of the day, including Josiah Strong, William E. Dodge, Edward Judson, Cortland Myers, Graham Taylor, as well as the league's president Frank Mason North and its tireless corresponding secretary E. B. Sanford. The Open and Institutional Church League not only sponsored a forum for the discussion of urban work through conferences and its official organ the *Open Church*, but more importantly it intended to create "a bond of union and fellowship between churches and individuals who are seeking to advance the principles and work expressed in the platform."[42] The League was trans-denominational and its leaders (including Sanford and North) formed the foundation for later ecumenical endeavors culminating in 1908 in the Federal Council of the Churches of Christ in America.

The motivations of many institutional church leaders showed how a changing conception of church mission, or vocation, directly influenced the way they understood the identity and role of the church. Rainsford, for example, took exception to critics who accused him of neglecting his duty to convert souls because of his emphasis on social programs. Responding to a parishioner who left the congregation in 1892 for this reason, he replied, "You gladly admit that we in St. George's are doing all that we can to present, at least, Christian character and practice to men. This, in my view, is the chief thing to-day. Christ's law obeyed is what men want to see; it is the best way to present the person and work of Christ to a community that can only be saved by these."[43] A moral environmentalist at heart, Rainsford believed that if evangelicals provided the masses what they wanted and needed, they would come to church; once inside, the church could influence their character to be good Christians.[44] N. McGee Waters epitomized this view, writing that "Christianity is character; Christianity is man-making and man-building. Its is taking for raw materials humanity as we find it, with all its faults, with all its sins, and with all its vices, and transforming it into the humanity as it should be, with all the fulness [sic] of the stature of Jesus Christ."[45]

---

[42] Ibid., 3. Cf. *The Open and Institutional Church League: Our Work* (New York: The Open and Institutional Church League, n.d.) 2.

[43] Quoted in Anstice, *History of St. George's*, 327.

[44] Ibid., 171–72.

[45] N. McGee Waters, *A Young Man's Religion and His Father's Faith* (Thomas Y. Crowell & Co., 1905) 178. Cf. Judson, *Institutional Church*, 153. Judson reminded his readers that the church's "main work...is in the realm of motive and character, rather than of environment...But a man will not listen when he is in pain. To believe in

In the same way that secular reformers believed city parks, art museums, and libraries were valuable because they lead to the moral uplift of urban dwellers, institutional church leaders claimed that various contacts with churches provided the very means by which individuals could develop a godly and moral character.[46] Rainsford wrote: "What we want is to have the most beautiful churches in the crowded districts, and the best music. Where life is sordid, you want beauty; where life is crowded you want the big church; where there is discord, you want the most beautiful music. ...the beauty of it [a city church] will draw people; and if we cannot make use of that beauty to help people to the Source of all beauty, we fail."[47] One New York Presbyterian commented, "I say, open those doors and let that voice of piercing sweetness reach the sidewalks unobstructed, with its heavenly, 'Come.'...An invited guest is sure of welcome, an invited guest enters boldly, enters and meets—God."[48]

Institutional church advocates claimed that this influence of character provided a valuable service of the church for American society as a whole. "'Bums...need religion," wrote Rainsford, "and when one of them is converted and feels that the Church needs him, and needs what he can do, he becomes a grand working man."[49] Taking this logic even further, Huntington defended the opening of church doors by asserting that "the exemption of ecclesiastical property from taxation by the State can only be defended on the score of the usefulness of the Church as a bulwark for public morals."[50] Sociologist E. M. Fairchild agreed, claiming "that church which produces men and women who live intelligently and in perfect devotion to the fulfillment of the highest ideals, is the church that is the greatest, because it serves society's needs."[51] Goals to inculcate citizenship received high praise from New York's social elite. President Theodore Roosevelt, writing of his friend Rainsford, declared that "not only New York

---

God, he must first believe in man." Also see Samuel Zane Batten, "The Church as the Maker of Conscience," *American Journal of Sociology* 7/5 (March 1902): 611–28.

[46] See Paul Boyer, *Urban Masses and Moral Order in America, 1820–1920* (Cambridge: Harvard University Press, 1978, 1997) 233–51.

[47] Rainsford, *Preacher's Story*, 170.

[48] A Presbyterian, "The Padlocked Church," *Outlook* 70/7 (15 February 1902): 446.

[49] Rainsford, *Preacher's Story*, 129.

[50] Anstice, *History of St. George's*, 184.

[51] E. M. Fairchild, "The Function of the Church," *American Journal of Sociology* 2/2 (September 1896): 223.

City but the nation as a whole owes him a debt of gratitude for his molding of American citizenship in the form in which it should be cast. The kind of citizenship for the upbuilding of which he labored is that which rests its sense of duty to city and country on the deep and broad foundation of the eternal laws of spiritual well-being."[52]

Interestingly, these evangelicals often disapproved of coercive reforms such as Sunday blue laws or prohibition of drink. In 1892 Rainsford caused no small stir among evangelicals for suggesting that saloons be allowed to open on Sunday. With typical candor he later asserted that "your Puritan who insists on passing his own peculiar law is the ally of the bad element in the city. His stupid insistence to pass laws that cannot be enforced is disastrous; there can be nothing worse."[53] According to Rainsford, only the church could provide the environment to mold men and women into the image and character of Christ. Graham Taylor agreed, suggesting that "the churches should be the last to tolerate, much less to claim, or secure, class legislation for their own benefit or others' benefit, for they stand for all, if for any."[54] In the final analysis, noted Graham, "formatories are the best reformatories."[55]

Because many advocates of Christian nurture asserted that the vocation of the church was primarily to influence of the character of individuals, their conception of the identity of the church began to be depicted in terms that had been relegated previously to the family. In essence the church became a household. One Methodist thinker observed:

> The hundreds of thousands of bachelors and spinsters who have been too poor or without opportunity to wed have no home…And the other thousands who have been fortunate enough to be able to marry cramp themselves and their families into one, two, or three rooms in a flat or tenement; they too have no home. The Church is their only home. Here they come to know those who 'do the will of the Father in heaven,' and who are to them in a very real sense fathers and mothers and brothers and sisters. Here or no where do they learn the fundamentals of our social life—the lessons of 'authority, inequality, fraternity'—to teach which the family was divinely instituted.[56]

---

[52] Hodges and Reichert, *Administration of an Institutional Church*, x.

[53] Ibid., 163. Cf. Anstice, *History of St. George's*, 332–37.

[54] Graham Taylor, "The Social Function of the Church," *American Journal of Sociology* 5/3 (November 1899): 310.

[55] Ibid., 311.

[56] J. W. Magruder, "The Open Church and the Closed Church," *Methodist Review* 14/5 (September 1898): 772–73.

Similarly, Russell H. Conwell's biographer noted that "he determined the church should be a home, a church home, but nevertheless a home in its true sense, overflowing with love, with kindness, with hospitality for the stranger within its gates."[57] The mission of the church to reach the masses through institutions, therefore, changed the understanding of the church from a place where the lost were converted and the converted worshipped to a family environment that shaped the character of all who entered. A new shibboleth began to emerge among evangelicals concerned with the relationship between the church and the laboring classes as well: "The Fatherhood of God and the brotherhood of man." This slogan, which became the watchword for social Christianity and the later ecumenical movement, pointed to a shift in an understanding of the role of the church as the nurturing family with God as its father and members as equal siblings.[58] In fact, wrote one evangelical, "if the Church fails to stand...as veritable Embodiment of the truth that the children of men, being the offspring of God, are brethren and are called to come again into the fellowship in the Father's Household...I know not what agency, or what social institution or order may take its place."[59]

In this context one can better understand these evangelicals' preoccupation with getting men and boys into their churches.[60] Cortland Myers, pastor of the Baptist Temple in Brooklyn and an OICL vice president, proclaimed that the concern of "'why men do not go to church,' is one of the burning questions of the hour."[61] Along the same lines another author noted that "the church must win the boys and it is not winning them. They are not at its preaching services; the vacant seats on the 'boys' side' of

---

[57] Agnes Rush Burr, *Russell H. Conwell: Founder of the Institutional Church in America* (Philadelphia: John C. Winston Company, 1905) 141.

[58] Cf. W. C. Helt, "The Liberalistic Shibboleth—'The Fatherhood of God and the Brotherhood of Man,'" *Homiletic Review* 35/1 (January 1898): 41–42.

[59] William Frederic Faber, "The Real Question: Why We Have a Church?" *Andover Review* 9/50 (February 1888): 125–26.

[60] For a general historical context of the concept of "manliness" during this period see Gail Bederman, *Manliness and Civilization: A Cultural History of Gender and Race in the United States, 1880–1917* (Chicago: University of Chicago Press, 1995) 1–44.

[61] Cortland Myers, *Why Men Do Not Go to Church* (New York: Funk and Wagnalls Co., 1899) vii.

the Sunday-school room are the despair of the superintendent."[62] These evangelicals believed that a church with no men did not constitute a complete family; without men, no one could be an example in helping build the character of boys. Because women did not have the social power to help evangelical churches solve the dilemma of democracy, the retention of men, who dominated the culture-forming spheres of business and politics, had to be a top priority.[63] Fatherly example for many evangelicals provided the key to getting boys into the church. Writing of the hypothetical and typical American man named "Smith," Harry H. Beattys observed, "Not withstanding the fact that his mother is quite likely more religiously inclined than his father, still Smith, Jr. is far more influenced, in the matter of church going, by his father than by his mother."[64]

Not long after the creation of the Open and Institutional Church League, Washington Gladden provided a much-needed theological rationale for the institutional church movement. He agreed that the projects of institutional churches, though perhaps untraditional, "are not furnished in any furtive fashion—as a kind of Christian cajolery to entrap and convert souls; they are provided for what they are worth in themselves."[65] However, he defended this view theologically by positing the immanence of Christ in all social institutions, arguing that "there is no kind of work in which any

---

[62] Harry H. Beattys, *Smith and the Church* (New York: Frederick A. Stokes Company, 1915) 78–79. The average American "Smith" and his relationship to the church caused an editorial stir on the pages of the *Atlantic Monthly* three years earlier. See Meredith Nicholson, "Should Smith Go to Church?" *Atlantic Monthly* 109/6 (June 1912): 721–33; "The Church and Smith," *Atlantic Monthly* 110/2 (August 1912): 270–72; "Smith and the Church," *Atlantic Monthly* 110/2 (August 1912): 272–76.

[63] Besides those listed above, the following citations provide a representative sample of the literature of this type: Judson, *Institutional Church*, 178–84; Gerald H. Beard, "Church Work for Men" *Open Church* 2/3 (July 1898): 324–26; J. H. W. Stuckenberg, "Questions: How Can I Win Men to the Church...?" *Homiletic Review* 42/6 (December 1901): 557–58; Charles Stelzle, "Reaching the Street-Boy," *Outlook* 72/11 (15 November 1902): 649–52; Edward Bok, "The Young Man and the Church," *Outlook* 76/16 (16 April 1904): 934–38; anonymous, "The Church and the Young Man: A Discussion," *Outlook* 76/18 (30 April 1904): 1019–23; N. Waters, *Young Man's Religion*; "Why Men Do Not Go to Church" *Outlook* 96 (3 September 1910): 10–10a.

[64] Beattys, *Smith and the Church*, 87.

[65] Washington Gladden, *Ruling Ideas of the Present Age* (Boston: Houghton, Mifflin and Company, 1896) 128.

man has a right to engage that is not in its deepest meaning sacred work."[66] This doctrine of the immanence of Christ, declared Gladden, "makes the old distinction between the sacred and the secular meaningless and almost blasphemous."[67] "Citizenship is a sacred duty," he continued, "the voters are the sovereigns. It is with them that the final responsibility rests. It is they who are ordained of God to establish justice, to defend liberty, to promote common welfare."[68] The church, according to Gladden, had as its primary task the institution of the kingdom of God on earth; it provided the leaven by which all society would eventually be redeemed.[69]

As suggested by Gladden's apology, the idea that the church was the herald and catalyst for the institution of the kingdom of God often walked hand-in-hand with the view of the church as a formatory of character. In 1888 Congregationalist William Faber lamented that Protestants seemed to miss the idea that the church constituted "a miniature redeemed society" through which all secular realms of society would be redeemed and made rightfully sacred.[70] Just over a decade later Lyman Abbott stressed to the congregation of the Broadway Tabernacle in New York City that the church should not be confused with the kingdom of God. The kingdom, he explained, "is uprightness, peace, and joy. It is honesty in business, justice and liberty in government, truthfulness and sincerity in society; it is good will and service one toward another; it is compassion to the erring and the sinful; it is tenderness and sympathy and love binding the family together in the bond of perfectness."[71] Through the church, he continued, Christians heralded the coming kingdom and participated in its institution on earth:

> This is your power, your mission, your message: that God is in his world; that he is such a God as Jesus Christ was when Jesus Christ was on the earth;...and that you are banded here together in this church, that you may be his ministers, the almoners of his life, the teachers of his doctrine, the heralds of his presence; that you may do what in you lies, by your messages from the pulpit, by your work in the Sunday-schools, by your industries, by your political services in the State, by your personal services in the domestic

---

[66] Ibid., 295.
[67] Ibid.
[68] Ibid., 174.
[69] Ibid., 110.
[70] Faber, "The Real Question," 123–25.
[71] Lyman Abbott, "The Mission of the Christian Church," *Outlook* 70/5 (12 April 1902): 911.

circle—that you may do what you can to bring about the kingdom of God in the city of New York.[72]

Episcopalian and economist Richard T. Ely agreed with Abbott's assessment, noting that "Christianity is primarily concerned with this world, and it is the mission of Christianity to bring to pass here a kingdom of righteousness and to rescue from the evil one and redeem all our social institutions."[73] The University of Wisconsin professor put into action the idea that God redeemed all facets of human endeavor. Publishing his last distinct work on the church and Christianity in 1895, he went on to concentrate his efforts solely in the field of political economy.[74] While he never repudiated his convictions of a social Christianity, Ely concentrated on such "sacred" topics as municipal reforms and land economics.[75]

While Gladden, Abbott, and Ely made central to their understanding of the church that it was not to be conflated with the coming kingdom of God, exactly how advocates of social Christianity believed the church instituted the kingdom varied. On the one hand, leaders of the institutional church movement certainly saw their activities as a means to bring about the kingdom. As suggested by its motto, "Fellowship in Common Service," the Open and Institutional Church League wished to unite evangelical churches through cooperative efforts of reaching the unchurched masses and "advancing the interests of the Kingdom of God."[76] Its vision statement went so far as to assert that the League aimed to "save all men, by all means, abolishing so far as possible, the distinction between the religious and the secular, and sanctifying all days and all means to the great end of saving the world to Christ."[77]

However, some advocates of social Christianity, notably Walter Rauschenbusch, thought the work of the institutional church a "necessary evil."[78] Writing from his church in "Hell's Kitchen" in New York City, he

---

[72] Ibid., 915.

[73] Richard T. Ely, *The Social Aspects of Christianity and Other Essays* (New York: Thomas Y. Crowell & Company, 1889) 53.

[74] Ely went on to write *The Social Law of Service* (1918).

[75] Robert T. Handy, *The Social Gospel in America, 1870–1920* (New York: Oxford University Press, 1966) 182.

[76] *Open and Institutional Church League: Our Work*, 4.

[77] *Institutional Churches—A Vision* (New York: Open and Institutional Church League, n. d.) 3.

[78] Walter Rauschenbusch, "The Stake of the Church in the Social Movement," *American Journal of Sociology* 3/1 (July 1897): 26. In a chapter in his *Christianity and*

asserted that "The people ought to be able to provide for themselves what the churches are trying to provide for them. If the people had comfortable homes, steady work, and a margin of income for the pleasures of life, they could look out for themselves and the churches could prune off their institutional attachments. ...Make social life healthy and you can simplify church work. Let poverty and helplessness increase, and the work of the churches will increase too."[79] Rauschenbusch based his argument upon the idea that institutional churches required an inordinate amount of money and energy to exist. Not only did he think that pastors of such churches were bad life insurance risks, but he also noted that the concentration of wealth in American society meant that even institutional churches ironically depended upon the rich, who caused the very problem the churches felt compelled to assuage.[80] The church could only solve these problems, according to Rauschenbusch, by changing rather than acting society's part.

Advocates of the social gospel, a movement whose name became linked with Rauschenbusch, tended to see the mission of the church in terms of its prophetic capacity and practical attempts to institute the kingdom of God within American society. Methodist J. W. Magruder fully acknowledged that the institutional church played a role in the uplift of society by cooperating with municipalities in charitable work; however, he believed that such work was "only the outgrowth of others' neglect of social duty."[81] He continued, "If a church playground is opened let it be under protest, and as a standing rebuke to the authorities for not multiplying the number of open spaces and breathing places in the congested downtown districts. Have it clearly understood that the Church is averse to doing other people's business;...that for every such neglect [of their social duty] on the part of private citizens or public officials they will one day be brought to judgment."[82] Further, he added, if such a prophetic voice does not shame the social order to act, "cooperation sometimes must be changed to coercion."[83]

The belief that the church must be a prophet of and activist for the institution of the kingdom of God on earth in American society motivated

---

the Social Crisis (New York: Macmillan Company, 1907, reprint, 1913) based upon this article and donning the same title, Rauschenbusch considerably toned down his criticisms. See 304–305.

[79] Rauschenbusch, "Stake of the Church," 26–27.

[80] Ibid., 25, 23.

[81] Magruder, "The Open Church," 771.

[82] Ibid.

[83] Ibid.

some dramatic scenes of American evangelical political activism during the late nineteenth and early twentieth centuries. Delivering the Beecher Lectures at Yale Divinity School in 1913, Presbyterian minister Charles H. Parkhurst proclaimed that "it is the kingdoms of *this world*, Scripture tells us, that are to become the kingdom of our Lord, and of his Christ....We ought to work to redeem this world, not merely to populate the *next*."[84] The church, according to Parkhurst, had a responsibility for civic conditions. He expected that the duty of the church today, "as much as it was the duty of Elijah and Jeremiah, is to take eternal principle, and to measure existing conditions and institutions against the principle as standard and as frankly and eloquently as possible to declare the amount of discrepancy between the two."[85]

Parkhurst knew of what he spoke. Almost twenty years before he held the prestigious lectureship at Yale, he led a crusade against the abuses of power within the New York City police department and the misrule of the Tammany Hall political machine. In February of 1892, the Presbyterian minister shocked city ministers and public officials by preaching against Tammany Hall right from the pulpit and accusing public officials of political corruption: "In its municipal life this city is thoroughly rotten. Here is an immense city reaching out arms of evangelization to every quarter of the globe; and yet every step that we take looking toward moral betterment of this city has to be taken directly in the teeth of the damnable pack of administrative bloodhounds that are fattening themselves on the ethical flesh and blood of our citizenship."[86] Tammany accused the minister of spreading falsehood and caricatures. Parkhurst answered them on 13 March

---

[84] Charles H. Parkhurst, *The Pulpit and the Pew* (New Haven: Yale University Press, 1913) 105.

[85] Ibid., 104. In a letter to the editor, Parkhurst wrote, "Legislation proper is not a process of making law, but of interpreting the law that is unwritten and eternal, and translating it into terms required by the exigencies of the occasion. It is a process of straining up the people to a level of the ideal, not diluting the ideal to the taste of the people." See "Creed of Deed?" *Outlook* 61/2 (13 January 1900): 101.

[86] Charles H. Parkhurst, *Our Fight with Tammany* (New York: Charles Scribner's Sons, 1895; reprint, New York: Arno Press and the New York Times, 1970) 10. Cf. "Reverend Charles H. Parkhurst, D. D., Denouncing Tammany Misrule," *Review of Reviews* 10/5 (November 1894): 468. The editor of the *Review* misdated the sermon as 13 March 1892. Also see Tammany's response to Parkhurst: Richard Croker, "Tammany Hall and Democracy," *Atlantic Monthly* 165/423 (February 1892): 225–30.

with another sermon. He even went so far as to substantiate his claims, providing his audience with packets of copied affidavits against the police department and the New York political machine. He concluded his sermon with a challenge to Tammany: "For four weeks you have been wincing under the sting of general indictment, and have been calling for particulars. This morning I have given you particulars, two hundred and eighty-four of them."[87] Parkhurst founded the City Vigilance League in May 1892 and covertly investigated and collected evidence of city corruption.[88] Capitalizing upon his prestige as a Presbyterian minister, Parkhurst helped topple the Tammany domination of New York politics with the election of the Reform candidate William L. Strong as mayor in 1894. The November issue of *Reviews of Reviews* credited Parkhurst with the fall of Tammany and noted that through his persistence "a great lesson has thus been taught to reformers everywhere."[89]

Following Parkhurst's example, in 1900 Episcopal bishop Henry C. Potter similarly tried to influence change within the New York City police department. Appalled by organized vice and corruption around his parish on the East Side, Bishop Potter demanded that the captain of the precinct make a concerted effort to clean up the neighborhood.[90] The department's unenthusiastic response enraged him.[91] Left with few options, he waged a public relations campaign against the city police. Using the prestige of his episcopal rank, Potter wrote an open letter to mayor Robert A. Van Wyck, stating, "I come to you, sir, with this protest, in accordance with the instructions lately laid upon me by the Convention of the Episcopal Church of the Diocese of New York.... Months have passed since the incidents occurred to which I have alluded in this communication. But, in all these months, the condition of things in whole neighborhoods have not improved, but rather grown worse.... Such a state of things cries to God for vengeance, and calls no less loudly to you and me for redress."[92] Potter's letter made

---

[87] Ibid., 78.

[88] Cf. Boyer, *Urban Masses*, 163–65.

[89] Anonymous, "Dr. Parkhurst's Triumph," *Review of Reviews* 10/5 (November 1894): 469.

[90] Anonymous, "Police Uphold a Reign of Vice," *New York Times*, 17 November 1900, 1.

[91] Anonymous, "Police Defence Delayed," *New York Times*, 18 November 1900, 1.

[92] Anonymous, "Bishop Potter's Letter," *Outlook* 66/13 (24 November 1900): 732–33.

headlines, and consequently Van Wyck publicly chastised the board of police commissioners and called for change. Furthermore, he assured Potter that he would exert all legal means possible to secure the cooperation of the police department to clean up the neighborhood. Potter's complaints led to the indictment of two officers.[93] Although the officers were eventually cleared of the charges against them, Potter's action brought the force under serious public scrutiny.[94] While evangelicals such as Parkhurst and Potter typically tried to cooperate with city officials, they believed that Christian duty called them to political activism if such efforts failed.

Importantly, however, most supporters of Christian nurture, whether involved with the institutional church or social gospel movements, did not typically create bipolar division between the salvation of society and the salvation of souls. Walter Rauschenbusch, in his opus *A Theology for the Social Gospel* (1917), admitted that "the salvation of the individual, of course, is an essential part of salvation."[95] His concerns with revivalism had little to do with the primacy of social Christianity; rather, he worried that modern revivalism addressed social concerns ineffectively if at all.

> The social gospel furnishes new tests for religious experience. We are disposed to accept the converted souls whom individualistic evangelism supplies without looking them over.... To one whose memory runs back twenty or thirty years to Moody's time, the methods now used by some evangelists seem calculated to produce skin-deep changes. Things have simmered down to signing a card, shaking hands, or being introduced to an evangelist. We used to pass through some deep-soil ploughing by comparison. It is time to overhaul our understanding of the kind of change we hope to produce by personal conversion and regeneration. The social gospel furnishes some tests and standards.[96]

While he certainly critiqued the revivalism of his day, Rauschenbusch hardly rejected it whole cloth. Regardless of whether his 1917 critique was fair, he acknowledged that Dwight L. Moody's generation had produced socially relevant revivalism. Anson Atterbury also agreed that, insofar as evangelical churches must use "experimental efforts" to "adapt itself to

---

[93] Anonymous, "Olcott to Prosecute Cross and Herlihy," *New York Times,* 25 November 1900, 3.

[94] Anonymous, "Herlihy Charges Are Dismissed," *New York Times*, 21 February 1901, 2.

[95] Walter Rauschenbusch, *A Theology for the Social Gospel* (Nashville: Abingdon Press, 1945) 96.

[96] Ibid., 96–97.

changed conditions of modern times," even the Salvation Army movement, despite its "unfortunate separation" from establishment churches, "is directly or indirectly an effort of the Christian Church to meet the needs of the world."[97] Revivalism and rescue missions, to which we now turn, also provided time-tested, nature-oriented strategies for engaging American culture alongside of the nurturing church.

He Who Winneth Souls Is Wise:
Soul Saving as Social Salvation

In 1913 a retired Methodist preacher, reflecting upon his career, lamented that revivalism had lost its respectability in his denomination.

> A great change has come to the Methodist Church since I entered the pastorate thirty-five years ago. Conversions such as were the rule then, are the exceptions now. A pastor in those days must know how to deal with a soul in the agonies of conviction for sin and the bitter pangs of repentance. He must know how to pray and sing and exhort and wait.
> ...but we have grown too refined for such manifestations of interest in our souls and the souls of others. We have shortened and straightened and macadamized the way into the Kingdom so that one may travel easily and comfortably...Meanwhile poor human nature is the same; honest souls are conscious that they cannot by reasoning nor by an effort of the will bring themselves to love God nor persuade themselves that they have not sinned, nor repress a longing for pardon. There are two fundamental facts in the Gospel....One of these is, Man is a sinner; the other is, Man has a Saviour.... To preach the latter without the former is folly. To preach the former without the latter is cruelty.[98]

During the thirty-five years of this man's ministry, evangelicals, drawing upon the soul-saving traditions of revivalism, adapted their methods to meet the needs of the day. Evangelicals from this revivalistic heritage believed that the church's primary mission lay in its proclamation of this gospel message to the lost, and they employed a well-developed tradition of techniques at their disposal as a means to convert the unchurched masses. Indeed, "convert" was the operative term. Although revival technically meant to bring life into a lifeless or backslidden church, Presbyterian

---

[97] Anson P. Atterbury, "The Church Settlement," *Open Church* 1/3 (October 1897): 163.
[98] A retired methodist preacher, "If I Were a Pastor Again," *Independent* 74/3354 (13 March 1913): 577–78.

evangelist J. Wilbur Chapman claimed that a revival in the popular sense embraced "not only the idea of the quickening of the saints but the conversion of sinners."[99] He noted, as Finney had fifty years before, that wherever the Holy Spirit renewed church bodies, the conversion of sinners closely followed.[100]

Conversion, according to these evangelicals, provided an important remedy for the dilemma of democracy and the ailments of society. Just as advocates of social Christianity had concerned themselves with regaining the masses for the churches, those who promoted revivalism intended to use their techniques toward the same end. In an edited "how-to" volume on revivalism, a reprinted article by Edwards A. Park stated that "various methods of moral reform have been proposed, but we have reason to believe that chief and radical reformation of men will be the effect of the Divine Word orally delivered, and accompanied with the influence of Divine Grace."[101] Baptist minister George Vosburgh proclaimed this message, too:

> A genuine revival of religion, sweeping over a community, will do more to right its ethical and social life than all things else. Make the heart right, and the life will be right. Christ saw as we can never see the evils of humanity of man toward man. But He knew that government would never be right until men who made government were right. Men will not be right until they are right with God. Christianize the world and you will have civilized it. The converse is not true. It is as difficult to Christianize a Godless civilization as it is to Christianize barbarism. There is no hope for an unregenerate world.[102]

Of urban evangelism A. T. Pierson also argued that "we believe that the Gospel, the Spirit of God, the love of souls, are just as mighty to-day as ever, and if these were really depended on, and practically operative, the churches would again regain and retain hold on the people."[103] Baptist Russell H. Conwell considered that all aspects of church work existed for its "only mission": saving souls of the lost. He proclaimed that "every concert, every choir service, every preaching service, every Lord's Supper, every

---

[99] J. Wilbur Chapman, *Revivals and Missions* (New York: Lentilhon & Company, 1900) 2.

[100] Ibid. Cf. Finney, *Lectures on Revivals*, 8.

[101] Edwards A. Park, "Power in the Pulpit," in *Revivals: How to Promote Them*, enlarged ed., ed. Walter P. Doe (New York: E. B. Treat, 1895) 23.

[102] George B. Vosburgh, "The Mission of the Church," *Watchman* 76/44 (31 October 1895): 10–11.

[103] A. T. Pierson, "The Problem of City Evangelization," *Missionary Review of the World*, 2d series 12/6 (June 1899): 409.

agency that is used in the church must have the great mission plainly before his eye. We are here to save the souls of dying sinners."[104]

Education of lay persons for the work of evangelism was critical to this endeavor. Virginia Lieson Brereton noted that early revivalists, such as Dwight L. Moody, A. B. Simpson, and A. J. Gordon, founded educational institutions to promote home and foreign missionary activity. These schools, including Moody's Chicago Bible Institute and the Northfield schools, A. B. Simpson's Missionary Training Institute, and Gordon's Boston Missionary Training School, taught not only courses in the Bible but also techniques in evangelism, revivalism, and "personal work." Often courses in social work or sociology appeared on the course offering as well.[105] Other local church colleges also offered training. J. Wilbur Chapman's Bethany College, for example, had a "Christian Work Department" to train laypersons interested in ministry.[106] Russell H. Conwell's Temple College likewise had a school of theology that offered a bachelor of divinity course; however, its evening department focused upon nontraditional students who hoped to work as YMCA secretaries, colporteurs, home and foreign missionaries, and Bible readers. The Temple School of Theology was "undenominational...upon the basis of church unity" and it emphasized practical studies available at Grace Baptist Church, which at the time was one of the largest churches in the United States.[107]

Beside training schools, how-to manuals covering the topic of "soul-saving" also proliferated during the late nineteenth and early twentieth centuries. These texts, among them such descriptive titles as *The Soul-Winning Church, Revivals: How to Promote Them, Method in Soul-Winning, Soul Winning Songs for Soul Winners, How to Win Men to Christ,* and *The Art of Taking Men Alive,* concentrated on methodology in a fashion similar to advocates of the institutional church movement.[108] One conspicuous feature

[104] Smith, *Conwell,* 184.

[105] Virginia Lieson Brereton, *Training God's Army: The American Bible School, 1880–1940* (Bloomington: Indiana University Press, 1990) 55–77.

[106] Williams, "The New Era of Church Work," 70.

[107] Anonymous, *Temple College Catalogue* (Philadelphia: Temple College, 1896) 28–31. This course catalogue is housed in the Conwellana-Templana collection at Temple University, Philadelphia PA; cf. Agnes Rush Burr, *Russell H. Conwell,* 237.

[108] Len G. Broughton, *The Soul-Winning Church* (Chicago: Fleming H. Revell Company, 1905). Although a Southern Baptist, Broughton was a popular lecturer on revivalism and soul-winning through the urban North and England. Other manuals included, but were not limited to, R. A. Torrey, *How to Bring Men to Christ* (Chicago:

of these manuals included their appeal to revivalism's long and successful history, associated with many of the most memorable American and English evangelicals, such as Jonathan Edwards, George Whitefield, John and Charles Wesley, Charles G. Finney, Charles H. Spurgeon, and Dwight L. Moody. One article on revivals claimed that one of the most important steps in successful soul-winning included "a further needed study on the human side of the methods of the most successful Christian workers."[109] J. Wilbur Chapman's manual, *Revivals and Missions* (1900), included two full chapters on revivals in American history and another chapter on the "Prince of Modern Revivalism," Charles Finney.[110] The first chapter of Henry Mabie's *Method in Soul-Winning* (1906) contained anecdotes of successful evangelists and missionaries in order to underscore the elements of their success.[111]

These "soul-winning" evangelicals, however, typically looked toward Dwight L. Moody as their best model of contemporary revivalism, and with few exceptions his evangelistic efforts directly influenced the manual writers. Henry C. Mabie, R. A. Torrey, and J. Wilbur Chapman, for example, had all worked with Moody in his various evangelistic campaigns. "We cannot all have Mr. Moody...," wrote one author, "but we can all be taught by him."[112] Moody himself did not necessarily fit the mold of a typical evangelist. Never ordained in a denomination nor theologically trained, Moody had given up a successful career as a shoe salesman to work with poor children through his Sunday school efforts in Chicago. After the Great Fire in 1871, he left with his chorister Ira Sankey on an evangelistic tour in the British Isles, where the

---

Fleming H. Revell Company, 1910); Henry C. Mabie, *Method in Soul-Winning* (Chicago: Fleming H. Revell Company, 1906); P. P. Bilhorn, *Soul Winning Songs for Soul Winners* (Chicago: P. P. Bilhorn Publisher, 1896); *Revivals: How to Promote Them*, 2d ed., ed. Walter P. Doe (New York: E. B. Treat, 1895); James Burns, *Revivals: Laws and Leaders* (New York: Hodder and Stoughten, 1909); J. C. Massee, *How to Be a Soul-Winner*, Evangelistic series 555 (Philadelphia: American Baptist Publication Society, n.d.); and R. A. Torrey, ed., *Individual Soul Winning: Its Obligation and Its Methods* (Philadelphia: Sunday School Times Company, 1906).

[109] T. W. Hunt, "The Grace of Soul-Winning," *Homiletic Review* 42/5 (November 1901): 414.

[110] Chapman, *Revivals and Missions*, 12–58.

[111] Mabie, *Method in Soul-Winning*, 11–33.

[112] J. E. Franklin, "What Mr. Moody Can Do for Us," in *Revivals*, 332. For another appreciative interpretations of Moody see William C. Wilkinson's two articles: "Dwight L. Moody as Preacher," *Homiletic Review* 36/2 (August 1898): 110–19 and "Dwight L. Moody as a Man of Affairs," *Homiletic Review* 36/3 (September 1898): 201–208.

two became a sensation. The duo returned to the United States as famous revivalists and between 1875 and 1879 conducted campaigns in Brooklyn, New York, Philadelphia, Boston, and Chicago.

"Soul-winning" evangelicals borrowed from Moody and Sankey several revivalistic techniques to meet the demands of modern, urban evangelism. One of his biographers noted that "Moody's name has grown to be a synonym of method. He had a method in everything. ...he felt that no detail was too small in the supreme business of winning souls for Christ."[113] One of his important practices included a shrewd use of advertising. "The more publicity given evangelistic meetings and addresses the better," explained Moody, and "there is no method of circulation like the press."[114] Not only did Moody advertise his engagements with placards, but also he always used the press to his advantage and gave reporters good seats at his meetings. He noted that, while he could reach a few thousand a night in a church or auditorium, thousands more could be reached by the newspaper the following morning.[115]

Like Whitefield and Wesley before him, Moody also showed a preference to preach in free churches, auditoriums, or open-air assemblies. Reflecting on this practice, A. T. Pierson believed that in Moody's career, "God has shown us that the non-church-going masses are best reached by a free, plain house of assembly, in which the poorest can feel at home, and have the Gospel without money and without price. No candid, reflecting mind can well avoid or evade the conviction, that the large free tabernacles erected in the great cities where his greatest work has been done were inseparable from his success."[116] In effect, the use of such spaces addressed many of the same concerns of the institutional church movement: the creation of a free, open, and hospitable place to reach people with the gospel of Christ.

Another prominent method employed by Moody was the "after-meeting" call for an immediate decision to follow Christ. The evangelist used the pulpit, much like Finney before him, to move his hearer to a point

---

[113] Edward Leigh Pell, *Dwight L. Moody: His Life, His Work, His Words* (Richmond VA: B. F. Johnson Publishing Co., 1900) 188.

[114] Ibid., 191. Cf. Dwight L. Moody, "How to Develop and Make Pastoral Evangelism General," *Homiletic Review* 35/5 (May 1898): 408–409.

[115] Pell, *Dwight L. Moody*, 191.

[116] A. T. Pierson, "Dwight L. Moody, the Evangelist," *Missionary Review of the World* 13 (February 1900): 91.

of decision. Moody's contemporaries debated about his abilities in oratory and preaching. He generally spoke reservedly, occasionally showing a tear of emotion; however, most observers, even those perplexed by his success, admitted that his strength lay in his "clearness, force, and earnestness."[117] Intending to move his audience to pledge themselves to Christ, Moody carefully orchestrated a call for inquirers to come forward, so that he and other chosen ministers might teach, counsel, and pray for them.[118] Most important, according to the next generation of his interpreters, his success was due to his commitment to the essential gospel message with his three R's: "ruin by sin, redemption by Christ, and regeneration by the Holy Ghost."[119] Moody delivered this message in plain and simple terms that could be understood by any of his hearers. Pierson noted that the evangelist, while neither ordained nor educated, had an ability to "make much of the blood" in his presentation of the gospel of Christ.[120]

The heirs of Moody's revivalism, including G. Campbell Morgan, J. Wilbur Chapman, R. A. Torrey, A. C. Dixon, and William Bell Riley, not only used Moody's techniques but often improved upon or adapted them in new situations. Chapman, who worked with Moody in his 1893 World's Fair campaign in Chicago, made method a top priority in his evangelistic campaigns. His recommendations for revivals, typical for the time, exemplified the extraordinary degree to which evangelism began to be conceived as an applied science for divine purposes. "The Holy Ghost is not bound by rules," he admitted, "but it certainly cannot be displeasing to Him to have a well-defined plan and as nearly as possible a perfect organization."[121] Chapman began his evangelistic crusades by contacting all

---

[117] Pell, *Dwight L. Moody*, 173–78; cf. Pierson, "Dwight L. Moody," 90–91 and R. W. Dale, "Elements of Success in the Services of Messers. Moody and Sankey," in *Revivals*, 324–31. Dale wrote, "Of Mr. Moody's own power I find it difficult to speak.... Mr. Moody's address was simple, direct, kindly, and hopeful; it had a touch of humor and a touch of pathos; it was lit up with a story or two that filled most eyes with tears; but there seemed nothing in it very remarkable. Yet it *told*." Ibid., 324–25. Emphasis in the original.

[118] Pierson, "Dwight L. Moody," 91.

[119] George M. Marsden, *Fundamentalism and American Culture: The Shaping of Twentieth-Century Evangelicalism, 1870–1925* (New York: Oxford University Press, 1980) 35. R. A. Torrey wrote of Moody that he lived these very things he preached. See *Why God Used D. L. Moody* (Chicago: Moody Press, 1923).

[120] Pierson, "Dwight L. Moody," 88.

[121] Chapman, *Revivals and Missions*, 83.

the ministers in a target city up to a year in advance of his visit, assuring them of his intention to save souls and not detract from local churches. He encouraged these pastors to begin preparing their congregations for revival by initially preaching on subjects such as: "1. Confessing sin. 2. Personal consecration. 3. Our responsibility for the unsaved. 4. What must I do to be saved?" A later series of sermons he suggested included the topics: "1. Revivals in history. 2. How we may promote a revival? 3. Hindrances to revivals. 4. Are we ready?"[122]

The pre-campaign groundwork advocated by Chapman also included a union, or ecumenical, Bible class taught by the participating pastors for church members six months in advance in order "to quicken and enlarge our faith, to awaken our expectations, and to stir our souls to go out in search of the lost."[123] Three months prior to Chapman's visit, the target city was divided into sections, each assigned with a supervisor and about fifteen workers. The workers then went door-to-door to meet and befriend neighborhood residents, especially the unchurched and the needy.[124] Next, Chapman advocated the institution of a "union prayer meeting," which floated from church to church each Sunday, as well as similar groups gathering in private homes within each city section on Friday nights.[125] He also suggested that an executive committee consisting of representative members from all participating churches be elected to oversee the work delegated to committees on finance, advertising, canvassing, music, ushers and assistants, free will offerings, and devotion.[126]

Chapman expected everything to be planned expertly, including where the audience should be seated in relation to the choir, building ventilation, and the timing of when the church or auditorium doors should be opened before the service. Most important, he trained the ushers and assistants (he expected no less than one usher per sixty persons expected to attend the service) to pass out inquirer's cards and to work with card signers during the "after-service." He required that the men and women appointed to be ushers and assistants have upstanding moral character, qualifications of a typical Sunday-school teacher, and a "willingness to do anything for Christ."[127]

---

[122] Ibid., 84.
[123] Ibid., 86.
[124] Ibid.
[125] Ibid., 87.
[126] Ibid., 88–106.
[127] Ibid., 100.

These members of the laity had the job to speak one to one with those who had been convicted of sin or wanted to renew their faith. Finally, Chapman introduced the method of simultaneous campaigning within urban revivalism. In order to maximize effective results, he placed an evangelist and chorister in each of the pre-campaign city divisions. During his 1906 Boston meetings, Chapman and his chorister Charles M. Alexander conducted services in central Boston at the famous Tremont Temple. Simultaneously, twenty-six other meetings took place throughout the Boston metropolitan area, each with its own evangelist, chorister, and local church volunteers.[128] The revival conducted by Chapman received national attention and continued for nearly one month from 26 January to 21 February.

Evangelicals in this revivalistic tradition also placed great emphasis on participation of the laity in converting the lost. Congregationalist Reuben A. Torrey, superintendent of Moody Bible Institute and pastor of Chicago Avenue Church, provided individuals a manual for personal evangelism in his *How to Bring Men to Christ* (1910). In the preface of the book, he explained that while there existed many books on providing Bible texts to use with inquirers, "this book is intended not only to point out passages to be used but to show how to use them, illustrating this use by cases from actual experience."[129] Torrey's manual covered ways to share Christ with many different types of unbelievers, including nine chapters covering the indifferent, careless, anxious, complaining, willful, deluded, procrastinators, backsliders, skeptics, and infidels. He also made clear that any layperson had the potential to successfully bring people to Christ so long as he or she had a love for souls, a working knowledge of scripture, an active prayer life, and experienced baptism of the Holy Ghost.[130] Henry C. Mabie's text went so far as to give specific advice on how to be tactful in the evangelism of possible converts.[131] Giving time to home and foreign missions, he considered how to approach agnostics, Roman Catholics, and adherents to non-Christian religions.[132] Chapman devoted an entire chapter to personal

---

[128] Arcturus Z. Conrad, *A Complete Account of the Great Boston Revival under the Leadership of J. Wilbur Chapman and Charles M. Alexander* (Boston: The King's Business Publishing Company, 1909) 227–88.

[129] Torrey, *How to Bring Men to Christ*, 3–4.

[130] Ibid., 7–13.

[131] Mabie, *Method in Soul-Winning*, 86–110.

[132] See especially ibid., 111–28.

evangelism and soul-winning in his *Present-Day Evangelism* (1903), noting that the success or failure of the evangelistic church ultimately depended upon the extent of active participation by the laity.[133] Torrey, Mabie, and Chapman emphasized the duty of all believers to bear witnesses to the gospel message with an eye to save the souls of the unregenerate.

Another timed-tested resource for evangelicals included the use of rescue missions. While some participants of the institutional church movement, like Rainsford, claimed that these organizations did more harm than help, evangelicals influenced by revivalism saw them as a good way to win souls and at the same time ameliorate social ills. Urban missions gained a new following with the success of the English-imported Salvation Army. Started by William and Catherine Booth in the slums of London, the first Salvationists, "the splendid seven," arrived in the United States on 10 March 1880. By the mid-1890s the Salvation Army missions, brass bands, and open-air meetings were a familiar sight on the streets of urban America.[134] General Booth's *Darkest England and the Way Out* (1890), particularly his idea of the "City Colony," became the catalyst for the American Army's social activism among the urban poor and destitute. The City Colony consisted of a fourfold plan: receive houses for the destitute, factories for those out of work, regimentation of the unemployed, and household salvage brigades.

American Salvationists most visibly transplanted Booth's idea of receiving houses in the United States.[135] In his original conception, Booth wished to ensure "food and shelter for every man" by opening food depots and rescue missions.[136] He sold the food to Londoners only to cover expenses, and rooms (including use of a washroom and a meal) could be purchased for the minimal cost of four pence per night. While at the shelter, Army workers asked boarders to attend "a rousing Salvation meeting"

---

[133] J. Wilbur Chapman, *Present-Day Evangelism* (New York: Baker Taylor Co., 1903; reprint, Chicago: Fleming H. Revell Company, 1913) 137–44, 168–78.

[134] Edward H. McKinley, *Marching to Glory: The History of the Salvation Army in the United States, 1880–1992*, rev. and expanded 2d ed. (Grand Rapids: William B. Eerdmans Publishing Company, 1995) 91.

[135] This is not to suggest that the other ideas were ignored. See Commander Booth Tucker, "The Winter Relief and Christmas Dinners of the Salvation Army," *Social Service* 6/6 (December 1902): 119–21.

[136] General Booth, *In Darkest England and the Way Out* (London: International Head Quarters of the Salvation Army, 1890) 95.

complete with banjoes, tambourines, testimonies, and addresses.[137] While admitting that many boarders remained, at best, only curious, Booth noted that the meetings gave the Army a most important opportunity to labor for the salvation of individuals while meeting their physical needs.[138] With their emphasis on evangelism, Salvationists had a lot in common with many of their American evangelical brothers and sisters and eventually influenced them with their combined fervor for soul-saving and social outreach.

Of those North American evangelicals influenced by the Salvation Army, Henry Wilson provides an interesting case. When the Army arrived in 1884 at Kingston, Ontario, where he served as an Anglican priest, Wilson, much to the dismay of his bishop, began to attend their meetings regularly. He admitted that going to the altar with the poor of the city made him realize he was as spiritually decrepit as any of them. He claimed that this experience became the most formative spiritual event in his life. That same year his involvement with the Army cost him his position in Kingston, but, upon hearing of Wilson's situation, William Rainsford offered him a position at St. George's Episcopal Church in New York. Rainsford placed him in charge of the Avenue A Mission run by the parish, where he preached each day, led Bible studies, worked with children, and diligently visited local members of the community. Rainsford reminisced of Wilson that "if we are really honest with ourselves we must admit that it is a rare thing to know a man who, without hesitation or backward look, is willing to place his very all on the altar. Such was he."[139]

Despite such sentimental admiration for a friend, however, Wilson's sentiments and zeal also provided the greatest source of tension with his rector. Of Wilson's work at Avenue A Rainsford more candidly noted: "Never was a more persistent painstaking effort made to apply what is called old-fashioned Gospel preaching to the community than we made for six years on distinctly Salvation Army lines; and I satisfied myself that the testimonies and all the rest were mostly trumped up. The effect was bad."[140] Despite his later misgivings about Wilson's seven years at St. George's Church, Rainsford remained remarkably tolerant of his associate minister's extra-ecclesial associations. Wilson continued to work with the Salvation Army in New York City, even convincing Rainsford to open a drawing room

---

[137] Ibid., 97–100.
[138] Ibid., 98.
[139] Rainsford, *Varied Life*, 247.
[140] Rainsford, *Preacher's Story*, 137.

in his own rectory so the Army could hold meetings there.[141] He not only maintained many Salvationist friends throughout his life, including periodic correspondence and visitation with General Booth, but credited them as the catalyst for his own conversion and source of his methods in urban evangelism.[142]

While at St. George's, Wilson also became friends with the Christian and Missionary Alliance founder and president A. B. Simpson. In fact, his initial association with Simpson and his Gospel Tabernacle was made possible by the Christian Alliance's position that participants need not leave their regular church connections; this is not to mention the willingness of Rainsford and Bishop Henry C. Potter to abide these associations. Wilson was attracted to Simpson's vision of his organization as a "fraternal organization of all evangelical denominations" seeking to promote conversions, personal evangelism, higher Christian living, and healing.[143] While working with Simpson, Wilson experienced the healing of his own bodily ailments, and this experience validated his belief that Christ could meet the spiritual and bodily needs of all converted persons.[144] In 1891 he resigned his assistantship at St. George's and became the associate pastor of Simpson's Gospel Tabernacle.

A. B. Simpson's path was similar to Wilson's. While serving as a Presbyterian minister at Thirteenth Street Presbyterian Church in New York City, he ran into resistance from his congregation for encouraging the poor and homeless to attend services. In 1881 he resigned his pulpit because the congregation refused to admit to membership 100 Italian immigrants converted through street evangelism and neighborhood visitation. That same year Simpson founded the Gospel Tabernacle, a theater converted into a place of worship at Forty-fourth Street and Eighth Avenue. He immediately sought to bring evangelicals together in order to promote home and foreign evangelism and in 1884 organized a conference to this end. Within a decade, Simpson had held similar conferences throughout Eastern and Midwestern cities, and in 1887 the regular participants officially formed the Christian Alliance "of all those in all the world who hold in

---

[141] Madele Wilson and A. B. Simpson, *Henry Wilson: One of God's Best* (New York: The Alliance Press Company, 1908) 67.

[142] Ibid., 63–75.

[143] Ibid., 77.

[144] Ibid., 82–93.

unison the faith of God and the Gospel of full salvation."[145] Alliance members included such evangelical luminaries as A. J. Gordon, R. A. Torrey, Dwight L. Moody, J. Wilbur Chapman, Frances Willard, Robert E. Speer, and A. T. Pierson.[146]

Simpson's emphasis on personal evangelism was rooted in the holiness beliefs in sanctification. He believed that Christ prepared the convert to receive the Holy Spirit; the Spirit, then, gradually sanctified the convert, which resulted in good works toward his or her neighbor.[147] Such an understanding meant that all Christians "are here as missionaries, every one of us with a commission and a trust." He therefore exhorted Alliance members, "Let us find our work, and like Him, 'whatsoever thy hand findeth to do, do it with thy might.'"[148] Besides foreign missions, the Gospel Tabernacle and the Christian Alliance supported rescue missions, orphanages, hospitals, children's ministries, prison work, and evangelism among immigrants. By 1897, when the Christian Alliance, focused upon urban missions, merged with its sister organization the International Missionary Alliance to form the Christian and Missionary Alliance (CMA), the urban work of the organization was so extensive that Simpson himself could no longer keep track of all the charitable work in which his associates participated in New York.[149] Interestingly, the CMA founder noted his success with the urban masses over and against techniques of advocates of religious environmentalism. Only converted souls, he believed, could begin to live the higher Christian life through which God called them to reach out to all persons, especially the poor and neglected of the city.[150]

The Pacific Garden Mission (PGM) in Chicago provided an exceptional example of the results that soul-saving evangelicals expected from their urban missions work. Founded in 1877 by a former Union colonel, George R. Clarke, and his wife, Sarah Dunn Clarke, the mission ministered to bums and drunkards in Chicago's "whiskey row." Three years later the mission moved to 100 East Van Buren Street into the old Pacific Beer Garden; Dwight L. Moody suggested to Clarke that he remove the

---

[145] Quoted in Magnuson, *Salvation in the Slums*, 15.

[146] Ibid., 18.

[147] A. B. Simpson, *The Fourfold Gospel* (Camp Hill PA: Christian Publications, 1984) 31.

[148] Ibid., 79.

[149] Magnuson, *Salvation in the Slums*, 17.

[150] Anonymous, "Varieties of Christian Work," *Christian Alliance and Missionary Weekly* 11/21 (24 November 1893): 322.

word "beer" from the building and add the word "mission" as testament that all things can be redeemed.[151] Theologian Carl F. H. Henry remarked that under the leadership of the Clarkes and their successor and convert, Harry Monroe, PGM became "a growing cradle of American evangelism" because such a large number of its converts went on to do ministerial work.[152] One reason for this included it's leaders' insistence that the mission keep as its primary goal the transformation of all converts into personal ambassadors for Christ whether they entered full-time Christian work or not.[153]

The Pacific Garden Mission's two most famous converts, Billy Sunday and Mel Trotter, went on to become national figures in revivalistic evangelism and urban missions, respectively. In fact, Sunday and Trotter often worked together in their early careers. Sunday, after completing a campaign, often called Trotter to deliver his dramatic testimony the last day. Trotter electrified crowds with his story of how he intended to commit suicide by throwing himself into Lake Michigan. An alcoholic and laden by debt, Trotter explained that he had nothing else to live for when Harry Monroe pulled him from the street into PGM. After giving his life to Jesus, he told them, he kicked his drinking habit, reconciled with his wife, and began to work full-time at the mission.[154] After the testimony, Sunday moved on to the next city, leaving Trotter behind to attempt to organize the local Christians and new converts in order to found another city mission.[155]

While it is unclear how many missions took root because of Trotter's teamwork with Sunday, Trotter did found a national network of missions throughout the United States. He established the City Rescue Mission in Grand Rapids, Michigan, in February 1900 at the behest of the city's Christian businessmen. Trotter's mission was an old storefront in a seedy section of town on Canal Street. The outside of the mission was painted with messages such as "Jesus Saves" and "Hope for All Who Enter Here." By 1907 the work had expanded and Trotter raised money to purchase Smith's Opera House. According to Trotter, the key to a successful mission

[151] Carl F. H. Henry, *The Pacific Garden Mission: A Doorway to Heaven* (Grand Rapids: Zondervan Publishing House, 1942) 29.

[152] Ibid., 50.

[153] Ibid., 62.

[154] Trotter's personal testimony can be found in "Life Story: Told by Mel Trotter at the Rescue Mission," Mel Trotter papers (hereafter cited as Trotter papers) collection 47, box 8, folder 22, Billy Graham Center archives, Wheaton IL.

[155] Henry, *Pacific Garden Mission*, 69; cf. Fred C. Zarfas, *Mel Trotter: A Biography* (Grand Rapids: Zondervan Publishing House, 1950) 83–87.

was preaching "the simple gospel" 365 nights every year in order to transform "miserable men into modern miracles."[156]

Trotter, however, gave as much attention to method as message. He argued that successful mission needed the support of local churches regardless of denominational affiliation. The board of directors should be men of high standing who were not only willing to support "soul-winning, old-time religion" but who could sustain the mission financially as well. The placement of the mission was also carefully planned. Trotter thought the best locations were centralized, preferably near pawn shops, second-hand stores, or saloons. Most important, Trotter did not see the mission as a competitor with the church; rather, missions acted as an arm of the true church itself. For this reason, converts did not become "members" of the mission; however, Trotter did write down their names and addresses. If converts did not attend local churches, he would make efforts to keep them coming to the mission. This often meant providing child care, children's Sunday school, and mothers' meetings. Ultimately, Trotter hoped that men would dedicate themselves to Christ and then to their home and family life.[157] Within forty years Trotter expanded the number of urban missions to sixty-six in such cities as Milwaukee, South Bend, Muskegon, Kalamazoo, St. Paul, Pittsburgh, and Los Angeles.[158]

It is well worth noting that the methods of those evangelicals running rescue missions often resembled those used within the institutional church movement. The New Grand Army of the Redeemed (NGAR) Mission in New York, for example, assisted U.S. Army veterans. Saloon keepers often cashed veterans' pension checks for a small fee, hoping they would stay and patronize the establishment. In order to undermine the saloon keepers' tactic, rehabilitated drunkard Henry H. Hadley convinced Presbyterian minister T. DeWitt Talmage and publisher Louis Klopsch to provide the funds to cash veterans' checks free of charge, outside the influence of morally questionable establishments.[159] Talmage claimed that the NGAR Mission's efforts kept thousands of pension checks out of saloon tills.

---

[156] Anonymous, "City Rescue Mission, Grand Rapids, Mich.," Trotter papers, collection 47, box 8, folder 22.

[157] Mel Trotter, "Rescue Missions," Trotter papers, collection 47, box 7, folder 35.

[158] Henry, *Pacific Garden Mission*, 69–70.

[159] Anonymous, "To the Rescue of the Veterans," *Christian Herald* 15/21 (25 May 1892): 325.

Episcopalian Henry Y. Satterlee's Galilee Mission in New York maintained a reading room, library, and lodging house. The mission also instituted an alcohol-free restaurant that sold prepared food at cost to counteract saloons that sold cheap food to attract thirsty patrons.[160] Founded by four former hoboes, Philadelphia's Inasmuch Mission coupled its preaching and Bible studies with classes in "better living."[161] The mission housed homeless men, taught them proper hygiene and manners, and acted as an employment agency. The four superintendents, Arthur W. Taylor, George A. Tyler, Randolph M. Lawrence, and George Long, made business contacts with several steel companies in Pennsylvania, including Lukens, Cambria, and Carnegie, to place mission residents into full-time jobs.[162] Rescue missions, therefore, exemplified how soul-saving revivalism concretely impacted the social order. Indeed, even those with inclinations toward moral environmentalism often recognized the positive contributions of revivalism and rescue missions toward the social order.[163] In the words of one *Biblical World* editorial, "Our immediate duty, then, is plain. It is not that the educator shall oppose the revival or that the revivalist shall declaim against education, but that each shall endeavor to make his own work more effective by more perfectly adapting it to the nature and needs of those for whom he works.... Together they call, not for mutual opposition, but for intelligent co-operation."[164]

Theological Minimalism and Denominational Ambivalence

The attempts by evangelicals to gain cultural relevance, whether through the methods of social Christianity or soul-saving revivalism, tended to promote theological minimalism, which in turn lent itself to denominational ambivalence. Moltmann argued that the effort to successfully make the gospel sensible to the wider culture typically results in a watering down of the very distinctions and peculiarities that create religious identity. The

---

[160] Anonymous, "A Successful Mission," *Christian Herald* 15/32 (10 August 1892): 499.

[161] Blair Jaekel, "The Inasmuch Mission," *World's Work* 25/2 (December 1912): 205–213.

[162] Ibid., 212.

[163] Charles H. Richard, "Some Needed Factors in the New Evangelism," *Bibliotheca Sacra* 62/246 (April 1905): 354–55.

[164] "Education vs. Revivals, or Education and Revivals?" *Biblical World* 25/5 (May 1905): 326.

denominational identity within the Northern Protestant establishment was particularly vulnerable because so many evangelicals within it shared a common sense of mission and focus upon method. Both advocates of the techniques of soul-saving revivalism and social Christianity promoted theological minimalism, a minimalism that aided in their extra-ecclesial associations promoting particular methods of engaging American culture.

Many advocates of social Christianity found that the methods they promoted required close association and practical cooperation with evangelicals of like mind. However, the problem, as they saw it, was a tenacious sectarianism that often scuttled practical cooperation. In a paper submitted to the World's Parliament of Religion in 1893, publisher William T. Stead claimed that "The work of the Civic Church is to establish the Kingdom of Heaven here among men—in other words, to reconstitute human society, to regenerate the State and inspire it with an aspiration after a Divine ideal" based upon "intelligent and fraternal co-operation."[165] Advocates of the social gospel learned quickly that the social victories by individuals like Parkhurst and Potter were few and far between and surmised that full evangelical Protestant cooperation was a necessary component for the church to carry out its prophetic mission to institute the kingdom of God on earth. Stead continued: "[While] men may differ about original sin, they agree about the necessity of supplying pure water; they quarrel over apostolic succession, but they are one as to the need for cleansing cesspools and flushing sewers. It is in the fruitful works of righteousness, in the practical realization of humanitarian ideals that the reunion of Christendom, and not of Christendom only, is to be brought about."[166] Stead's statement, intimating the reunion of the world's great religions, was extreme for most evangelicals; however, mainstream social gospel advocates, such as Washington Gladden, echoed Stead's sentiments. "When the Church whose high calling it is to be the healer of breaches and the promoter of unity so far departs from the word and ways of our Lord as to give place to these schisms in her own body, the case is indeed deplorable.... The champions of the sects have had to exalt their own peculiarities; not one of these is of any vital importance; and to emphasize these is to make unity impossible."[167]

---

[165] William T. Stead, "The Civic Church," *Review of Reviews* 8/4 (November 1893): 428.

[166] Ibid., 429.

[167] Washington Gladden, *Social Facts and Forces* (New York: G. P. Putnam's Sons, 1897) 210. Cf. "The Church" *Chautauquan* 29/2 (May 1899): 127.

Schism, sectarianism, and church divisions, according to the Ohio Congregationalist, thwarted the church's central mission to institute the kingdom of God on earth.

Rauschenbusch's *A Theology for the Social Gospel* provided the social gospel with a mature theological rationale. The Rochester Theological Seminary professor realized that this work was meant to serve an existing social gospel movement and, in this sense, was derivative in nature. "We have a social gospel," he began the book. "We need a systematic theology large enough to match it and vital enough to back it."[168] The theological readjustment that he advocated surrounded the idea of unity. "The dogmas and theological ideas of the early Church were those ideas which at that time were needed to hold the Church together, to rally its forces, and to give it victorious energy against antagonistic powers.... The social gospel does not need the aid of church authority to get hold of our hearts.... It will do for us what the Nicene theology did in the fourth century."[169]

According to Rauschenbusch the crux of the social gospel was not statements of dogmas or religious rites but ethics. "Every forward step in the historical evolution of religion has been marked by a closer union of religion and ethics by the elimination of non-ethical religious performances. This union of religion and ethics reached its highest perfection in the life and mind of Jesus.... Any new movement in theology which asserts the union of religion and ethics is likely to be a wholesome and christianizing force in Christian thought."[170] Ten years earlier in his *Christianity and the Social Crisis*, the work that catapulted him to fame as a spokesperson of the social gospel, Rauschenbusch declared that dogmatism constituted "one of the chief anti-social forces" within Christianity.[171] So long as the church was primarily dogmatic, it continued to be "churchly," or focused inwardly upon itself. Such a focus, however, ignored the true vocation of the church, which existed "to create the force which builds the kingdom of God on earth, the better humanity."[172] In Rauschenbusch's view, the church of the twentieth century had thus far continued to be unfaithful to its calling by focusing upon statements of dogma, creeds, and religious forms of worship. Such arguments clearly implied that the church could not be identified by its

---

[168] Rauschenbusch, *Theology for the Social Gospel*, 1.

[169] Ibid., 13.

[170] Ibid., 14–15.

[171] Rauschenbusch, *Social Crisis*, 206.

[172] Ibid., 207.

beliefs and creeds; rather, only its common commitment to the moral and ethical truths of Jesus validated its claim to be the true church. Not all advocates of the social gospel were willing to go as far as Rauschenbusch on matters of dogma and creed, but most had sympathies, at least, with his wish to set dogmatic disputes aside and de-emphasize theology in order to allow evangelical Protestant churches to reach the masses.

As in the case of advocates of social Christianity, the promotion of soul-saving as the primary mission of the church shaped the way these evangelicals understood the church's identity. Chapman epitomized the view of the church held by the heirs of revivalism. Of the church's mission he explained that "to evangelize is the first duty in the order of time, for there must be believers to be baptized and converts to become believers in order to form the Church."[173] Understanding the church as a body of converted believers typically resulted in an emphasis upon doctrines as opposed to ethical behavior as a litmus test for determining the true church. However, an irony must be noted. Although the focus upon individual conversion usually meant that faith (or belief) became a locus of religious experience, distinctive theological dogmas and systems were typically distilled to "basic" or essential truths.

Simply, faith (or belief) always has an object or set of objects toward which it points. Soul-saving evangelicals, therefore, expected that the Holy Spirit used the basic truths of the gospel proclaimed by the church to awaken the sinner, who then confessed how he had experienced these very truths in his own life. Len G. Broughton, a Southern Baptist who regularly lectured among Northern urban evangelicals, claimed, therefore, that "there are THREE ESSENTIAL TRUTHS which need especial emphasis in a soul-winning church: The Integrity of the Scriptures, the Deity of Christ, and Salvation by the Cross."[174] While he admitted that these doctrines had an old history, the goal of soul-saving made them particularly important and vital to the vocation of the church. These three doctrines, according to Broughton, formed the necessary foundation for the church's message to the world. "No apology will be tolerated," he warned. "The moment one shows signs of wavering about the Deity of Christ, the Infallibility of the Scripture, or Salvation by Grace *his power to win souls is gone.* Sinners themselves have

---

[173] Chapman, *Evangelism*, 13–14.
[174] Broughton, *Soul-Winning Church*, 43–44.

no respect for faithless teaching."[175] An editorial in the Northern Baptist *Watchman* sounded a similar admonition:

> Let the ministers preach the affirmative, pivotal truths of Christianity. This is no time for them to occupy the attention of their people with discourses which only touch the fringes of the Christian revelation; it is not a time for a series of sermons on "Bible Cities," and the "Women of the Bible," or for lectures on ethical relations, or on "Municipal Reform," or the "Higher Criticism." ...The great things in the Bible are the claims of Christ and His revelation to men as Saviour and Lord. We do not hesitate to affirm that the ministers who wish to see revival of religion in their churches will not stray far from those central and controlling themes.[176]

Presbyterian Robert E. Speer, in a speech before the New England Evangelistic Association in 1906, went even further, asserting that "the churches whose growth has been slight have been churches regarding which the impression prevails that they have relinquished a little hold upon the central evangelical convictions," preaching "a poor, washy, tepid Gospel."[177]

The publication between 1910 and 1915 of the twelve-volume work *The Fundamentals*, funded by millionaires Lyman and Milton Stewart, most dramatically illustrated the importance of doctrine for church identity as presented by evangelicals in the revivalist tradition. A. C. Dixon, Louis Meyer, and R. A. Torrey edited these volumes under the supervision of a committee consisting of, among others, Charles R. Erdman, L. W. Munhall, T. C. Horton, and Henry C. Mabie.[178] A short perusal of the volumes confirms that the compilation is a menagerie of theological treatises, cultural critique, and personal testimony from American, British, and Canadian contributors of various Protestant traditions; however, for all of their disparate opinions, the authors uniformly found themselves concerned about those groups claiming to be the true church while abandoning evangelical orthodoxy.

---

[175] Ibid., 48.

[176] "Working for a Revival," *Watchman* 76/1 (3 January 1895): 7.

[177] Quoted in "The Message of Christianity," anonymous, *Outlook* 83/11 (17 March 1906): 591, 592.

[178] Volumes 1–5 were published between 1910 and 1911 and edited by A. C. Dixon. Louis Meyer edited volumes 6–10 between 1911 and 1913, when he died. Torrey, while the head of the Bible Institute of Los Angeles, edited the final two volumes in 1915. Cf. "A Statement by Two Laymen," in vol. 12 of *The Fundamentals: A Testimony to the Truth* (Chicago: Testimony Publishing Company, n.d.) 3.

Of the articles dealing with the church's vocation, the *Fundamentals'* authors consistently advocated the coupling of dynamic evangelistic method with an orthodox presentation of the gospel message. Munhall, in his contribution to volume twelve of the series, asserted that "doctrinal preaching…is necessary to evangelistic success."[179] He illustrated his point with a moving (likely apocryphal) story about a conversation he had with Henry Ward Beecher, known to be a theologically liberal preacher.[180]

> While conducting an evangelistic campaign in Brooklyn Tabernacle I one day met Mr. Beecher. As he held my right hand in both of his, he said: "I hear you are having a great blessing in your meetings with Dr. Talmage. I very much wish we could have your campaign in Plymouth Church." He trembled as he held my hand. He then said, "But I fear my people would not stand for it." Then, after hesitating for a few minutes he added, "I would like to see an old-time Holy Ghost revival in Plymouth Church before I go hence." He then broke down and cried as if his heart would break. Three weeks later, to a day, his body was laid in the grave.[181]

J. C. Ryle, Anglican bishop of Liverpool, in his contribution to volume nine, expressed the importance of doctrine as a distinguishing mark of the true church in no uncertain terms. Members of the true church, according the evangelical churchman, "are entirely agreed on all the weightier matters of religion, for they are taught by one Spirit. About God, and Christ, and the Spirit, and sin, and their own hearts, and faith, and repentance, and the necessity of holiness, and the value of the Bible, and the importance of prayer, and the resurrection, and the judgment to come—about all these points they are of one mind."[182]

Ironically, evangelicals from the revivalistic tradition, while criticizing advocates of other forms of social Christianity for minimizing theology in an effort to reclaim America for the church, tried to package their presentation of the gospel message in the most rudimentary forms for the same reason.[183]

---

[179] L. W. Munhall, "The Doctrines that Must Be Emphasized in Successful Evangelism," in *Fundamentals*, vol. 12, p. 15.

[180] It is unclear to what extent this story has been embellished to make its author's point.

[181] Munhall, "Successful Evangelism," 23.

[182] Bishop Ryle, "The True Church," in *Fundamentals* vol. 9, p. 7.

[183] For examples of such critiques see Vosburgh, "Mission of the Church," 10; William B. Riley, *The Perennial Revival: A Plea for Evangelism* (Chicago: Winona Publishing Co., 1904) 136; and A. C. Dixon, "The Greatest Need of the Greater New York," *Homiletic Review* 38/6 (December 1899): 520.

Dwight L. Moody, at the twilight of his career, wrote that "in all my experience I do not recall one pastor who has proved a failure if he preacht the Word of God in simplicity and sincerity, and molded his ministry along Gospel lines."[184] Henry C. Mabie wrote an entire chapter along these lines in his soul-winning manual, noting that "he who would evangelize effectively needs to have a right view, first, of the divinely wrought basis on which evangelization is possible...[However,] if we are to be *skillful* as evangelists, we must learn to delimit the content of our message in the interest of strategic skill."[185] T. DeWitt Talmage, popular preacher and pastor of Central Presbyterian Church in Brooklyn, advised that "the Gospel has been kept back from the masses because we have been such sticklers for the mere technicalities of religion.... We must come in the plain vernacular or they will not understand us."[186]

The content of that basic gospel message generally had the same assumptions: 1. Individuals being sinful find themselves eternally separated from God; 2. Christ's substitutionary atonement is the only adequate gift to humanity that allows the possibility that all persons can be reconciled to God; and 3. Individuals must accept the gift whereupon they begin a new life in Christ with the help of the Holy Spirit. While these evangelicals presented that message in a variety of ways, they often moved from simple to simplistic expressions of faith. Henry C. Mabie declared that "the evangelizing message to a world of sinful men, is the proclamation of the new and relatively speaking, altered probation made possible to men through the sacrificial lamb eternally slain for them."[187] Likewise, Torrey noted that those intending to share Christ needed to know the Bible "so as (1) to show men their need of a Saviour, (2) to show them Jesus as the Saviour they need, [and] (3) to show them how to make this Saviour their own."[188] A. B. Simpson emphasized what he called the four essential truths of the gospel: "Christ our Saviour, Sanctifier, Healer, and Coming King." Talmage simply noted that "I should rather tell the people, 'Justification is this: you trust in Christ and God will let you off.'"[189]

---

[184] Dwight L. Moody, "How to Develop and Make Pastoral Evangelism," 409.
[185] Mabie, *Method in Soul-Winning*, 34–35. Emphasis added.
[186] T. DeWitt Talmage, "Preaching to the Masses," in *Revivals*, 314
[187] Mabie, *Method in Soul-Winning*, 47.
[188] Torrey, *How to Bring Men to Christ*, 10.
[189] Talmage, "Preaching to the Masses," in *Revivals*, 316.

As in the case of social gospel advocates, by simplifying the message of the gospel in order to evangelize, soul-saving evangelicals tended to minimize dogmatic constructions and symbolic forms of worship, which made denominational institutions theologically distinctive. Ryle's discussion of the true church in *The Fundamentals* was illustrative:

> It is a Church of which all the members have the same marks. They are all born of the Spirit; they all possess "repentance toward God, faith toward out Lord Jesus Christ," and holiness of life and conversion. They all hate sin, and they all love Christ. They worship differently and after various fashions;...but they all worship with one heart. They are all led by one Spirit; they all build upon one foundation; they all draw their religion from one single Book—that is the Bible. They are all joined by one great center—that is Jesus Christ. They all even now can say with one heart, "Hallelujah"; and they can all respond with one heart and voice, "Amen and Amen."[190]

More to the point, DeWitt Talmage claimed that "intense denomi-nationalism" provided a chief obstacle for reaching the masses. While stating that he believed denominations ought to remain separate, he greatly qualified this statement: "Now we need to show the world that we have a desire dominant over all sectarianism, and that our first desire is to bring people into the Kingdom of our Lord Jesus Christ, whether they join our Church or some other Church."[191] Trotter argued that missions constituted the church downtown and must have "no law but love, no creed but Christ."[192] Therefore, minimization of theological reflection for expedient evangelization led to the support of extra-denominational and parachurch organizations that had focused goals and missions. Whether nondenominational "faith missions," Booth's Salvation Army, a city rescue mission, or an evangelistic campaign by Dwight L. Moody, these evangelicals had few reservations about trying to reclaim American culture outside of clearly marked ecclesial institutions.

The demand of new methods to regain cultural relevance was not the only thing that shaped the ecclesiology of the Northern evangelical Protestant establishment. Pneumatology and eschatology provided important and defining sources for the development of evangelical ecclesiology in the establishment as well. Therefore, the next two chapters

---

[190] Ryle, "True Church," in *Fundamentals*, vol. 9, pp. 5–6.
[191] Talmage, "Preaching to the Masses," in *Revivals*, 312.
[192] Trotter, "Rescue Missions."

will examine these doctrines and show how they shaped the church idea among these evangelicals.

CHAPTER 4

Pneumatology:
The Holy Spirit and the Shape of Authority

In an oft-quoted passage C. I. Scofield observed in 1899 that "within the last twenty years more has been written on the doctrine of the Holy Spirit than in the preceding eighteen hundred years."[1] Professor Henry Collin Minton, one-time moderator of the Presbyterian Church in the U.S.A., argued that "no subject in all the range of Christian truth or thought is more important than that of the work of the Holy Ghost within us."[2] Religious author and Methodist minister James M. Campbell likewise believed that "no other subject is of more absorbing interest" than that of the Holy Spirit, and he anticipated that this particular doctrine would occupy the mind of the church for generations to come.[3] However, Frank Mason North, president of the Open and Institutional Church League, worried that this unprecedented focus upon the Holy Spirit had made the church "peculiarly liable to certain kinds of errors" that might subvert the mission and purpose of the church.[4] These four representative voices suggest the importance

---

[1] C. I. Scofield, *Plain Papers on the Doctrine of the Holy Spirit* (Grand Rapids: Baker Book House, 1966) 9. Cf. George M. Marsden, *Fundamentalism and American Culture: The Shaping of Twentieth Century Evangelicalism, 1870–1925* (New York: Oxford University Press, 1980) 72; Grant Wacker, "The Holy Spirit and the Spirit of the Age," *Journal of American History* 72/1 (Jun 1985): 55.

[2] Henry Collin Minton, "The Holy Spirit in Christian Experience," *Homiletic Review* 42/1 (July 1901): 31.

[3] James M. Campbell, "The Place of the Doctrine of the Holy Spirit in the Preaching of To-day," *Homiletic Review* 46/4 (October 1902): 297.

[4] Frank Mason North, "Above That Which Is Written," *Open Church* 2/1 (January 1898): 256–57.

placed upon pneumatology, or the doctrine of the Holy Spirit, by turn-of-the-century evangelical Protestants.

The two most important movements of pneumatology in the Northern Protestant establishment were the New Theology, or progressive orthodoxy, and the Keswick Holiness, or Higher Life, movements. Grant Wacker convincingly argued that evangelicals in the late nineteenth century, whether subscribing to the "new theology" or the pursuit of the "higher life," were actually cut from the same cloth. He further claimed that it is a "serious distortion" to depict these forms of evangelicalism as incompatible types of spirituality; rather, he suggested that the movements be compared to twins sharing the same genetic material.[5] This shared genetic material especially included their shared stress upon religious experience, or divine immanence. Simply, the Holy Spirit constituted the very presence of God whether dwelling within the individual, the church, or the modern world. However, their beliefs about the Holy Spirit were not simply abstract contemplation. Establishment evangelicals wished make their beliefs concrete and effective. To this end, one can observe a direct correlation between evangelicals' pneumatology and the structures they believed ought to govern the church. Depending upon whether evangelicals thought the Spirit worked primarily through individuals or institutions made a difference in the way theologians imagined the church community, called by God and guided by the Spirit.

The proponents of the New Theology and Keswick Holiness not only shared an emphasis on divine immanence, but they also shared concerns about the woeful state of the Protestant establishment, fretted over the alienation of the masses from its churches, and believed that the denominational status quo was not sufficient to address the dilemmas faced by the church. As theological critics of the denominational status quo, these thinkers typically aligned themselves with and defended the strategies employed to address evangelical concerns with American culture. A large majority of the thinkers in these movements actively promoted and participated in the reform efforts discussed in the previous chapter. Furthermore, these theologians provided a rationale for or against particular attempts to engage American culture, while actively attempting to shape the way their particular denominations would be the church in the world. Advocates of the Keswick Holiness movement placed emphasis upon the

---

[5] Wacker, "Spirit of the Age," 46, 49.

work of the Spirit, who sanctified the individual in this world through faith (as opposed to the after-life). This meant that God enabled believers to live a life of holiness necessary for change in society to occur from the bottom up. Conversely, advocates of the New Theology asserted God's immanence through developing creation. The Holy Spirit, according to them, continued the ministry of Jesus Christ by progressively revealing the will of God in the present time within the discoveries of science, the institutions of democratic government, the church, or modern intellectual insights. Reform of society, therefore, would occur from the top down through institutions that could influence the individual.

Not surprisingly, therefore, both groups' ecclesiology diverged, mirroring their differing pneumatology. On the one hand, advocates of progressive orthodoxy sought to influence the clergy and laity through "efficient" centralized structures; hence, they typically supported the strategies of social Christianity, ecumenical and cooperative efforts, denominational centralization, and educational endeavors. Proponents of the Higher Life movement favored a more populist approach, preferring to gain adherents through organizations that promoted conversion, personal moral reform, and individual growth through prayer and Bible study; therefore, they naturally preferred revivalistic techniques for reform. In each case, the group's pneumatology also bolstered evangelical denominational ambivalence, but for different reasons. Ideally, the New Theologians, in their quest for efficient, centralized structures, questioned the ultimate suitability of denominations to carry out the work of the church. Practically, however, they recognized the importance of denominational structures to promote their ecclesiological agenda. Likewise, the egalitarian impulses of Keswick Holiness also questioned denominational authority. However, Keswickers also recognized that denominations had particular gifts that helped promote the gospel of Christ. This chapter will explore the pneumatology of the New Theology and the Higher Life, giving special attention to the ecclesiological implications this doctrine provided theologians in the Protestant establishment churches.

Be Ye Baptized with the Holy Ghost:
Keswick Holiness in Establishment Churches

The strategists of revivalism did not invent the ideas concerning the Holy Spirit that informed and bolstered their vocational vision of the church.[6] During the 1870s the American husband-and-wife team of Robert Pearsall Smith and Hannah Whitall Smith promoted many of the basic theological elements that constituted the Higher Life theology, associated with the holiness conferences held in the resort town of Keswick, England. Both Smiths were products of the famous 1858 urban revivals in the United States and sought to experience the "second blessing" of baptism of the Holy Spirit in order to live a holy life pleasing to God. Although they "waited upon the Lord" almost a decade before finally receiving this blessing, their dramatic and emotional experience convinced the two to promote holiness teaching in the United States and abroad. Their popularity rose with the publication of Pearsall Smith's *Holiness Through Faith* (1870) and Whitall Smith's *The Christian's Secret of a Happy Life* (1875).

Pearsall Smith extended the Protestant dogma of justification by faith alone and advocated "the principle of sanctification by faith, and not by works or effort."[7] According to him, Jesus Christ had won our sanctification (as our justification) on the cross; therefore, holiness came through faith as "the gracious operation of the Spirit, taking the glorious things of Christ and his salvation, and showing them to us."[8] Although the Smiths did not participate in the first Keswick Conference in 1875, they had spoken at its precursors in Oxford (1874) and Brighton (1875) and their doctrine of "sanctification by faith" became an important idiom of the new movement for the promotion of scriptural holiness.[9] By the turn of the century Keswick was not only an English evangelical movement but had many American

---

[6] For a nice introduction to American pneumatology in the antebellum period see Bruce M. Stephens, "Changing Conceptions of the Holy Spirit in American Protestant Theology from Jonathan Edwards to Charles G. Finney," *St. Luke's Journal of Theology* 33/3 (June 1990): 209–223.

[7] Robert Pearsall Smith, *Holiness Through Faith: Light on the Way of Holiness* (New York: Anson D. F. Randolph & Co., 1870) 15; reprinted in *The Devotional Writings of Robert Pearsall Smith and Hannah Whitall Smith*, ed. Donald Dayton (New York: Garland Publishing, Inc., 1984).

[8] Ibid., 91.

[9] David Bebbington, *Evangelicalism in Modern Britain: A History from the 1730s to the 1980s* (Grand Rapids: Baker Book House, 1989) 151.

participants and supporters as well. A. J. Gordon, who called Keswick speaker Andrew Murray a mentor, sounded as if he had been discipled by Pearsall Smith when he stated that Christ "is rewrought in us through the constant operation of the Holy Ghost, and thus the cross and the resurrection extend their sway over the entire life of the Christian." The movement's prominent watchwords, such as "rest in the Lord," "complete surrender," and "victorious Christian living," found a new homecoming on American shores within the Protestant establishment, particularly its traditionally Calvinistic denominations (i.e., Presbyterianism and Congregationalism).[10]

American revivalism had a natural affinity with the Holiness movement. Many historians of the United States have suggested that a major religious theme in the context of American democracy included the gradual triumph of limited free will over an extreme Augustinian version of predestination, Arminianism over strict Calvinism.[11] Princeton theologian Benjamin Breckenridge Warfield, however, also observed that "history verifies the correlation of Perfectionism and Libertarianism, and wherever Libertarianism rules the thoughts of men, Perfectionism persistently makes its appearance."[12] Warfield's point is well taken when considering the typical progression from revivalist assumptions of how the Christian received justification of sin to holiness views about leading the holy life. At the same time that revivalists attempted to persuade potential converts they needed to accept Jesus as their savior, they expected these same men and women would forsake their old sinful ways. While many traditional Protestants had suggested that sanctification was gradual and only completed after death, the biblical rejoinder to such ideas by holiness thinkers was "how shall we that

---

[10] For a history of the movement by a contemporary participant see A. T. Pierson, *The Keswick Movement in Precept and Practise* (New York: Funk & Wagnalls Company, 1907). Methodism did not seem as open to Keswick teaching, primarily because those who might have found its teachings theologically palatable had left the denomination during the holiness schisms of the late nineteenth century.

[11] See Jon Pahl, *Paradox Lost: Free Will and Political Liberty in American Culture, 1630–1760* (Baltimore: Johns Hopkins Press, 1992); Nathan O. Hatch, *The Democratization of American Christianity* (New Haven: Yale University Press, 1989); and William G. McLoughlin, *Modern Revivalism: Charles Grandison Finney to Billy Graham* (New York: The Ronald Press Company, 1959).

[12] B. B. Warfield, "Albrecht Ritschl and His Doctrine of Christian Perfection," in vol. 1 of *Perfectionism* (New York: Oxford University Press, 1931; reprint, Grand Rapids: Baker Book House, 1981) 3.

are dead to sin live any longer therein?"[13] In the words of Whitall Smith, Jesus "came to destroy the works of the devil, and dare we dream for a moment that He is not able or not willing to accomplish His own purposes?"[14]

Being filled with the Spirit's power became an important feature and contribution of the holiness tradition to American revivalism in the late nineteenth and early twentieth centuries. Soul-saving manuals almost without exception covered this topic in one form or another. Typical of the manual writers, R. A. Torrey claimed that baptism of the Holy Spirit, or his "infilling with power," constituted "an absolutely necessary condition of acceptable and effective service for Christ."[15] Even revivalists not specifically associated with the Higher Life movement characteristically asserted the importance of Holy Ghost power in their evangelistic work, showing the influence of the teaching. Dwight L. Moody, while intentionally avoiding watchwords used by holiness advocates, claimed that "every believer has the Holy Ghost dwelling in him. ...yet he is not dwelling within them in power." Similar to Keswickers, he distinguished between the Spirit "in" the believer at the time of conversion and the Spirit's descending "upon" the Christian enduing him with power for service.[16] In a similar vein, William Bell Riley stated that "the Holy Spirit is pleased to impart His power to God's people"; however, he lamented that "some good Christian men and women speak as if it were presumption to ask the Holy Ghost [for his blessing] and expect to be infilled with His power."[17]

Upon reading authors connected with the Keswick Holiness movement, one is immediately faced with a problem of terminology. Watchwords such as "baptism of the Holy Spirit," "the second blessing," "infilling of the Spirit," "sealing of the Spirit," "enduement of the Spirit," and "consecration" litter the writings with no agreed systematic definition. Nonetheless, there existed a common understanding and consistent pattern about the function of the Holy Spirit in the life of the Christian individual and the church. Englishman James Elder Cumming, who frequently spoke at the

---

[13] Romans 6:2 (KJV); cf. Pearsall Smith, 21–22.

[14] Hannah Whitall Smith, *The Christian's Secret of a Happy Life* (Boston: The Christian Witness Co., 1885; reprinted in *Devotional Writings*) 22.

[15] Torrey, *How to Bring Men to Christ*, 104.

[16] Dwight L. Moody, *Secret Power, or Success in Christian Life and Work* (Chicago: Fleming H. Revell, 1881) 34; 21–39.

[17] William B. Riley, *The Perennial Revival: A Plea for Evangelism* (Chicago: Winona Publishing Co., 1904) 99.

Keswick Conferences, noted that, despite the inconsistent use of
terminology, those influenced by Keswick admitted a difference between a
Christian having the "new life" and one who has it "more abundantly."[18] In
other words, they distinguished the role of the Holy Spirit in the regeneration of the Christian at the time of conversion from the Spirit's subsequent
work of empowering the believer to lead a holy life in the service of God.

   Therefore, despite the different use of terminology, one can outline the
general contours of Keswick theology. Proponents of the Higher Life
generally believed that the Spirit's initial work in the Christian at conversion
was described as a "baptism of the Holy Spirit" through which activity God
incorporated mystically the new convert into the body of Christ (or the
church).[19] In the same way that the ritual of water baptism offered entrance
into a church institution liturgically, so baptism of the Holy Ghost, they
contended, was its more important spiritual counterpart. Furthermore,
because they accepted the Calvinistic belief that once saved a Christian
could not fall from grace, they argued that baptism of the Holy Spirit
occurred only one time at the moment of conversion. Upon meeting certain
spiritual conditions after this initial work of the Holy Ghost, the Christian
next expected the "infilling of the Spirit" that provided the power to carry
out Christian service and holy living.[20] The conditions of this infilling
included repentance from all known sin, "absolute surrender" (or
"consecration") of the human will to the control of the Spirit, and faith that
the subsequent power promised by Jesus would be granted by the Spirit.[21]
Finally, the believer "waited" upon the Spirit by pleading and praying for

   [18] James Elder Cumming, *Through the Eternal Spirit: A Biblical Study on the Holy
Ghost* (Chicago: Fleming H. Revell Co., 1896) 109.
   [19] R. A. Torrey is a notable exception in the terminology scheme laid out here.
He distinguished between the Spirit's work of regeneration at conversion and the
baptism of the Holy Spirit for the purpose of empowering the Christian for service.
Despite the terminology differences, however, Torrey clearly accepts the basic
tenants of Keswick pneumatology. See R. A. Torrey, *The Baptism of the Holy Spirit*
(Chicago: Fleming H. Revell Co., 1895) 9–17.
   [20] A helpful contemporary defense of Keswick Holiness views of sanctification
can be found in J. Robertson McQuilken, *Five Views on Sanctification* (Grand Rapids:
Academie Books, 1987) 149–95.
   [21] For American examples, see J. Wilbur Chapman, *Received Ye the Holy Ghost?*
(Chicago: Fleming H. Revell, 1894) 81–85; Torrey, *Baptism*, 41–42; C. I. Scofield,
Plain Papers on the Doctrine of the Holy Spirit (Chicago: Fleming H. Revell, 1899;
reprint, Grand Rapids: Baker Book House, 1969) 60; and A. J. Gordon, *The Ministry
of the Spirit* (Chicago: Fleming H. Revell, 1894) 117–18.

the blessing of infilling. Under these conditions, Higher Life theologians believed, the Holy Ghost inevitably descended upon the believer and endued him with grace and power.

Keswickers distinguished themselves theologically from other American Protestants by their rejection of progressive eradicationist views of sanctification. Both Wesleyan Holiness thinkers and conservative Calvinists typically claimed that sanctification of human nature was a gradual process that began at the time of conversion. These two camps differed over the possibility of the Christian to attain perfection before death. On the one hand, Wesley himself had claimed that the Christian had the ability to attain eventually "entire sanctification" within this life if he or she sought and strove toward it.[22] On the other hand Old School Presbyterians such as B. B. Warfield, an outspoken critic of Wesleyan and Keswick Holiness theology, claimed that the eradication of sin in the Christian occurred progressively in this life only to be completed in the next.[23] According to Keswickers, the corrupted sinful nature of human beings was not gradually transformed into a godly nature; rather, sinfulness remained until death but was suppressed, or "counteracted," by the power of the Spirit, making a life of holiness possible.[24]

Keswick advocates, therefore, effectively steered a mediating course between orthodox Calvinists and Wesleyans on the matter of sanctification. Within the believer there remained a sinful and corrupt human nature that contended against the Spirit for the allegiance of the will.[25] Presbyterian

---

[22] John Wesley, "A Plain Account of Christian Perfection," in vol. 11 of *The Works of John Wesley*, 3rd ed. (London: Wesleyan Methodist Book Room, 1872; reprint, Peabody MA: Hendrickson Publishers, 1991) 387–91.

[23] B. B. Warfield, "The Victorious Life," in *The Works of Benjamin B. Warfield*, vol. 8 (New York: Oxford University Press, 1932; reprint, Grand Rapids: Baker Book House, 1981) 583. For a comparison between Warfield and Lewis Sperry Chafer, which helpfully compares the Princetonian and Keswick positions on sanctification, see Randall Gleason, "B. B. Warfield and Lewis S. Chafer on Sanctification," *Journal of the Evangelical Theological Society* 40/2 (June 1997): 241–56.

[24] W. H. Griffith-Thomas, "The Victorious Life II," *Bibliotheca Sacra* 76/304 (October 1919): 464. Cf. Griffith Thomas, "The Victorious Life I," *Bibliotheca Sacra* 76/303 (July 1919) 271.

[25] One possible implication of this sanctified will without a sanctified nature, which did not receive universal Keswick approval, included a peculiar dual understanding of human nature within the Christian. Lewis Sperry Chafer, for example, stated that "Into this whole 'natural man' a new divine nature is imparted when we are saved. Salvation is more than a 'change of heart.' It is more than a

Lewis Sperry Chafer, founder of Evangelical (later Dallas) Theological Seminary, categorized Christians as either "carnal" or "spiritual."[26] The carnal Christian lived by his own power, or "the flesh," while the spiritual believers had received the blessing of the Spirit's infilling and continued to abide in him, submitting to his wishes.

The Spirit's power, while dependent upon Christ's sacrifice upon the cross, nonetheless remained contingent upon the believer's faith and cooperation. J. Wilbur Chapman summed this up in his four "As" of the Spirit-filled life: *acknowledge* you need the Spirit; *ask* for your birthright and privilege; *accept* the gift of the Spirit; and *act* on His strength.[27] Furthermore, the Christian needed to beware that he or she did not "grieve" or "quench" the Spirit by resisting his will or leaving any sinful action unconfessed to God.[28] Indeed, wrote A. T. Pierson, "the Spirit of God is like a dove which is eager to alight and rest in the dove-cote, but it is also timid and easily driven away. He never takes control of any man or body of men without their will."[29] Therefore, unlike baptism of the Holy Spirit, the indwelling potentially (though not ideally) might take place several times throughout the earthly life of a Christian. Keswickers often quoted Presbyterian evangelist William J. Erdman's rule of thumb on this issue: "one baptism, many fillings."[30]

---

transformation of the old: it is regeneration, or creation, of something wholly new which is possessed in conjunction with the old nature so long as we are in the body. The presence of two opposing natures (not two personalities) in one individual results in conflict." See *He That Is Spiritual* (Chicago: Fleming H. Revell, 1918; reprint, Chicago: Moody Press, 1943) 142.

[26] Chafer, *He That Is Spiritual*, 13. This distinction had been used before Chafer's use by popular Keswick speaker Andrew Murray. See Murray's *The Master's Indwelling* (Chicago: Fleming H. Revell, 1896) 7–25.

[27] J. Wilbur Chapman, *Present-Day Evangelism* (New York: Baker Taylor Co., 1903; reprint, Chicago: Fleming H. Revell Company, 1913) 52.

[28] Typical of this terminology is Scofield, *Doctrine of the Holy Spirit*, 54–57. Cf. Chafer, *He That Is Spiritual*, 81–118.

[29] A. T. Pierson, *The Acts of the Holy Spirit: Being an Examination of the Active Mission and Ministry of the Spirit of God in the Acts of the Apostles* (Chicago: Fleming H. Revell, 1898) 63–64.

[30] G. Campbell Morgan, *The Spirit of God* (Chicago: Fleming H. Revell, 1900) 193. Cf. William J. Erdman, *The Holy Spirit and Christian Experience* (New York: Gospel Publishing House, 1909) 24; "The Holy Spirit and the Sons of God," in vol. 10 of *The Fundamentals: A Testimony to the Truth*, ed. Louis Meyer (Chicago: Testimony Publishing Company, n.d.) 70–71.

Although the views of Keswick concerning the relationship between the Holy Spirit and the individual dominated the movement's literature, this brand of holiness had important and decisive ecclesiological implications for its promulgators. A 1900 editorial in A. T. Pierson's *Missionary Review of the World* contained the basic theological components of Keswick sympathizers' strategy within and critique of the Protestant establishment:

> Nevertheless it should be understood that the Holy Spirit bears to the Church collectively a similar relation to that borne to the individual believer. And that, as the individual, so the Church may "resist," "grieve," and "quench" the Spirit.... Wherever the individual or the local church seeks to be guided and controlled by Him, He is ever active and powerful. But all of the history of the Church since Pentecost demonstrates that to all intents and purposes He is *practically absent* from any church, or any believers where there is a habitual life of sin and unfaithfulness to truth and God.[31]

The implications of this statement are clear: so long as the church seeks the infilling of the Spirit, collectively asking his guidance on all matters, it will succeed in its mission to bear witness to Christ and the gospel message. Negatively, the failure of the church to carry out its divine vocation provided an indication of its unfaithfulness to God.[32] Some Keswick theologians took the logic of this argument and attached it to doctrinal belief as well, claiming that the Spirit also was the "Conservator of Orthodoxy." In the words of one Boston preacher, "wherever and whenever the Holy Spirit has been prominent in the church and proved its presence by the fruits, love, joy, peace, there Orthodoxy has been honored." Conversely, the truth of orthodoxy lay in its correlation with profound religious awakening.[33]

Keswick Holiness advocates also understood the church as the place where the Holy Spirit resides on earth. Further, the Spirit directed and empowered the Christian community to carry out its divine vocation to know Christ and to make him known. Most of the movement's authors, therefore, typically referred to the Holy Spirit as the "administrator" of the church. G. Campbell Morgan noted that God resided in the church as administrator "in order that the work which He had done as Saviour might

---

[31] Anonymous, "The Holy Spirit and the Church," *Missionary Review of the World* 13/2 (February 1900): 137.

[32] The terms "practical" or "practically" are important here because the editor, most likely Pierson, suggested that the Spirit never fully leaves the Church, although the Church may not abide in the Spirit and follow the Spirit's will. Ibid.

[33] J. Cook, "The Holy Spirit as the Administrator of the Church," *Our Day* 15/90 (December 1895): 293–94.

become a real fact within the experience and the character of men of whom He should be able to obtain full possession, and in whom, therefore, He should be able to exercise control. By the Holy Spirit, Jesus is henceforth to be Lord, while loyal subjects to his dominion are, by the indwelling of the Spirit, to pass into the realization of the will of God."[34] Morgan further believed that this gave the work of the Spirit within the church cosmic significance; he reminded his readers that the realization of the will of God within individuals had been God's intention for all humanity at the creation of the world.[35]

Keswickers used the biblical model of the Pentecost story in the Acts of the Apostles as their model for the modern church and its relationship with the Spirit. The order of the Spirit's work in the Pentecost story, they observed, began with the regeneration of individual sinners, then their spiritual incorporation into the body of Christ (the church), and, finally, the Spirit's filling them with his power for service and action.[36] One typical Keswick advocate, James Elder Cumming, depicted Pentecost like a baptism in the Holy Spirit writ large. The creation of the church by the Spirit and his subsequent abiding presence occurred once for all at that time. The event also inaugurated the "Pentecostal Dispensation" wherein "the experience of Pentecost is ever being renewed" within the members of the church.[37] Much like the individual, the Spirit abided continually within the church; however, as an editor of the *Missionary Review of the World* noted, "He does not *compel* submission. And where there is either organized resistance to His authority, or such carnality and worldliness as make His effective working impossible, is it too much to suppose that...He withdraws as into some inner chamber, and leaves such Laodicean churches to their own devices?"[38] However, insofar as the church, like individuals, had the ability to resist, grieve, or quench the Spirit, it also had the possibility to renew itself many times, seeking the Spirit's power to continue to carry out its divine vocation. The theological explanation and pattern of revivalism, therefore, found a new and able defender in Keswick Holiness.

---

[34] Morgan, *Spirit of God*, 132.
[35] Ibid.
[36] Cumming, *Through the Eternal Spirit*, 14.
[37] Ibid.
[38] Anonymous, "The Holy Spirit and the Church."

The Spirit not only called the church into being and resided within it but administered it as the "Vicar of Christ on earth."[39] He manifested his administration of the church through two primary means: Scripture and spiritual gifts (*charismata*). Without exception, those influenced by Keswick asserted that the Bible comprised the "Spirit's utterances in written form."[40] A. J. Gordon asserted that at Pentecost the Holy Ghost had given the apostles an "*ad interim*" authority to direct the church; however, since the writing of the New Testament, the Holy Ghost had transferred this authority (*ad perpetuam*) to the Scriptures, which embodied his thoughts in written form.[41] "As coal has been called 'fossil sunlight,'" the Spirit claimed, "so the New Testament may be called fossil inspiration which fell upon the apostles being herein stored up for the use of the church throughout the ages."[42] The church, therefore, not only had an important and infallible source of revelation in the Scriptures (since they were authored by God), but it also did not have the right to throw off the Spirit-ordained authority of the Bible. In most cases, Keswick Holiness thinkers defended infallibility, or inerrancy, with a *reductio ad absurdum* argument, asserting that any falsehood in the Bible was tantamount to saying that none of it could be trusted for spiritual guidance. They, of course, assumed that no one would want to admit this. One looks in vain for sophisticated defenses of inerrancy like those defended by A. A. Hodge and B. B. Warfield in the Princeton tradition. A. J. Gordon, perhaps, provided the exception that proved the rule. He claimed that "humans can only understand thoughts through language," or "the idea embodied in speech." Based upon this philosophical assumption, he asserted that verbal inerrancy in the Scriptures (the embodied ideas of the Spirit) provided the logical way in which God communicated with human beings in a permanent manner. Of course, he agreed that language had its limitations, but this was a matter of human limitation, not Divine.[43]

The other means by which the Holy Ghost administered the church was through the dispensing of the *charismata*, or spiritual gifts. Through

---

[39] Gordon, *Ministry of the Spirit*, 150.

[40] Cumming, *Through the Eternal Spirit*, 138. Cf. Gordon, *Ministry of the Spirit*, 179; R. A. Torrey, *How to Study the Bible*, new ed. (Chicago: Fleming H. Revell, 1896; reprint, New Kensington PA: Whitaker House, 1985) 7.

[41] Gordon, *Ministry of the Spirit*, 167.

[42] Ibid., 168.

[43] Ibid., 172–81.

baptism in the Spirit all the members of the church received different spiritual gifts, such as prophecy, teaching, hospitality, healing, or speaking in tongues, which God expected each believer to use in the power of the Holy Ghost to carry out the church's mission of revealing Christ to a lost world. The differentiation of charismata further meant that the corporate church was more than the sum of its parts, because individual believers were not complete in themselves to accomplish God's will upon the earth. Each believer not only needed the power of the Spirit, who resided only in the church, but also his or her fellow believers to carry out the church's mission. Applied denominationally, the universal church was also more than the sum of its denominational expressions, each of which contributes some gift that benefits the whole church.

Because, in Keswick thinking, the Spirit always initiated redemption through individuals, revivalism provided an obvious means for the church to achieve the purposes of God. Conversion provided the seminal Christian experience, beginning with the Spirit's convicting of the potential convert of his or her sin and separateness from God. The church, armed with the "sword of the Spirit" (the Bible), acted as the Spirit's voice of conviction by witnessing to the Lordship of Christ and his work on the cross for a lost humanity.[44] In this vein Chapman asserted that "the Spirit of God always leads us into the world, that we may go to the lost and tell them of life, bidding them in the Name of Jesus and on the authority of the Word and by the power of the Spirit to believe in him, that their position may be changed."[45] In other words, Keswickers believed that revival, both in the sense of renewal and conversion, comprised the natural result of allowing the Spirit to administer the church unhindered. In the words of R. A. Torrey: "When any church can be brought to the place where they will recognize their need of the Holy Spirit, and take their eyes from all men, and surrender absolutely to the Holy Spirit's control, and give themselves as His agents, having stored the Word of God in their heads and hearts, and then look to the Holy Spirit to give power as it falls from their lips, a mighty revival in the power of the Holy Ghost is inevitable."[46] Not only did they believe that Pentecost inaugurated the pattern of revival, but in modern

---

[44] Morgan, *Spirit of God*, 198.

[45] Chapman, *Holy Ghost*, 103–104.

[46] R. A. Torrey, "The Holy Spirit in a Revival," in *How to Promote and Conduct a Successful Revival with Suggestive Outlines*, ed. R. A. Torrey (Louisville: Charles T. Dearing, 1901) 18.

times, through the Spirit's continued prompting and indwelling power, the church could employ its methods in the modern world.

The Keswick emphasis upon sanctification by faith and the indwelling of the Spirit also had an important egalitarian dimension not lost upon its advocates. Historian David Bebbington noted that in Keswick "holiness was becoming democratised."[47] Clearly Keswickers assumed the holy life to be attainable by any faithful believer, not something reserved as the crowning achievement of a few hard-working saints. In this spirit, A. J. Gordon supported even women's suffrage and their right to speak and participate as leaders at revivals.[48] In terms of engendering mobilization among the laity, therefore, Keswick thinkers preached a brand of holiness that anticipated Christian service, including social activism, as the normative fruits of the Spirit-filled life. Not surprisingly, American Keswick leaders not only organized revivals but participated in philanthropic and social work. J. Wilbur Chapman encouraged soul-saving evangelicals to do their duty to meet the social demands of the gospel. He further concluded that seeking conversions while turning a blind eye to the plight of the poor ignored half of Christ's message.[49] In fact, Chapman and R. A. Torrey ran institutional churches in Philadelphia and Minneapolis, respectively.[50]

Keswick Holiness helped create and reinforce a populist ecclesiological orientation and denominational ambivalence among its advocates at the same time that political Populism reached its height in American politics. This natural emphasis and promotion of the common Christian vocation shared by average believers directly related to the way proponents of the Higher Life organized their work within the Protestant establishment. Typically, they were suspicious of centralized organizational super-structures. Influencing individuals to promote ecclesiological and cultural change remained the primary objective. Their cultural projects, therefore, tended to be local, grass-roots operations and organizations that focused on one or two issues of popular concern. "Faith missions," such as the China Inland Mission and the African Inland Mission, provide examples of organizations that depended upon individual contributors and churches for

---

[47] Bebbington, *Evangelicalism in Modern Britain*, 173.

[48] A. J. Gordon, "The Ministry of Women," *Homiletic Review* 7/12 (December 1894): 910–21. Cf. Donald Dayton, *Discovering an Evangelical Heritage* (New York: Harper & Row Publishers, 1976) 93.

[49] Chapman, *Evangelism*, 57–65.

[50] Wacker, "The Holy Spirit and the Spirit of the Age," 51–52.

their support as opposed to moneys distributed from a centralized denominational fund. Not surprisingly, associates of Keswick typically ran,
supported, and promoted these types of endeavors. A. T. Pierson's
Missionary Review of the World chronicled and promoted this type of mission
work for an American audience. Other extra-denominational organizations
supported by soul-saving evangelicals included Frances Willard's Women's
Christian Temperance Union, William Booth's Salvation Army, and a host
of independent Bible schools and institutes, in such cities as Chicago, Los
Angeles, Philadelphia, Boston, and New York, whose initial purpose consisted in training individuals for home and foreign missionary work. Revivals
and urban missions, as described in the last chapter, also promoted popular
involvement on a local level. Revivals required an enormous amount of
support from local churches and individuals to function properly. There was
a job, therefore, for anyone who wanted to help—from speaking, counseling,
and praying to ushering—and each job was labeled indispensable.

Progressive Orthodoxy and the Spirit of Truth

Keswick, however, was not the only pneumatological system active among
evangelicals. The career of Charles Augustus Briggs of Union Theological
Seminary in New York represented well the success and travails of the New
Theology, or progressive orthodoxy, within the establishment. In 1890 he
published his book *Whither? A Theological Question of the Times*, precipitating
a series of events that eventually led to his heresy trial and dismissal from the
Presbyterian ministry three years later. Even before the publishing of
Whither? he was not a stranger to controversy; in fact, he reveled in it. A
decade earlier he had dueled with Old School Princetonians A. A. Hodge
and B. B. Warfield over the inspiration of Scripture. Hodge and Warfield
defended the "verbal, plenary" inerrancy of the Bible, while Briggs defended
the higher criticism and a corresponding weaker view of inspiration that the
Scriptures only "contained" the word of God.[51]

---

[51] The debate was published as a series of exchanges in the *Presbyterian Review*.
Cf. Archibald A. Hodge and Benjamin B. Warfield, "Inspiration," 2/2 (April 1881):
225–60; Charles Augustus Briggs, "Critical Theories of the Sacred Scriptures in
Relation to Their Inspiration: I. The Right, Duty, and Limits of Biblical Criticism,"
2/3 (July 1881): 550–79; William Henry Green, "Professor W. Robertson Smith on
the Pentateuch," 3/1 (January 1882): 108–156; Henry Preserved Smith, "The Critical
Theories of Julius Wellhausen," 3/2 (April 1882): 357–88; Samuel I. Curtiss,
"Delitzsch on the Origin and Composition of the Pentateuch," 3/3 (July 1882):

Throughout the pages of *Whither?* Briggs opined that one of the travesties of "orthodoxism," by which he meant Old School Presbyterianism, included its inability to take seriously the doctrine of sanctification.[52] He asserted, "It is high time that a holy life of sanctification should be the ideal life for which every Christian should strive. The error that sanctification cannot be accomplished in this life paralyzes every effort."[53] Remarkably, he endorsed the comments of premillennialist James H. Brookes, who claimed that making sanctification ostensibly a postmortem event, as Old School Presbyterians such as Hodge and Warfield did, was unscriptural.[54] Briggs tied the idea of sanctification to the institution of the kingdom of God on earth. He believed that God intended human beings to strive to live in a holy and godly manner, thereby manifesting in themselves Christ's presence for the benefit of their neighbor and the nation as a whole.[55]

On the surface, Briggs's comments about sanctification sound remarkably similar to the ideas of Keswick Holiness. As representative of the New Theology, or "progressive orthodoxy" as he preferred, he questioned the vitality of Old School Presbyterianism defended by the theological guard at Princeton Seminary. Briggs knew that he was in for a fight, and that was exactly what he wanted. He confidently ended *Whither?* with a battle cry:

> The Holy Spirit will guide the Church and the Christian scholar in the present and the future as He has in the past..:. The more conflict the better. Battle for the truth is infinitely better than stagnation in error. Every error should be slain as soon as possible.... Error is our greatest foe. Truth the most precious possession.... Let us unite in the truth already gained and agree to contend in Christian love and chivalry for the truth that has not yet

---

553–88; Willis J. Beecher, "The Logical Methods of Professor Kuenen," 3/4 (October 1882): 701–731; Charles A. Briggs, "A Critical Study of Higher Criticism with Special Reference to the Pentateuch," 4/1 (January 1883): 69–130; and Francis L. Patton, "The Dogmatic Aspects of Pentateuchal Criticism," 4/2 (April 1883): 341–410.

[52] Charles A. Briggs, *Whither? A Theological Question for the Times* (New York: Charles Scribner's Sons, 1890) 287–89.

[53] Ibid., 288. Cf. 147–48.

[54] Ibid., 199–200.

[55] Ibid., 288–89. Cf. 60–61. In this latter passage Briggs claims that "dead orthodoxy" ignores the religious element in Christianity, "a life of union with the living God," and, therefore, has "little value for the reformation of the individual, the nation, or the world."

been sufficiently determined, having faith that in due time the Divine Spirit will make all things clear to us.

Briggs got his fight and ended up one of its first casualties. After Union Theological Seminary conferred upon him its new title Chair in Biblical Theology, conservatives in the denomination accused Briggs of heresy based on his inaugural address, in which he denied Mosaic authorship of the Pentateuch and verbal, plenary inerrancy. In a well publicized heresy trial in 1893, Briggs was defrocked from the Presbyterian ministry for not upholding the doctrine of the inspiration of Scripture as stated in the Westminster Confession.[56] This event also precipitated the withdrawal of Union Seminary, whose board of directors and faculty defended their colleague on the grounds of academic freedom, from under the official auspices of the denomination. Briggs promptly became an Episcopalian and was ordained a priest in the diocese of New York by Bishop Henry C. Potter.

The New Theology had as many important similarities to as difference from Keswick Holiness regarding the role of the Holy Spirit and authority in the church. Besides a common understanding that the old orthodoxy was unable to meet the vocational crisis in the church, the two movements shared the belief of the unity of truth in God. In other words, understood properly, truth did not develop; however, with the aid of the Holy Spirit, it could be discovered more completely by humanity. Differences existed in the understanding of the means by which the Spirit revealed this truth and humankind's capability to receive and accept it. On the one hand, Keswick advocates claimed that the Holy Spirit revealed truth mediately and infallibly through the Bible and immediately through his indwelling. The New Theology, on the other hand, posited God's immanence in his creation; therefore, the Spirit, while having the ability to reveal truth in an immediate fashion, typically revealed it through the evolutionary processes of nature and history. Truth, according to the New Theologians, was gradually revealed as humanity progressed, or evolved, to the point where it could be accepted and applied faithfully.

---

[56] For a concise sequential history of the events, see Max Gray Rogers, "Charles Augustus Briggs: Heresy at Union," in *American Religious Heretics: Formal and Informal Trials*, ed. George H. Shriver (Nashville: Abingdon Press, 1966) 89–147. For Briggs's own defense of his position see Charles A. Briggs, "Response to the Charges and Specifications Submitted to the Presbytery in New York," *Andover Review* 16/96 (December 1891): 623–39.

As with Keswick Holiness, terminology also becomes a problem for those wishing to discuss the role of the Holy Spirit among the advocates of progressive orthodoxy. These theologians differed notably from Keswick in their typical reference to the Holy Spirit as "it" instead of "he." Because they perceived the Spirit, more often than not, generically as the spiritual, moral, and immanent presence of God within creation and humanity, they alternately called the Holy Spirit the Divine Spirit, the Spirit of Jesus Christ, the Spirit of Truth, or the Presence of God. Nonetheless, a common pattern of emerged from these thinkers. Most important, advocates of progressive orthodoxy based their ideas on the thought of Horace Bushnell; therefore, a precursory look at his thought will be valuable, since his theological imprint appeared throughout the work of the New Theologians.

Near the end of his life, Bushnell began writing a book he feared he might never finish. His premonition proved true, and, upon his death in 1876, he left incomplete a treatise entitled "Inspiration by the Holy Spirit." Despite the fact that he only completed what might be called an introductory chapter on the topic, those who know Bushnell's work will find throughout the piece themes present in his previous work. At the beginning of this theological fragment he claimed that "inspirableness…is the supreme faculty of man," while the Spirit of God was an "inspiration, because it inbreathes something of a divine quality and configures the subject in some way to itself."[57] On the basis of humanity's "inspirableness" Bushnell asserted that God intended to manifest and communicate himself to each individual, a doctrine he called the Holy Spirit's "universal inspiration," which, "by unnumbered and persistent ways of discipline, he trains experimentally to the knowledge of himself."[58] This universal inspiration could be either "nutritive" or "corrective": "The former is absolute, entering without leave into all the growths of sentiment and intelligence. The latter is distinguishable in two degrees, either as act or fact. As act, it is to God the permeation of his will in corrective and restorative impulses, while to the subject it is either a grace unobserved, or a grace resisted, or a grace accepted in true welcome. Wherein it becomes a grace as fact, having found a true lodgment and become the seed of a true character, a living, everlasting inspiration."[59] The individual, in Bushnell's view, depended upon the Spirit

---

[57] Horace Bushnell, "Inspiration by the Holy Spirit," in *The Spirit in Man: Sermons and Selections*, centenary ed. (New York: Charles Scribner's Sons, 1910) 7.

[58] Ibid., 14–15.

[59] Ibid., 15.

to operate efficiently within him in order to uplift his sinful nature so that he could be swayed by his "better sensibilities;" however, the Holy Spirit, never acting in an domineering manner upon the human spirit, waited for its subject to yield his will to that of the Divine.[60] Although much of this thinking is reminiscent of Keswick, the outline left by Bushnell for "Inspiration of the Holy Spirit" shows he continued to have an aversion to revivalism.

In this outline, Bushnell objected to the idea that the Holy Sprit was occasional in his working; rather, "he is all-present, all-permeating, all-searching, correcting, nourishing. He loves all men alike, is for and with all men, pressing in upon them, even as the atmosphere."[61] This statement provided an important clue that Bushnell, in his most mature thinking, continued to assert the immanence of God within all creation. Rejecting what he called the "Spirit of scenes" of the revivalists, he held to "the faith of an abiding Spirit, present to every good thought and righteous struggle, upholding and cherishing all weakness, drawing us ever to a closer and purer fellowship with God, pervading the family [and] filling the church."[62] Bushnell believed that this doctrine of the "abiding Spirit" constituted a fundamental Christian truth. The Christian family and its natural extension, the church, he contended, existed as redeemed communities being continually drawn by the Holy Spirit into closer relationship with God.

This idea of the abiding Spirit had important ramifications for Bushnell's understanding of the mission of the church. In 1844 he had admonished New England Congregationalists that Christian progress within the church can only be the result of growth, "not conquest."[63] The church, according to Bushnell, existed as the body of Christ on earth in the sense that through its "practical and internal spirit," it became a perpetual manifestation of the Divine Nature.[64] Furthermore, "her Christ-like graces of love, purity, truth, and beneficence, are a divine atmosphere about her, and her atmosphere enters the breath and blood." All humanity, he therefore concluded, would eventually yield to the divine will because of the spiritual quality of the gospel message and character of the church as a

[60] Ibid., 23–24.
[61] Ibid., 33.
[62] Horace Bushnell, "Growth, Not Conquest, The True Method of Christian Progress," in *Views of Christian Nurture* (Hartford: Edwin Hunt, 1847) 222, 224–25; this article originally appeared as "The Kingdom of Heaven as a Grain of Mustard Seed," *New Englander* 2/8 (October 1844): 600–619.
[63] Ibid., 148–50.
[64] Ibid., 174.

manifestation of the divine nature. "To approach her is to be convinced of sin, righteousness, and a judgment to come. To be thus, in her Christian growth, a demonstration of the Spirit, to have the divine nature flowing out thus impalpably but really on the world, gives her an *assimilative power* in the nature of vitality. So that if she gains a convert, whether at home or in the ends of the earth (for place means nothing) it is not by external conquest but by virtue of her own internal life—the life of God."[65] The problem with revivalists, in Bushnell's assessment, was that they asserted the Spirit immediately and coercively conquered the individual's will, labeling it a conversion experience. He countered that the Spirit's influences, whether immediate within the individual or mediated through the church, had a fixed relation to one another, such that if "the church unfolds her piety as a divine life, which is one, the divine life will display its activity as much more potently and victoriously without, which is the other."[66]

Bushnell noted that on a practical level even Jesus' disciples had to come to terms with the fact that the redemption of the world required growth and not conquest.

> They [the disciples] discovered that it is not so much extasies [sic] that men want in religion, as it is principles, and that no romantic, or enthusiastic flights, unaided by habit, can settle a new principle into practical dominion over the mind...influences that operate gradually, imperceptibly and through the medium of godly exercise of truth, became more important, and the Holy Spirit, being now fully revealed was accepted as the attendant of ordinary life, the support of its struggles and the hope of all Christian effort.[67]

In fact, he argued, once the early Christians realized that the divine plan of redemption primarily consisted in the gradual growth of the Christian into divine principles, they discovered a new understanding of piety, which was domestic in nature. At that moment the Christian family became a divine institution for the educating of children in Christ, "a school of love...for Christian nurture and training."[68] The church, therefore, acted as an extended redeemed family, "taking the whole society of man into its bosom and becoming the school of the race."[69]

---

[65] Ibid. Emphasis in the original.

[66] Ibid., 175.

[67] Horace Bushnell, "The Scene of Pentecost, and a Christian Parish," in *Views*, 217.

[68] Ibid., 217–18.

[69] Ibid., 220.

If the family and the church accepted the reality of the abiding Spirit, Bushnell estimated that the impact upon American Christianity would include results of practical import. First, faithful parents and ministers, as Christian educators, would expect that their children could and should bear the fruits of the Spirit, thus manifesting the divine nature.[70] This expectation and the godly habits instilled through Christian training coupled with an atmosphere of worship and adoration of the divine would form "disciples of the truth" who would embody the ethical character of Jesus "received...in the Spirit, and by the Spirit apply it to this life."[71] Finally, this common commitment to the truth manifested by "the fruits of righteousness" would encourage a catholic understanding of the Christian faith, "subordinating diversities of form and thought, and moderating over terms of partial conflict, so as to bring them [different church communities] into cordial and fully acknowledged brotherhood."[72]

According to Bushnell, this catholic brotherhood, the *telos* of human society from its inception by God, existed as the primary means through which the Divine Spirit would redeem the world. "One thing is clear," he explained:

> that the highest form of piety can never appear on earth until the disciples of Christ are able to be in the Spirit...The Spirit of God is a Catholic spirit, and a universal movement, penetrating gradually and quickening into power the whole Church of Christ on earth. Then and then only, in the spiritual momentum of such a day, when the Spirit of God is breathing inspirations into all believing souls, and working graces in them that are measured, no longer by the dogmas of sect, but by the breadth of his own character—then, I say, feeling the contact of every man, of a universal fellowship, and rising with the flood that is lifting the whole church into freedom and power, it will be seen what possible heights of attainment—hitherto scarcely imagined—what spiritual completeness and fullness of life the gospel and the graces of Christ are able to effect, in our sinful race.... We are to receive the Spirit in his own measures, not anymore in ours, and prepare ourselves gradually, for an outspreading era of life, that shall be as the manifested Life of God.[73]

---

[70] Ibid., 235.
[71] Ibid., 243.
[72] Ibid., 237.
[73] Horace Bushnell, "A Discourse of Dogma and Spirit, or the True Reviving of Religion," in *God in Christ* (Hartford: Brown and Parsons, 1849) 354.

The catholicity engendered by living in the Spirit was crucial, because without this "temperament consciously cherished," Bushnell believed that the church would be impotent to meet the true conditions of Christian piety and progress required for the nineteenth century.[74] Consequently, dogmatism provided the church with the biggest road-block to its growth, not to mention that it essentially denied "the true idea of Christianity, as a ministration of the Spirit."[75] Those who retreated into dogmatism, he surmised, did so because they feared the Holy Spirit would topple their platforms and dissolve their doctrines.[76] The essence of true Christianity, however, "is that the disciple shall be led out one moment to the next, through all his life, by a present union with God and a constant guidance— that he shall be the child of the Spirit."[77] Indeed, he asserted, "Christian character itself, and all its graces are forms of inspiration;" apart from such a spirit there was no law or authority which could give life to the world.

Bushnell's work found a ready audience with the authors of progressive orthodoxy in the late nineteenth century. After the Civil War, his thought seemed to take on a prophetic character. In the wake of the social discord that sounded the opening of the last quarter of the nineteenth century, his notions of social redemption, ethical atonement, and the role of the church as a school for souls seemed to offer a solution to a world marred by Haymarket, saloons, and urban bossism. More important, Bushnell provided them with an intellectual basis for a critique of the Protestant establishment that had spurned his message a generation earlier. The New Theologians so imbibed his thinking that it is fair to imagine they could wear the label "Bushnellian" as an earlier generation had worn the label "Puritan." If they often lacked the depth and texture of their progenitor, they ably used this theology to address the pressing issues of the day as well as made efforts to propagate his thought in evangelical seminaries and popularize it in preaching and public addresses. Through the New Theologians Bushnell had more influence after his death than in his own day.

The New Theologians also utilized Bushnell's thought concerning God's immanence and the progressive nature of revelation in their own ideas surrounding the nature and role of the church. New Haven Congregationalist Theodore T. Munger became one of the first architects

---

[74] Bushnell, "Pentecost," in *Views*, 239.
[75] Bushnell, "Dogma and Spirit," in *God in Christ*, 348.
[76] Ibid.
[77] Ibid., 351.

of the New Theology. In his essay "On Reception of New Truth" (1883) he stated that the purpose of the Acts of the Apostles "is to unfold the broadening spirit and form of the church of God."[78] His interpretation of Acts was quite different than that of the holiness advocates who believed it to be a history describing the inaugural era of the church, which, filled with the Spirit, had all the truth, sanctity, and power necessary to preach successfully the gospel message to a perishing world. Munger countered that "valuable as this book of Acts is as a record of events, and as the *nexus* between Dispensations, it is more valuable as introducing the life of the Spirit, and as showing how the faith of the ages develops into the liberty and the full revelation of God evoking the full life of man."[79] The Spirit, he claimed, acted immanently everywhere and continually within nature and humanity unfolding and revealing truth. Therefore, he argued, "it is a mistake to regard the truths of the Christian faith, even those that are called leading and fundamental, as having a fixed form."[80] He believed that the doctrines, forms, and practices of the church perpetually evolved, through the revelation and guidance of the Spirit, as Truth continued to unfold within creation. The allegiance of the church, according to Munger, if clinging to dogma, ecclesiastical platforms, liturgical forms, or denominational polity, was misplaced. Were such things "revelations *from* God," he noted, they might require strict allegiance; however, "being revelations *of* God, they imply a process of unfolding. Truth is not something handed down from heaven, a moral parcel of known size and weight, but it is a disclosure of God through the order of the world and of the Spirit."[81]

Munger suggested that all inspirations, which reveal truth, have a divine and a human element.[82] The human element evolved slowly in accord with the advance of society, science, and the individual, while the divine element entailed the instantaneous appropriation of truth through the quickening of human nature and intellect by the Spirit.[83] "I gain knowledge slowly," he explained. However, "I gain the meaning of knowledge instantly;

---

[78] Theodore T. Munger, *The Freedom of Faith*, 11th ed. (Boston: Houghton, Mifflin and Company, 1885) 47.

[79] Ibid., 49.

[80] Ibid., 59.

[81] Ibid.

[82] The echoes of Bushnell's human "inspirableness" and the Spirit's inspiration rings clear here.

[83] Munger, *Freedom of Faith*, 68–69.

it is a revelation of the Spirit that acts when knowledge has done its work."[84] Therefore, one did not properly speak of inspired things, such as the sacraments, creeds, or the Bible; instead, the Holy Spirit inspired human beings, according to their evolved capabilities. The forms surrounding inspired individuals, said Munger, were appropriate to the needs of a particular age but remained time-bound artifacts in the context of a later historical milieu.[85] He believed that the church needed an attitude of passivity and alertness: "passive to the Spirit that is ever breathing upon us, and alert to note and follow the unfolding revelation of God in the world."[86] In particular, this latter statement meant assimilating the truths gradually discovered in the fields of science and history and proclaiming their appropriate religious import, which was instantaneously revealed by the Spirit, so that Christ would be all in all.[87] Munger confidently proclaimed that once Christianity "contemplates itself under development, it has the key of its interpretation; it can account for its changes; it can defend its history; it can separate its substance from its forms…it can once more take its place at the head of the sciences, and demand loyalty of all."[88] The essays in *Freedom of Faith* (which included "On the Reception of New Truth") became a virtual theological handbook for progressive orthodoxy.[89]

Typical of other advocates of progressive orthodoxy, Episcopal bishop Phillips Brooks asserted that Christianity was "a world-embracing power," and the church must take into itself all of the parts of society considered secular thereby expanding the kingdom of God:

> If we will not claim [the home, the school, and the shop] for their best use, and by our use of them exalt them to the best explanations, we need not wonder at the low and godless explanations which men give of them. When we are willing to see them as the ministrations of God; when men, asking us for the means of grace, are pointed, first of all, to the duties and relations of

---

[84] Ibid., 69.

[85] Ibid., 67.

[86] Ibid., 58.

[87] Ibid., 59.

[88] Ibid., 67.

[89] William R. Hutchison, *The Modernist Impulse in American Protestantism* (Cambridge: Harvard University Press, 1976; reprint, Durham NC: Duke University Press, 1992) 95–96.

their lives as the places where they will meet God..., then how the dead earth and all that is upon it will glow with a fire that no materialism can quench.[90]

George A. Gordon, pastor of Boston's Old South Church, agreed, stating that "Christianity might be called the Holy Spirit of assimilation. It has an organism of eternal vitality; it is able to take in all fact and all truth, to absorb the universe, and to turn it into its own substance."[91] In the words of Boston University professor Borden P. Bowne, the mission of the church, therefore, included the "building of men into the realization of their Divine sonship."[92]

The theologians of progressive orthodoxy also had intimate connections with the advocates of social Christianity. Both often believed that the Spirit progressively revealed God in all facets of life; therefore, they claimed that the church had a duty to adapt its doctrines and methods in order to preach the gospel in the modern world. William Rainsford, reflecting on the religion of his parents' generation, represented the way advocates of social Christianity often utilized the central tenants of progressive orthodoxy:

> One of my chief reasons for writing it [my second autobiography] is to insist on the comparative unimportance of creeds and doctrines. If true religion is to live, and men cannot live without it, their creeds must change and doctrines once precious and useful perish. The God who indwells man—the Holy Spirit, ever living, ever in action—pushes aside, transcends, finally destroys, those forms of words in which successive generations have sought piously but vainly, to find a final expression for His voice. So much is inevitable. The Kingdom of good and God can come no other way. Jesus said the Gospel he preached was a SEED—a growing, expanding thing—Truth to be sown and re-sown, not to be husbanded in ecclesiastical granaries. Not in the doctrines they held lay my parents' power—and power they had. Not to

[90] Phillips Brooks, *The Best Methods of Promoting the Spiritual Life* (New York: Thomas Whittaker, 1897) 29–30.

[91] George A. Gordon, *The New Epoch for Faith* (Boston: Houghton, Mifflin and Company, 1901) 79.

[92] Borden P. Bowne, *The Christian Life: A Study* (Cincinnati: Curts and Jennings, 1899) 143. Other examples of Bushnell's thinking can be found in Washington Gladden, *How Much Is Left of the Old Doctrines? A Book for the People* (Boston: Houghton, Mifflin and Company, 1899) 2–4, 63, 149–50, 175, 233–35; William Newton Clarke, *An Outline of Christian Theology*, 2d ed. (New York: Charles Scribner's Sons, 1898) 383–85; George Park Fisher, *The Nature and Method of Revelation* (New York: Charles Scribner's Sons, 1890) 48; and James M. Campbell, *The Indwelling Christ* (Chicago: Fleming H. Revell, 1895) 22–31.

one of those doctrines could I subscribe now. Yet well I know that anything I am, anything worth while that I have done, I owe to the spirit they imparted, which indeed was a perpetual possession.[93]

Rainsford's statement, published in 1922, is worth quoting at length, because he made no pretensions about being a theologian himself; nonetheless, one clearly observes the influence of Bushnell in the crediting of his parents for passing on to him the Christian spirit, his dismissal of dogmatism, and the way he understood the expansion of the kingdom of God. Furthermore, he believed his own life, beliefs, and institutional church projects found justification in the way God, specifically the Spirit, worked within humanity and the world. The theologians of progressive orthodoxy and their popularizers aided and abetted those like Rainsford by providing them with a theological rationale for their strategies of church vocation. Their close relationship meant that the successes of each lent credence to the viability and vitality of the other.

The New Theologians' understanding of the immanence of God and Christianity in perpetual development, if taken seriously, not only critiqued but undermined any static form of ecclesiastical identity that claimed its authority based upon tradition. The practical question remained for proponents of progressive orthodoxy who argued that truth had no fixed forms: what distinguishes this people claiming to be called by God as the church? William Hutchison correctly noted that the assumption of God's immanence within all creation and the progressive revelation of truth posed a problem that required the solution to the question, "But why Christianity?"[94] If this question seemed pressing to progressives in the Northern Protestant establishment, one might be willing to excuse the often contentious concerns of conservatives who valued their distinctive denominational institutions.

The New Theologians, under the influence of the theological systems of Albrecht Ritschl and his student Adolf von Harnack, located the uniqueness and finality of Christianity in its founder Jesus Christ. Further, Jesus' authority, according to the adherents of progressive orthodoxy and their heirs, centered upon his concrete ethical character. Bushnell himself had suggested this was the case; however, the New Theologians broadened

---

[93] William Rainsford, *The Story of a Varied Life: An Autobiography* (New York: Doubleday, Page & Company, 1922), 34–35.

[94] Hutchison, *Modernist Impulse*, 111–13.

and expanded this idea.[95] The ethical life and teachings of Jesus not only became the unifying symbol of Christianity but became the visible identification of the true church. Both Ritschl and Harnack had sought to answer positivistic critiques of Christianity (and religion in general), which claimed that its truth in absolute terms was neither objective nor scientifically meaningful.[96]

German theologian Albrecht Ritschl believed that the scientific study of history provided a means by which Christians could answer the positivistic critique. Ritschl described Christianity as a positive experience of fact that could be shown to be true. This experience consisted in nothing other than divine power indwelling the individual and thereby transforming and giving him the freedom to live the ethical life of Jesus practically and visibly within the world. The apologetic value of Ritschl's thinking lay in his assertion that the substance of the Christian ideal, epitomized in the ethical command and example of Jesus, could be documented concretely in the history of the church and distinguished from its historical accidents. This argument attempted, therefore, not only to explain the development of the various historical forms of Christianity but to insulate the gospel from the implication that the church's failures, development, and changes intimated its lack of universality and absoluteness.[97]

Against such implications, Adolf von Harnack, Ritschl's most influential student, argued that Jesus' message focused upon humanity, which "fundamentally, always remained the same, whether...moving upwards or downwards, whether...in riches or poverty, whether...strong or weak. It is the consciousness of all these oppositions being ultimately beneath it, and of its own place above them, that gives the Gospel its sovereignty."[98] In other words, because the gospel of Jesus Christ centered

---

[95] See Bushnell, *The Character of Jesus: Forbidding His Possible Classification with Men* (New York: The Chautauqua Press, 1888). This text constituted chapter 10 in his *Nature and the Supernatural*, new ed. (New York: Charles Scribner and Company, 1869) 276–332.

[96] See William Adams Brown's discussion of Ritschl's school in *The Essence of Christianity: A Study in the History of a Definition* (New York: Charles Scribner's Sons, 1906) 223–27.

[97] Ibid., 252–53.

[98] Adolf von Harnack, *What Is Christianity?* (Philadelphia: Fortress Press, 1986) 17. These lectures were originally published in 1900 under the title *Des Wesen des Christentum* (*The Essence of Christianity*).

upon humanity and its spiritual, moral, and physical development, its core message always had relevance, even if its forms became passé.

American students of Ritschl and Harnack, in particular Presbyterian William Adams Brown, professor at Union Theological Seminary (New York), and Methodist Borden Parker Bowne, professor at Boston University, used these continental theologians' arguments to augment their understanding of the church as the ethical community of Christ. William Adams Brown wrote of Ritschl that he believed that "the great duty of the theologian, therefore, is to discover, and to define as accurately as he can, what is the particular fact in history which calls forth the distinctively Christian experience."[99] This experience of the divine in its particular historical circumstances provided an objective and observable expression in the ethical life. He further saw both Ritschl and Harnack's thinking not only as an apology against positivistic critiques of Christianity but also as a defense of social Christianity. Objective historical study, he believed with Harnack, showed that "Christianity...is the religion of divine sonship and human brotherhood revealed and realized through Jesus Christ."[100] "As such," he continued:

> it is the fulfilment [sic] and completion of all earlier forms of religion, and the appointed means for the redemption of mankind through the realization of the kingdom of God. Its central figure is Jesus Christ, who is not only the revelation of the divine ideal for man, but also, through the transforming influence He exerts over His followers, the most powerful means of realizing that ideal among men. The possession in Christ of God's love and power constitutes the distinctive mark of Christianity and justifies its claim to be the final religion.[101]

Ecclesiologically, Brown suggested that the fact that the church could claim Christianity as the final religion had valuable consequences for its understanding of its own identity and relationship with the world. He noted that so far as the Christian community uncovered the true essence of the gospel message and ideals of Christ, it would bring needed "definiteness to its thought and direction to its activities" because "the church that expects to win the world to Christ must know what Christ wants of the world, and what He is able to do for it."[102]

---

[99] Ibid., 233.
[100] Brown., *Essence of Christianity*, 309.
[101] Ibid. Cf. Harnack, *What Is Christianity?*, 63–74.
[102] Brown, *Essence of Christianity*, 315–16.

Brown further asserted that this uncovering of the essence of true Christianity through historical and scientific study would have the residual effect of forcing the church to focus upon living issues that met the needs of the masses and taught and formed them into the way of divine sonship and human brotherhood.[103] The theology of the future, he proclaimed, "will be a theology for the people":

> It will address itself to permanent human interests, and present Christ as the Lord and the light of life. Believing in the present God, it will find evidences of His presence in the movements of the time, and will take up into its catalogue of sanctities the familiar experiences and duties now too frequently relegated to a lower sphere. Like its Master, it will seek to hallow all of life by carrying into everything the Christian spirit. Above all, it will emphasize service as the true bond of union between God and man.[104]

It is an important point of contrast from the Holiness movement that this "theology for the people" did not necessarily constitute a theology *of* (or *from*) the people. In other words, theology as the New Theologians understood it was not an orthodoxy developed within a community of individuals, equally guided by the Spirit (so long as they remained faithful); rather, it increasingly became understood as a science practiced by theological engineers and used to meet the needs of the people through human institutions.

The New Theologians typified this type of thinking by the emphasis they placed upon the role of the religious teacher within the Christian community. In the spirit of Bushnell's ideas of religious nurture, they believed that the Christian educator, whether a parent, minister, or professor, had the most critical role in the spiritual formation of individuals. The understanding of the parent, minister, and theologian as a teacher and former of souls had its best expression in the thought of Borden Parker Bowne. In a few lectures he published under the title *The Christian Life* (1899), Bowne advised Christian teachers that their primary "aim must be to help men to a consciousness of the Divine purpose, and to bring them into obedience to it. This recognition of the Divine will, this filial trust and obedience, are the heart of religion and the central meaning of salvation."[105] Such obedience, as might be expected, manifested itself in the life of the

---

[103] Ibid., 316.
[104] Ibid., 317–18.
[105] Bowne, *Christian Life*, 89.

Christian as ethical service and love toward humanity.[106] As Bushnell previously asserted and social Christianity practiced, Bowne thought that the nurture of children provided the most important object of the Christian teacher's work because "it is no quick and easy process this building of men into the realization of their divine sonship."[107]

The importance of the Christian teacher, however, went beyond the important task of spiritual formation. Bowne, greatly interested in the emerging field of psychology, believed that the religious educator had a duty to help the developing Christian to interpret properly his or her experience of the divine Spirit and distinguish it from false experiences similarly named. While he believed that the "heart religion" of his own Methodism had rightfully brought religion back to the masses, he warned that Christian educators must vigilantly protect the faithful from entering into the unwholesome thralls of religious enthusiasm.[108] His distinction on this point was nothing other than an uncharitable attack upon revivalism and the holiness conception of the role of the Spirit in the Christian life.

> In order to be wholesome and rational, emotions must spring from ideas; and religious emotions spring from religious ideas. When sought by themselves and for themselves, they have neither rational nor moral significance but are purely neurological or pathological. Religious emotions of this sort differ in nothing from the excitement of the howling or whirling dervishes. This is the source of the marked ethical weakness of popular revival services, and of the lack of moral fiber in so many alleged conversions.[109]

Religious ideas, from which sprung proper religious affections, had to be taught, and Christian teachers, of course, became the true evangelists of humanity. Bowne did not, however, wish to revert to dogmatism as a means to deter enthusiastic religiosity; in fact, he asserted that theological symbols were essentially metaphorical in nature. Better, he believed, that the Christian teacher should emphasize the practical, moral, and volitional elements in conversion and not the emotional.[110] True Christian devotion, he claimed, "is not a *statement* of an experience but shows itself chiefly in

---

[106] Ibid., 129.
[107] Ibid., 143; cf. 131–43.
[108] Ibid., 85–97.
[109] Ibid., 91.
[110] Ibid., 146–48.

service."[111] It is important not to misunderstand the importance of experience for Bowne. On the one hand, he believed that the experience of the Holy Spirit, while essential for the formation of the individual, could only be evaluated via the actions of the Christian; on the other hand, an expression of conversions and fillings of the Spirit without outward proof was nothing more than empty words.

During Bowne's tenure, Boston University produced another important thinker in Christian education, George A. Coe. A Methodist, Coe became a leading theorist in liberal religious education, teaching at Northwestern University, Union Theological Seminary, and finally Columbia University's famed Teacher's College. While at Northwestern he published his most important works including *The Spiritual Life* (1900), *The Religion of a Mature Mind* (1902), and *Education in Religion and Morals* (1904). In these works, Coe directly appealed to Bushnell's arguments concerning Christian nurture to question the techniques of revivalism and defend "salvation by education."[112] Equating God's providence with the divine education of the human race, he claimed that God used parents and teachers as "instruments in the divine hand for playing upon the divinely constructed strings of human nature."[113] The religious vocation of the teacher, in Coe's estimation, even surpassed that of the minister, preacher, or evangelist. "The process of redemption is at root all one with the process of education. A parent who is true to his parenthood, or a teacher who is true to his calling, not less than a priest who ministers at the altar, distributes the bread of life to hungry souls; he drinks the cup that Jesus drank, is baptised [sic] with the baptism where with he was baptised [sic], becomes a part of the great process of incarnation whereby God reconciles the world to himself!"[114] Revivals had their place, according to Coe, but they had a basic limitation: they were remedial in nature, an attempt to correct the failures of the church to retain and properly train their children.[115] Religious education, however, was a constructive enterprise consisting in the growth of the

---

[111] Ibid., 92. Emphasis added.

[112] Cf. chapters 9–10 of George A. Coe, *The Religion of a Mature Mind* (Chicago: Fleming H. Revell Co., 1902) 255–326.

[113] Coe, *Education in Religion and Morals* (Fleming H. Revell Co., 1904) 35, 39.

[114] Ibid., 406.

[115] Ibid., 395.

kingdom of God by feeding the individual's religious impulse "to realise [sic] its full manhood through voluntary obedience to Christ."[116]

Coe determined that salvation by education had a dual goal of redeeming the individual and society, and he reinterpreted the doctrines of the incarnation and atonement accordingly.

> Even when we advance to the notions of incarnation and atonement, we are not outside the circle of educational ideas. For the incarnation is the supreme instance of the sharing of life through which an incomplete life attains unfoldment or education. As to atonement, whatever tragedy of the divine heart is suggested by the term, the working out of the fact in the world, the historical at-one-ment of man and God, is accomplished by the essentially educational method of revelation through personality in the sharing of life.[117]

The process of redemption addressed both the individual and social aspects of the human being. According to Coe, religious education "must begin with a sense of membership in a community of persons of whom Christ is one in exactly the same way as other persons."[118] The church, therefore, needed to focus its energies, not on restrictive doctrines or liturgical forms, but rather upon the educational example of the historic Jesus.[119] The message from the Jesus of history, he observed, did not center on mystical or dogmatic interpretations of Christ, but simply the fatherhood of God and the brotherhood of man. In other words, the individual found meaning in relationship with God and fellow human beings; in the Christianity of Jesus, individualism and social organization find their unity in the realization of the kingdom of God on earth.[120]

Advocates of progressive orthodoxy believed that the church's role in the institution of the kingdom of God on earth not only involved the education of individuals but also the assimilation of all aspects of human endeavor under the life-giving example and message of Jesus Christ. Coe lamented that the church's educational vocation was hindered by its lack of professional standards for religious teachers, attention to age-appropriate catechetical content, and competition and uncoordinated efforts with organizations outside of the church, such as the YMCA, Christian Endeavor

---

[116] Ibid., 39.
[117] Ibid., 406.
[118] Ibid., 405.
[119] Ibid., 403–406.
[120] Ibid., 399–401.

societies, religious camps, and even Sunday schools.[121] His observation coincided with the most important feature of ecclesiological change: a more coordinated and centralized church governance.

As was the case for the Keswick understanding of Spirit, the New Theologians' pneumatology correlated with the ecclesiological orientation they preferred within the Protestant establishment. While holiness advocates stressed that the Spirit's redemptive work began with the individual, the New Theologians believed that salvation began with society. As George A. Gordon put it, "Society is the full expression of man, and religion is the complete expression of society."[122] God, through the divine Spirit, therefore, drew humanity to himself by the conforming of individuals' characters to the divine will through the nurture of social institutions. The church needed only to bring, by means of example and persuasion, all human cultural institutions (considered secular by the world) under the influence of the gospel and the will of the Spirit. In the words of renowned preacher and Episcopal bishop Phillips Brooks, "the salvation of Christ is nothing less than this, the entire occupation of the human life by the Divine life."[123]

Not surprisingly, therefore, advocates of progressive orthodoxy naturally gravitated toward the use of the ecclesiastical machinery of their denominations, which were consolidated and bureaucratized in the early twentieth century. Ironically, the impetus for such consolidation came because the move toward bureaucratization often pushed progressive social reform outside civil government venues.[124] Organizations that had existed outside of denominational auspices, whether focusing on such issues as temperance, labor, or race relations, began to be incorporated into established denominational structures. Through the use of church agencies they expected to influence and form the characters of their church membership and the wider society from the top down.

The success of the New Theologians can be gauged by the institutionalization of their vision within the Northern establishment churches. By the time of, or soon after, the First World War, most of their denominations had created agencies to promote the Christianization of the social order because of their activism. In 1901 the Protestant Episcopal

---

[121] Ibid., 289–318.

[122] Gordon, *New Epoch*, 14.

[123] Brooks, *Spiritual Life*, 49.

[124] Robert H. Wiebe, *The Search for Order, 1877–1920*, American Century series ed. (New York: Wang and Hill, 1968) 208–209.

Church created a Joint Commission on the Relation of Capital to Labor to promote a spirit of Christian harmony between employers and the working classes.[125] That same year, Congregationalists appointed a Committee on Labor Organizations, upon which sat luminaries such as Washington Gladden, William Jewett Tucker, and Graham Taylor.[126] In 1903 the Presbyterian Church in the U.S.A. created a Department of Church and Labor under the auspices of its Board of Home Missions.[127] In 1908, the Methodist Episcopal Church issued its famous "Social Creed," which was adopted by the Federal Council of Churches (and subsequently by most other establishment church bodies) that same year. The Social Creed among other things officially denounced child labor practices and called for living wages and shorter working hours for laborers. In 1909 the Northern Baptist Convention (NBC) not only officially adopted the Social Creed but issued a series of pamphlets on "Social Service." By 1913, the NBC had created a Department of Social Service and Brotherhood.[128] The department was headed by Samuel Zane Batten, professor of social science at Des Moines College, who along with Walter Rauschenbusch had promoted social gospel programs among Northern Baptists.

Also, the arguments progressives employed to bolster the finality and uniqueness of Christianity, having its fullest expression in the life of Jesus, not only downplayed dogmatic distinctions but made Christian disunity an embarrassment. The ecumenical movement became a natural outgrowth and goal from these projects of progressive orthodoxy. If character provided the only tangible evidence of the true disciple of Christ, then there appeared to be little, besides unfaithful church leaders or a spiritually immature laity, to prevent communities of Christian disciples from visibly and practically becoming "one body" in the present time. The New Theologians and their theological heirs, however, did not agree on the exact form Christian unity should take. The failure of the Evangelical Alliance, which steadily waned in power during the mid-1890s, lay in its organization as a league of individuals rather than church organizations. While the Alliance clearly expressed the sentiments of a large cross-section of the Protestant establishment, its

---

[125] James Thayer Addison, *The Episcopal Church in the United States, 1789–1931* (New York: Charles Scribner's Son's, 1951) 322.

[126] C. Howard Hopkins, *The Rise of the Social Gospel in American Protestantism, 1865–1915* (New Haven: Yale U. Press, 1940) 286.

[127] Ibid., 280–81.

[128] Ibid., 294–95.

leaders and participants did not officially represent their church denominations. This model clearly needed to be avoided if serious ecumenism was to occur.

One alternative, held by such thinkers as Charles Briggs and New Haven Congregationalist pastor Newman Smyth, advocated the complete organic unity of all Christians, including Roman Catholics.[129] Indeed, as early as 1870, pioneering ecumenist William Reed Huntington argued that churches could unify under the beliefs of the "quadrilateral of pure Anglicanism": the Scriptures as the Word of God; the ancient creeds as the rule of faith; practice of the sacraments of baptism and the Eucharist; and the episcopate "as the keystone of governmental unity."[130] However, as was often the case for plans of organic unity, Huntington's appeal appeared to many evangelicals as more a sectarian invitation to become Anglican than a genuine discussion of unifying different denominations with real claims to be the true church.[131]

The majority of New Theologians and their theological heirs promoted a federationist understanding of union based upon common Christian work within the world. Groups such as the Open and Institutional Church League (OICL) already employed the federationist model on a small scale, and, not surprisingly, two of its prominent leaders, Frank Mason North and Elias Sanford, became the primary architects of the Federal Council of the Churches of Christ in America in 1908. Sanford tirelessly advocated practical cooperative union, stating that "organic unity is still a dream of the future," but "federation is a present possibility."[132] Federationist models of ecumenism looked remarkably like the progressive orthodoxy's vision of centralized denominations. By creating unity through coordinated social outreach, federationist models of church unity obviated the sticky practical difficulties of organic unity, which surrounded polity,

---

[129] See Briggs, *Whither?*, 268–72, 289–98, and Newman Smyth, *Passing Protestantism and Coming Catholicism* (New York: Charles Scribner's Sons, 1908). Also of interest by Smyth is his essay "Concerning Schism," in *Approaches Toward Church Unity*, ed. Newman Smyth and Williston Walker (New Haven: Yale University Press, 1919) 65–73.

[130] William Reed Huntington, *The Church-Idea: An Essay Towards Unity* (Harrisburg PA: Morehouse Publishing, 1870, 2002) 114–15.

[131] See Peter Ainslie, "The Rapprochement of the Churches," *Christian Century* 44/38 (22 September 1927): 1099–1101.

[132] E. B. Sanford, "The Relation of the Church to the Kingdom of God," *Open Church* 3/31 (March 1899): 30–31.

dogma, and liturgical form, while genuinely and officially expressing a unified voice and cooperation on concrete social, moral, and religious issues faced in the United States. Also, by avoiding such difficulties, many conservatives and revivalists were willing to consent to allow their denominations to participate in organizations such as the Federal Council.[133]

Summary

Historians William Hutchison and George Marsden have convincingly argued that the New Theology and Keswick Holiness laid important theological foundations for the development of modernism and fundamentalism, respectively.[134] The pneumatology of these theological movements also profoundly shaped the ecclesiological vision of their respective advocates and their heirs. Progressive orthodoxy naturally promoted the development of more centralized and efficient structure through which the Holy Spirit could act. The proponents of the Higher Life theology gravitated toward a more bottom-up model that valued egalitarian structures. However, pneumatology was not the only doctrine that intimately shaped the ecclesiology of evangelicals of the late nineteenth and early twentieth centuries. The next chapter will examine how eschatology, or the doctrine of the end, had an equally important effect.

---

[133] See John A. Hutchison, *We Are Not Divided: A Critical and Historical Study of the Federal Council of Churches of Christ in America* (New York: Round Table Press, Inc., 1941) 41–42. For B. B. Warfield and the the idea of a "formal federation of denominations for prosecuting tasks common to the federated bodies, so far as federation involves no sacrifice of principle or testimony." See "True Church Unity: What It Is," *Homiletic Review* 20/6 (December 1890): 489.

[134] Hutchison, *Modernist Impulse*, 226–56; Marsden, *Fundamentalism*, 93–101.

CHAPTER 5

The Church, the Kingdom of God, and Evangelical Eschatology

William Adams Brown, professor of systematic theology at Union Theological Seminary in New York, wrote in the 1900 edition of *A Dictionary of the Bible* an entry on "the Millennium" that stated: "Premillenarian views have, indeed, been revived from time to time..., and have never been without their advocates in the Church; but they have failed to win general acceptance. The Church, as a whole, Protestant as well as Catholic, has either adopted Augustine's identification of the Millennium with the Church militant, or else looks for a future period of prosperity preceding the second advent of Christ."[1] Despite Brown's dismissal of premillennial views of the Second Advent of Christ, he correctly identified the most important views concerning the second coming of Christ and the establishment of the millennial kingdom of God on earth that prevailed in the late nineteenth and early twentieth centuries. Eschatology, specifically an understanding of Christ's coming kingdom and his return, had an important influence on evangelicals' view of the church. In short, eschatology is that branch of Christian theology that, among other things, attempts to explain consummation of God's plan on earth. Therefore, role of the church in that divine plan is necessarily part of this branch of theology.

As noted by Brown, St. Augustine's influential identification of the millennial kingdom of God with the church militant in book 20.9 in his *City*

---

[1] William Adams Brown, "Millennium" in *KIR–PLEIADES*, vol. 3 of *A Dictionary of the Bible Dealing with its Language, Literature, and Contents including Biblical Theology*, ed. James Hastings et al. (New York: Charles Scribner's Sons, 1900) 373.

of God became one of the most important statements of "realized" eschatology in Western Christian theology. Reflecting upon Revelation 20, Augustine noted:

> The Church even now is the Kingdom of Christ, and the kingdom of heaven. Accordingly, even now His saints reign with Him, though otherwise than they shall reign hereafter; and yet, though the tares grow in the Church along with the wheat, they do not reign with Him.... It is then of this kingdom militant, in which conflict with the enemy is still maintained, and war carried on with warring lusts, or government laid upon them as they yield, until we come to that most peaceful kingdom in which we shall reign without an enemy, and it is of this first resurrection in the present life, that the Apocalypse speaks in the words just quoted. For after saying that the devil is bound a thousand years and is afterwards loosed for a short season, it goes on to give a sketch of what the Church does or of what is done in the Church in those days...It is not to be supposed that that this refers to the last judgment, but to the seats of the rulers and to the rulers themselves by whom the Church is now governed.[2]

This position, often labeled amillennialism, influenced segments of the Protestant establishment in the late nineteenth and early twentieth centuries. This position was often coupled with belief affirmed by Augustine that the unfulfilled prophecies concerning Israel or Jerusalem in the Old Testament have or would find their fulfillment in the church.[3]

Those advocating an earthly reign of Christ in the future (though this belief might be debated historically) often perceived amillennialism as an unfortunate status quo among Protestants in the United States. The many types of American millennialists all agreed that amillennialists had made a theological error. Premillennialists, who believed that Christ's Second Advent would occur before the institution of the millennial kingdom of God on earth, especially argued against an identification of the biblical reference about Israel with the church. This biblical hermeneutic affected the way these evangelicals understood ecclesiology and left them ambivalent about their denominational affiliations. Postmillennialists, who believed the Second Advent would be the consummation of the gradual growth of the kingdom of God on the earth, as well as those social and theological liberals who held to a symbolic rather than literal millennium, also believed

---

[2] Philip Schaff, ed., *Augustine: City of God, Christian Doctrine*, vol. 2 in ser. 1 of *Nicene and Post Nicene Fathers* (Peabody MA: Hendrickson Publishers, Inc., 1995) 430.

[3] Ibid., 338–39.

amillennialists conflated the church with the kingdom of God. This postmillennial eschatology equally affected how these evangelicals viewed the identity and mission of the church. Like their premillennial coreligionists, their eschatology increased their ambivalence to denominational affiliations. Despite their common assertion that amillennialists espoused an erroneous eschatology, however, these two groups perceived one another as rivals within their denominational institutions. In fact, the first rumbles of the fundamentalist-modernist controversies within the establishment surrounded the issue of eschatology.

Ecclesiology and the Development of Dispensationalism

John Nelson Darby was the most important early promoter and developer of a theological system called dispensational premillennialism, or dispensationalism. In 1831 Darby, an Anglican priest, left the Church of Ireland and joined the Plymouth Brethren movement. The Plymouth Brethren focused upon biblical instruction, sought simple forms of worship, and avoided hierarchical ecclesiastical structures and distinctions. Because of Darby's influence, dispensationalism became the most important theological system among the Plymouth Brethren; however, its popularity in England, Canada, and the United States spread well beyond the movement. Darby made seven trips to North America between 1859 and 1874. Further, his eschatology, or doctrine of the end times, formed the bedrock for thought of the most important dispensationalists in the United States, including James H. Brookes, A. J. Gordon, C. I. Scofield, and A. C. Gaebelein.[4]

Simply put, dispensationalism is an eschatological system that delineates time (past, present, and future) into periods, or dispensations, using narrative cues found in the Bible. Further, dispensationalism is a kind of premillennialism, which argues that Christ's Second Advent will initiate the Millennium, or the 1000-year reign of Jesus on the earth, depicted in the twentieth chapter of the book of Revelation. Oddly, perhaps, neither Darby's employment of dispensations to divide time nor his belief in the premillennial second coming of Christ made his eschatology unique. Rather, as historian Ernest Sandeen rightfully noted, the distinctive points of Darby's eschatology developed directly from his understanding of the nature

---

[4] Larry V. Crutchfield, *The Origins of Dispensationalism: The Darby Factor* (Lanham MD: University Press of America, 1992) 10–16.

of the church.[5] Sandeen's observations echoed mid-twentieth-century dispensationalist theologian Charles C. Ryrie, who noted that "ecclesiology...is the touchstone of Dispensationalism."[6] Indeed, it appears that Darby developed his most unique and well-known eschatological ideas, such as the secret rapture of the church and the division of the New Testament between Jewish and Christian proclamations, to solve theological (particularly ecclesiological) problems.

In order to understand the influence of Darby's ecclesiology upon his version of dispensationalism, it is important to define his idea of "church." First, his definition of the church made a distinction between what he called the "body of Christ" and the "habitation of God": "We may consider the Church in two points of view. First, it is like the formation of the children of God into one body united to Christ Jesus ascended into heaven, the glorified man; and that by the power of the Holy Ghost. In the second place, it is the house or habitation of God by the Spirit. The Saviour gave Himself, not only to save perfectly all those who believe in Him, but also to gather together in one the children of God that were scattered abroad."[7] The body of Christ included all those who had been redeemed by Jesus in the power of the Holy Spirit and through faith. The phrase "body of Christ," according to Darby, pertained to individual Christians and their relationship to Jesus Christ. The church, therefore, properly included all redeemed Christians. This church was heavenly in character insofar as it was presently connected to Jesus Christ, who ascended to heaven and now sits at the right hand of God the Father.

Darby did not believe, however, that the church was just a spiritual entity. He rejected the Augustinian distinction between the "visible" and "invisible" church.[8] He rhetorically asked, "What is the value of an invisible light?"[9] Darby believed that the local assembly, as the habitation of God, still acted as an earthly vessel of the truth, corporately manifesting the body of Christ with a full complement of the gifts of the Holy Spirit.[10] In fact, the

---

    [5] Ernest Sandeen, *The Roots of Fundamentalism: British and American Millenarianism, 1800–1930* (Chicago: University of Chicago Press, 1970) 66–67.

    [6] Charles Caldwell Ryrie, *Dispensationalism Today* (Chicago: Moody Press, 1965) 132.

    [7] William Kelly, ed. *The Collected Writings of J. N. Darby*, 34 vols. (Kensington-on-Thames: Stow Hill Bible and Tract Depot, 1957) 14:76.

    [8] Ibid., 14:30.

    [9] Ibid., 14:85.

    [10] Ibid., 14:31–32.

local assembly was the only place Darby believed one could possibly find an earthly manifestation of the church in the present age. He noted that very soon after the founding of the church at Pentecost, the habitation of God, or the "professing" church as he often called it, became mixed with "vessels of dishonour," gradually degenerating into apostasy.[11] This state of apostasy occurred because those within the professing church had departed from the faith once delivered and practiced worldly evils that mimicked true Christianity. Worse, the professing church had countenanced such error and immorality rather than purging it from its midst.[12]

This perceived state of apostasy, however, created a theological dilemma for Darby. On the one hand, if God did not ultimately "cut off" the professing church because of its corruption, then "the responsibility of man in and by any given economy is lost."[13] On the other hand, if the individual member of the body of Christ found himself or herself cut off because of the failure of the professing church, "the security of the Lord's faithfulness" to the believer would be compromised. The secret rapture of the church, or the removal of the true believers in Christ from the earth, solved this particular theological dilemma. "That the saints are caught away before vengeance bursts upon the professor is quite certain, because it is when Christ appears that He executes vengeance…. Now when Christ appears, we appear with Him…. Matthew xiii. 41, 43 only proves that, when the wicked are judged, the righteous shine forth."[14] In Darby's view the future rapture of individual Christians provided one of many biblical examples of God preserving both his justice and faithfulness by calling a remnant from out of a corrupt people. "The responsibility of man, or any set of men under any dispensation of God, is quite distinct from the salvation of any individuals of that dispensation. The confounding of these things renders the apprehension of the dealings of God with man impossible…. So decided is this distinction, it is just where the dispensation entirely fails, that the faithfulness of the saved remnant is most conspicuously manifest."[15] In fact,

---

[11] Ibid., 14:67. Darby believed such apostasy could already be seen in 1 John 2. See ibid., 1:118.

[12] Ibid., 1:115.

[13] Ibid., 1:114.

[14] *The Letters of J. N. D. Volume 3, 1879–1882* (Sunbury PA: Believer's Bookshelf, 1971) 334–35.

[15] *Collected Writings*, 1:114.

argued Darby, God had called the church itself from Israel after the Jews had rejected its Christ.

Darby also maintained a clear distinction between Israel and the church. "The subject of prophecy," he noted, "divides itself into two parts: the hopes of the church and those of the Jews."[16] Darby rejected the practice of applying the unfulfilled biblical prophecies regarding Israel to the church.[17] Any dispensation and any Old Testament prophecy concerning Israel, claimed Darby, had as its subject God's calling of his chosen people and God's government on the earth. Therefore, the church technically could not be understood to belong to a dispensation (as Darby typically understood the term) or to be the subject of "earthly" Old Testament prophecies, because it is already united to Christ, who reigns in heaven.[18]

> Prophecy applies itself properly to the earth; its object is not heaven. It was about things that were to happen upon the earth; and the not seeing this has misled the church. We have thought that we ourselves had within us the accomplishment of these earthly blessings whereas we are called to enjoy heavenly blessings. The privilege of the church is to have its portion in heavenly places; and later blessings will be shed forth upon earthly people. The church is something altogether apart—a kind of heavenly economy, during the rejection of the earthly people, who are put aside on account of their sins, and driven out among the nations, out of the midst of nations God chooses a people for the enjoyment of heavenly glory with Jesus Himself. The Lord, having been rejected by the Jewish people, is become wholly a heavenly person.[19]

Such an argument led Sandeen to argue that Darby believed the church to be "so spiritual that it existed outside of history."[20] This somewhat misrepresents his ecclesiology.

God had inhabited the created order, according to Darby, since the time of the nation of Israel. Corporately, Israel was the "dwelling-place and habitation of God," that is until the nation rejected its Christ. With the martyrdom of Stephen the "Jewish central successional order closed" and the church was called from the midst of Israel.[21] Its calling did not, however,

---

[16] Ibid., 2:373.
[17] Ibid., 1:114.
[18] Ibid., 11:41–54.
[19] Ibid., 2:376.
[20] Ibid., 14:67.
[21] Ibid., 1:112.

create a new dispensation; rather the church existed in parentheses between the 69th and 70th week of Daniel 9.[22]

Darby understood that the Jewish rejection of Christ and martyrdom of Stephen completed the 69th week; however, the Great Tribulation, which signaled the beginning of the 70th week, had not yet occurred. God had stopped the prophetic clock; a new dispensation would not occur until the last had concluded. Therefore, the age in which the church existed was anomalous and unique.[23] In other words, the church found itself separated from, or outside, the dispensations of history. Furthermore, the church would not see the conclusion of the incomplete dispensation, because it will have been secretly raptured before it starts.

Darby also coupled the logic of prophetic separation with practical separation. He believed that the Scriptures demanded that believers separate from the professing church. "Evil exists. The world is lying in wickedness, and the God of unity is the Holy God. Separation, therefore, from evil, becomes the necessary and sole basis and principle, I do not say power, of unity. For God must be the center and power of that unity, and evil exists: and from that corruption they must be separate who are to be in God's unity; for He can have no union with evil."[24] Darby further repudiated both sectarianism and "independency." He argued that a sect "signifies a doctrine, or a system, whether philosophy or religion, which has its adherents united as adopting this doctrine."[25] Darby claimed that nowhere do the Scriptures admit, as a proper idea of the church, the voluntary association of individual believers or individual groups of believers.[26] Rather, "the Church of God in one place represents the whole and acts in its name."[27] Therefore, while these churches are local in character they cannot act independently of one another because they are *"one* in thought word and deed by the operation of one Spirit, as the Father and the Son in the unity of the divine nature (will)."[28] Theoretically, Darby's position may have seemed theologically cogent; however, on a practical level, as American dispensationalist leader A. C. Gaebelein observed, "the party-split among these different divisions [of

---

[22] Ibid., 13:155.
[23] Ibid., 1:93–94.
[24] Darby, *Collected Writings*, 20:356.
[25] Ibid., 14:362.
[26] Ibid., 14:306, 363.
[27] Ibid., 14:302.
[28] Ibid., 14:363.

the Plymouth Brethren] was even more sectarian than the sectarianism of the larger denominations."[29] Ironically, in Darby's own lifetime, Plymouth Brethren unity became a casualty of the fight over who would be welcomed to the communion table, the very symbol of Christian community.

Dispensationalism and Denominational Ambivalence in the United States

Darby influenced many important North American premillennialists, especially those connected with the prophetic ideas associated with Niagara Bible Conference. The Bible conference movement began in 1875 as an attempt by conservative, soul-saving evangelical Protestants to create a forum for doctrinal orthodoxy. Dispensationalists quickly became the dominate leadership within the group, and by 1878 a newly drafted fourteen-point "Niagara Creed" included a plank on premillennialism.

The Niagara Creed's drafter, James Hall Brookes, helped found the conference and subsequently presided over its annual meetings for two decades. Ordained in the Presbyterian Church in the U.S.A. in 1854, he ministered most of his career in St. Louis, Missouri, at the Second and later 16th & Walnut Street Presbyterian Churches. Brookes was also editor of the periodical *The Truth*, which along with A. J. Gordon's *Watchword* provided an important vehicle for the early dissemination of premillennialist thought in the United States. Whether Brookes actually met Darby in St. Louis remains a mystery. The well-know Plymouth Brethren preacher H. A. Armstrong made a passing remark in his *Historical Sketch of the Brethren Movement* that Darby preached in Brookes's pulpit; however, Sandeen rightfully noted that this lone reference to a direct meeting of the two ministers was proffered with no accompanying historical evidence.[30] Nonetheless, within five years of Darby's 1872 visit to St. Louis, Brookes became an important leader in the American prophecy conference movement and an advocate of dispensationalism.

Brookes clearly borrowed many facets of Darby's ecclesiology and is representative of American dispensationalism in general. He argued that

---

[29] Arno Clemens Gaebelein, *Half a Century: The Autobiography of a Servant* (New York: Publication Office of "Our Hope," 1930) 85.

[30] H. A. Ironside, *A Historical Sketch of the Brethren Movement: An Account of Its Inception, Progress, Principles and Failures, and Its Lessons for Present Day Believers* (Grand Rapids: Zondervan Publishing House, 1942) 196. Cf. Sandeen, *Roots of Fundamentalism*, 74–75.

"the Old and New Testaments respect two entirely distinct and different dispensations of God's dealing with his people."[31] Therefore, Israel had an earthly calling while the church had a heavenly calling.[32] According to Brookes, the mistake of confusing the vocation of the church with the calling of Israel had led many Christians astray. "[In the New Testament or the church dispensation] the saints are addressed as 'partakers of the heavenly calling,'...There is not a word to indicate that they had any portion on the earth.... If the Christian puts himself back on Old Testament grounds, and therefore expects to be great and rich and powerful on the earth, he will entirely lose view of his real calling."[33] That "real calling" was simply the preaching of the good news of Jesus Christ until all those whom God intended had become united to the Body of Christ.[34]

Brookes contrasted the true calling of the church to preach the gospel with what he believed to be the mistaken claim that the church would convert the world. Those who made this mistake, he thought, erred by claiming that the church was synonymous with the kingdom of God. Brookes argued that the belief of many professed Christians that the church's vocation included a mission to civilize or convert the whole world was unscriptural and false.

> The Church after eighteen hundred and fifty years of existence has not succeeded in converting the world, not all of the inhabitants of the smallest province or neighborhood of the world, but the world has well nigh succeeded in converting the church. Where is the line of distinction between them? With the exception of a few, it may be hoped in each congregation, who can note any difference? The members of the church as a rule are just as eager in the pursuit of money and pleasure, and just as dishonest in their practices, and rush to balls and theatres and operas with as much avidity, as the children of the devil.[35]

In fact, according to Brookes, the greatest danger to the church's mission was the beliefs and actions of its "professed followers."[36] He further contended that the Bible had predicted this turning from the church's true calling. "The professing church," he noted, "will continue in its formality

---

[31] James H. Brookes, *Israel and the Church: The Terms Distinguished as Found in the Word of God* (Chicago: The Bible Institute Colportage Association, n.d.) 7.
[32] Ibid., 12.
[33] Ibid., 14–15.
[34] Ibid., 185.
[35] Ibid., 194. Cf. 198–99.
[36] Ibid., 195.

and worldliness, and semi-infidelity, and ridiculous travesty upon the faith and practice enjoined in the New Testament until it reaches the Laodicean state."[37] While Brookes believed that a faithful remnant would continue the preach God's truth, the lukewarm, professing church would finally be spit from the mouth of God, as warned in Revelation 3:16.

The belief that a great apostasy would occur in the last days before Christ's return coupled with their expectation of the imminent Second Advent left typical dispensationalists ambivalent about denominational institutions. This ambivalence was both theological and practical. They felt uncomfortable associating with those they perceived to be heretics within their own denominations. However, their acknowledgment that the Bible predicted the apostasy of the professing church did not clearly answer questions concerning practical church association. Although John Nelson Darby believed that the true Christian remnant should not remain united with in institutions containing "vessels of dishonour," American premillennialists did not universally find Darby's demand for theological and moral purity persuasive.[38] Often practical considerations made them far more tolerant of denominational associations containing both "wheat and tares." Although American dispensationalists usually admitted that denominational institutions necessarily manifested a sinful and divided professing church, they also argued that such institutions provided a practical venue through which large audiences of people could be reached with the true gospel message. Because of this fundamental ambivalence the practical effect of dispensationalist thought upon the ecclesiology of its American adherents was varied.

The thought of Cyrus Ingersoll Scofield also provides a key to understand how American dispensationalists related with denominational institutions. After his conversion Scofield met James Brookes in St. Louis and, according to Charles G. Trumbull, the latter become a mentor to the former.[39] Scofield popularized dispensationalism for his generation through his participation at prophecy conferences, a successful correspondence course begun in 1890, and finally his opus, an edited reference bible. Oxford University Press published the Scofield reference Bible in 1909, thereby making Scofield's notes and his dispensational theology accessible to a wide

---

[37] Ibid., 197–98.

[38] For Darby's view of separation, see *Collected Writings*, 20:356.

[39] Charles Gallaudet Trumbull, *The Life Story of C. I. Scofield* (New York: Oxford University Press, 1920) 34–36.

THE CHURCH, THE KINGDOM OF GOD, AND EVANGELICAL ESCHATOLOGY   121

audience of Protestants. It also had the psychological effect of virtually making Scofield's notes part of the Holy Writ, next to which they were printed.

Scofield proclaimed in the introduction of his *Reference Bible* that "the Editor disclaims originality" and suggested that he summarized and organized the teachings and thought of the many contributing editors.[40] The contributing editors included some of the preeminent dispensationalists of the generation, such as James M. Gray, dean of Moody Bible Institute; Henry G. Weston, president of Crozer Theological Seminary; Presbyterian evangelist and speaker William J. Erdman; W. G. Moorehead, president of Xenia Theological Seminary; Elmore Harris, president of Toronto Bible Institute; A. T. Pierson; and evangelist and editor of *Our Hope*, A. C. Gaebelein. The Reference Bible, therefore, provides a representative lens to understand dispensationalist views of the church that reached a large audience.

Several years before the publication of his reference Bible, Scofield published a small booklet entitled *Rightly Dividing the Word of Truth*, in which he noted that the professing church was characterized by an "admixture" of true believers with "mere formalists, hypocrites, or deceived legalists."[41] He warned, however, that "the judgment of professors is not committed to us, but is reserved to the Son of Man."[42] Thirteen years later in the Scofield reference Bible, he expanded his notion that the church was an admixture. In his notes on Exodus 12:38 and Numbers 11:4–6, Scofield argued typologically that the description of Israel as a "mixed multitude" stood for "unconverted church-members" who "clamour for things pleasing to the flesh in the work and way of the church: sumptuous buildings, ornate ritual, and easy doctrine."[43] The parable of the wheat and the tares found in Matthew 13 provided another support for Scofield's position. "The wheat of God at once becomes the scene of Satan's activity. Where the children of the kingdom are gathered, there, 'among the wheat' (vv. 25, 38, 29), Satan "sows" "children of the wicked one," who profess to be the children of the kingdom, and in outward ways are so like the true children that only the

---

[40] C. I. Scofield, ed., *The King James Study Bible*, reference ed. (Uhrichsville OH: Barbour Publishing, Inc, n.d.) iv.

[41] C. I. Scofield, *Rightly Dividing the Word of Truth* (Neptune NJ: Loizeaux Brothers, 1896) 57.

[42] Ibid., 61.

[43] Scofield, *King James Study Bible*, 85, 181.

angels may, in the end, be trusted to separate them."[44] Furthermore, Scofield added that the burning of the tares, which occurs at the end of the parable, "does not imply immediate judgment."[45] Rather, the wheat is gathered first, which Scofield believed was an allusion to the rapture, and only at the end of the age did judgment commence.[46] Scofield's interpretation clearly suggested that the professing church would never be pure, and only God (or perhaps the angels) had the right and ability to properly separate the believer from the pretenders. While association with apostasy seemed undesirable, the ministry of the true children of God did not include condemning the professing church.

Scofield's notes also softened what might otherwise have seemed a clear biblical command supporting ecclesial separatism in 2 Corinthians 6:11–18. St. Paul communicates to the Corinthian congregation God's wish that they should "come out from among them, and be ye separate" (v. 17, KJV). Following a much earlier argument made by Darby, Scofield noted that in a "moral universe it is impossible for God to fully bless and use His children who are in compromise or complicity with evil."[47] "Separation from evil implies (a) separation in desire, motive, and act, from the world, in the ethically bad sense of this present world-system (see Rev. xiii.3, note); and (b) separation from believers, especially false teachers, who are 'vessels unto dishonour' (2 Tim. ii,20, 21; 2 John 9–11)."[48] The language used by Scofield unmistakably echoed Darby; yet, unlike Darby, Scofield did not demand ecclesial separation. Biblical separation, he claimed, "is not from contact with evil in the world or the church, but from complicity to it."[49] Scofield reminded his readers that the Pharisees were rebuked by Jesus for having a "mechanical and ascetic conception of separation."[50] Jesus, he observed, remained holy and pure, all the while having much contact with the sinners who needed his message of salvation.

While Scofield clearly stated that complicity with evil (including false teachers) was unacceptable, he also argued that true Christians did not have the qualifications to judge between unbelievers, misled believers, or children

---

[44] Ibid., 1015.
[45] Ibid., 1016.
[46] Ibid.
[47] Ibid., 1234.
[48] Ibid.
[49] Ibid.
[50] Ibid.

of the devil. Practically, the best and simplest way to preach the gospel to the largest audience meant membership within a denomination. Scofield himself left the Congregationalist denomination because he argued that "it stands for certain liberties which I do not allow myself, and for a certain attitude toward the Bible and historic Christianity which is not my attitude."[51] However, he subsequently joined the Southern Presbyterian Church in the U.S.A., a denomination he believed expressed true historic Christianity.[52] He consistently worshipped with a Plymouth Brethren congregation in Oxford while working on his *Reference Bible*. Such association led one reader of the *Sunday-School Times* to ask: "How far did Dr. and Mrs. Scofield share the peculiar beliefs of these people?" Scofield responded that the members of the church, with whom he worshipped, were "Open Brethren" and, therefore, not emphatic about the idea of separatism, an idea he noted that neither he nor his wife supported.[53] While leaving one's denomination was neither the expected nor obvious solution to apostasy in the professing church, denominational infidelities often left dispensationalists uneasy.

The story of Arno Clemons Gaebelein also exemplifies well the am-bivalence of American premillennialists toward denominational institutions. A German immigrant, he was ordained in the Methodist Episcopal Church in 1886. His exposure to premillennialism instilled in him an interest in the Jewish people and he began a mission to Jews at Allen Street Memorial Methodist Church in New York City. After participating at the Niagara Bible Conferences, Gaebelein became convinced that the Old Testament prophecies surrounding Israel still applied to modern Jews. He therefore learned Hebrew and Yiddish and began publishing *Tiqweth Israel—The Hope of Israel Monthly*. In 1893 he met Ernst F. Stroeter, who resigned a professorial post at Denver University to begin working with Gaebelein's newly formed Hope of Israel Mission, later called Our Hope.

Gaebelein and Stroeter believed that Jews who came to believe that Jesus was the Messiah should not become "Gentilized" because of the special dispensational status of Israel.[54] In his autobiography Gaebelein stated that, when he founded the Hope of Israel Mission, he believed that "the attempt to make Methodists, Baptists, Lutherans or Presbyterians out

---

[51] Trumbull, *C. I. Scofield*, 120.
[52] Ibid., 119.
[53] Ibid., 116–17.
[54] Gaebelein, *Half a Century*, 2.

of them would be a mistake.... Our conception was that a believing Hebrew should not sever his connection with the nation, but though a believer in our Lord as Israel's true Messiah, he should not separate himself from his brethren."[55] This meant that the mission's principles made its connection with the New York City Church Extension and Missionary Society of the Methodist Episcopal Church awkward. Although local bishops and the Society's secretary, Frank Mason North, gave Gaebelein and Stroeter latitude to enlarge the ministry outside of Methodist auspices, by 1897 Our Hope became officially nondenominational and severed all financial ties with the Methodist Church.[56]

Gaebelein continued his association with the Niagara Bible Conference and by 1898 had befriended and shared the lectern with many of its dispensationalist leaders, including C. I. Scofield and William J. Erdman. Soon, he decided that his view about converted Jews remaining in Israel was unscriptural.

> In that body [the church] there is neither Jew nor Gentile; all are one in Christ. So long as this body is forming the believing Jew is added by the Spirit of God as a member to the body of Christ. It will be far different after the body of Christ, the true Church, is completed. There will then be called a remnant, God-fearing, Bible-believing, and Messiah-expecting, from the people of Israel. They will continue in connection with the unbelieving nation and bear witness to the coming King, whom they know is our Lord Jesus Christ. It is this believing remnant of the future which will receive the promises [made in the Old Testament].[57]

This change in ecclesiology, as it related to converted Jews, had dramatic consequences for Gaebelein's ministry. First, it led to his parting ways with Ernst Stroeter, who refused to relinquish the view that Jews who believed Jesus to be the Messiah should remain within the Jewish community.[58] Next, it made Gaebelein start thinking about his denominational affiliation. Bible passages such as Colossians 2:10–18, Ephesians 4:3, 1 Corinthians 12:13, and John 17:11 suggested to him that denominationalism appeared to him "not as the work of the Spirit, but as the work of the flesh."[59]

---

[55] Ibid.
[56] Ibid., 68.
[57] Ibid., 53.
[58] Ibid., 76.
[59] Ibid., 77–78.

Gaebelein later claimed that this study of the church became the turning-point in his career. "Then it gradually came to me that my future ministry whether to Jews or Gentiles, believers in Christ, must be exercised according to this truth [found in Ephesians 4:12]. The new commission came to me in the early part of 1899 to go forth denominationally unaffiliated, to minister to the body of Christ, wherever it is found and wherever my Lord would open the door."[60] If Bible study helped begin his journey away from the Methodist Church, his attendance at the weekly Methodists' Preachers Meeting in New York strengthened his resolve to sever his denominational ties. At the April 1899 meeting, he heard Congregationalist minister Samuel Parkes Cadman present an address that denied Mosaic authorship of the Pentateuch and the historicity of the Jonah story. Gaebelein wanted Cadman and his address officially condemned but was rebuffed by denominational leaders. He perceived the inaction of officials against Cadman to be complicity with heresy. Ultimately, this incident became the straw that broke the camel's back, and Gaebelein left the Methodist fold.[61]

The reactions to Gaebelein's decision by his dispensationalist colleagues are instructive insofar as it clearly reveals the fundamental ambivalence by dispensationalists with denominational institutions. Evangelist L. W. Munhall, a Methodist coreligionist, advised that Gaebelein ought to remain in the Methodist church and fight the apostasy. Notably, Munhall remained, if only as a gadfly, in the Methodist Episcopal Church until his death in 1934. Presbyterian William J. Erdman also counseled against leaving but for practical reasons. Gaebelein reported that Erdman warned that leaving a denomination "cannot be done in this country. You will not have any calls to service...when people find out you are an independent."[62] Erdman incorrectly projected a two-year life span for Gaebelein's nondenominational ministry. C. I. Scofield, however, encouraged Gaebelein's resolution to leave, as did E. P. Marvin who reasoned that "if the apostasy continues in the different denominations, we all must take the same step sooner or later."[63]

If one considers that Gaebelein left Methodism well before the controversies of the 1920s and 1930s, then his tolerance of colleagues that

---

[60] Ibid., 79.
[61] Ibid., 80–81.
[62] Ibid., 81.
[63] Ibid., 80–81.

remained in their denominations during these later controversies is notable. While never sorry for leaving the Methodist Episcopal Church, he argued as late as 1930 that the true believers should neither denounce denominations nor those who remain within them. "Laodicea is all about us. It is the final state of Protestant Christendom, lukewarm, indifferent, modernistic. Yet the work of the true servant of God is not to denounce the professing church, but to go and bear a loving faithful testimony to those in Laodicea."[64] Following the thought of C. I. Scofield, Gaebelein interpreted the churches of Philadelphia and Laodicea in the third chapter of Revelation as simultaneously applying to the professing church of the last days. "Prophetically, Philadelphia stands for that portion of the professing church during the end days of our age which remains faithful; it is the believing remnant. The modernistic portion of the professing church is represented by Laodicea.... The inspiration and revelation of the Bible and the Deity of Jesus Christ our Lord—this is the battlefield of these days."[65] Although his conscience moved him to separation, his prophetic hermeneutic allowed that one could remain within a denomination and still be part of the believing remnant. Furthermore, practical considerations along the lines of Erdman's thought influenced his unwillingness to denounce denominationalism as a key component of his ministry. In his autobiography, he admitted, "denominationalism exists, and there is nothing that will change it. But my commission was to go and minister the Truth wherever the Lord would open a door for His servant."[66]

While these evangelicals considered evangelism a divine mandate, their premillennialism often left them ambivalent about the future of American society and culture as well. Illustrating well this ambivalence, A. C. Dixon wrote in one sermon that "Our citizenship is in heaven. We are now part of the heavenly Jerusalem; but we have duties here as citizens. The fact that I have citizenship in heaven does not free me from the responsibility of voting.... But it makes me unworldly.... I stop for a while, enjoy the sights, profit from what I hear and see, perform the duties of each day, but I make no large investments.... So we are strangers here."[67] Premillennialists influenced by the Holiness movement, such as Dixon, A. B. Simpson, A. J. Gordon, and A. T. Pierson, considered cultural engagement a Christian

---

[64] Ibid., 102.

[65] Ibid., 196. Cf. Scofield, *King James Study Bible*, 1333–34.

[66] Gaebelein, *Half a Century*, 85.

[67] A. C. Dixon, *Heaven on Earth* (Greenville SC: The Gospel Hour Inc., n.d.) 9.

duty and a mark of the indwelling of the Holy Spirit. Gordon proclaimed that Christians had a duty to ensure that the state uphold, at least legally, the highest Christian values, particularly on the issue of alcohol prohibition: "When God says 'Woe,' no government has a right to say 'Weal.' …It is for Christians to resist evil to their utmost; if then the wrong goes on, let it go branded with the trademark of the devil, and not legalized by the revenue stamp of the state."[68] However, Gordon understood that a state influenced by evangelical churches did not necessarily obviate the dilemma of democracy if those churches ignored the voice of the Holy Spirit. "Let us remember," wrote Gordon speaking of evangelical churches, "that a democracy may be guilty of the same sin as a hierarchy, in settling issues by a 'show of hands,' instead of prayerfully waiting for guidance of the Holy Spirit, in substituting the voice of a majority for the voice of the Spirit."[69]

Other premillennialist leaders, such as L. W. Munhall and Nathaniel West, not only believed that the dilemma of democracy existed but insisted that it was an unavoidable reality in a fallen world prophesied to get worse before Christ returned. Munhall questioned the great advances of the church attempting to institute the kingdom of God on earth: "What government was ever more corrupt than that of the United States at the present time?…Don't we all know that 'John Barleycorn' comes more nearly dominating civil and social affairs in the United States than Christian principles?"[70] Nathaniel West went so far as to proclaim that the idea of a Christian state was patently unbiblical:[71] "Herein consists the *gigantic lie and narrow mindedness* of our generation, that our civilization is thought to be the highest thing, accepted as a surrogate for grace, and for regeneration by the Spirit of the living God. *It is the idol of the modern world.*"[72] Favorably quoting bishop Hans Lassen Martensen of Seeland, West explained that the observant student of prophecy expected democracy's decay. "No false Democracy, or Red Republic," he explained, "will be the last of historical events to precede the Coming of the Lord. *The last development will be Caesarism, Absolute Despotism, a Scarlet Caesarism, and Revolution,* the

---

[68] A. J. Gordon, *Ministry of the Spirit*, 131–32
[69] Ibid.
[70] Munhall, *The Lord's Return and Kindred Truth* (Philadelphia: E & R Munhall, 1888) 59–60.
[71] Nathaniel West, *The Thousand Years in Both Testaments* (Chicago: Fleming H. Revell, 1889) 439.
[72] Ibid., 442. Emphasis in the original.

128   YET SAINTS THEIR WATCH ARE KEEPING

necessary pre-supposition of the Antichrist."[73] Such predictions sounded remarkably like de Tocqueville's vision of a democracy without religion. For premillennialists, such as Munhall and West, the apocalyptic visions of the Bible implied an unfashionable America, "a Beast whose power is now *in check* for the present, but soon to be *unchecked* and drive Christianity to the wall."[74]

The Kingdom of God, the New Theology, and the Social Gospel

As was the case for dispensational premillennialists, the eschatological dimension of this doctrine of the kingdom of God also affected the way advocates of the postmillennialism, particularly those that also professed the New Theology, understood the role of the church. Washington Gladden wrote, in his *Ruling Ideas of the Present Age* (1895), that the three key doctrines of the modern period included the immanence of Christ, the vital and organic relations of all members of society, and the presence of the kingdom of God on earth.[75] He further noted that the kingdom of God, while currently present, had not completed its dominion over the earth; rather, he believed that the kingdom would gradually grow within society and at a future time would finally be established in its fullness. Gladden represented well the eschatology of his fellow advocates of the social gospel and New Theology. The effects of this vision of the kingdom both mirrored and differed from their dispensational coreligionists. On the one hand, both groups agreed that the church and the kingdom of God must not be conflated with one another. Further, the eschatology of both groups made their proponents ambivalent about denominational affiliation. On the other hand, the proponents of these two groups differed about the relationship between the church and the kingdom as well as the specific vocation of the church in the world.

The theologians who promoted what Oberlin professor of theology Henry Churchill King called the new "social consciousness" argued that a deepening sense of the brotherhood of all humanity has led to "recognition of the vital and essential importance of the mutual influence in the

---

[73] Ibid., 459–60. Emphasis in the original.
[74] Ibid., 448. Emphasis in the original.
[75] Washington Gladden, *Ruling Ideas of the Present Age* (Boston: Houghton, Mifflin and Company, 1896) 273–91.

attainment of character, in the individual relation to God, [and] in the creed."[76] Therefore, he claimed that a person could no longer see himself as a separate entity responsible only for his individual salvation. King asserted that the socially conscious Christian understood human society as an organism in which each part had a mutual effect and responsibility for his brother or sister in Christ.[77]

The defense of this liberal Protestant notion of the "social consciousness," of which King spoke and represented, inevitably led to a revitalized significance of ecclesiology. He claimed that older ideas about the church no longer sufficed to meet the needs of the modern world.

> On the one hand, it [the church] cannot derive its importance from having to do with an unalterably fixed and infallibly organized external authority; and, on the other hand, it can be no longer be an unimportant addendum concerned only with methods of organization and government, and with ecclesiastical ordinances and procedure. So far as the social consciousness has influenced theology at this point, theology must see that the doctrine of the church is the doctrine of that priceless, living, personal fellowship, in which Christian character, Christian faith, and Christian confession can arise and continue. The doctrine of the church becomes thus the doctrine of the very life and growth of Christianity in the world. It is the doctrine of the real kingdom of God, Christ's own great central theme.[78]

Simply put, the advocates of postmillennialism (whether they believed in a literal millennium or not) believed that they had discovered "a new sense of the importance of the doctrine of the church" because they properly understood the kingdom of God as Christ taught it.[79]

The eschatology connected with the doctrine of the kingdom of God often walked hand in hand with the social programs of the New Theology and the social gospel. Baptist Walter Rauschenbusch, in his landmark book *A Theology for the Social Gospel* (1917), wrote an entire chapter on eschatology. He argued that Christian eschatology played a crucial role in a proper understanding of the social gospel; however, such eschatology must be based upon the tradition of the Hebrew prophets rather than the

---

[76] Henry Churchill King, *Theology and the Social Consciousness* (New York: Macmillan Company, 1902) 177).

[77] Ibid., 9, 163.

[78] Ibid., 177–78.

[79] Ibid., 177.

apocalypticism practiced by modern premillennialists.[80] As a church historian, Rauschenbusch contended that apocalypticism had historical importance; nonetheless, in the present day it was promulgated by the "untaught and pagan mind" and nothing short of "dangerous."[81] In the final analysis, Rauschenbusch contended that "the issues of future history lie in the moral qualities and religious faith of nations. This is the substance of all Hebrew and Christian eschatology."[82] This eschatology of which Rauschenbusch spoke was compatible with postmillennialism, although many of the advocates of the social gospel, including Rauschenbusch, denied any literal interpretation of a thousand-year reign of Christ. "Our chief interest in any millennium is the desire for a social order in which the worth and freedom of every last human being will be honored and protected; in which the brotherhood of man will be expressed in the common possession of the economic resources of society; and in which the spiritual good of humanity will be set high above the private profit interests of all materialistic groups. We hope for such an order for humanity as we hope for heaven for ourselves."[83] Such a view embodied the progressive and optimistic character of postmillennialism; however, Rauschenbusch noted that "the duration of a thousand years is a guess and immaterial."[84]

The church had a distinct function within the eschatology of the kingdom of God promoted by advocates of the New Theology and the social gospel. Specifically, the church was ancillary to the kingdom. In the words of Rauschenbusch, "since the Kingdom of God is the supreme end of God, it must be the purpose for which the Church exists."[85] Washington Gladden compared the church to the human brain. Just as the brain constitutes the most important organ to direct the body to its end, so too God called the church to be a key catalyst to institute the kingdom of God on earth.[86] In particular Gladden understood the church as "the training

---

[80] Walter Rauschenbusch, *A Theology for the Social Gospel* (Nashville: Abingdon Press, 1945) 216.

[81] Ibid., 216, 225.

[82] Ibid., 224.

[83] Ibid.

[84] Ibid.

[85] Ibid., 143.

[86] Washington Gladden, *The Christian Pastor and the Working Church* (New York: Charles Scribner's Sons, 1914) 43.

school, ordained by God, in which men are fitted for the life of the Kingdom."[87]

The positive, practical ways the church advanced the kingdom on earth by those who promoted the New Theology and social gospel has been presented in previous chapters; however, describing those activities of the church that these individuals believed did not or insufficiently advanced the kingdom of God is equally instructive. Rauschenbusch warned that the church had too often promoted itself rather than the kingdom of God, and this led the church astray from its social vocation toward a religious individualism. He contended that ever since Augustine argued that the church fully embodied the kingdom of God, Christians had lost touch with Jesus' ethical thought, which developed from his idea of the kingdom.

> When the Kingdom ceased to be the dominating religious reality, the Church moved up into the position of the supreme good. To promote the power of the Church and its control over all rival political forces was equivalent to promoting the supreme ends of Christianity.... When the doctrine of the Kingdom of God is lacking in theology, the salvation of the individual is seen in its relation to the Church and to the future life, but not in its relation to the task of saving the social order.[88]

This perversion of the function of the church, according to Rauschenbusch, primarily manifested itself in an exaggeration of individual salvation and election.[89] Henry Churchill King agreed, asserting that Christians do not "climb to heaven by some sure little individual ladder of our own."[90] Gladden decried what he alternately called "churchism" or "ecclesiasticism," the belief that the church could separate itself from the world.[91] He claimed that the moment the church promoted being "religious just for the sake of being religious," as opposed to advancing the kingdom of God on earth, it became "dead and accursed," "worse than useless," "a bane and a blight to all society in which it stands."[92]

The polemic of social gospel advocates against the church's abrogation of its heavenly duty typically led to an ambivalence concerning denominational affiliation. Rauschenbusch downplayed the importance of

---

[87] Ibid., 41.
[88] Rauschenbusch, *Theology for the Social Gospel*, 134, 137.
[89] Ibid., 123.
[90] King, *Theology and the Social Consciousness*, 163.
[91] Gladden, *Christian Pastor*, 45.
[92] Ibid., 44.

denominational distinctions. "The saving power of the Church," he claimed, "does not rest on its institutional character, on its continuity, its ordination, its ministry, or its doctrine. It rests on the presence of the Kingdom of God within her."[93] King insisted that true unity of humanity, which ought to characterize the social consciousness of the church, "not only tolerates differences, but welcomes and justifies them...It believes in equality, but not in identity."[94] Such a statement went hand in hand with his arguments that the church must reject any position that made itself its own end. Gladden likewise believed that the educated servant of Christ never strove or prayed for the success of his denomination. Instead, he argued that the church affiliation was analogous to political affiliation. "Every Christian's first loyalty is to the Kingdom, and not to the church. The church, in its best estate, holds much the same relation to the Kingdom that the political party, at its best estate, holds to the government of the country; it is an instrument which men employ to secure the progress and the permanence of the Kingdom."[95] Denominational institutions, therefore, existed primarily as a means to an end. While this meant that distinctions of doctrine and practice, which differentiated denominations, had limited importance, local churches justified themselves insofar as they vitalized and spiritualized "business and politics and amusement and art and literature and education and every other interest of society."[96]

The Opening Salvos of Controversy

It is, perhaps, curious that the first rumblings of discord between those who would soon identify themselves as fundamentalists and modernists surrounded eschatology. Premillennialists, as previously mentioned, believed that the kingdom of God would be established only when Jesus Christ returned bodily to inaugurate a thousand years of theocratic reign of peace and prosperity. They further viewed the present world in a pessimistic light, expecting it to grow increasingly worse until Christ returned. This apocalyptic outlook seemed an unlikely focus against which the heirs of social Christianity and progressive orthodoxy would unite in protest, yet this is exactly what happened. Historian Timothy Weber noted that the First World War, coupled with the apparent accuracy of premillennialists'

---

[93] Rauschenbusch, *Theology for the Social Gospel*, 129.
[94] King, *Theology and the Social Consciousness*, 168.
[95] Gladden, *Christian Pastor*, 40–41.
[96] Ibid., 44.

predictions of its aftermath, lent credence to and bolstered the popularity of this prophetic movement, making theological liberals feel seriously threatened by this prophecy movement as a whole.[97]

Those theologians who attacked premillennialism, however, seemed far more concerned with the effects that the organized prophetic movement might have in the denominations of the Protestant establishment. The prophetic conferences that took place in Chicago (1914), Philadelphia (1918), and New York City (1918) drew large audiences because the war seemed to support the great cataclysms predicted by dispensational premillennialists. One critic, Presbyterian James M. Snowden of Western Theological Seminary in Pittsburgh, worried that premillennialism "lends itself to highly emotional types of religious experience...It is an aid to the emotional evangelist to move people to take his hand as an indication of their desire to flee from the imminent day of wrath. It finds a congenial atmosphere in the crowded tabernacle with its heated contagious air and audience easily swept by hysterical appeals and passions."[98] Because its attackers believed that premillennialism logically demanded social and political quietism, they argued that it posed a real danger to the mission of the church.

While the Great War did its part to expose weaknesses in the progressive view of human development that was central to liberal Protestantism, the growing popularity of these prophecy conferences made theologically and socially liberal evangelicals all the more anxious about their movement's security within the Protestant establishment. Harris

---

[97] Timothy Weber, *Living in the Shadow of the Second Coming: American Premillennialism, 1875–1925* (New York: Oxford University Press, 1979) 112–13. Anti-premillenarian works by liberals included: George P. Eckman, *When Christ Comes Again* (New York: Abingdon Press, 1917); Shailer Mathews, *Will Christ Come Again?* (Chicago: American Institute of Sacred Literature, 1917); Shirley Jackson Case, *The Millennial Hope: A Phase of War-Time Thinking* (Chicago: University of Chicago Press, 1918); James Snowden, *Is the World Growing Better?* (New York: Macmillan Company, 1919) *The Coming of the Lord: Will It Be Premillennial?* 2d rev. ed. (New York: Macmillan Company, 1919); James M. Campbell, *The Second Coming of Christ: A Message for the Times* (New York: Methodist Book Concern, 1919); George Preston Mains, *Premillennialism: Non-Scriptural, Non-Historic, Non-Scientific, Non-Philosophical* (New York: Abingdon Press, 1920); and Harris Franklin Rall, *Modern Premillennialism and the Christian Hope* (New York: Abingdon Press, 1920). This is not to mention a series of anti-premillenarian articles published in the journals *Biblical World*, *Christian Century*, and the Methodist *Sunday School Journal.*

[98] Snowden, *Coming*, 232.

Franklin Rall, professor of systematic theology at Garrett Biblical Institute, noted that he did not find himself concerned with the ideas of Russellites, Seventh-day Adventists, or Millennial Dawnists, who could be refuted easily; rather, the pernicious form of apocalyptism that worried him was that propagated by "undenominational" premillennialists who were "organized and aggressive, at times almost tending to be a church within our churches."[99] Rall was not the only one worried. James Snowden, editor of the *Presbyterian Banner*, complained of premillennialism: "It organizes itself into conventions, meetings, issues platforms, and proclamations, gratuitously distributes books and literature advocating its position, flooding our theological seminaries with them, appears to be gratuitously subsidized, holds 'prophetic conferences,' founds 'Bible schools' to teach it, and thus in many ways carries on an active propaganda."[100] University of Chicago professors Shailer Mathews and Shirley Jackson Case each published popular pieces against premillennialism as well. Mathews, in a pamphlet distributed through the American Institute of Sacred Literature, alleged that "Christian churches are being honeycombed by a movement liberally financed and widely organized which threatens the spiritual and moral nature of Christianity."[101] Case went so far as to suggest that premillennialists might wish the Germans to win the war in order to speed up Christ's return and then left his readers with an innuendo that the kaiser might be financing the movement.[102]

Underneath such uncharitable accusations, the attackers of premillennialism offered more substantive reasons for their grave concerns. Foremost, it was incompatible with their understanding of the church and its mission. Rall observed that:

> We are realizing that in this thoroughgoing modern premillennialism we are dealing not simply with the zealous advocacy of an isolated doctrine but with a whole system of theology. We have here an interpretation of Christianity which would rule out other conceptions. Further, it is directly and practically significant for our conception of the church and its work. For the heart of this teaching is its doctrine of world salvation and the conclusions

---

[99] Rall, *Modern Premillennialism*, 15.

[100] Snowden, *Coming*, 11–12.

[101] Shailer Mathews, *Will Christ Come Again?* (Chicago: American Institute of Sacred Literature, 1918) 2.

[102] Shirley Jackson Case, "The Premillennial Menace," *Biblical World* 52/1 (January 1918): 19.

of that doctrine cut the ground out from under the enterprises to which the church is committed to-day.[103]

Snowden agreed, arguing that premillenarianism "is not a theory which can be confined within narrow limits…It is a pervasive spirit that insinuates itself everywhere."[104] This incompatibility coupled with perceptions that premillennialists were well-financed and organized apart from denominational channels led the heirs of the social gospel movement and progressive orthodoxy to believe they saw the writing on the wall. A movement that formed churches within churches, yet was unable to be controlled or co-opted into denominational machinery, must have been frightening indeed. "Already the menace has reached such proportions," wrote Case, "that Christian leaders among Methodists, Baptists, Presbyterians, and similarly influential bodies are beginning to realize the necessity of actively opposing the pernicious propagana. …it has become nationwide."[105]

As one might expect, these attackers battled the "premillennial menace" by attempting to educate average evangelicals about undesirable results spawned by their opponents' teaching. They accused premillennialists of encouraging political, social, and evangelistic quietism.[106] They also believed that the premillenialists' pessimistic doctrine undermined the belief that Jesus Christ and the Holy Spirit had the ability to redeem the whole world.[107] The weapon of those attacking premillennialism was biblical criticism. The anti-premillenarians asserted that antiquated biblical literalism gave these evangelicals the veneer of orthodoxy, making incorrect interpretations of prophecy seem religiously sound to average churchgoers.[108] Rochester Theological Seminary professor Conrad Henry Moehlmann observed that "until Christianity is ready to help folks to a proper understanding of the Bible, the attempt to destroy millenarianism

---

[103] Rall, *Modern Premillennialism*, 16–17.

[104] Snowden, *Coming*, 10.

[105] Case, "Menace," 20.

[106] See for example Case, *Millennial Hope*, 240; Rall, *Modern Premillennialism*, 156; Mathews, *Will Christ*, 11–12; Eckman, *When Christ*, 154–55; Mains, *Premillennialism*, 101; Herbert L. Willett, "Activities and Menace of Millennialism: A Study of the Dangers Implicit in the Millenarian Propaganda," *Christian Century* 35/33 (29 August 1918): 8; and Snowden, *Coming*, 225–27, 233–34.

[107] Snowden, *Coming*, 224–25.

[108] Ibid., 220–21.

will prove abortive."[109] To this end, the anti-premillenarians wrote hundreds of pages attempting to explain to nonacademic audiences that the millennial hopes of the early church existed as non-Christian theological remnants of Jewish thought that had ended in disappointment.[110] This tactic backfired and further exacerbated the problem.

The premillennialists responded to their attackers in kind. The use of biblical criticism to discredit premillennialism only confirmed for its adherents that apostasy would mark the professing church of the last days. Baptist Cortland Myers, once a vice president of the Open and Institutional Church League, blamed German theology and higher criticism for the European war, claiming that "we see the harvest fields being reaped from these seeds of German rationalism and false philosophy."[111] I. M. Haldeman, pastor of First Baptist Church in New York City, responded to Mathews' pamphlet with his own *Professor Shailer Mathews' Burlesque on the Second Coming of Our Lord Jesus Christ.* Haldeman made a popular, commonsense appeal that the Bible meant what it said about a literal premillennial return of Jesus Christ and distributed his thirty-two-page pamphlet free of charge (compared with Mathews' twenty-three-page pamphlet costing two cents).[112] Haldeman also answered Mathews's specific charges that the movement was Jewish in nature, unbiblical, and historically non-Christian with pages of proof-texts and lists of persons who advocated premillennialism in the history of the church. Finally, he rhetorically asked his readers which attitude was saner, the opinions of biblical premillennialism or Professor Mathews, who "looking through an environment of smoke, the blood of battle, the failure of civilization, the unrest of the people,...believes the infusion of the spirit of Christ in the world to be that steady ample second coming which is to conquer it for

---

[109] Conrad Henry Moehlmann, "The Apocalyptic Mind," *Biblical World* 54/1 (January 1920) 68.

[110] Cf. Mains, *Premillennialism*, 56–83; Moehlmann, "Apocalyptic Mind," 64; Case, "Menace," 23; Mathews, *Will Christ*, 6–7; Rall, *Modern Premillennialism*, 127–48; Case, *Millennial Hope*, 48–205; and Snowden, *Coming*, 223–24.

[111] *Light on Prophecy, a Coordinated, Constructive Teaching Being the Proceedings and Addresses at the Philadelphia Prophetic Conference, May 28–30, 1918* (New York: Christian Herald, 1918) 176–77.

[112] I. M. Haldeman, *Professor Shailer Mathews' Burlesque on the Second Coming of Our Lord Jesus Christ* (New York: First Baptist Church, n.d.) 10–11.

righteousness and truth and bring in abiding rest to the troubled hearts of men."[113]

Other premillennialists claimed that the attackers had misunderstood their movement; they also argued against the "logic" of premillennial quietism. A typical response included that of Baptist pastor of Tremont Temple, J. C. Massee, who reminded his readers that when Christ returned he would not only judge unbelievers but the works of the church as well; therefore, Christ's imminent return motivated true believers to lead lives of personal holiness and perform acts of Christian service within the world.[114] R. A. Torrey agreed, stating that the knowledge that Christ might return at any time provided the believer with the greatest incentive to Christian service, especially evangelism.[115] Charles R. Erdman, Princeton professor and son of William Erdman, admitted to being baffled by the charge of quietism when the leading missionaries and evangelists of recent time were premillennialists, including Robert E. Speer, John R. Mott, Hudson Taylor, Charles Spurgeon, Billy Sunday, Moody and Sankey, Whittle and Bliss, Chapman and Alexander, Torrey and Varley, and L. W. Munhall.[116] As to the allegations that premillennialism logically led to the abandonment of the church's social service, Erdman's rhetorical rejoinder placed him clearly in the camp of soul-saving evangelicalism. "It is a fair question," he contended, "whether evangelism, which leads men to submit their whole lives to Christ, does not do more to destroy intemperance and to check crime and to remove causes of poverty and to increase sympathy between employers and employees, and so to improve all social conditions, than all others factors in our modern life; and we have seen that premillennialists do not fail here."[117] Robert McWatty Russell, Westminster College president and moderator of the United Presbyterian Church, noted at a prophecy conference at Moody Bible Institute that the premillennialists even found themselves "interested in all true efforts of civic righteousness and national purity and peace

---

[113] Ibid., 35.

[114] J. C. Massee, *The Second Coming* (Philadelphia: Philadelphia School of the Bible, 1919) 101. Cf. the comments of Presbyterian Aquila Webb in "The Doctrine of the Lord's Coming as a Working Force in the Church and Community: a Symposium," in *Coming and Kingdom*, 137.

[115] Torrey, "The Lord's Second Coming a Motive to Personal Holiness," in *Coming and Kingdom*, 231–35.

[116] Charles R. Erdman, "Premillennialism Defended Against Assailants," *Christian Workers Magazine* 16/12 (August 1916) 917–18.

[117] Ibid., 917.

because through right conditions of society the gospel can spread more rapidly and the day of the King's advent be brought nearer."[118] Evangelist Billy Sunday similarly asserted that "every time we do personal work or try to get anybody saved, we may be doing something that will bring the coming of the Lord…That gives us something definite and tangible to work for."[119]

Eschatology and the Apostolicity of the Church

The attacks upon and defenses of premillennialism just before and after the war also revealed two different views of history tied with dissimilar understandings of how modern Christians connected themselves to the church founded by Jesus Christ, the Holy Spirit, and the apostles. By connecting themselves to the early church, advocates on both sides attempted to legitimate their own understanding of the church and its cultural vocation. In other words, if postmillennialists had conceded that premillennialists might be correct (though ever so slightly) in their view of prophetic history, they simultaneously conceded that their own vision of the church might be incorrect. Likewise, premillennialists could not concede the evolutionary view of historical development defended by progressives without calling into question their ecclesiology.

Premillennialists connected themselves to the early church by suggesting that they subscribed to the same essential faith and teachings of the apostles, teachings now preserved by the Holy Spirit in an inerrant Bible. Subscription to the idea of an infallible (or inerrant) Bible as the sufficient source of faith and practice, therefore, typically became premillennialists' theological shorthand for connection with apostolic Christianity and its litmus test for true church membership. This test could be asserted with confidence, according to premillennialists, because the Holy Spirit, who authored and protected the Scriptures, also regenerated the sinner. Put another way, because the Holy Spirit divinely inspired the Scriptures (making them inerrant), belief in the teachings of Scripture constituted one of the marks of true conversion and spiritual regeneration.

---

[118] Robert McWatty Russell, "Wrongly Dividing the Word of Truth: A Reply to Assaults on Premillennialism," in *The Coming and Kingdom of Christ: A Stenographic Report of the Prophetic Conference Held at Moody Bible Institute of Chicago February 24–27, 1914* (Chicago: The Bible Colportage Association, 1914) 63.

[119] William Ashley Sunday, *The Second Coming* (Sturgis MI: Journal Publishing Company, 1913) 12.

James Gray, dean of Moody Bible Institute, insisted in typical fashion that "everything in the church is according to the record of His [the Holy Spirit's] will, which is found in the holy Scriptures which He caused to be written."[120] Furthermore, in the same way that the Spirit regenerated the sinner and thereby grafted him or her within the body of Christ, He provided this church, through the Bible, its very message and mission. In this sense one can understand William Bell Riley's assertion that "the real point of all inspired teaching, and the real point of all revealed prophecy, and the real intent of all Biblical preaching is the salvation and sanctification of man, not the mere retention and defense of truth. Skepticism, therefore, does not endanger the Bible, it endangers the people!"[121] Rejection of the inerrant Bible, therefore, became the chief mark of apostasy; it manifested a rejection of the mission and identity of the church required by the Spirit, its administrator.

Proponents of the progressive view of Christian history also claimed to connect themselves to the church of the apostles but not by doctrines, beliefs, or an inerrant Bible. Rather, they saw themselves at the end of a long chain of spiritual evolution guided by the Holy Ghost. Presbyterian Henry Sloane Coffin noted that "the same Spirit who lived and ruled in the Church of the first days has been breathed on us, through the long line of apostolic-spirited men and women who reach back to Jesus, and lives and rules in us."[122] Therefore, he believed that those in the church of today, being guided by the Spirit, had the liberty to pick and choose from the past that which helps the modern Christian community spread the kingdom of God on earth.[123] At a meeting of the Brotherhood of the Kingdom, an American social gospel organization, Leighton Williams expressed a similar view: "Christianity is a great historical movement; taking its rise from Judaism, it has passed through a score of centuries in unbroken continuity." Moreover, he argued, if the church expected to carry out its divinely ordained mission to help institute the kingdom of God on earth, it must be "truly

---

[120] James M. Gray, "The Holy Spirit—His Person and Purpose," in *God Hath Spoken: Twenty-five Addresses Delivered at the World Conference of Christian Fundamentals* (Philadelphia: Bible Conference Committee, 1919) 205.

[121] William B. Riley, *The Menace of Modernism* (New York: Christian Alliance Publishing Co., 1917) 131.

[122] Henry Sloan Coffin, *Some Christian Convictions: A Practical Restatement in Terms of Present-Day Thinking* (New Haven: Yale University Press, 1915) 195.

[123] Ibid., 195, 203.

comprehensive of all genuine [new] manifestations of the Christian spirit and life."[124]

Shailer Mathews claimed that "loyalty" to Christ and his teachings constituted the true test of church membership and identity.[125] The Bible, therefore, rather than being an infallible guide to faith, existed merely as an historical record expressing the values of Jesus Christ in a particular cultural milieu. Even so, Shirley Jackson Case admitted that the Bible still remained important because it contained the essential ideas of Jesus' mission; however, these ideas could only be discovered by meticulous historical research. This research sought to divide the outdated theological assumptions of the biblical writer from the underlying convictions, or theological "garments," they expressed.[126] In the words of Mathews, theology only existed as "the variant legitimization of constant attitudes and convictions."[127] Not surprisingly, perhaps, the Jesus discovered by the research of heirs of social Christianity and progressive orthodoxy demonstrated the possibility of all persons to live pure lives, maintain an optimistic spirit, and cherish an attitude of cooperative brotherhood and social service.[128] Ironically, scholars like Mathews and Case claimed that the essential message of the Scriptures undermined any effort to use biblical inerrancy as a litmus test for true Christianity. The Jesus of the Bible, according to them, only required of his church loyalty to his ethical principles coupled with a life of active service.

Advocates of premillennialist and postmillennialist views of Christian eschatology both maintained an intimate connection between church vocation and identity. They both likewise attempted to legitimize the particularities of their ecclesiological outlook by demonstrating that their views of the church stemmed from Jesus and the apostles. These views of history not only played the crucial role of upholding particular views of the church but also connected their advocates with the ecclesiology of the previous generations of Christians. Eschatology became the theological symbol of an evangelical version of apostolic succession.

---

[124] *Report of the Sixteenth Annual Conference of the Brotherhood of the Kingdom Held at Marlborough-on-Hudson, New York, August 9th to 12th, 1910* (Kingston NY: R. W. Anderson & Son, 1910) 5.

[125] Shailer Mathews, *The Faith of Modernism* (New York: Macmillan Company, 1924) 55.

[126] Shirley Jackson Case, "Modern Belief about Jesus," *Biblical World* 37/1 (January 1911): 7–8.

[127] Mathews, *Modernism*, 71.

[128] Case, "Jesus," 15.

Although these clashes between premillennialists and their detractors were intense, they did not have direct institutional repercussions within establishment denominations. The spat was only a foretaste of future debates. Eschatology helped develop evangelical ecclesiology by shaping its adherents' understanding of the church's purpose in the divine plan of redemption. It also suggested views of cosmic history that legitimized particular strategies for cultural engagement. Evangelical eschatology, whether progressive or premillennial, also spawned a natural denominational ambivalence that would help cement denominational loyalty for some and leave open the possibility of schism for others.

PART 2

1920–1937

The times are out of joint, O cursed spite that ever
I was born to set them right.
—William Shakespeare, *Hamlet*, Act I Scene V

Theologically, the times are out of joint!
—William B. Riley, *The Menace of Modernism* (1917)

For all is not right in the world. On this men are agreed.
—Shailer Mathews, *The Faith of Modernism* (1924)

CHAPTER 6

Catalysts for Contention

As the next generation of evangelicals began to supplant the former, they like their religious forebears looked to the past as they attempted to shape the ecclesiology of their denominations. Not surprisingly, the previous generation's methods of engagement with American culture, pneumatology, and eschatology became the sources that shaped the ecclesiology of the next generation. Fundamentalism and modernism, trans-denominational movements of the new generation within the establishment denominations, drank deeply from the wells of Keswick, the New Theology, dispensationalism, postmillennialism, revivalism, and the social gospel movement. In the last several chapters I showed how these sources promoted often quite different visions of ecclesiological change in the Northern establishment. However, while these evangelicals often quibbled about the best ways to be America's church, they managed to coexist within their denominations. The question remains, then, why did fundamentalism and modernism have such an explosive conflict in the 1920s and 1930s, when only a generation before, different visions of the church—both practical and theological—lived under the same denominational tents with relative tolerance?

Polarized models of American evangelicalism provide the most persistent explanations of the fundamentalist-modernist controversies within Northern evangelical Protestantism. Historians have often suggested that after the Civil War evangelicals embodied the conservative and capitalistic American values of a Horatio Alger-style individualism, or gospel of wealth, which by the late 1880's had begun to be criticized by liberal theologians and the developing social gospel movement.[1] Fundamentalism, therefore, embodied an old, passé form of individualistic religion, while modernism embraced its critics. The variations of this argument find their roots in Max Weber's Protestant ethic thesis. In *The Protestant Ethic and the Spirit of Capitalism* (1904–1905), he contended that Protestantism (in particular, those varieties influenced by Calvinism) "forms one of the roots of that disillusioned and pessimistically inclined individualism which can even to-day be identified in the national characters and the institutions of the peoples with a Puritan past in contrast to the quite different spectacles through which the Enlightenment later looked upon men."[2] Weber's analysis constitutes the major element common to typical theses about evangelicals in the late nineteenth and early twentieth centuries: the division between traditional, individualistic Calvinism and the modern, humanitarian Enlightenment.

Weber's bipolar division between the traditional individualism and the modern humanitarianism has informed one of the more long-standing theses on the fundamentalist-modernist split in American evangelical Protestantism: the "two-party system." Jean Miller Schmidt and Martin Marty advanced the argument that evangelical Protestantism fractured into "private" and "public" parties in 1912.[3] In the words of Miller Schmidt, Protestantism was divided between those who wished to re-Christianize

---

[1] See C. Howard Hopkins, *The Rise of the Social Gospel in American Protestantism, 1865–1915* (New Haven: Yale University Press, 1940); more recently see Susan Curtis, *A Consuming Faith: The Social Gospel and Modern American Culture* (Baltimore: Johns Hopkins University Press, 1991).

[2] Max Weber, *The Protestant Ethic and the Spirit of Capitalism*, trans. Talcott Parsons (New York: Charles Scribner's Sons, 1904–1905, 1958) 106–107.

[3] Miller Schmidt identified the creation of the Commission on Evangelism in the Federal Council of Churches to counterbalance the Commission on the Church and Social Service as the watershed event that indicated the split between the public and private parties; however, one might reasonably argue that the creation of the commission on evangelism meant the FCC became properly representative. Schmidt's reasoning also ignores J. Wilbur's participation in the FCC from its very beginning. To Schmidt's line of reasoning, Marty added the public attack of Billy Sunday upon Washington Gladden in Columbus OH in the same year. One wonders when Sunday previously maintained restraint to make this attack momentous. Cf. Jean Miller Schmidt, *Souls or the Social Order: The Two-Party System in American Protestantism* (Brooklyn: Carlson Publishing, Inc., 1991) 131; Martin Marty, *Righteous Empire: The Protestant Experience in America* (New York: The Dial Press, 1970) 183.

America by addressing "souls or the social order."[4] The most important outcome of this split, according to its proponents, was that it signaled the eclipse of denominationalism in American religion and life.[5] Marty is not alone in his thinking.

A bipartite division in American Protestantism (or even American religion in general) signaling the end of denominationalism has continued to provide an attractive model for scholars to explain the character of American religion. Using Timothy Smith's expression "the Great Reversal," sociologist David O. Moberg noted that between 1910 and 1930 conservative evangelicalism exchanged its long tradition of social concern and philanthropy for evangelistic enterprises.[6] George Marsden also invoked this expression to describe how fundamentalists between 1900 and 1920 began to reject vehemently programs of social amelioration. Marsden argued that the growing identification of the social gospel with liberal theology, in a way that seemed to exclude the evangelistic enterprise of soul-saving, led to conservative suspicion of progressive social concern and provoked negative fundamentalist reactions.[7] Sociologist Robert Wuthnow has argued that after the Second World War American religion split trans-denominationally between liberal and conservative factions.[8] More recently,

---

[4] Miller Schmidt, *Souls or the Social Order*, xxxii. Marty's descriptions of these two parties echo Weber's division: "One party, which may be called 'Private' Protestantism, seized that name 'evangelical' which had characterized all Protestants early in the nineteenth century. It accentuated individual salvation out of the world, personal moral life congruent with the ideals of the saved, and its fulfillment or absence in the rewards or punishments in another world in a life to come. The second informal group, which can be called 'Public' Protestantism, was public insofar as it was more exposed to the social order and the social destinies of men. Whereas the word 'evangelical' somehow came to be part of the description of the former group, the word 'social' almost always worked its way into designations of the latter." Marty, *Righteous Empire*, 179.

[5] Ibid., xxxii–xxxiii.

[6] David O. Moberg, *The Great Reversal: Evangelism and Social Concern*, rev. ed. (Philadelphia: J. B. Lippincott Co., 1977) 13–14, 30. Moberg stated that Smith used the expression "the Great Reversal" in his lectures.

[7] George M. Marsden, *Fundamentalism and American Culture: The Shaping of Twentieth-Century Evangelicalism, 1870–1925* (New York: Oxford University Press, 1980) 92–93.

[8] Robert Wuthnow, *Restructuring of American Religion: Society and Faith since World War II* (Princeton: Princeton University Press, 1988); Ferenc Morton Szasz argued that this phenomenon occurred as early the 1930s. See Szasz, *The Divided*

he suggested that the split is better labeled a division between those who practice "religion" and those who espouse "spirituality."[9] Harold Bloom claimed that American religion could be divided between the gnostic and the traditional forms of religion.[10] James Davison Hunter went further, arguing that the two-party system properly describes America's "culture war" between the orthodox and the progressive parties in the United States generally.[11] Regardless of the grounds of division, the model presents two opposite poles that transcend institutional affiliation and therefore eclipse those institutions.

A flurry of critiques of the two-party model have appeared since Marty's *Righteous Empire* (1970). Those advocating a "pluralist model" of American religion, including among others Catherine Albanese, R. Laurence Moore, and (perhaps ironically given the present discussion) Martin Marty, implicitly challenged simplistic divisions within American religion.[12] Also, scholars within the evangelical tradition began to argue against the two-party thesis. Donald Dayton and Norris Magnuson claimed that a two-party system did not accurately describe their alleged "side" of the division, especially when traced through the Methodist-Holiness-Pentecostal traditions.[13] More recently, in a collection of essays published under the auspices of the Re-Forming the Center Project at Messiah College, David Edwin Harrell summarized the judgment of all but one of the contributors with his expression, the "myth of bipolar Protestantism."[14]

Mind of Protestant America, 1880–1930 (University: University of Alabama Press, 1982) 106.

[9] Robert Wuthnow, *After Heaven: Spirituality in America since the Late 1950s* (Berkley: University of California Press, 1998).

[10] Harold Bloom, *The American Religion: The Emergence of the Post-Christian Nation* (New York: Simon & Schuster, 1992).

[11] James Davison Hunter, *Culture Wars: The Struggle to Define America* (New York: Basic Books, 1991).

[12] See Catherine Albanese, *America: Religions and Religion*, 2d ed. (Belmont CA: Wadsworth Publishing Company, 1992); R. Laurence Moore, *Religious Outsiders and the Making of Americans* (New York: Oxford University Press, 1986); and Martin Marty, *The Irony of It All, 1893–1919*, vol. 1 of *Modern American Religion* (Chicago: U. of Chicago Press, 1986).

[13] Donald Dayton, *Discovering an Evangelical Heritage* (New York: Harper & Row Publishers, 1976); Norris Magnuson, *Salvation in the Slums: Evangelical Social Work, 1865–1920*, paperback ed. (Grand Rapids: Baker Book House, 1990).

[14] David Edwin Harrell, "Bipolar Protestantism: The Straight and Narrow Ways," in *Re-forming the Center: American Protestantism, 1900 to the Present*, ed.

The two-party system has some explanatory power when applied to the Northern evangelical establishment; however, in the final analysis it is unsatisfactory on several counts. First, while the thesis rightly labels the two major strategies evangelicals used to approach American culture, its partitions are too neat. Even after 1900, the division that existed between souls and the social order was more of a chicken-and-egg question rather than a rejection of one or the other. Theological conservatives such as J. Wilbur Chapman, John Roach Straton, and Mark Matthews stood beside their liberal counterparts as social critics of their day.[15] Also, theological and social liberals such as Josiah Strong and Walter Rauschenbusch argued the importance of individual conversion in the salvation of society.[16] Evangelicals facing the dilemma of democracy used (often indiscreetly) any and all methods they thought might reach the unchurched of America. In other words, evangelicals often saw the methods of revivalism and social Christianity as two compatible weapons in their Christian arsenal. In short, evangelicals tried everything and initially disparaged little. Second, while the two-party thesis accurately describes many methodologically and theologically consistent leaders of extra-ecclesial movements, it does not describe the whole of evangelicalism inside or outside the Northern Protestant establishment. If the leadership promoting souls versus the social order presaged the fundamentalist-modernist controversies within establishment churches, then the tradition of unreflective coexistence showed the possibility of future toleration within these same denominations. Finally, the two-party thesis does not accurately describe the dynamic of conflict within establishment denominations, which, as we shall see, was typically multiparty rather than bipolar in nature.

Models of declension provide another important interpretive model for describing the controversy. Sydney Ahlstrom claimed that urban change had

Douglas Jacobsen and William Vance Trollinger (Grand Rapids: William B. Eerdmans Publishing Company, 1998) 15–30. Not surprisingly, the dissenting voice in the volume is Marty's. See Marty, "The Shape of American Protestantism," in *Reforming the Center*, 91–108.

[15] For a fine recent discussion of theologically and economically diverse "social Christianity," see Gary Scott Smith, *The Search for Social Salvation: Social Christianity and America, 1880–1925* (Lanham MD: Lexington Books, 2000).

[16] Strong claimed that "all quick and easy processes for regenerating society without regenerating the individuals who compose it are delusions." See Josiah Strong, *The New Era or the Coming Kingdom* (New York: The Baker & Taylor Co., 1893) 118; Rauschenbusch, *Theology for the Social Gospel*, 95–109.

the "devastating" consequence of many new urbanites having no contact with Protestant churches.[17] Few would follow Ahlstrom's exaggerated statement; however, the idea that Protestantism declined during the first several decades of the twentieth century seems taken for granted. Like the two-party model, this model has certain explanatory power. First, it accurately portrays the rhetoric of many establishment Protestants that they were losing the masses. Using the U.S. Census Bureau's tally of the distribution of total membership by principle denomination between 1890–1916 (see table 6.1), it becomes clear that the major evangelical denominations had lost ground when compared with religious rivals such as Roman Catholics.

Table 6.1: Percent Distribution of Total Membership of Principle Evangelical Establishment Denominations Compared with Roman Catholics: 1890, 1906, and 1916.[18]

Denomination	1890	1906	1916	Change
Northern Baptists	3.7	3.0	2.9	-0.8
Congregationalists	2.4	2.0	1.9	-0.5
Disciples of Christ	3.0	2.8	2.9	-0.1
Methodist Episcopal Church	10.3	8.5	8.9	-1.4
Presbyterian Church in the U.S.A.	3.6	3.4	3.8	+0.2
Protestant Episcopal Church	2.5	2.5	2.6	+0.1
Total Evangelicals	**25.5**	**22.2**	**23.0**	**-2.5**
Total Roman Catholics	**33.8**	**40.5**	**37.5**	**+3.7**

Furthermore, if one couples this information with the relative strength of evangelicals in the cities compared with Roman Catholics, the fears by the majority of urban evangelicals that their influence continued to wane appears justified (see table 6.2).

[17] Sydney Ahlstrom, *A Religious History of the American People* (New Haven: Yale University Press, 1972) 738.

[18] Information compiled from "Diagram 2.—Distribution of Total Membership By Principle Denominations: 1890, 1906, and 1916. Membership 13 Years and Over: 1916," in *Summary and General Tables*, part 1 of *Religious Bodies, 1916* (Washington: Government Printing Office, 1919) 31.

Table 6.2: Percent Total Distribution of Membership of Principle Northern Evangelical Denominations Compared with Roman Catholics in Cities of 25,000 Inhabitants or More: 1916.[19]

	% Distribution of Church Membership in Cities with Inhabitants Numbering . . .			
Denomination	**Over 300k**	**300k-100k**	**100k-50k**	**50k-25k**
Northern Baptist Convention	2.6	3.4	3.1	3.7
Congregationalists	1.2	2.6	2.1	2.7
Disciples of Christ	0.6	2.0	2.3	2.2
Methodist Episcopal Church	4.2	6.0	6.5	8.1
Presbyterian Church in the U.S.A.	3.7	3.8	3.7	4.7
Protestant Episcopal Church	4.1	4.0	3.7	3.9
Total Evangelicals	**16.4**	**21.8**	**21.4**	**25.3**
Total Roman Catholic	**66.1**	**51.4**	**52.3**	**46.1**

In other words, the picture these statistics paint explains why proponents of revitalization movements, like revivalism, social Christianity, the New Theology, and Keswick Holiness, felt the need to act and implement denominational change. Indeed, many evangelicals of the time pointed this out. Charles Graves, for example, wrote in 1902 that an examination of recent religious statistics showed a slackened growth when compared with the American population as a whole (see table 6.3).[20]

---

[19] Information compiled from "Table 44—Members Distributed According to Classes of Cities, By Principle Denomination: 1916," in *Religious Bodies*, 121.

[20] Charles Graves, "Are the Churches Declining?" *World's Work* 4/1 (May 1902): 2076–80.

Table 6.3 The Increase or the Decrease in the Membership of Evangelical Churches Between 1885–1900.[21]

For four years ending

Denomination	1894	1895	1896	1897	1898	1899	1900
Baptists, three bodies*	208,341	140,431	82,814	-9,332	204,470	286,189	11,425
Congregational	76,607	19,018	12,638	10,669	2370	1,640	1640
Disciples	229,966	52,646	80,009	47,407	34,536	32,781	31,586
Episcopal**	59,263	25,526	19,930	21,867	21,064	19,978	16,849
Methodist Episcopal	110,372	279,259	45,040	14,394	12,038	-3,747	18,727
Presbyterian, North	88,296	26,237	20,758	15,784	15,643	6,392	12,099
Total	**772,845**	**543,117**	**261,215**	**100,789**	**290,123**	**143,233**	**92,326**

* Graves questioned the returns for the Baptists in 1897 and 1898, considering them doubtful.

** The figures for the Episcopalians include their foreign fields, except in 1900.

The growth rate of evangelical Protestant churches, Graves pointed out, declined between 1880 and 1900 from 2.6 percent to 1.72 percent of the American populace.[22] Thomas Dixon, Jr., pastor of the People's Church in New York, agreed with Graves's evaluation and boldly proclaimed that Protestantism had failed in New York City.[23]

The statistical information, however, may not have been as bleak as some evangelical Protestants and later historians believed. Sociologists Roger Finke and Rodney Stark have dismissed models of Protestant declension. Using the same census statistics, they argued that church membership rates in the cities were not only higher in the principal cities (those with 25,000 residents or more) than the nation as a whole but continued to widen between 1890 and 1906.[24] On the basis of this data they

---

[21] Compiled from Graves, "Churches Declining?" 2078.

[22] Ibid., 2077.

[23] Thomas Dixon, Jr., *The Failure of Protestantism in New York and Its Causes* (New York: The Strauss and Rehn Publishing Co., 1896) 11–22.

[24] Roger Finke and Rodney Stark, *The Churching of America, 1776–1990: Winners and Losers in Our Religious Economy* (New Brunswick NJ: Rutgers University Press, 1994) 204. The statistical table recorded that in the principle cities of the United States, membership percentages of the total population in 1890 equaled 37.9 and

hypothesized that "the primary impact of religious pluralism is to provide a broad spectrum of specialized religious firms competing to attract and hold a segment of the market."[25] They also claimed that cities with the highest degree of religious pluralism had the greatest religious adherence rate.[26] Because the majority of Northern evangelical Protestants in 1930 lived in urban areas, Finke and Stark concluded that evangelicals were well suited to meet the demands of their urban environment as specialized religious firms.

Historian Jonathan Butler also challenged the theme of Protestant declension during the Gilded Age. He argued that Congregationalist Walter Laidlaw's analysis of New York City in the early twentieth century debunked the common assumption that urbanization caused denominational decline.[27] He noted that, according to Laidlaw's calculations, religious institutional affiliation in New York City rose from about 21 percent in 1855 to approximately 40 percent in 1916.[28] Other turn-of-the-century religious statisticians, such as Henry King Carroll, editor of the New York *Independent*, also painted a rosy picture of evangelical health in 1896 and 1906, claiming that evangelical Christianity continued to grow and dominate the cultural landscape of America.[29]

One must use such statistics cautiously. Membership may not and likely does not reveal participation levels, and evangelicals attempting to revitalize their denominations were far more concerned with the latter than the former. This perhaps explains why revitalization movements, like revivalism, social Christianity, the New Theology, and Keswick Holiness, thought they needed to act despite membership increases. However, models of declension tend to mask the actual successes of these movements in stabilizing denominations and helping them adapt to new cultural contexts. If

---

only 32.7 nationwide. In 1906 the principle cities recorded a membership rate of 46.7 percent of the population with only 39.1 percent nationwide.

[25] Ibid., 205.

[26] Ibid.

[27] Jonathan Butler, "Protestant Success in the New American City, 1870–1920," in *New Directions in American Religious History*, ed. Harry S. Stout and D. G. Hart (New York: Oxford University Press, 1997) 296–333.

[28] Ibid., 307.

[29] H. K. Caroll, *The Religious Forces of the United States: Enumerated, Classified, and Described*, rev. ed. (New York: Charles Scribner's Sons, 1912) lxxx. Cf. anonymous, "Progress of the Churches," *American Review of Reviews* 15 (1897): 206–207, and anonymous, "Is the Power of Christianity Waning?—No," *Forum* 21 (May 1896): 376–84.

evangelicals failed to create religious hegemony in American culture generally, they nonetheless succeeded in revitalizing their denominations to meet the needs of the day. Rather than signaling denominational eclipse, evangelicals rightfully saw their denominations as one of the successful fruits of their labors. This, in part, explains why these denominational institutions provided the battlegrounds of later conflict. It also suggests that denominations, rather than being eclipsed, took on new and greater significance.

It is also important to note that the conflict between fundamentalists and modernists within their establishment denominations was not inevitable. Keswick Holiness, dispensational premillennialism, and revivalism informed (though not exclusively) the fundamentalist movement. Likewise, the New Theology, postmillennialism, and social Christianity shaped modernism. However, each establishment denomination in the late nineteenth century managed to house all of these disparate movements of theological and ecclesial reform. Therefore, new conditions acted as catalysts that sparked conflict within many of the denominations of the Protestant establishment. Denominational centralization, massive denominational fund drives, and the collapse of the Interchurch World Movement in 1920 took shrinking resources and put them in the hands of a few, causing contention about the use and alleged abuse of denominational funds, machinery, and institutions. The fact that the three denominations having the most conflict—the Northern Baptists, Northern Presbyterians, and the Disciples of Christ—met annually also helped keep the fires of contention regularly fanned.

Catalysts: Denominational Centralization

One important reason the controversies erupted in the 1920s was evangelical churches' push for the centralization of denominational structures and organizational efficiency, paralleling the bureaucratization of American industry and government. With few exceptions, the establishment denominations gradually consolidated church agencies under centralized denominational control during the early twentieth century. The goal of this consolidation was efficiency. By consolidating ecclesiastical machinery, denominations discouraged agencies or individuals from competing with one another for money, personnel, or endorsements. Centralized agencies allocated resources in an effort to avoid duplication of effort and waste. Those in control of the resources, therefore, maintained an enormous amount of power to influence the direction of church mission within their denominational communities. Furthermore, as denominational structures centralized they curtailed opportunity for competing strategies of cultural engagement to have an official voice. This shift in organizational power gradually upset the equilibrium between various parties within denominational tents.

The Northern Baptist Convention (NBC) was established in 1908 under the aegis of creating a more unified and efficient organization for advancing Baptist interests. The NBC for the first time brought together under one umbrella the missionary, publication, and educational enterprises of Baptist congregations north of the Mason-Dixon Line. Upon incorporation in 1910, a centralized executive committee directed what had been the American Baptist Home Missionary Society, American Baptist Foreign Missionary Union, American Baptist Publication Society, and American Baptist Educational Society. This placed the missions, seminaries, denominational schools, and publication houses in the hands of a select few elected at the annual convention.[30]

The Disciples of Christ followed suit in 1912, ratifying a constitution for the General Convention of the Churches of Christ, leading to the consolidation of its denominational machinery.[31] In 1913 it merged together five other periodicals of various Disciples' agencies into the *World Call*, its new official organ.[32] By 1917 the General Convention had created a representative Committee on Recommendations through which all resolutions brought to the convention floor had to pass. That same year, delegates called for the creation of a United Christian Missionary Society (UCMS), combining into one the six existing Disciples' mission boards. The UCMS was organized not only to centralize missionary work, but also to perform the administrative, educational, promotional, and service functions for the denomination as a whole.[33]

Presbyterians and Episcopalians consolidated as had their Disciples and Baptist cousins. Created by two denominational mergers in 1870 (the

---

[30] H. Leon McBeth, *The Baptist Heritage: Four Centuries of Baptist Witness* (Nashville: Broadman Press, 1987) 563–64.

[31] Lester G. McAllister and William E. Tucker, *Journey in Faith: A History of the Christian Church (Disciples of Christ)* (St. Louis: Chalice Press, 1975) 340.

[32] These included the *American Home Missionary*, *Missionary Tidings*, *Missionary Intelligencer*, *Business in Christianity*, and *Christian Philanthropist*. Cf. *Journey in Faith*, 342–43.

[33] Ibid., 346–49.

reunion of the Old and New school churches) and 1906 (with the Cumberland Presbyterian Church), the Presbyterian Church in the U.S.A. (PCUSA) further consolidated its denominational agencies between 1920 and 1923 into four boards: foreign missions, home missions, education, and sustentation.[34] The Protestant Episcopal Church, at its 1919 General Convention, created a central administrative body, the Presiding Bishop and Council. For the first time Episcopalians voted to have their primate elected by the House of Bishops (the title traditionally had been granted to the eldest bishop in order of consecration) and then confirmed by the House of Deputies. Two years later the Presiding Bishop and Council was reorganized as the National Council of the Protestant Episcopal Church in the U.S.A., bringing all the agencies and boards of the denomination under its direction. The National Council consisted of the presiding bishop, four bishops, four priests, and eight laypersons; its departments, each with its own executive head, included Missions and Church Extension, Religious Education, Christian Social Service, and Finance & Publicity.[35]

Centralization during this period, however, had less effect upon Methodists and Congregationalists. The Methodist Episcopal Church (MEC) did not need to push toward centralization in the early twentieth century because it had already done so earlier in the 1870s. Bishops and general superintendents oversaw regional annual conferences and appointed district superintendents. The bishops and superintendents (general and district) also maintained control of ministerial appointments to local churches and often transferred these ministers annually. In 1872 the General Conference, the MEC's national gathering, brought all the boards of its societies under national boards. Therefore, national executive boards and committees ran the common tasks of the denomination, tasks that had previously been accomplished through the regional annual conferences. By the turn of the century, the General Conference with its advising Board of Bishops affected virtually all of the political considerations of the denomination, diminishing the annual conferences' influence.[36] Having a generation of experience with denominational centralization helps explain

[34] James H. Smylie, *A Brief History of the Presbyterians* (Louisville: Geneva Press, 1996) 112.

[35] Raymond W. Albright, *A History of the Protestant Episcopal Church* (New York: Macmillan Company, 1964) 341–42.

[36] James Kirby et al., *The Methodists* (Westport CT: Greenwood Press, 1996) 135–46.

why Methodism had less conflict than most of the establishment churches. Congregationalists provided the only exception to this consolidation trend, which may be accounted for by the fact that its congregational sensibilities, small constituency, and regional orientation left it a much more theologically homogenous and organizationally manageable denomination. Virtually no conflict affected the Congregationalists during the 1920s and 1930s.

Within denominations such as the Presbyterian Church in the U.S.A., the Northern Baptist Convention, and the Disciples of Christ, however, advocates of the New Theology and social Christianity, having a natural affinity with institutional machinery in order to carry out their ecclesiological vision, often found themselves in what appeared to be greater positions of power. In effect, denominational consolidations dispropor-tionately placed eager modernists in stronger positions to implement their ideas of church vocation and their attendant programs. Furthermore, disputes were exacerbated within these denominations because they historically valued less centralized forms of church polity. This meant that heirs of revivalism, premillennialism, and Keswick Holiness often feared that their rivals usurped their official place within Protestant establishment by creating new forms of polity.

The creation of the World's Christian Fundamentals Association depicts this fear clearly. The attacks by denominational leaders made many premillennialists and revivalists believe they needed to organize outside their denominations to defend their positions within their denominations. The well-organized prophetic conferences, therefore, became the foundation of this trans-denominational movement. While attending a Bible conference at Montrose, Pennsylvania, in 1918, Baptists William Bell Riley and A. C. Dixon planned to establish a confederacy of those Christians and institutions wishing to counteract the growth and influence of modernism within the Protestant establishment. They met at the summer home of Congregationalist R. A. Torrey along with six other conservative evangelicals including Anglican W. H. Griffith Thomas and United Presbyterian Robert McWatty Russell.[37] A confederation of "Bible-

---

[37] Anonymous, "Introduction," *God Hath Spoken: Twenty-five Addresses Delivered at the World Conference of Christian Fundamentals* (Philadelphia: Bible Conference Committee, 1919) 8. Cf. William B. Riley, "What Is Fundamentalism?" *Bible Champion* 33/8 (August 1927) 409, and Stewart G. Cole, *The History of Fundamentalism* (New York: Richard R. Smith, Inc, 1931) 298–99.

believing" evangelicals—those adhering to the Bible as an infallible rule for faith and practice—had been a dream of Riley's for at least a year.[38] In May 1919 he realized his dream in the World's Christian Fundamentals Association (WCFA), which was founded at Music Hall in Philadelphia with approximately 6,000 participants.[39] Further, the WCFA conference helped solidify what would shortly be labeled a fundamentalist agenda and indicated its possible implementation within the Protestant establishment churches.

Many leaders among premillennialists, Keswickers, and independent Bible institutes, as well as popular revivalists and evangelists, joined the WCFA. These included R. A. Torrey, Paul Rader (radio evangelist and pastor of the famous Moody Tabernacle in Chicago), J. C. Massee, W. H. Griffith Thomas, William L. Pettingill (dean of Philadelphia School of the Bible), John Roach Straton, L. W. Munhall (premillennialist conference speaker and Methodist evangelist), I. M. Haldeman, Joseph Kyle (president of Xenia Theological Seminary in St. Louis), and C. I. Scofield.[40] The WCFA had emerged from the prophetic conferences during wartime but under the leadership of Riley broadened its vision beyond premillennialist concerns. Although the 1919 meeting included speakers on prophecy, the conference focused upon the fact that "thousands of false teachers, many of them occupying high ecclesiastical positions, are bringing in damnable heresies" within the denominations of the Protestant establishment.[41] The populist tenor of the speakers also surfaced as they optimistically claimed that revival was just over the horizon because average evangelicals in the pews hungered for true Bible teaching.[42] This conference aspired to speak for those experiencing the pangs of spiritual hunger during this biblical "famine" caused by the "deepening apostasy" within the Northern Protestant denominations.[43]

The WCFA created subcommittees that standardized a creedal subscription for independent Bible schools, evaluated the orthodoxy of denominational schools and seminaries, promoted fundamentalist aims and goals, organized future Bible conferences and local WCFA chapters, and

---

[38] Riley called for a confederation of this type in his book *The Menace of Modernism* (New York: Christian Alliance Publishing Co., 1917) 154–81.

[39] Riley, "Fundamentalism."

[40] Ibid.

[41] Anonymous, "Introduction," *God Hath Spoken*, 7.

[42] Ibid., 8.

[43] Ibid.

supported the activities of nondenominational international faith missions. James M. Gray (dean of Moody Bible Institute), Charles Blanchard (president of Wheaton College), Charles G. Trumbull (who oversaw American Keswick conferences), William B. Riley, and Orson Palmer headed these committees, respectively.[44] Further, a Resolutions Committee, chaired by Griffith Thomas, drafted a nine-point doctrinal statement encapsulating the WCFA's fundamentals of the faith. The first article affirmed the verbal inerrancy of the Bible and followed with statements on the Trinity, the deity of Christ, the fall of humanity, substitutionary atonement, the bodily resurrection and ascension of Christ, Jesus' premillennial Second Advent, justification by faith and regeneration by the Holy Spirit, and the resurrection of the body followed by judgment. These basic statements, the Resolutions Committee believed, presented a minimal doctrinal test of true Christianity. The statement also provided a short and efficient test of orthodoxy broad enough to unite many premillennialists, Keswickers, and revivalists.

Among the other concerns voiced by the Resolutions Committee was the growing centralization of the denominations dominated by "modernists." The report lamented that denominational machinery consolidated its publication efforts only to litter them with modernist propaganda.[45] It asserted that, although the WCFA wished to set up regional centers for more Bible conference activity, this program should not be confused with a program of central unification.[46] The language of constriction also peppered the report's attack upon the movement for church federation:

> We note with interest the determined endeavor to force the various evangelical denominations into a federation in which the 'the fundamentals of the faith' will play little or no conspicuous part. We believe that the accomplishment of such a religious corporation, at the cost of truth, would provide a flashing spectacle of apparent church success to be speedily succeeded by the most colossal failure that has characterized Christianity

---

[44] Anonymous, "Resolutions and Reports," in *God Hath Spoken*, 12–25; cf. Ernest Sandeen, *The Roots of Fundamentalism: British and American Millenarianism, 1800–1930* (Chicago: University of Chicago Press, 1970) 243.

[45] Ibid., 14.

[46] Ibid., 15.

since the dark days when an ecclesiastical corporation (the Roman Catholic Church) controlled the religious thinking of the world.[47]

With this prospect in mind, the leaders of the conference voiced their "determined protest" and warned that formal adoption of such a policy would lead to schism.[48]

An interesting feature of this protest was the belief of many conference speakers that the modernist conception of the church weakened its ability to carry out its mission to the world because it excluded the average church member. The result of the modernist program, claimed John Roach Straton, was an "inactive pew."[49] Modern Christians "have tended to shift the emphasis," he explained, "from the individual off on to the organization. We imagine the church collectively can accomplish the ends desired, or that the Sunday school, as a well-oiled machine, will grind out results. Thus it is that pompous ecclesiasticism has more and more taken the place of personal evangelism, and in place of self-sacrificing efforts for the salvation of others, we have substituted the comforts and inspiration of upholstered pews for ourselves."[50] Riley also made such an appeal, claiming that all regenerate Christians are expected to partake in the church's mission to preach the gospel to all nations.[51] Between the lines of such populist visions of the church lay the conference leaders' conviction that within the Protestant establishment the typical Christian still adhered to the fundamental doctrines of the faith and the mission of the church to evangelize the lost.[52] Therefore, fundamentalist leaders believed that by consolidating denominational machinery, the heirs of social Christianity and progressive orthodoxy had purposefully isolated average church members and subverted their participation within the church's mission.

The papers delivered at the conference also exemplified fundamentalists' ambivalence to their denominational homes. On the one hand, the speakers argued for reform, suggesting the importance of denominations. On the other hand, they often argued that there existed within the Protestant establishment two irreconcilable visions of the church.

---

[47] Ibid.

[48] Ibid.

[49] John Roach Straton, "The Secrets of Success in the Early Church," in *God Hath Spoken*, 416.

[50] Ibid., 418.

[51] William Bell Riley, "The Great Commission," in *God Hath Spoken*, 431.

[52] Anonymous, "Resolutions and Reports," in *God Hath Spoken*, 14.

Riley compared the conference to the posting of Luther's Ninety-five Theses and asserted that the church had to reform corrupt doctrine if it expected to reform corrupt behavior. The infidelity to which he alluded was "Modernism...the whole attitude of which is inimical to the church and the Christ of God."[53] He claimed that a "Great Divide" had left evangelicalism torn in two and he included ecclesiology as one of the main items that divided these two camps. He noted that because the church consisted of those "called out" (the literal translation of *ekklesia*), it consisted of a "witness-bearing company" pointing to the truths of the faith.[54] He also chided the "modernist" program for cooperative church federation, noting that it was a "direct result" of its conception of the church. "For them to unite by the practical abolition of all 'fundamentals of the faith,'" he concluded, "is theological bolshevism."[55]

P. W. Philpot, pastor of the Gospel Tabernacle in Hamilton, Ontario, reminded his audience that:

> It is generally conceded that the Protestant Church has been losing ground at an alarming rate for these last few years, and there is a feeling that something must be done if she is to be saved, and all sorts of remedies are being suggested and undertaken, but...When the church is true to her calling and does that one thing [preach the gospel], she will not only accomplish the purpose of God in the saving of men, but she will do more to solve the problems that are disturbing the world than she ever will by any other service, no matter how good and commendable these enterprises may be in themselves.

These sentiments found sympathetic restatement in the papers of James Gray, William Pettingill, and John Roach Straton.[56] Straton, pastor of Calvary Baptist Church in New York City, went so far as to remind his audience that social reform had the positive effect of providing better opportunities for the church to carry out its mission to evangelize; however, he made the important caveat that "first things must be kept first. Even social service enthusiasm can lead us astray unless we balance it with the eternal truths of God. Failure will be written above the doors of the church,

---

[53] Ibid., 27.

[54] William Bell Riley, "The Great Divide, or Christ and the Present Crisis," in *God Hath Spoken*, 40–42.

[55] Ibid., 42.

[56] James M. Gray, "The Holy Spirit—His Person and Purpose," in *God Hath Spoken*, 203–208; William L. Pettingill, "Prophecy—Why Study It?" in *God Hath Spoken*, 321–26; Straton, "Secrets of Success," in *God Hath Spoken*, 411–12.

if she departs from her faith and if she surrenders her message of eternal life."[57]

The WCFA also promised to withhold money from those denominational organizations that refused to expunge modernism from their ranks. Blanchard's report for the Committee on the Correlation of Colleges, Seminaries, and Academies asserted that true Christians must publicly protest and withhold financial support from church institutions affected by modernism.[58] Not surprisingly, perhaps, from a president of an independent evangelical college, he suggested that parents send their children to doctrinally sound colleges and Bible institutes. A similar call to withdraw financial support from any missionary enterprise that failed to require its agents to subscribe to the fundamentals of the faith came from the Committee on the Correlation of Interdenominational Foreign Missionary Societies.[59] Charles Trumbull's committee asserted that true believers must be selective in their use of religious literature and support those publishing houses and periodicals that printed materials edifying the fundamentalist vision for the identity and mission for the church.[60]

Despite its grand visions, the WCFA had no political clout or authority within the churches of the Protestant establishment. Moreover, its committees proved ineffective in implementing reform of Protestant churches and calling them back to what their members believed were their true identity and vocation. This failure was significant considering that much of its focus was on the subversion and reclamation of denominational institutions. The WCFA exemplified how centralization helped upset the equilibrium between different ecclesial visions within establishment denominations. The founding of the WCFA was a symptom of growing conservative concerns over denominational centralization and doctrinal infidelity rather than the spark that ignited conflict. Centralization coupled with the rise of denominational campaigns and the Interchurch World Movement ultimately laid the foundation for controversy.

---

[57] Straton, "Secrets of Success," in *God Hath Spoken*, 415.
[58] Anonymous, "Resolutions and Reports," in *God Hath Spoken*, 19.
[59] Ibid., 25.
[60] Ibid., 21.

Catalysts: Denominational Campaigns and the Interchurch World Movement

At the conclusion of the First World War, two other major catalysts for controversy impacted the Northern Protestant establishment: massive denominational campaigns and the Interchurch World Movement (IWM). These catalysts likely would not have ignited conflict on their own. However, national campaigns funneled denominational resources in a way that created competition for use of funds and newly centralized church machinery by those who could obtain political power. Furthermore, the collapse of the Interchurch World Movement, which left most of the denominations with millions of dollars of debt, appeared so colossal that the event seemed to beg that blame be affixed to someone or some group. The combination of these events set the stage for controversies that lasted the better part of a decade. A close consideration of these catalysts, therefore, will be instructive.

Riding the wave of optimism following the First World War, many leaders among the Northern evangelical Protestants envisaged great denominational promotional drives, often called "forward movements," to bring to the world peace and the message of Christ. To this end, evangelical denominations announced major financial campaigns. The Northern Baptist Convention had started the One Million Dollar Campaign in 1918 as an emergency fund to cover expenses incident to the war. The Victory Campaign followed the 1918 drive, and Baptist layman John D. Rockefeller, Jr. agreed to add $2,000,000 to the campaign if it received the full subscriptions for its $6,000,000 goal. The Methodist Episcopal Church's Centenary Fund had received pledges in excess of $107,000,000 by mid-1919.[61] The Presbyterian Church in the U.S.A.'s New Era Movement sought to raise $75,000,000 in five years. Not to be outdone, at its Denver convention in 1919 the Northern Baptists created a third campaign, the New World Movement, through which they intended to raise $100,000,000 over five years.[62]

These forward movements, along with the Congregationalist New World Movement, the Protestant Episcopal Church's Nation-wide

---

[61] Anonymous, "M. E. Drive 'Over the Top,'" *New York Times*, 25 May 1919, 12.

[62] Anonymous, "Baptists in Big Drive," *New York Times*, 18 January 1920, sec. X, p. 4. Cf. F. King Singiser, "The New World Movement: What It Is and What It Is Not," *Watchman-Examiner* 8/9 (26 February 1920): 285.

Campaign, and the Disciples of Christ's Men and Millions Movement (later folded into the Disciples' World Movement) intended to gain new converts and raise large sums of money in order to meet the spiritual and social needs of a postwar America and world.[63] The movements also reflected a naïve optimism of church leaders that American churchgoers could and would contribute huge financial sums to ambitious programs such as rebuilding European churches, fighting Bolshevism, solving American social ills, creating denominational survey and canvassing departments, and educating their coreligionists as to why financial drives were essential to the world's future.

No postwar forward movement was more grandiose or expensive than the nondenominational Interchurch World Movement of North America (IWM). Conceived in 1918 by Southern Presbyterian minister James I. Vance as a pan-Protestant movement to coordinate American missionary, educational, and benevolent programs, the IWM launched its brief career in Cleveland, Ohio, on 30 April 1919 with 500 delegates from 28 Protestant denominations. The key goals hammered out at the Cleveland conference sought to foster a unified evangelical front to advance Christianity worldwide, survey the state of evangelical Christianity in the nation and the world, inculcate religious vocations in young people, secure new American converts, and raise the money necessary to support its goals.[64]

Using military imagery common during the Great War, IWM leaders saw themselves and their churches on the eve of a great battle in the war to Christianize and civilize the world. They believed that they stood at a great crossroads of history. Methodist John R. Mott, chairman of the IWM executive committee, reminded American Protestants of Napoleon's dictum that "the time to bring up the cavalry is when the enemy's lines begin to waver, that you may turn defeat into route." While the war had not cured the world's social and spiritual ills, Mott encouraged Protestant churches that, if they mobilized for Christ, they would succeed in defeating the world's problems. Indeed, he concluded, "the lines, not only here in North

---

[63] The Disciples' Men and Millions Movement was eventually merged into the Disciples World Movement. Cf. anonymous, "The Campaign for Underwritings," *World Call* 3/5 (May 1921): 6.

[64] Anonymous, "Interchurch Facts for You," *Missionary Review of the World* 43/3 (March 1920): iv–v. Cf. Curtis Lee Laws, "The Interchurch World Movement," *Watchman-Examiner* 8/3 (15 January 1920): 74; Tyler Dennett, "The Interchurch World Movement," *World's Work* 39/6 (April 1920): 570.

America, but on every continent, that opposed the friendly and constructive ministry of pure Christianity are not only wavering—they are breaking. This is the moment of moments for us to find our unity, our spiritual solidarity, in order that we may win world wide spiritual victories for our Lord and Master."[65]

Although its spiritual rhetoric was that of war, the IWM took its practical cues from the world of big business. In fact, its leaders claimed it represented "the biggest business of the biggest man in the world."[66] The title from an IWM campaign pamphlet proclaimed that "The Church Takes a Leaf from Successful Business."[67] An editorial from the *Churchman* captured well the movement's business ethos: "As one walks through the great office of the Interchurch World Movement in the old Greenhut Building, New York, one receives a graphic impression of bigness. Two immense floors are in use at present; others being prepared for use. Hundreds of clerks, stenographers, heads of departments, office boys and messengers, typical of the largest business offices, are at work. It seems symbolical of the size of a movement which is catching the imagination of the American public."[68] In another news article, which sounded more like an advertisement than a story, Episcopal clergyman and journalist Lyman P. Powell described the IWM:

> This clearing-house for churches, called the Interchurch, is in a large sense not unlike the Stock Exchange in the financial world. It is first gathering facts, next aiding churches to achieve their highest end, and finally helping to ingather life and money and dedicate the same to religious uses of the churches. It would release all the hidden spiritual energies of the whole world. It exists—as Mr. Rockefeller says—to carry out the will of the churches. But it is no lifeless thing. It is as organic as it is colossal. It creates public opinion by laying world facts of religion, morality and education before the denominations it represents, bids them to take off the blinders of

[65] John R. Mott, "Growth of the Interchurch Movement," *Missionary Review of the World* 43/3 (March 1920): 176.

[66] From an Interchurch bulletin to American clergy. Quoted in Eldon G. Ernst, *Moment of Truth for American Protestantism: Interchurch Campaigns Following World War One* (Missoula MT: American Academy of Religion & Scholars Press, 1974) 89.

[67] *The Church Takes a Leaf from Successful Business* (New York: Interchurch World Movement, 1920). This pamphlet, #50–5734, is located at the Wisconsin Historical Society in Madison.

[68] Anonymous, "What Is the Interchurch World Movement?" *Churchman* 121/15 (10 April 1920): 14.

the past, and see the task before the churches in its cosmic sweep. Waste and amplication will wither before common knowledge. Constructiveness in missionary work in industrial relations in hospitals, schools, and colleges will take place of the haphazard.[69]

Powell reassured readers that leading financiers of the day thought the movement's goals and budget were in no way extravagant. However, with a proposed five-year budget of $1,320,214,551, one only can imagine Interchurch leaders such as John D. Rockefeller, Jr. finding the movement anything but extravagant. Nonetheless, in the words of one Interchurch advertisement, "the price of one tire for God" seemed to IWM leaders a small asking price for the creation of a civilized and Christian nation and world.[70]

Most Protestants, liberal and conservative, supported the ultimate goals of the Interchurch movement, often finding themselves swept away by its grand vision of a future Christian world of peace and equality. Baptist Shailer Mathews claimed that the IWM was "the greatest piece of co-operative activity Protestantism has ever undertaken."[71] Presbyterian Delavan L. Pierson, son of A. T. Pierson and editor of the *Missionary Review of the World*, called the IWM "tremendous and inspiring."[72] Premillennialist Robert Cameron's *Watchword and Truth* also printed a positive review suggesting "much good will come out of it."[73] Curtis Lee Laws, editor of the *Watchman-Examiner*, wrote that while the movement's "absurd" budget deserved criticism, his fellow Baptists ought to "co-operate with this great and prophetic effort to arouse Christians of all denominations to a new sense of duty and privilege."[74] Even local religious leaders, such as Wisconsin Baptist state superintendent D. W. Hulbert, felt swept up in the excitement of the movement, calling it "the greatest drive of Christendom known in the

---

[69] Lyman P. Powell, "Can the Churches Work Together?" *American Review of Reviews* 61/5 (May 1920): 520.

[70] This advertisement can be found in the *Christian Century* 37/9 (26 February 1920).

[71] Anonymous, "Dr. Mathews on Interchurch Movement," *Watchman-Examiner* 8/1 (1 January 1920): 20.

[72] Anonymous, "An Epoch Making Conference," *Missionary Review of the World* 43/2 (February 1920): 81.

[73] Anonymous, "Inter-Church Movement," *Watchword and Truth* 42/3 (March 1920): 69–70.

[74] Curtis Lee Laws, "The Interchurch World Movement," 75.

world's history."[75] IWM executive board member John D. Rockefeller, Jr. summed up the hope and optimism of the movement: "What forces can stand against this Movement? If it is complete in its cooperation, if the individual constituents are consecrated and in earnest, and the leadership able, there is no limit under God to what may be accomplished in the establishment of his Kingdom on Earth."[76]

Rockefeller's statement presaged problems with the movement because the complete cooperation the IWM needed was never forthcoming. In fact, serious attacks against the IWM began soon after it began to take shape publicly. The majority of the attacks centered on the extravagance of IWM spending, the alleged mismanagement of the IWM by its leaders, and the potential that the movement would harm denominational work. Mark Matthews, pastor of First Presbyterian Church in Seattle, represented the sentiments of many critics that the movement's expenditures were "excessive, needless and destructive, as evidenced by its large cost of rental, its great multitude of employees, its numerous and expensive conferences, and its excessive cost in publishing and distributing printed matter."[77] John Roach Straton, pastor of Calvary Baptist Church in New York City, went so far as to claim that participation in the movement would constitute "denominational suicide."[78] George A. Gordon, Congregationalist minister at Old South Church in Boston, confessed that he was "appalled by the magnitude of this scheme, by the secrecy in which it has been devised, by the utter disregard for the judgment of the ministers and laymen on whom the burden would fall, if the plan should be put into operation." The Interchurch movement, concluded Gordon, was nothing short of "wildcat campaigning by ecclesiastics."[79]

Other detractors of the IWM had specifically ecclesiological concerns, such as the fear that the movement would establish an autocratic

---

[75] Editorial, "The Drive of Christendom is Coming," *Wisconsin Baptist* 21/11 (November 1919): 8.

[76] Dennett, "Interchurch World Movement," 577

[77] Anonymous, "Fund Drive to Stir General Assembly," *New York Times*, 16 May 1920, 9. Cf. James H. Snowden, "The One Hundred and Thirty-first General Assembly of the Presbyterian Church in the U.S.A," *Union Seminary Review* 30/4 (July 1919): 311–12.

[78] Anonymous, "Dr. Straton against Interchurch Move," *New York Times*, 17 March 1920, 10.

[79] Anonymous, "Wildcat Ecclesiastical Campaigning," *Literary Digest* 64/4 (24 January 1920): 36.

ecclesiastical body or usurp denominational authority. Conservative Disciples ministers, represented primarily in the pages of the *Christian Standard*, doomed the IWM to failure because of its federative and denominational nature. Such characteristics, they argued, made the movement fundamentally opposed to proper Disciples ecclesiology, which was rhetorically anti-denominational.[80] Congregationalist Gordon proclaimed the IWM "the boldest and most ruthless form of autocracy that I have ever known...This is not Congregationalism it is Caesarism, and Caesarism gone mad."[81] Premillennialist Reformed Episcopalian James Gray, dean of Moody Bible Institute, agreed with Gordon, though for different reasons. Gray feared that the IWM would promote church union at the expense of denominations that, he believed, quite properly distinguished themselves by emphasizing common theological beliefs.[82]

In fact, premillennialists conspicuously attacked the movement based on ecclesiological grounds. William Bell Riley attacked the IWM's implicit postmillennialism and described the movement as "a violent endeavor at kingdom-making":[83]

> The leaders of the Interchurch World Movement...believe Christ has come as King already, making no distinction in time between His successive offices, Prophet, Priest, and King. They think He is to be made world ruler in this age. They also believe that His crown is in their hands, and that the day of His coronation will be determined by their endeavor. Here again they have fallen into the mistake of the people who would bring the kingdom by force and are following the Constantine conception even to the point of force. With them, however, it is not force of arms but rather that of educated intellect, sacrificial energy and consecrated gold.[84]

The biblical conception of the church, stated Riley, "is an *ecclesia*, a called-out company. It belongs to this age distinctly; its membership is made

---

[80] See S. S. Lappin, "The Interchurch World Movement" *Christian Standard* 55 (20 March 1920): 3–4; M. P. Hayden, "Interchurch World Movement" *Christian Standard* 55/25 (20 March 1920): 7.

[81] Anonymous, "Wildcat," 36.

[82] James M. Gray, "The Proposed World Church Union—Is It of God or Man?" *Christian Worker's Magazine* 19/9 (May 1919): 633–34.

[83] W. B. Riley, *The Interchurch or the Kingdom by Violence* (Minneapolis: W. B. Riley, n.d.) 8.

[84] Ibid.

up of flesh and blood men; its territory is only so much as it can conquer; its task is evangelism."[85]

The most public attack upon the IWM came from I. M. Haldeman, pastor of First Baptist in New York City and noted premillennialist speaker, who called the movement "the slickest scheme the devil has ever brought about." In a sermon titled "Is the Interchurch Movement of God or of Satan?" Haldeman argued that the movement was modern theology in disguise and that it would "produce an ecclesiastical autocracy on the one hand and a church sovietism on the other."[86] The Baptist preacher's sermon was covered by the *New York Times* and so vexed Interchurch leaders that they felt compelled to respond in the media to what they called a "deplorable" attack.[87] Thanks to the press coverage, Haldeman claimed that he received so many inquiries from sympathetic evangelicals that he felt compelled to publish his position in *Why I Am Opposed to the Interchurch World Movement*.[88] In this lengthy pamphlet, which he freely distributed to delegates at the 1920 Northern Baptist Convention in Buffalo, New York, Haldeman explicitly argued that the true nature of the church's calling made it incompatible with the goals and interests of the IWM: "[The Interchurch World Movement] fills the Church with the machinery of man and not the energy of God.... It is a menace to the authority of the Holy Scripture, the guidance of the Holy Spirit and the upbuilding of the spiritual Church. It is organizing an ecclesiastical autocracy, a compelling spirit of dictatorship that will override pastoral liberty and destroy assembly independence. It is one of the foretold signs of the Great Apostasy, the end of the age, the coming of Christ."[89] Like other dispensationalists, Haldeman argued that the IWM leaders based their ecclesiology upon an erroneous conflation of the church with the kingdom of God. This in turn led to the distortion of the church's mission by emphasizing social amelioration at the expense of saving souls. Furthermore, as he perceived it, this apostasy of the professing church regarding its mission was a prophetic sign that the Second Advent was nigh.

---

[85] Ibid., 12.

[86] Anonymous, "Assails Interchurch Drive," *New York Times*, 3 May 1920, 12.

[87] Anonymous, "Answers Attack on Church Drive," *New York Times*, 4 May 1920, 10.

[88] I. M. Haldeman, *Why I Am Opposed to the Interchurch World Movement* (New York: I. M. Haldeman, n.d.) 3.

[89] Ibid., 52.

Despite attacks against the movement, the IWM found the official support of most Protestant denominational bodies. The Interchurch meeting in Atlantic City brought around 1,800 delegates from 42 Protestant denominations. By March 1920 thirty of those denominations promised to raise most of the $336,777,572 needed for the first year of the IWM's budget.[90] The Northern establishment churches not only made up the majority of the delegates (1,237) but underwrote the lion's share of the bank loans used to pay the movement's starting expenses.[91] The Protestant Episcopal Church did not officially participate, much to the dismay of its more progressive members; however, many of its clergy and laity endorsed the movement individually.[92] Of the $6,561,261.73 spent by the IWM by 1920, Northern establishment churches had guaranteed 84 percent of those loans and provided virtually all of the movement's leadership (Southern Presbyterian James I. Vance was a notable exception).[93] The denominations that underwrote the IWM felt confident that the carefully planned and lavishly advertised financial drive of in the Interchurch would succeed at its conclusion in May 1920. However, the IWM's pledge drive fell well short of the anticipated goal. Not only were the denominational subscriptions less

---

[90] *History of Interchurch World Movement* (n.p., 1924?), pt. 3, pp. 134–41. IWM leaders expected $40,000,000 of the total to come from friendly, non-church-affiliated Americans. The *History of the Interchurch World Movement* is a collection of IWM documents compiled in ten parts around 1924 after the movement finally shut down all operations. These documents were microfilmed by the William Adams Brown Ecumenical Library at Union Theological Seminary in New York City.

[91] The delegates counted included 375 Northern Methodists, 363 Northern Baptists, 260 Northern Presbyterians, 115 Congregationalists, 95 Disciples of Christ, and 29 Episcopalians. However, only the affiliations of the first 1,527 delegates were recorded for the several press reports. Cf. Laws, "Interchurch World Movement," 73; anonymous, "Interchurch Budget to be $1,300,000,000," *Churchman* 121/3 (17 January 1920): 27.

[92] See, for example, anonymous, "800 Men Hear Plans for Church Movement," *Churchman* 121/13 (27 March 1920): 24; anonymous, "Will You Urge Your Rector to Attend?" *Churchman* 121/9 (28 February 1920):25; anonymous, "Clergy Endorse Interchurch World Movement," *Churchman* 121/12 (20 March 1920): 22; anonymous, "Our Clergy for the Interchurch W. M.," *Churchman* 121/13 (29 May 1920): 22.

[93] *History of the Interchurch World Movement* pt. 6, pp. 141–44. The Northern Baptist Convention underwrote $2,500,000; the Disciples of Christ $636,529.55; the Methodist Episcopal Church $1,333,565.78; the Presbyterian Church in the U.S.A. $1,000,000; and the Congregationalists $89,000.

than anticipated, but the expected $40,000,000 support from "friendly," non-Protestant citizens failed completely.

The timing of the financial shortfall could not have been worse. The General Assembly of the Northern Presbyterians met that same May, and the financial condition and viability of the IWM became a lightning rod of debate. Many presbyteries sent overtures condemning what they believed to be mismanagement of Presbyterian funds by the IWM. Maitland Alexander, pastor of First Presbyterian Church in Pittsburgh, voiced his outrage at Interchurch mismanagement by circulating a resolution to withdraw completely from the movement. Other opponents argued that the executive committee of the Presbyterian Church in the U.S.A. had overstepped its authority by committing resources to the IWM. Fifteen presbyteries (among them St. Louis, Cincinnati, Philadelphia, Seattle, Dayton, Baltimore, Pittsburgh, and Grand Rapids) sent their own or concurred with others' overtures against the Presbyterian Church's involvement in the IWM. [94]

Supporters of the movement found themselves on the defensive in the face of the movement's financial crisis. Prominent Presbyterian laymen James M. Speers and Robert E. Speer, both IWM leaders, argued the importance of maintaining support of the organization.[95] On the floor of the General Assembly, Speers admitted that "the movement was projected on too large a scale, but not too large for a world struggling under a burden of sin."[96] Speer echoed this sentiment, noting that "it had shortcomings but it had values."[97] After several days of argument, the assembly ultimately voted to maintain a connection with the Interchurch if it limited its annual budget to no more than $1,000,000.[98] While this was a compromise measure in the assembly, it was a serious blow to IWM. On the one hand, if the IWM accepted the Presbyterians' condition, its executive board would appear to lose its autonomy to make financial decisions; on the other hand, if it rejected the resolution it risked losing the support of one its major financial backers.

---

[94] Anonymous, "Presbyterian Row over Interchurch," *New York Times*, 26 May 1920, 17.

[95] Ibid.

[96] Ibid.

[97] Ibid.

[98] *Minutes of the General Assembly of the Presbyterian Church in the U.S.A.*, vol. 20 (Philadelphia: Office of the General Assembly, August 1920) 174–76; cf. anonymous, "Presbyterians Quit Interchurch Plan," *New York Times*, 28 May 1920, 17.

The next month, the Northern Baptist Convention met in Buffalo, New York. Rumors of Interchurch mismanagement coupled with the convention's substantial underwriting of the movement's expenses led the NBC to cut its ties completely with the IWM. After the Baptist withdrawal the movement quickly began to unravel and collapse. The Disciples of Christ had originally authorized the denomination to participate in the IWM for only one year; the following fall at their convention in St. Louis they took no action to renew membership. In November, the Board of Bishops of the Methodist Episcopal Church severed its ties from the movement as well.[99]

The IWM's collapse had a devastating effect upon the minds of American evangelicals. In particular, the financial burden left to the denominations that underwrote the movement strained their resources. Curtis Lee Laws observed that the "crushing" debt was "the bitterest pill the Baptist denomination has ever had to swallow."[100] The NBC had to take out bank loans to pay off Interchurch creditors the $2,500,000 it had voted to underwrite the prior year. The $600,000 the Disciples of Christ underwrote for the Interchurch movement seriously hurt the denomination's financial stability. The *Christian Standard* snidely commented that because of the IWM the Disciples' newly-created United Christian Missionary Society "makes [the] worst possible start as it prepares to pay penalty for an alliance which is wholly contrary to the genius of the restoration movement."[101] Another editorial in *World Call* complained that "our underwritings are a debt that we owe on an old nag that has bitten the dust. Confessedly that makes our debt harder to pay."[102] Worse, the Disciples of Christ found themselves in the awkward position of needing to organize a new campaign

---

[99] Anonymous, "Twenty Questions and Answers Regarding the Underwritings," *World Call* 2/12 (December 1920): 52; anonymous, "Quit Interchurch Body," *New York Times*, 26 November 1920, 12. Cf. Ernst, *Moment of Truth*, 148–51; Congregationalists had to wait until 1921 to discuss the movement's failure. Cf. National Council of the Congregational Churches of the United States, *Reports of Commissions and Mission Boards Moderator's Add, Council Sermon, Minutes, Roll of Delegates, Constitution and By-laws, Etc.* (New York: Office of the National Council, 1921) 222.

[100] Editorial, "The Interchurch Movement," *Watchman-Examiner* 8/42 (14 October 1920): 1253.

[101] Anonymous, "The Interchurch Gamble Fails," *Christian Standard* 55/35 (29 May 1920): 7.

[102] W. W. Phares, "The Dead Horse," *World Call* 3/5 (May 1921): 7.

to pay off the money they underwrote to the IWM.[103] The collapse also left the Methodist Episcopal Church and the Presbyterian Church in the U.S.A. with large financial burdens. The Methodist Episcopal Church had to borrow the $1,300,000 it had sunk into the Interchurch as well as pay interest on the loans as high as 7 percent.[104] Like the Baptists, Disciples, and Methodists, Northern Presbyterians had to procure loans (excluding interest) for their Interchurch debt of $1,000,000.

Speaking before the International Congregational Council, Charles R. Brown, dean of Yale Divinity School, declared that the Interchurch had "left a dark brown taste in the mouths of Protestant Christianity in this country":

> If our recent unhappy experience [of the collapse of the IWM] stood alone it might not deserve remark. But it is a symptom of a tendency which in my judgment has brought hurt and loss to our American Protestantism. The Men and Religion Movement, the Laymen's Missionary Movement, the Interchurch World Movement and all the rest have resulted in disappointment.... They all made more difficult, rather than less, the work of the regular pastors and discriminating laymen in carrying forward those agencies upon which Protestant Christianity must continue to rely for its life. The generous people of our Church have to be taken in before they realize that they cannot always safely follow the leadership of small groups of religious promoters whose good intentions no one doubts, but whose judgment everyone questions.[105]

Brown correctly observed that the movement seemed to damage the credibility of its leadership; however, the failure of the IWM did much more than tarnish the reputation of a few prominent churchmen. The collapse of the IWM forced different evangelical parties to compete for resources within establishment denominations.

---

[103] Anonymous, "The Underwriting Campaign," *World Call* 3/8 (August 1921): 5. See also anonymous, "Day Set for Drive to Raise Interchurch Underwriting," *Christian Standard* 56/8 (20 November 1920): 11; anonymous, "Twenty Questions and Answers Regarding Underwritings," *Christian Standard* 56/10 (4 December 1920): 16–17; anonymous, "The Interchurch Underwritings," *Christian-Evangelist* 57/46 (11 November 1920): 1172; anonymous, "The Interchurch Underwritings: Why Pay the Obligation" *Christian-Evangelist* 57/49 (2 December 1920) 1277.

[104] Anonymous, "The Inter-Church Failure and the Foreign Board's Debt," *Central Christian Advocate* 65 (6 December 1922): 1133.

[105] Anonymous, "Decries Interchurch Drive," *New York Times*, 7 July 1920, 29. Cf. anonymous, "Sees Interchurch Idea a Nightmare," *Washington Post*, 7 July 1920, 11.

The failure of such a colossal, well-publicized, and costly movement begged for explanation and a bearer of blame. On the one hand, many conservatives, like Curtis Lee Laws, believed the movement exchanged evangelical doctrine and character for an "emasculated" Christianity that emphasized "world betterment and Christian civilization."[106] Presbyterian minister Clarence E. Macartney registered his outrage with the movement as well: "Woe to that man or that church which advocates Christianity because it enhances the value of real estate, drives brigands off the highways, reduces the death-rate from contagious diseases or purges the political stables! These are the things that accompany the spread of the gospel. Wherever the river of temple truth goes, the desert shall live. But the by-products of Christianity are not to be mistaken, or substituted, for its demands upon the life and conscience of the individual."[107] The *Missionary Review of the World* concluded that "the mistake came when the inclusion of all forms of philanthropy and social and industrial betterment in the program tended to obscure the main objective" of preaching the gospel to a "sin-infected world."[108]

On the other hand, Rae D. Henkle in the *Christian Herald* admitted that the movement suffered from ineffective programming and lack of focus. Nonetheless, he defended the IWM leaders against charges of extravagance and argued that the movement's opponents misrepresented the IWM, causing its ultimate failure.[109] *The Churchman*'s editor noted that unfavorable economic conditions, extravagant spending, and a miscalculation for non-Protestant support of the movement helped lead to its downfall. Further, he argued that the most serious problem of the IWM was its "individualistic and evangelical" character, which did not properly "appreciate the social character and obligation of the religion it proclaimed."[110]

---

[106] Editorial, "Baptists and the Interchurch Movement," *Watchman-Examiner* 8/24 (10 June 1920): 751.

[107] Clarence Macartney, "The Fall of the Colossus," *Christian Standard* 56/23 (5 March 1921): 1977–78.

[108] Anonymous, "The Interchurch Movement—Some Conclusions," *Missionary Review of the World* 43/7 (July 1920): 580.

[109] Rae D. Henkle, "A Plain Statement Concerning the Interchurch World Movement," *Christian Evangelist* 57/25 (10 June 1920): 576–77, 592; cf. anonymous, "Why the Interchurch Movement Failed," *Literary Digest* 66/6 (7 August 1920): 42.

[110] Anonymous, "The Interchurch World Movement Failure," *Churchman* 122/4 (24 July 1920): 8.

The demise of the Interchurch also coincided with a dampening of both American Protestant enthusiasm and generosity to contribute to great causes. An editorial in the Presbyterian periodical *The Continent* claimed that the collapse hinged upon a psychological fatigue of massive fund drives and campaigns.[111] Whether or not it was true that a "failure of psychology" led to its demise, the IWM's collapse overlapped with a decline of denominational finances and a weariness of forward movements. The *Nation* rightfully observed that the IWM "came as the last of many 'drives' to a tired and indifferent nation. Folks had grown excited and generous because of liberty loans, 'Y,' Red Cross, Salvation Army, till they had neither enthusiasm nor cash."[112] The American economic situation also did not help. The postwar economy slumped into a brief depression in 1920 followed by a sharp recession in 1923, causing many pledges to remain unfulfilled. In March of 1921 several Northern evangelical denominations held a conference on forward movements in New York City, presided over by Robert E. Speer, recently elected president of the Federal Council of Churches. The conference leaders intended to examine their campaign failures and share success stories. Leaders tried to put a positive face on what otherwise appeared to be lagging and uncollected pledges.[113] It did not take long for such discussions to become much more public in denominational periodicals and meetings.

Protestant leaders ultimately had to admit that their denomination's financial goals were not being met. The Northern Baptist New World Movement had received $55,000,000 in pledges (of which $45,000,000 was actually paid at the conclusion of the campaign).[114] As extraordinary as this sum was, it was considerably less than their $100,000,000 goal. By 1922 Baptists found themselves compelled to cut their national budget by 50 percent.[115] Three years into its five-year campaign, the Northern Presbyterian New Era Movement looked worse than the Baptists, having collected only $8,000,000 of its $75,000,000 goal. This is not to mention that the New World Movement found itself in debt to the tune of

---

[111] Anonymous, "Why the Interchurch Movement Failed."

[112] Anonymous, "The Collapse of the Christian Soviet," *Nation* 111/2871 (10 July 1920): 34.

[113] Anonymous, "Denominational Forward Movements," *Missionary Review of the World* 44/7 (July 1921): 507.

[114] McBeth, *Baptist Heritage*, 566–68.

[115] Anonymous, "Baptists End Work of Annual Council," *New York Times*, 21 June 1922, 2.

$600,000.[116] By November 1920 Presbyterian leaders found themselves in the embarrassing situation of facing bankers' threats for late payments on the loans procured to service their IWM and New World debts.[117] The Protestant Episcopal Church could only garner a 38 percent subscription rate of its three-year $45,000,000 goal. In 1922 the Disciples' Men and Millions Movements reported that their "task had been made unusually difficult because of the state of unrest and unfavorable financial conditions that have prevailed throughout the country."[118] They further reported a $2,150,000 deficiency from their $6,000,000 goal set in 1913.[119] The Congregationalists managed to collect only a third of its comparatively modest goal of $3,000,000. The Methodist Episcopal Church's Centenary Fund fared better than most other denominations' drives with a 93 percent subscription rate of its $113,000,000 goal.[120] Even so, by 1922 denominational leaders still found it necessary to host special fund-raisers to cover a $2,000,000 deficiency.[121]

Conclusion

Not all the denominations of the Northern Protestant establishment experienced serious conflict following the war. As mentioned before, the polity and theological homogeneity of Congregationalists helped maintain denominational peace. Although both Methodists and Episcopalians had centralized denominational structures, the conflicts only minimally affected these denominations. Quadrennial and triennial national meetings respectively helped mitigate conflict by limiting the ability of individuals or groups to give controversial topics a national platform. Also, both the Methodist Episcopal Church and the Protestant Episcopal Church had suffered schisms in the late nineteenth century with those most likely to have conservative evangelical affinities. The Reformed Episcopal Church

---

[116] *Minutes of the General Assembly*, 142.

[117] Anonymous, "Appeal for Interchurch Loan," *New York Times*, 10 November 1920, 4.

[118] Anonymous, *1922 Year Book of Organizations of Disciples of Christ* (St. Louis: United Christian Missionary Society, 1923) 32.

[119] Ibid., 33.

[120] Anonymous, "Denominational Forward Movements," 507–509. Cf. John Lankford, "Methodism 'Over the Top': The Joint Centenary Movement, 1917–1925," *Methodist History* 2/1 (October 1963): 27–37.

[121] Anonymous, "Methodists at Dinner Help Centenary Fund," *New York Times*, 31 October 1922, 36.

left the Protestant Episcopal Church in 1873, and a variety of holiness churches left the Methodists in the 1880s and 1890s.[122] Although one cannot be sure that controversies would have ensued had these schisms not occurred, these groups removed a critical mass of likely fundamentalist sympathizers.

This is not to say there was no conflict among Methodists and Episcopalians. Premillennialist L. W. Munhall remained a controversialist in the Methodist Episcopal Church. As early as 1913, in *Breakers! Methodism Adrift*, he attacked what he believed was growing modernist control of Methodist institutions, including schools, seminaries, literature, and the episcopacy.[123] Although he held no position in the Methodist hierarchy, Munhall was a nationally recognized revivalist and prophecy speaker. Even so, his voice really echoed a previous generation of such traditionalist Methodist bishops, such as Bible League of North America members C. H. Fowler, Charles C. McCabe, and W. F. Mallalieu, all of whom Munhall counted as personal friends.[124]

The essentialist movement, led by Harold Paul Sloan and John A. Faulkner, had better but limited success influencing the Methodist Episcopal Church (MEC). As a primarily traditionalist movement attempting to defend theological orthodoxy in the MEC, essentialists had an uneasy relationship with the wider fundamentalist movement. Bishop Adna W. Leonard coined the term "essentialist" in 1926 as "a reaction against fundamentalism and modernism." According to Leonard, essentialists rejected the doctrinal innovations of both movements by maintaining a scholarly approach to the scriptures and traditional doctrines of historic

---

[122] Timothy Smith, *Called Unto Holiness: The Story of the Nazarenes, The Formative Years* (Kansas City MO: Nazarene Publishing House, 1962) and Allen C. Guelzo, *For the Union of Evangelical Christendom: The Irony of Reformed Episcopalians* (University Park: University of Pennsylvania Press, 1994).

[123] L. W. Munhall, *Breakers! Methodism Adrift* (New York: Charles C. Cook, 1913).

[124] These three bishops along with L. B. Wilson were charter members of the "interdenominational" Bible League of North America, which was founded to defend the Bible from radicalism. See anonymous, "To the Ministers of the Methodist Episcopal Church," *Bible Champion* 17/3 (June 1914): 263–64. Munhall dedicates *Adrift* to the memories of McCabe and Mallalieu, among others. See Munhall, *Adrift*, 3.

Christianity.[125] Sloan immediately latched on to the name for his Methodist League of Faith and Life.[126] While he professed to be part of the fundamentalist movement, he often downplayed his connection with "organized fundamentalism" and noted that he wished to guard constitutionally protected doctrines of Methodism.[127] Between 1916 and 1924, he successfully drew attention to the course of study mandated for Methodist seminary students, which he claimed favored unorthodox, modernist theology.[128] At the 1924 General Conference in Springfield, Massachusetts, he presented a statement asking the conference to reaffirm traditional Methodist doctrines; the memorial passed in a slightly altered form.[129] He further helped convince the conference to pass a provision that required the Commission on the Course of Study to submit its text recommendations to the Board of Bishops for approval.[130] Sloan was pleased not only with the conference's result but with its aura of tolerant orthodoxy, remarking that "Modernism was not antagonized and excluded, nor was Fundamentalism organized and triumphant."[131]

In 1925 Sloan founded his Methodist League for Faith and Life, an organization to promote and preserve traditional Christian orthodoxy in the MEC. Under the League's auspices, conservative Northern Methodists networked with conservative Southern Methodists, such as Bishop Warren A. Candler, and even some conservative Lutherans, notably Wittenberg College professor Leander S. Keyser. While Sloan personally participated in many fundamentalist organizations, such as the World's Christian

[125] Adna W. Leonard, "Essentialist," *Northwestern Christian Advocate* 77/16 (21 April 1927): 372; "'I'm an Essentialist,' Says Bishop Leonard," *New York Times*, 29 March 1926, 22.

[126] Anonymous, "Bishop Leonard's Great Statement," *Call to the Colors* 1/12 (April 1926): 192–94; anonymous, "An Essentialist," *Call to the Colors* 2/1 (May 1926): 1–2.

[127] Harold Paul Sloan, "Fundamentalism: Organized and Unorganized," *Christian Advocate* 98/44 (1 November 1923): 1336–37.

[128] Harold Paul Sloan, *Historic Christianity and the New Theology* (Louisville: Pentecostal Publishing Company, 1922); Sloan, "The Law of the Church Not Fulfilled by the New Course of Study," *Methodist Review* 37/5 (September 1921): 792–99.

[129] James R. Joy, "Editorial Letter: The General Conference," *Christian Advocate* 99/19 (8 May 1924): 573–74.

[130] Harold Paul Sloan, "The Value of the General Conference of 1924 for Faith," *Christian Advocate* 99/26 (26 June 1924): 806–807.

[131] Ibid., 807.

Fundamentals Association and the Winona Lake School of Theology, other fundamentalist leaders found his unwillingness to embrace premillennialism and the verbal inerrancy of the Scriptures troublesome. He found more kindred spirits in the Bible League of North America and the Evangelical Student League. He was also attracted to Presbyterian J. Gresham Machen's vigorous defense of Christian orthodoxy. In fact, because he was sympathetic to Machen's views, Sloan encouraged many Methodist students to attend Princeton Seminary and later Westminster Seminary, and he unsuccessfully tried to garner a teaching position at the latter.[132] Machen not only ignored Sloan's overtures, but many "Westminster Methodists," most notably Harold Ockenga, defected from Sloan's movement to become Presbyterians.[133]

Methodism provided a reasonably hospitable and tolerant home for liberals as well as conservatives. Edwin Lewis, John Faulkner's colleague at Drew University, early came under the scrutiny of the Methodist League and Sloan for his modernistic views. Lewis, most publicly in his book *Jesus Christ and the Human Quest* (1924), wished to make Jesus accessible and believable for those individuals who had rejected supernaturalism.[134] At the 1928 Kansas City General Conference, Sloan and Lewis butted heads over a petition of around 10,000 signatures from 522 churches in 41 states calling for a committee of 15 to investigate charges of heresy in the MEC. The house voted to drop Sloan's case.[135] Responding to the controversy, the Board of Bishops took a mediating position against "controversial intolerance or intolerant controversialism."[136] They felt that "[i]f the preacher assumes to answer every adversary of Christianity, he will make the place a battlefield, instead of a sheepfold.... You have a right to insist and expect that the preacher will be intellectually loyal to his task, but you must not attempt to fetter him either with the bonds of an arrogant mechanistic

---

[132] Ockenga claimed that one-fourth of the students at Westminster were Methodist. See H. J. Ockenga, "Methodists among the Princeton Secession," *Essentialist* 5/6 (November 1929): 131.

[133] Floyd T. Cunningham, "Harold Sloan and Methodist Essentialism," *Asbury Theological Journal* 42/1 (Spring 1987): 69.

[134] Edwin Lewis, *Jesus Christ and the Human Quest* (New York: Abingdon Press, 1924).

[135] James R. Joy, "Editorial Letter: The General Conference," *Christian Advocate* 103/10 (10 May 1928): 581.

[136] Ibid., 580.

philosophy or with those of a despotic traditionalism."[137] Such a mediating position also won the day when Sloan and Lewis battled over a conservative statement of Methodist faith debated in the subcommittee on doctrinal standards. Lewis and Fred Spence of Jackson, Michigan, supported a substitute that simply affirmed belief in the fatherhood of God, brotherhood of man, and lordship of Jesus. The subcommittee made a final report that affirmed the traditional beliefs of Methodism, while adding a section "recognizing reverent science and scholarship."[138] This doctrinal affirmation was subsequently passed by the General Assembly 700 to 25.[139] Such action suggests that Methodism's lack of conflict had less to do with its being thoroughly modernist than its wish to consistently steer a middle course of compromise. Bishop Francis McConnell claimed that compromise was the secret of Methodism's freedom from conflict: "there are no distinctively Methodist doctrines. There are rather Methodist accents, on such phases of experience as conversion, assurance, and sanctification."[140] However, the guiding hand of a strong, mediating episcopate equally ensured prevailing compromise.

With its long tradition of the Elizabethan *via media*, strong episcopal control of the individual, relatively independent dioceses, and triennial conventions, the Protestant Episcopal Church (PEC) faced few controversies of national significance. Furthermore, the PEC had virtually no clergy connected with the fundamentalist movement and did not participate in financially disastrous ventures such as the IWM. Several conservative bishops, however, did raise the specter of modernism within their own dioceses and took action to undermine its influence.

William T. Manning, bishop of the diocese of New York, clashed with modernist clergymen in his diocese several times. Percy Stickney Grant, rector of the Church of the Ascension in New York, especially irritated him. In January 1923, Grant preached a sermon in which he claimed that Jesus did not have equality with God. All the New York papers carried the sermon, and it received national attention. Cries against Grant arose from

---

[137] Anonymous, "Methodists Rebuke Fundamentalist," *New York Times*, 3 May 1928, 56.

[138] Harold Paul Sloan, "Faith's Story in the General Conference of 1928," *Essentialist* 4/3–4 (June–July 1928): 53–54.

[139] Ibid., 54. Cf. James R. Joy, "Editorial Letter: The General Conference," *Christian Advocate* 103/22 (31 May 1928): 677–78.

[140] Francis J. McConnell, "The Methodist Church and Fundamentalism," *Homiletic Review* 87/2 (February 1924): 94.

many corners of the PEC, the majority of which claimed that liberalism was acceptable but denial and unbelief were not.[141] Manning, whose personal relationship with Grant had been quite rocky well before he became a bishop, demanded that the priest "publicly correct the impression given in your recent sermon and state clearly that you do accept the faith of the Church as set forth in the Creed, or if you do not accept this faith you should voluntarily resign from the ministry of this Church."[142] Grant avoided a heresy trial because Manning's investigation found that Grant's Christology was sufficiently vague to offer no grounds for a trial.

The House of Bishops' pastoral of 1923 and subsequent presentment for heresy of Lee W. Heaton for denying the virgin birth also caused much dissention in the PEC. On the thirtieth anniversary of his consecration as a bishop, William Lawrence of the diocese of Massachusetts preached a sermon in which he affirmed that one could deny the virgin birth and remain a faithful churchman.[143] Lawrence's sermon disturbed many Episcopalians in general and some of his fellow bishops in particular. Not long after the sermon, the House of Bishops met in Dallas, Texas, and issued a pastoral letter warning clergy that their doctrine must conform to the content of the Apostle's Creed.[144] Bishop Manning was a major advocate of the pastoral.[145] The issuing of the bishops' letter coincided with a presentment for heresy of Lee W. Heaton, rector of Trinity Church in Fort Worth, Texas. During his Palm Sunday sermon the previous April, Heaton like Lawrence had preached that an Episcopalian could faithfully deny the virgin birth.[146] Harry T. Moore, bishop coadjutor of the diocese of Texas, had already threatened to depose Heaton. The pastoral letter only emboldened the bishop to proceed with a trial.

---

[141] Anonymous, "Calls Dr. Grant a Radical," *New York Times*, 29 January 1923, 6; anonymous, "The Right to Stay in a Church and Deny Its Creed," *Literary Digest* 76/7 (17 February 1923): 35, 51–52; anonymous, "In Defense of Rationalism," *Watchman-Examiner* 11/5 (1 February 1923): 133–34.

[142] Anonymous, "Right to Stay," 32.

[143] William Lawrence, *Fifty Years* (Boston: Houghton Mifflin Company, 1923) 71–72.

[144] Anonymous, "Doffs Church Vestments," *New York Times*, 17 December 1923, 1.

[145] Hugh M. Jansen, "A Threatened Heresy Trial in the Twenties," *Anglican Theological Review* 49/1 (January 1967): 18–23.

[146] An excerpt from the sermon was printed in "Modernists Will Fight," *New York Times*, 17 December 1923, 2. Cf. Jansen, "Threatened Heresy Trial," 25–26.

The publication of the pastoral letter coupled with the publicity of Heaton's presentment caused a fury of reaction among modernist clergy. Leighton Parks, rector of St. Bartholomew's Church in New York, attacked the pastoral from the pulpit on 16 December. With dramatic flare, he doffed his surplice, cassock, and stole and donned his doctoral robes to preach.[147] He reminded his congregation that a pastoral letter simply presented advice from the bishop and only the General Convention could legally interpret doctrine.[148] He then denied the doctrinal necessity of virgin birth from the pulpit and dared the bishops to bring a presentment against him or Bishop Lawrence.[149] A large outcry against the pastoral letter and the Heaton presentment followed, including those by Percy Stickney Grant; Karl Reiland, rector of St. George's Church in New York; the Modern Churchman's Union; and the faculty of the Episcopal Divinity School in Boston.[150]

Manning wished to avoid a heresy trial in his own diocese, and he was not convinced that one in Fort Worth would further the cause of orthodoxy. When Ernest M. Stires, rector of St. Thomas Church in New York, met with Heaton and asked Manning to intervene, the bishop contacted Moore to ask that a trial be avoided.[151] In a diocesan pastoral letter dated 20 December, Manning proposed a "Christmas Truce" to allow things to cool down.[152] Nine days later, Manning met in the home of George Zabriskie, chancellor of the diocese of New York, at the behest of Bishop James

[147] Anonymous, "Doffs Church Vestments," 1.

[148] Leighton Parks, "Intellectual Integrity," *Churchman* 129/1 (5 January 1924): 10.

[149] Ibid., 14–15.

[150] Anonymous, "Dr. Grant Assails Pastoral Letter," *New York Times*, 17 December 1923, 2; anonymous, "Church Challenged to Place Dr. Parks on Trial as a Heretic," *Washington Post*, 18 December 1923, 1; anonymous, "Dr. Parks Condemns Bishops' Pastoral and Heaton Trial," *Churchman* 128/25 (22 December 1923): 20–21; anonymous, "The Bishops' Pastoral Letter: A Statement by the Modern Churchmen's League," *Churchman* 128/25 (22 December 1923): 10; anonymous, "Clergy Disturbed by Pastoral Letter," *Churchman* 128/26 (29 December 1923): 20–21, 24; and anonymous, "The Faculty to the Alumni: A Statement on the Pastoral Letter," *Churchman* 129/3 (19 January 1924): 10–11.

[151] Anonymous, "Doubt if Bishop Can Try Dr. Parks on Heresy Charge," *New York Times*, 19 December 1923, 4.

[152] This pastoral letter is printed in anonymous, "Manning Proposes Christmas Truce in Church Dispute," *New York Times*, 21 December 1923, 1.

DeWolf Perry of Rhode Island.[153] Other participants who attended the informal meeting included H. E. W. Hobroke, dean of General Theological Seminary; Henry B. Washburn, dean of Episcopal Divinity School; bishop William Cabell Brown of Virginia; bishop Charles H. Brent of Western New York; and Theodore Irving Reese, bishop-coadjutor of Southern Ohio. Manning personally invited Parks to attend the meeting.[154] In a press release, the participants declared that "we believe that the right solution of difficulties within the church will be found not in controversy but through conference."[155]

Moore eventually capitulated and the Heaton trial was avoided. Leighton claimed that Moore had allowed the PEC to avert schism by his willingness to drop the charges against Heaton.[156] Manning, however, made clear that in his opinion Anglican comprehensiveness had limits. Quoting his predecessor David H. Greer, he noted that:

> The Church in this land has her standards of Faith embodied in the Creed and offices and Articles, which taken together with Holy Scripture, are her Rule of Faith. In the interpretation of these there has always been and always will be a certain latitude of construction for which every wise man will be devoutly thankful. But that that latitude exists is no more certain than that it has its limits and that the transgression of these limits, by whatever ingenuity it has been accomplished, has wrought only evil in lowering the moral tone of the Church and in debilitating the individual conscience, is, I think, no less certain.[157]

Manning continued to stand firm on his position that while modernists had room to interpret the creeds and the Scriptures they must not reject outright their content or intent.

The informal meeting of December led to another in March. However, Manning refused to sign a statement that acknowledged that "the Church cannot hope to deal with these questions effectively unless they are discussed in a spirit of mutual confidence and belief in one another's loyalty. We affirm our conviction that the Church will continue to minister to the truth

---

[153] Jansen, "Threatened Heresy Trial," 34.

[154] Anonymous, "Episcopal Bishops, Clergy and Laymen Meet to Talk Peace," *New York Times*, 29 December 1923, 1.

[155] Ibid.

[156] Anonymous, "Split in Church Is Averted, Says Parks," *Churchman* 129/3 (19 January 1924): 22.

[157] William T. Manning, "A Message to the Diocese: The Present Situation in the Church," *Churchman* 129/7 (16 February 1924): 17.

as it is in Christ Jesus to which it has ministered in the past and there will be found no essential contradiction between the truth into which the Holy Spirit shall lead and faith which has been held throughout the ages."[158] The statement, though never published, bore the marks of modernist leaders, especially Leighton Parks. Parks had made a similar plea in his *What Is Modernism?* published the same month.[159] Parks defended the place of modernists within the boundaries of the Episcopal Church. With concern, he declared, "What a tragedy it would be if it should be declared that the spirit of the Modernist must be incarnated outside the Christian Church."[160] Although the 1924 General Convention manifested some of the debates between modernists and conservatives, compromise typically prevailed. The worries of traditionalists and modernists notwithstanding, strong episcopal structures meant that bishops who practiced restraint and compromise within their dioceses helped maintain tradition and order while averting serious denominational conflict.

In other establishment denominations, however, a perception of crisis and defeat began to cloud optimism in the aftermath of the Interchurch failure. As denominational resources became constrained, those with different perceptions of the church's mission became less tolerant of one another's strategies for reaching and recapturing American culture. There was only so much money, time, and machinery. This meant that tensions and divisions that had coexisted under broad denominational tents for several generations flared into conflict. The remaining three chapters will examine the three denominations in which conflict was most pronounced and public: the Northern Baptist Convention, the Disciples of Christ, and the Presbyterian Church in the U.S.A.

---

[158] Quoted in Jansen, "Threatened Heresy Trial," 35.

[159] Leighton Parks, *What Is Modernism?* (New York: Charles Scribner's Sons, 1924). See especially the fifth chapter, "The Purpose of the Modernist," 125–50.

[160] Ibid., 144.

CHAPTER 7

Case Study:
The Northern Baptist Convention,
1919–1926

Denominational centralization coupled with large denominational and interdenominational fund drives became a catalyst for conflict by amassing and constraining resources. In the Northern Baptist Convention (NBC) there existed at least three identifiable parties involved in the conflict that took place between 1919 and 1926. One doctrinally conservative group identified themselves as "fundamentalists." Fundamentalists opposed a liberal group who alternately called themselves "modernists," "liberals," and more rarely "evangelicals." A third traditionalist party also shaped policy in the denomination; however, they rarely labeled themselves anything other than "Baptist." These traditionalists, however, should not necessary be understood to be centrists between fundamentalists or modernists. Typically they exhibited conservative theological orientation while maintaining a traditional toleration of those who differed from them theologically. However, traditionalists' primary goals included loyalty to denominational interests and the success of denominational enterprises rather than theological doctrines per se.

Traditionalists typically shared with fundamentalists a distrust of autocratic institutions. Yet their wish for Baptist agencies to succeed also led them to value modernist attempts at organizational efficiency embodied in schemes of centralization. Fundamentalists and modernists shared a history of theological reflection in terms of pneumatology and eschatology that often left them with a theoretical ambivalence toward denominational structures on the one hand and a practical need for those structures on the other. Therefore, the dynamics of conflict and compromise in the NBC must be understood in the following terms: on the one hand, certain fundamentalists and modernists negotiated with loyalists to make compromises to create viable denominational institutions; on the other hand, other fundamentalists and modernists, because of denominational ambivalence, sought separation from denominational loyalty in terms of separatism and ecumenism, respectively. In terms of denominational loyalty, separatism and ecumenism provided their pundits with a similar strategy: diminish denominational loyalty in order to promote a perceived good of greater importance.

Model 7.1
Northern Baptist
Convention

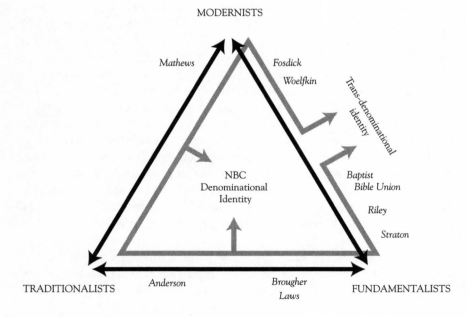

In terms of ecclesiology, this means that between 1919 and 1926 the development of ecclesiology in the Northern Baptist Convention is best described using Haight's notion of an "ecclesiology from below," or a clarification of Baptist practice of being the church based upon the contingencies of denominational structures and controversies. In other words, those fundamentalists and modernists who valued denominational loyalty sought and found compromises with one another and with loyalists in order to preserve the integrity of denominational structures and agencies. Those fundamentalists and modernists who valued loyalty less than another principle moved toward actual or practical separation from the denomination.

As argued in the previous chapter, a key catalyst of the controversies that plagued the Northern Baptist Convention during the 1920s was denominational centralization.[1] After the First World War, the organizational efficiency and centralization that had made the war effort possible seemed compelling to many self-interested Baptists. In May 1918 the NBC met in Atlantic City and charged a committee of five to make recommendations to promote denominational efficiency. The report of the committee, published the following spring, recommended the creation of a centralized Board of Promotion as a means by which to coordinate the budgets of the NBC's several missionary and educational agencies. The committee intended the board to raise and dispense money for the various Baptist agencies connected with the NBC. The NBC unanimously adopted the committee's report at the Denver convention in 1919.

The Denver convention, however, revealed many ecclesiological tensions present within the NBC. On the one hand, the convention unanimously voted to accept a report on comity penned by Shailer Mathews that declared that the Northern Baptist Convention "does not believe that organic unity with other denominations is possible." Mathews, a self-professed modernist with clear traditionalist proclivities, argued that Baptist ecclesiology precluded any discussion of organic church union: "The Baptist denomination is a collection of independent democratic churches. None of these churches recognizes any ecclesiastical authority superior to itself. They are grouped in associations. State conventions and a National Convention, but none of these groups has any control over a local church, beyond that

---

[1] A brief sketch of denominational changes in the NBC can be found in Robert Handy, "American Baptist Polity: What's Happening and Why," *Baptist History and Heritage* 14/3 (July 1979): 13–17.

which lies in common faith, practise [sic] and service.... By the very nature of our organization we are stopped from seeking organic unity with other denominations."[2] On the other hand, the NBC, by instituting the General Board of Promotion, created a centralized and relatively small delegated body with executive power to act on behalf of its "independent" congregations. Indeed, the NBC overwhelmingly voted to allow the board to act on its behalf in the Interchurch World Movement and the collection and dispersal of funds in the New World Movement.

Such apparent contradictions did not go unnoticed by many Northern Baptists, either. One proponent of organic union took issue with what he believed to be "a strange inconsistency between the Convention's statement regarding its lack of power to function organically and the very action the Convention took":

> If the Convention had ignored the overtures regarding organic unity its inaction would have been evidence of its impotency. But when it deliberated upon the matter and by vote consciously expressed its will to self-determination it functioned organically and thus repudiated its own declaration that "Baptist churches do not have organic unity among themselves." ...If we are going to maintain that we have a community of faith and practise [sic] amounting to "structural beliefs," consciously held throughout the denomination, then we must admit that we have some sort of organic fellowship.[3]

Many theologically conservative Baptists also began to have scruples about giving their financial resources to the Board of Promotion, upon which they had no direct control:

> Besides missionary activities the Board earmarked close to 33% of the anticipated $100 million in proceeds to help endow Baptist educational institutions. Further they underwrote millions of dollars for the Interchurch World Movement. The fact that the Board of Promotion dispersed funds to "unorthodox" endeavors exacerbated existing theologically conservative (fundamentalist and traditionalist) worries that their denomination had begun to drift away from the fundamentals of the Christian faith.[4]

---

[2] Anonymous, "Dr. Mathews Statement" *Watchman-Examiner* 7/23 (5 June 1919): 900–901.

[3] Robert Woods Van Kirk, "Organic Church Union and Structural Baptist Beliefs," *Watchman-Examiner* 7/43 (23 October 1919): 1479.

[4] Anonymous, "A Final Word about the Campaign," *Watchman-Examiner* 8/17 (22 April 1920): 527.

As the 1920 Buffalo convention approached, denominational conservatives became more and more alarmed about the spread of "rationalism" by means of denominational machinery and educational institutions. In April a group of 150 Baptist ministers and laymen publicly called for a General Conference on Fundamentals to meet immediately before the convention in Buffalo. The name of the conference was reminiscent of the World's Christian Fundamentals Association, and indeed many WCFA members like William Bell Riley and J. C. Massee participated. However, this General Conference was neither trans-denominational nor premillennialist. Between 21 and 22 June, the conservatives, whom Curtis Lee Laws famously dubbed "fundamentalists," complained that their voice had been marginalized by modernists and rationalists who controlled the denominational machinery.[5] Furthermore, they argued in the words of conference organizer J. C. Massee that within the NBC "certain small groups have constituted themselves steering committees of the Convention and have assumed for themselves responsibilities to determine in secret conferences courses of action for the whole body."[6] In fact, Massee imagined the pre-convention conference as the ecclesiological antithesis of the convention it preceded. The Conference on Baptist Fundamentals was not a legislative, delegated, or closed body of Baptists. Rather, according to Massee, conference leaders organized the gathering so that "all Baptists in the bounds of the Northern Baptist Convention, having open access to the Conference, may have privilege of participation in its counsels and thus in determining its influence upon the Convention."[7]

The speakers at the Buffalo convention bemoaned the abandonment of historic Baptist principles and fundamentals of the faith by modernist teachers, professors, missionaries, and convention leaders.[8] However, the overriding concern of the pre-convention conference was not simply one of doctrinal purity. Rather, conservatives feared that modernists and

---

[5] *Baptist Fundamentals Being Addresses Delivered at the Pre-Convention Conference at Buffalo, June 21 and 22, 1920* (Philadelphia: Judson Press, 1920) vii–viii, 4. Cf. Martin Marty, *Modern American Religion Volume 2: The Noise of Conflict, 1919–1941* (Chicago: University of Chicago Press, 1991) 164, 167.

[6] J. C. Massee, "Opening Address," in *Baptist Fundamentals*, 4.

[7] Ibid.

[8] See *Baptist Fundamentals*: Massee 4–7; F. L. Anderson, "Historical Baptist Principles," 18–19; A. C. Dixon, "The Bible at the Center of the Modern University," 119–40; W. B. Riley, "Modernism in Baptist Schools," 168–86.

rationalists used newly created centralized denominational machinery to gain access to resources that promoted a drift away from the fundamentals of New Testament faith. In fact, prior to the conference, Curtis Lee Laws consistently advertised that the meeting intended to discuss the "great doctrinal and ecclesiastical questions" of the NBC.[9] The pre-convention conference papers bear out this intent. Cortland Myers, for example, called modernists "ecclesiastical parasites" who "are trying to tell us, by a big piece of machinery, how to put it over [on the congregations of the NBC]."[10] There was surely no coincidence that the speakers did not target individuals or congregations they believed had fallen from distinctive Baptist principles; rather, they looked at Baptist institutions financially supported by the General Board of Promotion with funds contributed by their churches. William Bell Riley and A. C. Dixon hammered against the "menace of modernism" within Baptist schools that they claimed ultimately endangered a distinctive Baptist mission.[11]

Although doctrinally conservative, the fundamentalists never formulated the exact contents of the Christian faith apart from the sufficiency of the New Testament to determine all matters of faith and practice. One reason for this may have been that many of the pre-convention participants and speakers, including Myers, Laws, and Frank M. Goodchild, were not premillennialists like Massee and Riley. More likely, as the pre-convention papers reveal, there existed a deep ambivalence among many participants about the efficacy and propriety of attempting to promote a specific doctrinal test of orthodoxy at all. Many fundamentalist Baptists clung tenaciously to historical Baptist assertions such as "soul competency" and "no creed but the Bible." Principles such as "soul competency" provided most Baptists with more than a traditional window dressing around the core of their faith. Rather, such principles formed the cornerstone of Baptist ecclesiology. Baptists traditionally argued for the individual's freedom from religiously coercive institutions. They claimed that this standard logically led to the voluntary principle of church membership, which in turn precluded membership of children via infant baptism. In fact, Massee, during one conference session, called for an unofficial test vote on "open membership without emphasis on baptism." The *Watchman-Examiner*

---

[9] Anonymous, "That Fundamentals Conference," *Watchman-Examiner* 8/22 (27 May 1920): 688.

[10] Anonymous, *Baptist Fundamentals*, 161.

[11] Ibid., 117–40, 167–87.

reported that almost everyone in the hall "rose to express his adherence to the time-honored Baptist custom of a regenerate, baptized church membership."[12]

However, the tension between denominational traditionalism and separatism among fundamentalists became evident as speakers presented their addresses at the Fundamentals Conference. Many participants harbored a traditional Baptist distaste for the imposition of creedal or confessional statements of faith. Conference speaker Thomas Jefferson Villers of Detroit proclaimed that "it is the singular and distinguished honor of the Baptists to have repudiated from their earliest history all coercive power over the consciences and actions of men with reference to religion."[13] Newton Theological Seminary professor and conference speaker Frederick L. Anderson substantially agreed: "I oppose any creedal statement whatever in the Northern Baptist Convention, or any other formal gathering, because it would be sure to be regarded as an attempt to impose that creed on all Baptists contrary to their liberty in the gospel to differ from us, and, as we could not agree, it would be surely divisive and exclusive in its tendencies."[14] J. C. Massee also demurred from creating a creedal test, stating that "we would not write nor consent to the writing of a formal creed."[15]

Other fundamentalist speakers had a more sanguine assessment of imposing tests of orthodoxy. Riley, who constructed a de facto doctrinal test in his speech attacking wayward Baptist schools, emphasized the voluntary principle of Baptist ecclesiology more than soul liberty: "There is no difference between the Baptist creed and the Bible; ...the first is the succinct statement of the elaborate teachings of the second.... We would not at all be willing to have Baptist churches replace the Bible with a creed, but we did suppose when we united with this denomination...that there is a certain set of beliefs concerning God, Christ, the Scripture, and the Ordinances, etc., to which Baptists universally subscribe."[16] J. W. Porter, editor of the *Western Recorder*, felt less compelled to emphasize voluntary ecclesiology than the demand that profession of the unchanging faith once delivered was the qualification of any assembly to be recognized as a church at all. He

---

[12] Anonymous, "Northern Baptists at Buffalo," *Watchman-Examiner* 8/28 (1 July 1920) 839.

[13] *Baptist Fundamentals*, 30.

[14] Ibid., 21.

[15] Ibid., 7.

[16] Ibid., 170–71.

attacked organizations such as the Interchurch World Movement that underplayed the importance of dogma; he also asserted that "we are stewards not only of dollars, but also of doctrines."[17]

The pre-convention Conference on Baptist Fundamentals revealed two important features of its leaders' ecclesiology. First, given the different emphases on Baptist ecclesiology by the conference speakers, there existed no unanimity concerning the proper Baptist way to deal with the perceived menace of modernism present in the denomination and its institutions. Second, conservatives at the conference began to strongly assert the primacy of soul-saving and personal redemption over social amelioration. "Our distinctive mission is being disparaged," claimed Riley.[18] "We now draw lines, not in teaching at all, but at territory, and divide from any people that care to assume the name of Christ, not on the basis of doctrine, but to share the sphere of 'social service,' calling it 'the kingdom,' forgetting more and more that such federations put the soft pedal upon the great principles that have made our people a power."[19] Such endeavors, he concluded, have ended up "as incompetent as creedless."[20] One can find similar concerns in the addresses of most of the conference speakers, including Porter, Massee, Myers, Brougher, and W. W. Bustard.

The participants of the pre-convention conference, with some discussion, voted to bring to the national convention a resolution to create an investigating committee that would evaluate charges of doctrinal apostasy within Baptist educational institutions. At the convention, debate over this proposal was heated and interspersed with heckles and moans. Opponents to the resolution interrupted John Roach Straton's defense so often that he cried from the podium, "I will not be browbeaten or bullied. I will make this speech."[21] Other less-than-kind calls from the floor demanded that J. W. Brougher not be considered for the investigating committee because he had married the famous actor and divorcee Douglas Fairbanks to actress Mary Pickford.[22] In the end the convention authorized a committee of nine, including Brougher, to investigate the orthodoxy of Baptist schools.

---

[17] Ibid., 112.

[18] Ibid., 185.

[19] Ibid., 186.

[20] Ibid.

[21] Anonymous, "Baptists Attack 'Infidel' Teaching," *New York Times*, 24 June 1920, 16.

[22] Ibid. Cf. anonymous, "Demand Democrats Uphold 'Dry' Laws," *New York Times*, 27 June 1920, 16. Brougher's explanation and defense of the Fairbanks-

Anticipation and trepidation surrounding the investigation of the committee of nine became a focal point of a denominational debate concerning the importance of creeds and the authority of the NBC over its constituent churches. The tradition of Baptist liberty, or freedom from coercive institutions in matters of religion, became the rallying cry for both modernists (i.e., liberals) and fundamentalists. Modernists, especially those teaching in Baptist schools and seminaries, wanted freedom from doctrinal legislation as well as maintained centralization of denominational structures. Liberal Baptists applied such arguments and contended that the NBC did not have judicial power, the ability to assert a creed, or even the right to try a case of heresy. John R. Brown, professor at Rochester Theological Seminary, argued that "the Baptist principle is one, and only one...the competency of the soul before God."[23] Therefore, he contended, no true Baptist would assert a creed or confession as a binding statement of faith.[24] St. Louis pastor W. H. Geistweit stated that while Baptists may observe a "denominational consciousness," they could not claim to have a "denominational authority."

> This spiritual interpretation of the church, this refusal to submit to any authority—ecclesiastical, sacerdotal, ceremonial—carries with it the right for which our people steadily stand—the right of private interpretation of the Scriptures.... The church being a spiritual body, it follows that its members became so by conscious, voluntary action on their part; that they are therefore all believers before God, equal in every particular...[Therefore], our unity among ourselves—church with church, until it teaches something like national denominational expression—is entirely for the sake of enlarged service; our gatherings, therefore, are purely advisory, never judicial or legislative.[25]

Professor Theodore Gerald Soares of the University of Chicago agreed with Geistweit's conclusion. He noted the value (if not the necessity) of centralized bodies to carry out the missionary activities of the church. He nonetheless claimed that such recognition of missionary association did not

---

Pickford wedding can be found in anonymous, "Ask Brougher's Ousting as Film Wedding Sequel," *Los Angeles Times*, 28 June 1920, II1, II9; cf. anonymous, "Brougher Gives Wedding Views," *Los Angles Times*, 3 April 1920, II9.

[23] Anonymous, *Christianity in a New World* (Philadelphia: Judson Press, 1921) 77.

[24] Ibid., 76–85.

[25] W. H. Geistweit, "'The Church' and 'Church Unity': What Does My Denomination Mean by This Phrase?" *Watchman-Examiner* 9/7 (17 February 1921): 204.

entitle the denomination to function as a judicial body or to impose a binding creed on its constituent churches.[26] These Baptist liberals, as theological heirs of the New Theologians, postmillennialists, and social Christianity advocates, argued for the importance and necessity of centralized and efficient denominational structures. However, as good Baptists they appealed to Baptist liberty and soul competency in order to maintain freedom from creedal or confessional restraints.

Conservatives, or fundamentalists, also claimed the importance of independency and liberty. However, they claimed Baptist freedom from undemocratic Baptist bodies like the Board of Promotion or self-perpetuating boards of trustees at Baptist schools, which used denominational resources in ways they believed promoted heresy. A representative statement by J. C. Massee declared that "the conduct of our schools is undemocratic and un-Baptistic":

> They are governed almost without exception by self-perpetuating boards of trustees not subject either to direct or indirect selection by either the Northern Baptist Convention or the State Baptist conventions. Yet these schools, entirely independent in their constitution and control, assume the right to wear the Baptist name, claim the sponsorship of the Baptist conventions, and the right to make appeal for Baptist support through Baptist conventions, associations and other agencies. There is an age-long democratic principle "No taxation without representation." Baptist representation on the boards of trustees of so-called Baptist schools is not sufficiently demonstrated by the fact that members of the boards as individuals are members of Baptist churches.... Even where this is not true their membership on school boards is unofficial and irresponsible, except to themselves and the schools.[27]

Massee likened the $32,000,000 of the New World Movement earmarked for school endowment to an "unprecedented" denominational tax and an "unspeakable burden" upon the rank and file of Baptists, who were being forced to support financially doctrines and programs they would otherwise never support. Massee concluded, "If they wish to enlarge their equipment and endowment at the expense of the denomination let them tell us frankly...what limitation shall be put upon the beliefs, utterances and

[26] Theodore Gerald Soares, "Baptist Polity in the New Order," *Review and Expositor* 17/3 (July 1920): 307, 311–13.

[27] J. C. Massee, "The Churches and the Schools," *Watchman-Examiner* 9/11 (17 March 1921): 335.

teachings of the faculty employed."[28] Curtis Lee Laws, who often pleaded with disgruntled Baptists not to withhold money from the New World Movement, admitted that the campaign's association with the Interchurch World Movement and Baptist educational institutions had caused many Baptist churches not to cooperate with the drive.[29] Many fundamentalists concluded that, given the reality of the centralized Board of Promotion, a creedal test sanctioned by the NBC provided practical means by which to protect their financial gifts from promoting programs and institutions they found theologically problematic.

An anonymous donor exacerbated the conflict in the Convention in spring 1921. The donor offered a gift of $1,750,000 to the Baptist Home Missionary Society on the condition that the money only be used to support missionaries who subscribed to particular doctrines, such as the supreme authority of the Scriptures, the bodily resurrection, the physical return of Christ, and immersion as the proper form of baptism. Facing a budget deficit, the Home Missionary Society reluctantly accepted the gift. Dean Shailer Mathews of the University of Chicago registered his outrage in the *Independent*, arguing that such a gift constituted a backdoor means by which to assert a creed within the NBC and to subvert social Christianity.[30] Curtis Lee Laws snidely retorted in the *Watchman-Examiner* that Mathews ironically used the principle of Baptist liberty to attack this anonymous donor yet expected the donor to conform to Mathews's own particular wishes: "Now just a word about the creedal test bugbear. The donor was not seeking to establish a creedal test; he was simply insisting that the Home Mission Society should not use his money in supporting missionaries who do not believe in the great Christian verities."[31] The debate over the anonymous donor heightened concern over the possibility or necessity of some sort of doctrinal test for college and seminary professors and missionaries. With controversy looming, Baptist delegates braced themselves for a combative convention in Des Moines.

The second pre-convention Conference on Fundamentals met the day before the Des Moines convention, focusing its attention on Baptist

---

[28] Ibid., 337.

[29] Anonymous, "Our Denominational Finances," *Watchman-Examiner* 9/14 (7 April 1921): 423–24.

[30] Editorial, "Dean Mathews Criticizes," *Watchman-Examiner* 9/24 (16 June 1921): 741

[31] Ibid., 742

doctrines. The roll of speakers had a more North American flavor, including Southern and Canadian Baptists. In his opening address, J. C. Massee, president of the Conference on Baptist Fundamentals, noted that there existed a doctrinal, educational, and ecclesiastical cleavage in the Convention. "Without doctrinal cohesion there can be no denominational co-operation," claimed Massee, adding, "lying at the root of our doctrinal differences are the teachings permitted in our denominational schools."[32] To solve the problems surrounding the questionable orthodoxy of Baptist educational institutions, Massee proposed two possible solutions. First, he suggested that the New World Movement divorce itself from Baptist educational institutions and deal solely with missionary organizations. Alternately, he suggested that the NBC "adopt a statement of belief to which all teachers in all Baptist educational institutions shall be required to give annual assent in writing, cutting off from denominational support and sponsorship all schools refusing such fellowship of faith."[33] Finally, Massee warned his audience that denominational autocracy and centralization undermined Baptist democracy and independence.[34] T. T. Shields, pastor of Jarvis Street Baptist Church in Toronto, reinforced Massee's point. He decried those "Baptists who object to the 'tyranny' of those who are resolved to control their institutions and to see that the money they give is used for the propagation of principles in which they believe." Shields concluded that "standards are irksome to the man who would be a law unto himself."[35]

The pre-convention conference concluded with a controversial vote to adopt a confession of faith. Frank M. Goodchild presented to the conference a seven-point confession of faith on behalf of the executive committee of the Baptist Fundamentals movement. Laws reported a "prolonged and vigorous" debate that hinged not so much on the content of the statement as whether a statement should be made at all. Ultimately, the conference voted to adopt the confession; however, Laws conservatively reported that a significant 20 percent of the participants voted against the adoption.[36] The leaders of the Conference on Baptist Fundamentals insisted that the

---

[32] J. C. Massee, "Opening Address," in *Baptist Doctrines: Addresses at the North American Pre-Convention Conference, Des Moines, Iowa, June 21, 1921* (N.p.: J. C. Massee, 1921) 11, 14.

[33] Ibid., 19.

[34] Ibid., 20–23.

[35] T. T. Shields, "The Cross and the Critics," in *Baptist Doctrines*, 75–76.

[36] Curtis Lee Laws, "Pre-Convention Days at Des Moines," *Watchman-Examiner* 9/26 (30 June 1921): 812–13.

confession was voluntary in nature. However, it seemed clear given the content of Massee's speech that the confession provided a foundation upon which fundamentalists might practically solve the educational problem if they failed to disconnect schools from the New World Movement's budget.

The hot, humid June weather in Des Moines likely added to the humorlessness of the delegates as they prepared for debate. The convention ultimately voted for compromises that stymied any extreme position proffered by modernists or fundamentalists. The committee of nine failed to pen a unanimous report on the fidelity and efficiency of Baptist schools. While asserting that some heretical teachers marred the record of otherwise fine and faithful schools, the majority report representing the views of many fundamentalists was moderate in its assessment. The report also announced which schools required and which did not require specific doctrinal standards of its trustees, administrators, and faculty members.[37] A single committee member, Franklin W. Sweet, penned the minority report, which claimed that the majority report did not "affirm this vital loyalty to Christ on the part of Baptist teachers in secondary schools, colleges, and seminaries as clearly as the findings of the year demand."[38]

The Des Moines convention adopted both reports. Furthermore, the body concluded that it did not have the power to enforce orthodoxy. Denominational officers appealed to the NBC's charter, noting that the convention existed only for cooperative endeavors between congregations and not doctrinal conformity. The ruling was essentially a compromise. It asserted that there existed no constitutional means by which the "fundamentals" of the faith could be enforced as a test of faith, thereby protecting the liberty of modernist missionaries, teachers, and ministers. However, it also affirmed that the convention derived its power from its congregations, which remained sovereign political entities.

Two related issues also ended in compromise: the acceptance of the $1,750,000 gift to the Baptist Home Missionary Society and subsequently the right to designate the use of funds offered to the Board of Promotion. During the annual meeting of the Home Missionary Society, Judge F. W. Freedman offered a resolution to thank the anonymous donor who had attached doctrinal requirements to his gift. Further, he asked the society to

---

[37] *Annual of the Northern Baptist Convention 1921 containing the Fourteenth Meeting Held at Des Moines, Iowa June 22 to 28, 1921* (New York: American Baptist Publication Office, 1921) 49–94.

[38] Ibid., 98.

modify the doctrinal statement (at the donor's request) concerning the church so as to insist upon adult baptism. Modernists, unable to table the motion, offered a substitute motion asking that the donor reconsider the doctrinal requirement because it was not in accord with the Baptist principle of liberty. After intense debate and parliamentary maneuvering, the delegates passed the Freeman resolution by a vote of 662 to 422.[39] The fundamentalist victory on this issue modestly began groundwork that placed more power in the hands of the donor than the receiving agency. The following day, a report by E. R. Rhoads recommended that the Board of Promotion allow the designation of funds to particular areas, but it also suggested that general funds be distributed to meet the needs of other organizations that did not receive designated gifts. In other words, while the board intended to administrate the New World Movement, it would ensure that no one individual or congregation would be forced to put its money into a program it disapproved.[40] The Board of Promotion made this official policy at its November executive meeting later that year.[41] These policies acted as compromises that in principle allowed more conservative Baptists to maintain doctrinal scruples and denominational loyalty.

While many Baptists perceived the convention as a great success, some fundamentalists felt uneasy with the compromises. The third pre-convention conference on the topic of ecclesiology met before the Indianapolis convention in June 1922. The pre-convention conference revealed two diverging strategies about how to deal with modernists and rationalists in the convention. One group, led by William Bell Riley, argued that the legislation of a creed as a test of faith provided the only practical means by which to determine the boundaries of church identity. However, the executive committee of the Baptist Fundamentals movement, including J. C. Massee, disagreed, maintaining that dismantling the autocratic structures of the denomination remained a top priority. Massee supported a two-year commission to study the creation of a modern confession of orthodox Baptist faith to present to the NBC. Ultimately, Riley's supporters outflanked Massee's and resolved that the Convention should approve the

---

[39] Anonymous, "Fourteenth Annual Meeting of the Northern Baptist Convention," *Baptist* 2/22 (2 July 1921): 692–93.

[40] Anonymous, "A Storm Precipitated," *Watchman-Examiner* 9/27 (7 July 1921): 844.

[41] Anonymous, "Let Us Now Fall into Line," *Watchman-Examiner* 9/46 (17 November 1921): 1453.

New Hampshire Confession as a standard of Baptist faith. However, liberals under the leadership of Cornelius Woelfkin, pastor of Riverside Baptist Church in New York City, had planned for just such a contingency.

When Riley moved that the 1922 convention adopt the New Hampshire Confession, Woelfkin outmaneuvered him and offered a substitution declaring the New Testament as the sufficient statement of Baptist faith and practice. After a heated debate Woelfkin's motion carried by a vote of 1,264 to 637.[42] Laws was impressed and bemused by Woelfkin's parliamentary agility, writing that "General Woelfkin put General Massee to shame when it came to mobilizing forces. The liberals fought like well-trained regulars, the fundamentalists like raw recruits."[43] This setback, however, revealed a deeper split within the fundamentalists' ranks between those who believed in the feasibility of denominational loyalty and those who increasingly believed that fellowship with liberals was untenable.

The outcome of the Indianapolis convention infuriated many fundamentalists, who began to question the viability of the Baptist Fundamentals leadership. By September 1922, William Pettingill of Philadelphia, Pennsylvania, O. W. Van Osdel of Grand Rapids, Michigan, and R. E. Neighbor of Elyria, Ohio, made a public call for the creation of a new fundamentalist organization, the Baptist Bible Union. By 1923 the union had added T. T. Shields, J. Frank Norris, A. C. Dixon, and William Bell Riley to its ranks. John Roach Straton eventually aligned his newly created Fundamentalist League of Greater New York with the union as well.

The Baptist Bible Union was far more ambivalent about denominational connection than the Conference on Baptist Fundamentals. While the broadly North American character of the Bible Union reflected this ambivalence, the premillennialism espoused by the majority of the union's leaders certainly contributed to this feeling as well. In fact, the Bible Union's first creed included a premillennial plank; however, Riley argued that the premillennial statement should be removed so that non-premillennial but

---

[42] *Annual of the Northern Baptist Convention 1922 containing the Proceeding of the Fifteenth Meeting Held at Indianapolis, Indiana June 14 to 20, 1922* (New York: American Baptist Publication Office, 1922) 134; cf. George M. Marsden, *Fundamentalism and American Culture: The Shaping of Twentieth-Century Evangelicalism, 1870–1925* (New York: Oxford University Press, 1980) 172.

[43] Curtis Lee Laws, "Convention Highlights," *Watchman-Examiner* 10/26 (29 June 1922): 802.

sympathetic Baptists could join the movement in good conscience.[44] Removing the premillennial statement not only allowed the dynamic T. T. Shields to become a leader in the organization, but it also reflected Riley's optimism that the Baptist Bible Union would become the new voice for Baptist fundamentalists, of whom many were not premillennialists. Nonetheless, the core constituency of the Bible Union held premillennial convictions. As noted previously, American premillennialism typically demanded doctrinal purity in principle and allowed association within denominational affiliation for practical ends. Theoretically, the Bible Union allowed its members to belong to an organization that maintained the true faith, as it attempted to gain control of denominational machinery for practical ends. Realistically, however, the core membership's premillennialism planted a seed of separation.

Even with no premillennial doctrinal statement, the initial call for the creation of the Bible Union revealed a willingness to forego denominational loyalties as a founding principle. The union's "Call" highlighted that Baptist denominations found themselves under the grip of modernist-dominated "ecclesiasticism" that "has forced the Orthodox into an unholy and God-forbidden alliance with the Heterodox."[45] True Bible-believing Baptists, they concluded, must create a fellowship based upon right doctrine. A cartoon in J. Frank Norris's *Searchlight* concisely depicted their self-perception well: the fundamentalist battering ram (the Bible) cracking the towering brick wall of evolution, ecclesiasticism, closed policy, centralization, and autocracy.[46] The "Call" also revealed its authors' conviction that the minimal prerequisite for religious cooperation was doctrinal agreement. The stated aims of the movement, therefore, included opposing federative and denominational enterprises that included collusion with those of suspect faith. Furthermore, the Bible Union's manifesto intimated the union's willingness to support missionary and educational activities outside of current denominational structures.[47] Ultimately, practical separation became a reality. The Bible Union called for the

---

[44] Executive Committee of the Baptist Bible Union of North America, *A Call to Arms* (N.p.: n.p., n.d.) 19. Cf. Robert George Delnay, "A History of the Baptist Bible Union," Th.D. dissertation, Dallas Theological Seminary, 1963, 51–52.

[45] Anonymous, "The Baptist Bible Union of America: A Call," *Searchlight* 5/42 (1 September 1922): 3.

[46] Anonymous, *Searchlight* 8/52 (13 November 1925): 1.

[47] Anonymous, "Call," 3.

withholding of funds from denominational agencies, supported their own missionary union, and patronized nondenominational Bible schools and institutes.[48] The 1923 convention responded to Bible Union threats by passing a resolution denying representation to congregations that did not financially support at least one of the NBC's agencies. This only pushed the Bible Union further down the path of separation.

The Bible Union further polarized the NBC, especially with its tactics and stunts. John Roach Straton, for example, attempted to stop President W. H. P. Faunce of Brown University from taking the podium to deliver the convention sermon in 1924. Delegates booed Straton from the floor.[49] More important, however, the Bible Union split the ranks of the fundamentalists within the NBC by intentionally and directly competing with the Conference on Fundamentals. The Bible Union held its own pre-convention conferences and in 1924 made its conference overlap with the Fundamentals Conference's call to prayer before the Milwaukee convention. Having divided the fundamentalist forces, the Bible Union did not possess the political strength to determine NBC policies. Worse, its aggressive tactics helped precipitate several fundamentalist-modernist compromises to preserve the institutions of the NBC. Despite its claim that "the Union has been organized to preserve our beloved denomination," its policy of "no compromise with Modernism within the denomination" meant that each successive failure made schism the logical trajectory of their organization.[50] After a decade of disappointment, most of the Bible Union's small number of congregations withdrew from the Convention, in 1932 founding their own denomination, the General Association of Regular Baptists.

Modernists, such as Harry Emerson Fosdick and Cornelius Woelfkin, also manifested the logic of separation in their theology and practice. In the *Ladies Home Journal* Fosdick argued that the liberal "in his emphasis is utterly careless of sectarian distinctions. He is by conviction and ideal an interdenominationalist."[51] He also mirrored this trans-denominational

---

[48] The Bible Union eventually bought Des Moines University to create their own school in 1927. See Delnay, "Baptist Bible Union," 180–236, and anonymous, "Modernist Foes Acquire College," *New York Times*, 13 June 1927, 12.

[49] Anonymous, "Baptists in Uproar Silence Dr. Straton," *New York Times*, 24 May 1924, 1.

[50] The Baptist Bible Union of North America, *Information Concerning the Baptist Bible Union of North America with By-Laws and Aims* (n.p., n.d.) 9–10.

[51] Harry Emerson Fosdick, "What Christian Liberals Are Driving At?" *Ladies Home Journal* 42/1 (January 1925): 131.

conviction in practice, serving as the pastor of First Presbyterian Church in
New York City. A lightning rod for controversy, Fosdick always created
news for the press and galvanized the ire of fundamentalists. He once called
Rabbi Stephen Wise "the best Christian in New York," to which statement
the rabbi wryly quipped that Fosdick "seemed to know as little about New
York as he does about Presbyterian doctrine."[52] The *Watchman-Examiner*
noted with disdain that while the secular press insisted on attaching
"Baptist" to his name, "Dr. Fosdick holds these relations lightly and
frequently goes out of his way to speak of them slightingly."[53]

Yet Fosdick's controversial actions, rather than attempts to gain media
attention, were consistent with his vision of the church. In his Cole Lectures
at Vanderbilt University, Fosdick claimed that "one of the crucial problems
of American religious life" was the issue of ecclesiology. Fosdick rejected an
exclusivist conception of the church, advocated by those who claimed

> that we are the true church; that we have the true doctrines and the true
> practices as no other Church possesses them; that we are constituted as a
> Church just because we have these uniquely true opinions and practices; that
> all we in the Church agree about these opinions and that when we joined the
> Church gave allegiance to them; that nobody has any business to belong to
> our Church unless he agrees with us; that there are people outside the
> Church who disagree, they ought to be kept outside and if there are people in
> the Church who come to disagree, they ought to be put outside.[54]

Such an ecclesiology, argued Fosdick, limited one's view of God and
the ability of the church to carry out her mission to the world. Over and
against this view Fosdick promoted an "inclusivist" vision of the church,
suggesting

> that the Christian Church ought to be the organizing center for all the
> Christian life of a community; that the Church is not based upon theological
> uniformity but upon devotion to the Lord Jesus, to the life with God and
> man for which he stood, and to the work which he gave us to do; that
> wherever there are people who have that spiritual devotion, who possess that
> love, who want more of it, who desire to work and worship with those

---

[52] Anonymous, "Fosdick Calls Wise 'Best Christian,'" *New York Times*, 4
February 1925, 18; cf. anonymous, "Current Events," *Our Hope* 31/11 (May 1925):
674.

[53] Anonymous, "Dr. Fosdick on Baptism," *Watchman-Examiner* 13/12 (19 March
1925): 358.

[54] Harry Emerson Fosdick, *Christianity and Progress* (New York: Fleming H.
Revell Company, 1922) 232.

kindred Christian aspirations, they belong inside the family of the Christian Church.[55]

Such a vision, however, ultimately disavowed denominational commitments. Indeed, exclaimed Fosdick, "what wonder that multitudes of our youth, waking up to the facts about our vast and growing universe, conclude that it is too big to be managed by the tribal god of a Protestant sect!"[56]

Fosdick's "inclusivist" ecclesiology also caused him to question publicly many cherished Baptist practices. His avocation of "open membership" for those not baptized ultimately spawned controversy on the national level. Fosdick and his colleague and friend Cornelius Woelfkin argued that membership in a Baptist church should be made on a profession of faith rather than a ritual like baptism.[57] John Roach Straton, irritated by such a public claim, demanded that the New York Baptist Ministers' Association reaffirm its conviction in the necessity of baptism by immersion. The association voted that because it was a not legislative body it had no ability to reaffirm doctrine. This left open the question of whether a non-Baptist might be elected as a delegate to the national convention. The logic of Fosdick's conviction was clear: "If I had my way baptism would be altogether an individual affair. Any one who wanted to be immersed, I would gladly immerse. Any one who wanted to be sprinkled, I would glad sprinkle. If any one was a Quaker and had conscientious scruples against any ritual, I would gladly without baptism welcome him on confession of faith. Why not?"[58] When Cornelius Woelfkin retired from Park Avenue Church, the congregation called Fosdick as its minister. This meant that if his principles became the policy of the church, a non-baptized Christian could be a delegate at the NBC. In principle, adult baptism manifested the Baptist ecclesiological conviction that the church consisted of the voluntary association of competent souls. By diminishing this practice, Fosdick ultimately questioned how one defined church membership in a Baptist church; he questioned what it meant to be a Baptist church.

Both the Baptist Bible Union and the actions of Park Avenue Church helped all the parties see that the logic of separation was the most serious

---

[55] Ibid., 233.

[56] Ibid., 235.

[57] Ibid. Cf. anonymous, "Immersion Fight Lost by Straton," *New York Times*, 19 May 1925, 8.

[58] This passage is quoted from Fosdick's farewell sermon at First Presbyterian Church New York City on 2 March 1925. Quoted in "Dr. Fosdick on Baptism," 358.

threat to denominational integrity and efficiency. Therefore, between 1923 and 1926 the Northern Baptist Convention adapted its ecclesial structures and practice to accommodate the majority of fundamentalists, liberals, and traditionalists while rejecting separatist impulses. The 1923 Atlantic City convention had not only denied representation against congregations that did not financially support NBC agencies, but also approved of the designation of gifts to specific ministries.[59] Furthermore, the convention abolished the General Board of Promotion and replaced it with a much more broadly representative Board of Missionary Cooperation.[60] The delegates clearly voted for policies that rejected separation and encouraged board, inclusive cooperation within the denomination. The Bible Union had its peak of influence the following year at the Milwaukee convention. Straton argued for an investigation into the orthodoxy of the Baptist Missions and Riley presented an alterative course of study to the alleged modernist course demanded of Baptist seminarians. Both resolutions passed.[61]

Controversy once again erupted at the 1925 Seattle convention as representatives of the Bible Union attempted to block Park Avenue Baptist Church's delegation because of its pastor's promotion of an "open membership" policy for those not baptized. Because the church had just announced its call to Harry Emerson Fosdick as its minister beginning in October to replace the retiring Cornelius Woelfkin, C. S. Shank, chair on the Committee on Enrollment, protested the seating of Park Avenue delegates. Ultimately the convention voted to overrule Shank's protest because Fosdick, who promoted open membership himself, had not officially begun his duties and therefore did not officially represent the church. The committee of nine, on which J. C. Massee served, reported that the mission field was doctrinally sound except for a few bad apples.[62] Following the

---

[59] Anonymous, "Peace Reigns at Baptist Meeting," New York Times, 25 May 1923, 11.

[60] Anonymous, "Chicago University Freed by Baptists," New York Times, 27 May 1923, 10.

[61] Annual of the Northern Baptist Convention 1924 containing the Proceeding of the Seventeenth Meeting Held at Milwaukee, Wisconsin 28 May to 3 June 1924 (New York: American Baptist Publication Office, 1924) 267–72, 529–38. Cf. anonymous, "Northern Baptist Convention Orders Missions Inquiry," Washington Post, 30 May 1924, 3.

[62] Anonymous, "Baptist Conflict Looms at Seattle," New York Times, 1 July 1925, 2.

adoption of the report, above hisses of contempt Bible Union member W. B. Hinson of Portland, Oregon, offered a resolution that all missionaries not subscribing to New Testament faith (defined in twelve doctrinal principles) be recalled from the field. The resolution was tabled until the next day.[63] When consideration resumed, R. V. Meigs of Illinois (reminiscent of the 1922 Indianapolis convention) offered a substitute motion that acknowledged some missionaries had departed from traditional Baptist faith and that encouraged the foreign missions board to take action that would best conserve denominational interests. The substitution passed by a strong margin.[64]

After the defeat of the Hinson resolution, fundamentalists from the Bible Union resorted to personal attacks against modernist leader Cornelius Woelfkin. J. J. Ross demanded that Woelfkin's name be removed from a slate of candidates for a Ministers and Missionary Benefit Board. Woelfkin withdrew his name only to have it reinstated on the ballot on the motion of fundamentalist F. O. Belden of California.[65] Non-Bible Union fundamentalists not only disliked the aggressive attacks by unioners, but also believed that unioners' uncivil actions promoted divisiveness and undermined reasonable attempts to preserve denominational interests. In effect, the union's actions had pushed these fundamentalists toward the traditionalist camp. A group of primarily West Coast fundamentalists with traditionalist proclivities, led by J. W. Brougher and including F. O. Belden, offered a resolution to amend the NBC's constitution by defining a Baptist church as "one accepting the New Testament as its guide and composed only of Baptized believers, baptism being by immersion."[66] This they hoped would close the door on the "open membership" policy promoted by Fosdick, Woelfkin, and Park Avenue Church by promoting traditional Baptist ecclesiology.

The threat of schism loomed large at the conclusion of the Seattle convention. However, the aggressive tactics and separatist sensibilities of the Baptist Bible Union left a bad taste in the mouths of other fundamentalists.

---

[63] Anonymous, "Modernist Issue Raised Before North Baptists," *New York Herald Tribune*, 2 July 1925, 9.

[64] *Annual of the Northern Baptist Convention 1925 containing the Proceeding of the Eighteenth Meeting Held at Seattle, Washington June 30 to July 5, 1925* (New York: American Baptist Publication Office, 1924) 174–75.

[65] Ibid., 243–44.

[66] Ibid., 244–45.

Frank M. Goodchild felt compelled to differentiate the Bible Union from the Baptist Fundamentals movement. By November the Bible Union had shown its separatist stripes by officially severing its commitments with the American Baptist Foreign Missions Board and supporting an independent organization. J. C. Massee and J. W. Brougher became convinced that the controversy between fundamentalists and modernists was irreparably harming the mission enterprise of the NBC. In fact, their fears were well founded. Over the course of the previous five years the mission's budget had dropped from $11,000,000 to $5,000,000.[67] However, Brougher and Massee were not willing to capitulate to the non-sectarian separatism represented by the "open membership" policy of Fosdick, Rockefeller, and Park Avenue Church. As it turned out, many modernists were on the same page.

On 13 March 1926 sixty-eight Baptist leaders met in Chicago to forge a compromise. J. W. Brougher, J. C. Massee, M. P. Boyton, Judge F. W. Freedman, John Snape, John Roach Straton, and George W. Taft (among others) represented fundamentalist interests. Notable liberals such as L. C. Barnes, James C. Colgate, W. H. Geistweit, and Charles W. Gilkey also came to the table. A. L. Abbott, chairman of the Convention Law Committee, attended to advise the group constitutionality of any policy resolution to which they committed. These leaders, despite their different theological persuasions, shared a common commitment to the interests of the NBC as a denomination. After a day of debate and discussion they forged a new compromise resolution to be presented at the Washington convention the following May:

> Believing that the Northern Baptist Convention ought to devote its energies more completely to increased efficiency in its efforts for the evangelization of the world, in order that the day may be hastened when kingdoms of this world shall become the kingdom of our Lord and of his Christ, we recommend that when the amendment proposed at the Convention at Seattle is presented for consideration at the Washington, it be laid upon the table; and
>
> That the executive committee be requested to present the Convention for adoption the following standing resolution: The Northern Baptist Convention recognizes its constituency as consisting solely of those Baptist churches in which immersion of believers is recognized as the only Scriptural

---

[67] Anonymous, "Baptists Argue Immersion Test," *Boston Globe*, 25 May 1926, 15.

baptism; and The Convention hereby declares that only immersed members will be recognized as delegates to the Convention.[68]

The importance of the "Chicago compromise," as it was soon labeled, included its emphasis on cooperation and rejection of separatist impulses at work within the NBC. Inclusive in terms of doctrinal commitments, the resolution nonetheless rejected positions that either on the one hand denigrated the missionary agencies or policies of the denomination or on the other coerced the convention to recognize open membership.

The Baptist Bible Union predictably condemned the compromise. Straton, in fact, reversed his opinion within a week from his "yes" vote in Chicago. Straton and J. Frank Norris addressed the Bible Union, declaring that wealthy modernists such as J. D. Rockefeller, Jr. and Marshall Field used their influence and money to the "mammonize the Baptist church."[69] Further, Frank M. Goodchild, who replaced Massee as the head of the Baptist Fundamentals group, rejected the compromise as well. He also spoke before the Bible Union, denouncing the compromise as the beginning of the NBC's gradual disintegration.[70] Because he was president of the Baptist Fundamentals movement, Goodchild's rejection was a blow to the compromise. Newsmen noted the calm exterior of the convention's opening while hungrily waiting to report on the conflict they hoped boiled under the surface.

Brougher gave the convention's keynote address and made a plea for harmony. He declared that "extreme fundamentalists" and "extreme modernists" did not represent the sentiments or interests of the majority of Northern Baptists. The majority of Baptists, he claimed, had tired of the conflict within the denomination:

> They [the majority of Baptists] are irritated by the continual discussions in our convention; they are disgusted with the fighting attitude of both extreme Modernists and extreme Fundamentalists; they are weary of fractious talk and fractional dissentions. Their sympathies and activities are wholly given to putting over the program of our denomination and if they have their way they would put the extreme Modernists and extreme Fundamentalists

---

[68] Anonymous, "A Chicago Conference," *Watchman-Examiner* 14/16 (22 April 1926) 497.

[69] Anonymous, "Baptists Assail Rockefeller Gifts," *New York Times*, 22 May 1926, 20.

[70] Anonymous, "Baptists Threaten to Divide the Church," *New York Times*, 25 May 1926, 29.

into a room together, lock the door, throw the key away and let them argue and fight to their hearts content while the rest of us go on with the main and important work of the Kingdom.[71]

Brougher's keynote provided a rallying point for the compromisers. The following day he moved that the amendment to the bylaws, which he had authored in Seattle, be tabled. Having succeeded in tabling the amendment, Brougher moved that the Chicago compromise be adopted as a standing resolution. Riley countered with a substitute resolution that again defined Baptist churches as those that required baptism by immersion of all members.[72] After hours of debate the convention delegates voted against Riley's substitution 2,020 to 1,084, immediately after which the Brougher resolution was adopted. The following day, the NBC rewarded Brougher for his efforts by electing him as president of the NBC. J. C. Massee then proposed a six-month truce from doctrinal controversy so that the Convention could "devote itself, its energies, interests, agencies, machinery, and resources, exclusively to the business of winning lost souls."[73] Although Bible Union leaders such as Riley and Straton balked at Massee's proposed truce, the convention adopted it by a wide margin.

Bible Unioners predictably argued that the compromises made in Washington were a sell-out of truth to modernity. However, the compromisers defended their actions. Gordon H. Baker, an original participant in the 1920 Baptist Fundamentals Conference, argued that the compromises were indicative of wisdom rather than traitorousness:

At last the fundamentalists have started on the road to victory, but let it be remembered they have only started. When the proper time comes we shall take another step up the ladder. We must remember that it is not simply a question of fundamentalists climbing the ladder; we must lift the whole denomination with us and that is no easy task. ...They must be educated, reasoned with, and prayed into submission and loyalty to Jesus Christ. This

---

[71] Anonymous, "Northern Baptists Hear Harmony Plea," *New York Times*, 26 May 1926, 16.

[72] Anonymous, *Annual of the Northern Baptist Convention 1926 containing the Proceeding of the Nineteenth Meeting Held at Washington, D. C. May 25–30, 1926* (New York: American Baptist Publication Office, 1926), 80–81.

[73] Anonymous, "Dr. Massee Leads Baptists to Peace," *Boston Globe*, 29 May 1926, 12.

method may not appeal to the extreme belligerent fundamentalist, but it is a much more effective way to reach our goal.[74]

Baker's views represented well the position of many fundamentalists who deeply valued the denomination that had nurtured them. Massee also defended his actions at Washington by stating that coercion was neither prudent nor properly Baptist. He insisted that one ought to contend for the faith once delivered while letting one's moderation be known to all men.[75]

The promised counterattack of the Bible Union, however, did not amount to much in the end. Just after the convention, Bible Union leader J. Frank Norris was indicted on murder charges for shooting a man in his office. Shields and Jarvis Street Baptist church were expelled from the Toronto Bible Union. Straton faced problems in his own congregation over his alleged "Pentecostalism" and bad press because of his connection with the Supreme Kingdom, a Klan-affiliated antievolution league. Straton died a year later. Frank M. Goodchild, perhaps the Baptist Fundamentals leader most sympathetic with the Bible Union, died in 1928. The union's purchase and poor management of Des Moines College in 1927 ended in a public embarrassment. In 1932 several congregations affiliated with the Bible Union left the NBC with little fanfare and almost no notice to form the General Association of Regular Baptists. With great disappointment, leaders such as Robert Ketchum could not even persuade Riley to leave the NBC. Never giving up hope that his denomination might return to traditional faith, Riley himself remained in the NBC and created a fundamentalist "empire" in Minnesota.[76] Because of his grass-roots campaign, fundamentalists eventually dominated the state convention but never the national convention.[77]

Before the 1926 Washington convention, Elmer William Powell proclaimed, "Unbelievable! But it is a fact: a Baptist church has never been defined."[78] While Powell's statement was certainly exaggerated, it captured the art of ecclesiological compromise between modernists, fundamentalists,

---

[74] Gordon H. Baker, "Did the Fundamentalists Sell Out at Washington?" *Watchman-Examiner* 14/27 (22 July 1926): 906.

[75] J. C. Massee, "An Interesting Letter," *Watchman-Examiner* 14/35 (16 September 1926): 1162.

[76] William Vance Trollinger, *God's Empire: William Bell Riley and Midwestern Fundamentalism* (Madison: University of Wisconsin Press, 1990) 60–61.

[77] Ibid., 108–32.

[78] Elmer William Powell, "What Is a Baptist Church?" *Christian Century* 43/14 (8 April 1926): 446.

and traditionalists that culminated in Washington. Over the course of the previous seven years, modernists with traditionalist inclinations created centralized denominational structures to usher in with efficiency the kingdom of God on earth through the guidance of the Holy Spirit. Fundamentalists fought to promote a soul-saving, biblically grounded faith through evangelism and holiness of living in preparation for Christ's return. Traditionalists wanted to promote and protect denominational interests for the glory of God. The NBC ultimately developed an ecclesiology in practice that preserved traditional Baptist ecclesiology, including soul competency, congregational independency, and adult baptism. At the same time, modernists and fundamentalists shaped that traditional ecclesiology, creating a structure centralized enough to carry out efficiently denominational interests while unstructured enough to allow many fundamentalists to cooperate with easier consciences.

CHAPTER 8

Case Study:
The Disciples of Christ, 1919–1928

Denominational centralization and fund drives also helped spark controversy in the Disciples of Christ. The controversies, however, unfolded a bit differently than in the NBC because of the peculiarities of the Disciples' traditional ecclesiological concernsThe Disciples' idea of the church was decisively shaped by its development from early-nineteenth-century restoration movements. In other words, Disciples, like early-nineteenth-century restorationist leaders Barton Stone, Thomas Campbell, and Alexander Campbell, wished to restore the church to its original, divinely ordained shape as depicted in the New Testament. Throughout their history Disciples typically argued that the New Testament revealed the church as a local congregation with pastors, elders, deacons, and deaconesses. Membership in the church, they argued, required a profession of faith in Jesus as the Son of God and a subsequent baptism by immersion. Finally, because the local congregation constituted the highest ecclesiastical authority and because the Bible revealed that Jesus required church unity among Christians, Disciples typically repudiated official denominational affiliations and called themselves simply "Christians" or "disciples of Christ." The evil of denominationalism was two-fold: it subverted the authority of the Scriptures and the lordship of Jesus over the local church. Denominations, by distinguishing themselves on creeds and structures that were extra-biblical, undermined the liberty of Christian individuals on matters on which the Bible is silent. Disciples fondly claimed that "where the Scriptures speak we speak; where they are silent we are silent." By the early twentieth century, therefore, Disciples often identified several distinctive characteristics of their restorationist "plea," including anti-denominationalism, congregational polity, baptism by immersion as a requirement for church membership, the promotion of church unity, scriptural authority, and liberty of conscience on all matter outside of the Scriptures.[1]

Restorationism in the Disciples of Christ, with its principled anti-denominationalism, of course, complicates this discussion. One might reasonably question whether the Disciples should be considered in this study since they claim not to be a denomination. For this reason Richard T. Hughes doubted whether the restoration impulse in the Christian family of churches could even be classified as evangelical.[2] However, Alfred Thomas DeGroot, in his study on the sources of division among Disciples, argued that despite their theological proclivities, during the late nineteenth and early twentieth centuries they developed "toward a restoration denomination."[3] This very fact eventually caused problems for many Disciples. Ecclesiologically, what was at stake for traditional restorationists was not whether their denomination functioned properly as the true church but whether they had become a denomination and therefore relinquished any legitimate claim to be the church.

Disciples during this period had warrant to believe that their churches functioned like other Protestant denominations. Between 1890 and 1920 they created centralized bureaucratic structures, participated in federated movements like the Interchurch World Movement, and on the mission field

---

[1] A nice example of this can be found in Peter Ainslie, "The Message of the Disciples of Christ," *World Call* 1/3 (March 1919): 23–24. See also Mark Collis, "The Crisis in Missions," *Christian Standard* 57/11 (10 December 1921): 3.

[2] Richard T. Hughes, "Why Restorationists Don't Fit the Evangelical Mold; Why Churches of Christ Increasingly Do," in *Re-forming the Center: American Protestantism, 1900 to the Present*, ed. Douglas Jacobsen and William Vance Trollinger (Grand Rapids: William B. Eerdmans Publishing Company, 1998) 194–213. Hughes examines the Christian Churches rather than the Disciples of Christ in this piece; however, the criticism would seem to apply equally to the "strict restorationist" party in the Disciples. In another work, Hughes argued that the Disciples of Christ valued the ecumenism of Alexander Campbell above his restorationist views, upon which the Christian Churches centered; however, given the strong restorationist agenda of many Disciples, especially those connected with the *Christian Standard*, this division is too neat. See "Are Restorationists Evangelicals?" in *The Variety of American Evangelicalism*, ed. Donald W. Dayton and Robert K. Johnston (Knoxville: University of Tennessee Press, 1991) 113.

[3] Alfred Thomas DeGroot, *The Ground of Divisions among the Disciples of Christ* (Chicago: privately printed, 1940) 199.

practiced (if covertly) open membership of the unimmersed. What this suggests is that the denominational model suggested by DeGroot was being seriously entertained by many Disciples (some liberals even freely acknowledged the group's denominational status). Furthermore, the practical effects of centralization and cooperative efforts with other Northern evangelicals made the Disciples of Christ function like their evangelicals coreligionists in the Protestant establishment. In the words of Ronald E. Osburn, Disciples could be ironically characterized as "making into the mainline just at the time of its disestablishment."[4]

Like Northern Baptists, the Disciples of Christ had three identifiable parties that participated in their conflict. As early as 1926, Edward Scribner Ames, dean of the Disciples Divinity House at the University of Chicago, had recognized among the Disciples of Christ three parties he labeled fundamentalists, experimentalists, and institutionalists.[5] According to Ames, fundamentalists held to a fixed body of doctrine while experimentalists "believe not so much in revelation as in discovery and a creative continuing process of knowledge and faith." Institutionalists, he argued, valued expediency and compromise between the other two groups in order to preserve the church and its constituted agencies. Ames did not single out the Disciples for this typology; nonetheless, his typology describes his coreligionists uncannily. Historian Mark Toulouse described the parties within the Disciples using the terms "strict restorationists," "progressives," and "moderate restorationists," which, for all intents and purposes lined up with the groups identified by Ames.[6]

Adhering to a biblical literalism, strict restorationists, who simply called themselves "restorationists," argued that the New Testament alone could dictate the shape of the church and its mission. In essence, strict restorationists understood the church as a voluntary association of those individuals submitting themselves to the authority of their one Lord, one faith, and one baptism. They also voiced alarm at the "rationalism" and

---

[4] Ronald E. Osburn, "The Irony of the Twentieth-Century Christian Church (Disciples of Christ): Making it to the Mainline Just at the Time of Its Disestablishment," *Mid-Stream* 28/4 (July 1989): 293, 296–98.

[5] Edward Scribner Ames, "A Vital Church," *Christian Century* 43/7 (18 February 1926): 219.

[6] Mark Toulouse, "Practical Concern and Theological Neglect: The UCMS and the Open Membership Controversy," in *A Case Study of Mainstream Protestantism: The Disciples' Relation to American Culture, 1880–1989*, ed. D. Newell Williams (Grand Rapids: William B. Eerdmans Publishing Company, 1991) 197.

"ecclesiasticism" they perceived to be growing forces among Disciples. In particular, they believed that "open membership," or the allowing of unimmersed Christians to participate in the same manner as immersed members of the local congregation, threatened the very ecclesiological nature of the restorationist plea.

George Marsden argued that, because of their peculiar concerns, strict restorationist were really sympathetic but distant cousins to fundamentalists.[7] Nonetheless, while strict restorationists typically rejected premillennialism and suggested that denominational fundamentalists were, because of their affiliations, "out of harmony with the New Testament idea of the church of Christ," their concerns closely mirrored the understanding of church mission and identity professed by fundamentalists in denominations.[8] Kevin R. Kragenbrink showed that strict restorationists not only had sympathies with fundamentalists in denominations but gradually after 1925 cultivated those trans-denominational ties. He also convincingly noted that in the 1920s these conservative Disciples "entered the mainstream of Protestant religious debate, often leading the campaign to keep America Christian."[9] One can add that the *Christian Standard*, a periodical that voiced the position of the strict restorationists, printed articles by William Jennings Bryan, Clarence E. Macartney, W. H. Griffith Thomas, and William Bell Riley well before 1925.[10] One can also find

---

[7] George M. Marsden, *Fundamentalism and American Culture: The Shaping of Twentieth-Century Evangelicalism, 1870–1925* (New York: Oxford University Press, 1980) 178.

[8] Anonymous, "Our Relation to the Fundamentalists," *Christian Standard* 57/51 (16 September 1922): 10. Cf. Stewart G. Cole, *The History of Fundamentalism* (New York: Richard R. Smith, Inc, 1931)155. Interestingly, the *Christian Standard*, which voiced the concerns of strict restorationists, notably opened its pages to Baptist William B. Riley and Presbyterian William Jennings Bryan and acknowledged that the World's Christian Fundamentals Association was a good and important institution. Because restorationists saw Riley and Bryan as embodying "fundamentalism," it is understandable why they often associated the movement with creeds and confessions rather than the New Testament.

[9] Kragenbrink makes the point that sympathies and participation in the antievolution crusades show this commitment to American culture most clearly. See Kevin R. Kragenbrink, "The Modernist/Fundamentalist Controversy and the Emergence of the Independent Christian Churches of Christ," *Restorationist Quarterly* 42/1 (first quarter 2000): 17.

[10] William Jennings Bryan, "The Bible the Word of God," *Christian Standard* 56/43 (23 July 1921): 2453–54; Clarence Macartney, "The Fall of the Colossus,"

positive reviews of the World's Christian Fundamentals Association, an appreciation of the ecclesiology of the Plymouth Brethren, and an advertisement for the Scofield reference Bible.[11] By the time of the 1927 North American Christian Convention, T. H. Johnson, president of Kansas Bible College, preached a sermon on the Holy Spirit showing that Keswick Holiness had influenced strict restorationists as well, although one can see some influences of Keswick as early as 1899.[12] Since Disciples were new to the "denomination game," it is not surprising that strict restorationists only gradually cultivated relationships with other evangelicals in the establishment churches. The tie between strict restorationists and other fundamentalists (particularly Baptists) are particularly highlighted in the issue of ecclesiology. Centralization, congregational independence, adherence to a literal interpretation of the Bible, and concerns about who constituted a proper church member were issues shared by fundamentalists in other denominations.

Liberal, or progressive, Disciples, particularly those associated with the *Christian Century*, the Campbell Institute, and the Disciples Divinity House at the University of Chicago, challenged what they believed to be a naïve restorationist ecclesiology in the Disciples of Christ, often freely acknowledging that they practically constituted a "denomination." The influence of the New Theology, biblical criticism, and social Christianity coupled with these Disciples' ecumenical sensibilities often placed them in

---

Christian Standard 56/23 (5 March 1921): 1977–78; and W. H. Griffith Thomas, "The Bible as an Authority," *Christian Standard* 57/42 (15 July 1922): 8.

[11] William Bell Riley, "The Peril to Christian Education," *Christian Standard* 57/52 (22 October 1921): 3–4, 6–7; Edwin R. Errett, "The Fundamentalists' Rally," *Christian Standard* 58/38 (9 June 1923): 3–4; W. S. Martin, "The Plymouth Brethren," *Christian Standard* 58/48 (1 September 1923): 4; and advertisement for the Scofield reference Bible, *Christian Standard* 55/25 (20 March 1920): 640.

[12] T. H. Johnson, "The Office of the Holy Spirit," *Christian Standard* 62/49 (3 December 1927): 3–4; J. H. Garrison, ed., *Our First Congress Consisting of Addresses on Religious and Theological Questions, During the First Congress of Disciples of Christ Held in St. Louis, April 25–27, 1899* (St. Louis: Christian Publishing Company, 1900) 111–85. See especially the addresses on the Holy Sprit by R. T. Mathews ("Crucial Points Concerning the Holy Spirit—A Review," 111–50) and W. E. Ellis ("Crucial Points Concerning the Holy Spirit: A Supplementary Statement," 151–70). Another example of Keswick pneumatology evident among strict restorationists includes Irl R. Sidwell, "The Church The New Testament Missionary Society," *Christian Standard* 62/43 (22 October 1927): 8.

the vanguard of establishment modernism.[13] They also emphasized the idea of practical unity in Christian work. Therefore, they strongly pushed for the creation of efficient centralized Disciples organizations, such as the International Convention and the United Christian Missionary Society. They also argued that Christian duty necessitated participation in federative movements with other denominations, such the Interchurch World Movement, the Federal Council of Churches, or union movement[14] on the mission field. Progressives typically adhered to the New Theology and new forms of biblical criticism. For these reasons they often underplayed the significance of doctrines or dogmas they believed not only were divisive but properly fell under the category of Christian liberty. Progressives often advocated open membership. The techniques of biblical criticism, they argued, showed that much of the Bible was open to interpretation. Biblical criticism, therefore, allowed them to claim that open membership was a matter of individual conscience rather than clear scriptural mandate.

Moderate restorationists, like progressives, wished to promote ecumenism at home and on the mission field but not at the cost of unity among their coreligionists. In effect, they maintained a balancing act to preserve their restorationist heritage (especially individual liberty of conscience and congregational independency), avoid schism, and maintain the United Christian Missionary Society (UCMS), which they believed was crucial for the practical success of the Disciples plea. Mark Toulouse argued that many "moderate restorationists" within the UCMS found themselves between a rock and a hard place flanked by strict restorationists and progressives. Unlike strict restorationists, moderate restorationists believed that the International Convention and the UCMS existed as genuine expressions of the church. They were also convinced of the practical necessity of these organizations for the effective and efficient promotion of the Disciples plea. This meant that moderate restorationists found themselves particularly sensitive about practices or creeds that might prove divisive. In the case of open membership, for example, they believed that Disciples should neither legislate against it nor practice it. To forbid or to

---

[13] Osburn argued that the recognition granted by other Protestants to these progressives signified the arrival of Disciples into the establishment. It strikes me that one might perceive the growing connections between strict restorationists and fundamentalists similarly. See Osburn, "Twentieth-Century Christian Church," 297.

[14] The union movement was a push to combine the missions resources of various and different Protestant denominations to promote efficiency and avoid duplication.

practice open membership led to division and harmed the church (represented in the International Convention and the UCMS). The moderate restorationists, therefore, believed that loyalty to legitimate church institutions displayed faithfulness to the New Testament church and the Disciples plea. They often sided with strict restorationists by helping them make centralized Disciples agencies more democratic and banning divisive practices. They also attempted to maintain peace with liberals by actively promoting Christian liberty and charity in matters of theology and doctrine.

Model 8.1
Disciples of Christ

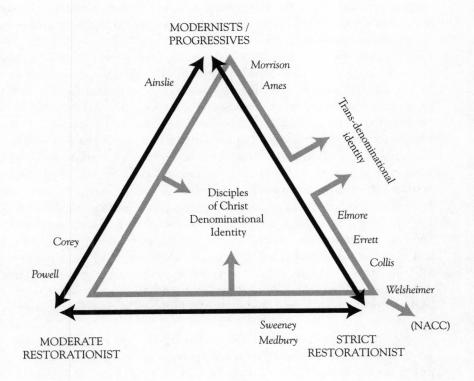

The three parties involved in the Disciples conflict each attempted to find concrete expression in their institutions and agencies. Not surprisingly, progressive Disciples like other modernists emphasized the creation of centralized denominational machinery, individual liberty in terms of doctrines and dogmas, and the promotion of practical Christian unity. Strict restorationists emphasized congregational autonomy, the voluntary nature of the church based upon a common faith and baptism, and an emphasis on soul-saving evangelism. Moderate restorationists tended to think of the newly created Disciples agencies and institutions as indispensable extensions of the church. Further, this loyalty to these institutions tended to make moderate restorationists suspicious of creed-like demands of strict restorationists and apparently divisive practices of progressives. Not surprisingly, therefore, the controversies among Disciples centered on the centralization of Disciples agencies and societies as well as the issue of open membership in the foreign missions field.

The first tremors of conflict began in 1917 when the Disciples' Kansas City convention adopted a new constitution to allow the convention to act as a clearinghouse of Disciples business on a national level.[15] Strict restorationists voiced their opposition to what they believed to be a "denominational" agenda of "ecclesiasticism" and centralization.[16] Strict restorationists rejected a proposal for a representative delegate convention and argued that all attending members of a given convention should be given the privilege to vote and make resolutions from the floor. Strict restorationists with institutionalist sympathies, such as Z. T. Sweeney, worked with other strict restorationists, especially *Christian Standard* editor Russell Errett, to create a compromise constitution. Sweeney suggested a "bi-cameral" constitution that allowed all Disciples members attending the convention a right to vote; however, a Committee on Resolutions presented all legislative proposals to the convention with their recommendation concerning its merit. The voting members then could accept, reject, or send back the resolution as presented by the committee. Sweeney's compromise won the day.

Many Disciples, like their establishment coreligionists, believed that efficient institutional consolidation and cooperation was imperative to claim practically the nation and the world for Christ. Therefore, the Kansas City

---

[15] Cole, *History of Fundamentalism*, 142.

[16] Russell Errett, "The 'Standard' vs. the 'General Convention,'" *Christian Standard* 52/2 (9 September 1916): 1686.

THE DICSIPLES OF CHRIST

convention also appointed a committee to consider the creation of a united society that could efficiently unify Disciples' efforts at home and abroad. Strict restorationists viewed the new constitution of the International Convention and the newly proposed UCMS as a betrayal of the "restorationist plea." In response, they announced in the pages of the *Christian Standard* a "Campaign for New Testament Evangelism," an effort to remind Disciples of their true "restorationist" mission and identity. One hundred ninety subscribers wrote to the *Standard* to express their support for the program.[17] One of the campaign coordinators, W. H. Book of Columbus, Ohio, declared that one of the goals of the program was to counter liberal influences in the denomination. The liberals, he claimed, had not only rejected the basic truths of the New Testament but forsaken the church's mission of soul-saving evangelism: "The apostacy [sic] from New Testament evangelism in these latter days may be seen in that men have minimized the moral and spiritual forces of Christ as revealed in the New Testament, and magnified the intellectual and material forces of men as set forth in human systems of philosophy, and, in the same ratio congregations and preachers have ceased to believe in or work for the salvation of sinners as the men who were commissioned of Christ."[18] P. H. Welshimer, pastor of the large, influential First Christian Church in Canton, Ohio, wrote that the gospel of the first century must be the same gospel for the twentieth, and this meant that the Spirit regenerated the sinner who upon professing his faith in Jesus Christ was baptized by immersion in water.[19]

The proposed United Society proved a lightning rod of debate. Individuals associated with the progressive Campbell Institute pushed for the proposed merger. In response, leaders of the Campaign for New Testament Evangelism waged a propaganda war against the United Society in the pages of the *Christian Standard* by identifying the UCMS and the members of the Campbell Institute with Baptist "modernists" at the University of Chicago, such as Shailer Mathews.[20] According to strict restorationist P. H. Welshimer, the consolidation would prove disastrous

---

[17] C. J. Sharp, "Campaign for New Testament Evangelism," *Christian Standard* 53/11 (15 December 1917): 331–36, 402–404.

[18] W. H. Book, "New Testament Meetings Instead of Modern Emotional or Mechanical Revivals," *Christian Standard* 53/11 (15 December 1917): 333.

[19] P. H. Welshimer, "New Testament Evangelism," *Christian Standard* 53/18 (2 February 1918): 500.

[20] Anonymous, "The Time Has Come for Action," *Christian Standard* 53/51 (21 September 1918): 1523.

because the Campbell Institute already had its advocates in key institutional positions, including four of seven members on the board of education, seven college presidents, seven college deans, and the president and secretary of the convention.[21] The Campbell Institute responded to the attacks by printing its own literature promoting cooperative church federation, open membership, and social Christianity.[22]

The Great War prevented a 1918 convention and a vote on the creation of the UCMS. Just prior to the 1919 St. Louis convention, the *Christian Standard* published a "call" with 183 signatories decrying the proposal of agency consolidation, which it claimed would allow modernists to dominate the denomination through an "ecclesiastical machine."[23] They argued that the UCMS was a subterfuge by modernists to allow "the placing of rationalistic teachers in our colleges and pulpits, and unimmersed into our congregations."[24] Furthermore, because the convention constituted all Disciples who registered there, they hoped to create a voting bloc to defeat the measure. Russell Errett, Z. T. Sweeney, W. N. Birney, and F. D. Kershner also sponsored a pre-convention "restorationist" congress immediately before the convention. Congress speakers identified the touchstone issues that would dominate Disciples disputes for the next eight years: centralization and open membership, both issues of denominational ecclesiology. The congress passed a resolution against the practice of open membership as unbiblical and expressed the belief that it undermined the identity of the church as having only a regenerate membership.[25] The strict restorationists also insisted that adult baptism by immersion upon the profession of a conversion experience constituted the test for true membership in the church. Further, they argued that the "open" membership advocated by liberals undermined church identity as a voluntary association of converted and "Bible-believing" individuals who promoted evangelism as the primary mission of the church. Finally, the congress passed resolutions claiming that no agency in the church had the

---

[21] Cole, *History of Fundamentalism*, 143–44.

[22] Ibid., 137–38.

[23] Anonymous, "Every Loyal Disciple of Christ in America Should Attend the St. Louis Convention," *Christian Standard* 53/51 (21 September 1918): 1523–24. Cf. Lester G. McAllister and William E. Tucker, *Journey in Faith: A History of the Christian Church (Disciples of Christ)* (St. Louis: Chalice Press, 1975) 381.

[24] Anonymous, "Time Has Come."

[25] Anonymous, "Resolutions Adopted by the Restoration Congress," *Christian Standard* 55/4 (25 October 1919): 1, 6.

right to act on behalf of all Disciples in an official, authorized, or exclusive manner.[26] This thinly veiled attack on the UCMS failed to persuade the majority of the Disciples, and the convention voted for the consolidation of the various boards of the restoration movement by a large margin.

Although strict restorationists like R. E. Elmore and Russell Errett had no intention to stop their crusade against the UCMS, the conflict might have become an historical footnote had it not been for a series of editorials published by the *Christian Century* that claimed missionary George Baird and the China Mission practiced open membership.[27] C. C. Morrison, editor of the *Christian Century*, published the editorials because he personally approved of open membership and wished to promote its successful practice within the China Mission. The *Christian Standard* publicized Morrison's editorials as proof that the UCMS approved of and allowed open membership.[28] The executive committee of the Foreign Christian Missionary Society vehemently denied the veracity of the *Century*'s claims.[29] UCMS officers, while openly considering new, practical ways to promote Disciples missions in the Chinese context and participation in the ecumenical union movement among Protestants in China, had made no official pronouncements. However, R. E. Elmore (once recording secretary of the Foreign Christian Missionary Society) knew that missionaries had long experimented with cooperative efforts with Methodists, Presbyterians, and Episcopalians in China, and the *Standard* gave him great editorial leeway to impugn the activities of the UCMS and the China Mission. Worse, Frank Garrett, secretary of the Central China Mission, was aware of Baird's approval of open membership, having specifically appointed him as the keynote speaker at the 1919 Kuling Mission Convention because of his position on the issue.[30] At the convention the mission churches in China voted their approval of open

[26] Ibid.

[27] Anonymous, "A Passing Dogma," *Christian Century* 37 (26 August 1920): 6–7; anonymous, "The Disciples Foreign Society and Its Missionaries," *Christian Century* 36/39 (23 September 1920): 5–6; anonymous, "The Freedom of Missionaries," *Christian Century* 36/40 (30 September 1920): 6–7; George B. Baird, "Church Membership in China," *Christian Century* 36/44 (28 October 1920):13–14.

[28] Stephen J. Corey, *Fifty Years of Attack and Controversy: The Consequences Among Disciples of Christ* (St. Louis: Christian Board of Publication, 1953) 74.

[29] Anonymous, "A Communication," *Christian Century* 36/38 (16 September 1920): 14–15.1

[30] Toulouse, "Practical Concern," 206.

membership, and Garrett subsequently requested that the UCMS give its opinion of the practice.

The publicity of the *Christian Century* concerning open membership succeeded in catching moderate restorationist officials at the UCMS off guard and raising the ire of strict restorationists who were already bent on dismantling the United Society. Elmore and Errett rallied against open membership as a betrayal of New Testament Christianity, not to mention traditional Disciples ecclesiology. In their eyes, the apparent revelation of open membership only further impugned the UCMS, suggesting, as they saw it, that the society had unilaterally legislated an unorthodox ecclesiastical position. In other words, the UCMS undermined the restorationist plea through open membership and autocratic ecclesiasticism. The *Christian Century* argued that the strict restorationist response revealed that the two visions of the church could no longer be reconciled among the Disciples:

> The one group hopes to find unity through correct organization, correct creed, correct forms, correct formulas—correct in the sense of conforming to a pattern assumed to have been laid down once for all in the New Testament. The other group hopes to find correctness, if at all, through the practice of unity. It is willing to concede, indeed it insists, that the formal basis of unity may be progressive in character, undergoing modifications as new times make new claims upon the church and bring fresh revealings of God's will, thus continually changing the perspectives in which forms and procedures and formulas are held, and sometimes rendering them obsolete.[31]

The editor further advocated that progressives resist strict restorationist demands, even if it meant losing financial support in the short run.[32]

The 1920 Winona Lake convention responded to Garrett's request for an opinion on open membership by passing a measure popularly known as the "Medbury resolution." Fearing that the divisive nature of open membership might lead to schism, more moderate restorationists attempted to create a resolution that would placate strict restorationists. Written by C. S. Medbury, the resolution demanded that the UCMS require the Disciples' churches abroad, missionaries, and mission administrators to maintain comity with American Disciples' historical position on immersion and church membership; it explicitly rejected open membership. Further, the

---

[31] Anonymous, "What Must the Disciples Do to Be Saved?" *Christian Century* 36/42 (14 October 1920): 6–7.

[32] Ibid.

resolution noted that if in "the liberty of conscience" one could not support proper membership requirements, he should tender their resignation to the United Society.[33] Finally, the resolution required that the UCMS distribute the resolution to its missions, investigate the possible practice of open membership on the mission field, and report its findings at the next convention. Progressives interpreted the resolution as the imposition of a creed by conservatives.[34] Frank Garrett, while claiming that open membership as defined by the convention did not occur in the UCMS's China missions, worried that the resolution would damage the credibility of Disciples missionaries in China and elsewhere.[35]

Responding to progressive anxieties, the executive committee of the UCMS explained to missionaries that the resolution should in no way be interpreted as the imposition of a creed or an impinging upon individual liberty of conscience.[36] Specifically, the UCMS interpreted the resolution to mean conformity to practice not belief. At the Winona Lake convention the following year, the UCMS reported that all missions had satisfactorily conformed to the resolution. Further, two conservatives with restorationist sympathies, John T. Brown and Z. T. Sweeney, were elected to the board. R. E. Elmore, however, was less than satisfied with the report, believing that the interpretation of the Medbury Resolution by the UCMS was an outright sham. Elmore claimed that the United Society employed "a mixed policy of evasion, compromise and surrender."[37]

Strict restorationists responded to the Winona Lake convention with another restorationist congress in Louisville, Kentucky, the following December. The Louisville congress attracted close to 700 participants. Congress organizer R. C. Foster intended to rally strict restorationist forces against the United Society and the International Convention. Participants at the congress resolved, after considerable debate, to call for true restorationist congregations to disassociate themselves from the UCMS. Welshimer's Canton Church had already withdrawn support from the UCMS, dealing a serious blow to the financially struggling agency. The

---

[33] R. E. Elmore, "An Intimate Review of the China Situation," *Christian Standard* 57/1 (1 October 1921): 4.

[34] Anonymous, "The Strange Psychology of the Disciples Convention," *Christian Century* 36/45 (4 November 1920): 7.

[35] Frank Garrett, "China Missionary Hurt by Convention Demand," *Christian Century* 37/1 (6 January 1921): 20.

[36] Anonymous, "Strange Psychology," 7.

[37] Elmore, "China Situation," 3.

Canton Church gave the United Society around $14,000 per annum, which supported about nine missionaries on the field.[38] Welshimer likely spoke for many strict restorationists, noting that while he did not oppose the UCMS in principle, he could not support an organization that would not allow his church to designate its funds to programs it believed represented the true gospel of Christ.[39] Other restorationists, such as Foster, Errett, and Elmore, did not believe that the United Society could be salvaged even in principle. To this end they proposed that independent Disciples organizations open their books to auditors so that "faithful" Disciples churches could support agencies true to the restorationist causes. Further, the congress authorized a committee to investigate all free missionary agencies and educational institutions in order to validate their orthodoxy.

The Louisville congress also organized a grassroots campaign to promote its agenda, including state and regional congresses and the creation of the New Testament Tract Society. As local congresses began to spring up, strict restorationists intended to use the Tract Society, along with the sympathetic *Standard*, as propaganda. Foster argued that they needed to use the power of the printed word. Given the fact the any Disciple who registered at the International Convention became a voting member, the propaganda strategy certainly seemed sound.

The well-publicized Louisville congress coupled with the withdrawal of financial support forced the UCMS's board of managers to attempt to negotiate between missionaries and the strict restorationists. In fact, the financial situation of the UCMS was critical. The United Society ended its fiscal year with a $271,717 deficit and several congregations promised no future funds.[40] Newly elected UCMS board members John T. Brown and Z. T. Sweeney worked to promote compromise. Brown used his personal capital among strict restorationists to promote cooperation with the United Society. He not only defended the UCMS against the charges of open membership on the floor of the congress in Louisville, but he also visited Welshimer personally to ask him to reconsider his congregation's

---

[38] John T. Brown, "Three Years a Member of the Executive Committee (U.C.M.S.) and Why I Resigned: Third in a Series," *Christian Standard* 59/9 (1 December 1923): 5.

[39] P. H. Welshimer, "Canton (O.) Church Withdraws Financial Support from U.C.M.S.," *Christian Standard* 57/10 (3 December 1921): 1–2

[40] Bert Wilson, "How the United Society Closed the Year," *World Call* 4/8 (August 1922): 60–61.

withdrawal of support.[41] Further, he announced that he would personally visit the missionary enterprises of the UCMS and make a report at the convention. To this end he visited India, China, and the Philippines to investigate missionary fidelity to UCMS policies. Z. T. Sweeney, in an effort to placate strict restorationist concerns, made a resolution to the UCMS board that it would not employ missionaries who were not "in sincere accord" with the policy that only "immersed penitent believers in Christ" be received as church members.[42]

The UCMS board of managers took great pains to show that strict restorationists' concerns about the United Society's infidelity to Christian principles were misplaced. They disavowed any intent to control state or local societies, repudiated federative efforts in denominational cooperation, and took steps to insure that individuals could not amass too much power within the society. However, they only reluctantly approved the Sweeney resolution. The resolution's rejection of "open membership" required almost immediate clarification. E. K. Higdon, a missionary in Manila, maintained two church roles for immersed members and active worshippers who were not members. Brown visited Higdon's congregation and claimed that the Manila church practiced open membership. Higdon balked at the accusation and requested clarification of the UCMS membership policies required by the Medbury and Sweeney resolutions.[43] Moderate restorationist leaders in the UCMS responded by arguing that the phrase "being in sincere accord" did not apply to personal opinion. The resolution, therefore, only meant the willingness to carry out the United Society's administrative policy. Furthermore, the board specifically stated that it did not wish to push the issue of open membership in a manner that promoted disunity or strife.[44]

At the 1922 Winona convention, the Sweeney resolution and the Higdon interpretation caused heated debate among modernists and strict restorationist, neither of whom approved of the legislation. In an address before the convention, Peter Ainslie pleaded for tolerance, claiming that opinions on the issue of open membership could only be determined by

---

[41] Brown, "Three Years," 5.

[42] Anonymous, "Convention Approves Action of the Board of Managers on So-called 'Sweeney Resolution,'" *Christian Standard* 57/50 (9 September 1922): 17.

[43] Corey, *Fifty Years*, 85–87.

[44] Anonymous, "Meeting of the Board of Managers of the U.C.M.S.," *Christian Standard* 57/19 (4 February 1922): 7, 15.

local congregations.[45] From the floor of the convention other progressives, including W. E. Garrison and E. S. Ames, argued against the resolution. According to Garrison, although in light of the Higdon interpretation the resolution did not constitute a creed, it still attempted to interpret to meaning of the New Testament regarding proper church membership. The resolution, therefore, undermined liberty of conscience and the "principle and genius" of the Disciples movement.[46] Ames argued that the resolution should be referred back to the committee because it failed on two counts. He claimed that the Higdon interpretation would not satisfy strict restorationists and, worse, too closely resembled a creedal statement to satisfy modernists.

The progressive arguments flabbergasted Sweeney, who noted that the resolution was administrative policy made by an agency that in no way claimed to be the church; therefore, he believed that the resolution by definition could not be a creedal statement. Strict restorationist J. B. Briney publicly supported the measure, claiming that it preserved liberty of conscience by requiring that opinions supporting open membership remain private. He reminded the convention that membership by immersion was not the divisive issue; rather, open membership had "been forced to the front and caused all of this trouble."[47] After the debate the Sweeney resolution passed with the Higdon interpretation. Furthermore, the UCMS made official its policy that financial gifts to the United Society could be designated to specific agencies and enterprises.

Ames's prediction that the Sweeney resolution would not satisfy strict restorationists or progressives proved correct. On the one hand, R. E. Elmore repudiated the Winona convention, suggesting that the Higdon interpretation took the teeth out of the resolution and that the UCMS's designation policy was a ruse by modernists to regain control of conservative money.[48] Errett and the *Standard* also reacted coolly to Winona.[49] On the other hand, progressives believed that the results of the convention had the marks of successful *Christian Standard* propaganda. Ames in particular

---

[45] Peter Ainslie, *The Disciples and Our Attitude toward Other Christians* (Baltimore: Association for the Promotion of Christian Unity, 1922) 16.

[46] Anonymous, "Convention Approves Action of the Board of Managers," 18–19.

[47] Ibid.

[48] Edwin R. Errett, "The Designation Hoax," *Christian Standard* 57/34 (20 May 1922): 5–6.

[49] Anonymous, "The 'Christian Standard's' Viewpoint," *Christian Standard* 57/53 (30 September 1922): 9, 15

believed that converting the convention to a representative delegate system might avert another Winona. The UCMS did, however, woo back some strict restorationists like Welshimer. The clarification on gift designation satisfied the Canton Church, and it cautiously reestablished financial ties with the UCMS.[50]

Between 1923 and 1924, strict restorationists and progressives continued with little success to promote their ecclesiological agendas. At the 1923 Colorado Springs convention, strict restorationists failed to block the Association for the Promotion of Christian Unity, whose board included self-professed liberals such as Ainslie and Ames, from official affiliation with the UCMS. A resolution by C. V. Dunn, president of Spokane University, calling for the cessation of "denominational nomenclature" such as "Disciples of Christ," also failed. Additionally the convention buried Ames's proposal that the convention become a representative delegation. Trouble arose, however, when the UCMS revealed in its annual report that it had accepted funds from the Men and Millions Movement to pay down about half of its continuing debt. The UCMS's debt was not only a combination of decreased revenue from churches refusing to support to United Society but also a leftover debt from the Interchurch World Movement (IWM). Strict restorationists wasted no time claiming that the UCMS and the Men and Millions Movement had broken trust with loyal Disciples by paying debts for programs and projects they did not wish to support (i.e., the IWM and the China Mission).[51] However, the complaints seemed to fall on deaf ears.

Strict restorationists were equally unsuccessful at the Cleveland convention the following year. The convention voted down three resolutions: the first attempted to strike from the Disciples Yearbook any congregation that practiced open membership; the second called for Peter Ainslie's resignation from leadership of the Association for the Promotion of Christian Unity; and the third requested the association's severance from the UCMS. The convention became so acrimonious that Z. T. Sweeney

---

[50] P. H. Welshimer, "The Canton Church and the United Society," *Christian Standard* 57/53 (30 September 1922): 8.

[51] Edwin R. Errett, "The Colorado Springs Convention," *Christian Standard* 58/51 (22 September 1923): 3–4, 9.

proposed the creation of a "peace" committee to negotiate peace between strict restorationists and the moderate restorationist UCMS leadership.[52]

The Peace Committee met twice during the year following the convention. The committee's final report called for solidarity among Disciples and recommended that "both our agencies and our brethren at odds with our agencies manifest the utmost consideration for the unity of the churches of Christ."[53] The wish to avoid divisiveness also drove the committee's condemnation of the practice of open membership. "In order to promote peace and unity" the committee recommended:

> 1. That no person be employed by the United Christian Missionary Society as its representative who has committed himself or herself to the belief in, or practice of, the reception of unimmersed persons into the membership of the churches of Christ. 2. That if any person is now in the employment of the United Christian Missionary Society as its representative who has committed himself or herself to the belief in, or practice of, the reception of unimmersed persons into the membership of the churches of Christ, the relationship of that person to the United Christian Missionary Society be severed as employee.[54]

The committee further recommended a constitutional amendment to allow that all business items brought to the convention via the Committee on Recommendations be amended from the floor. Finally, the Peace Committee acknowledged the "necessity of conference and co-operation with denominational bodies" but remarked that care should be taken to avoid interpreting the restoration movement in "denominational terms."[55]

The *Christian Standard* became so engulfed in the controversy that its editors felt they had neglected important, spiritually edifying topics. Therefore they spun off a new periodical called the *Spotlight* (later named the *Touchstone*) to tend specifically to current controversial topics. Intentionally modeled after J. Frank Norris's *Searchlight*, the *Spotlight*, under the editorial hand of Robert E. Elmore, served to "expose and counteract

---

[52] Anonymous, "Women's Jubilee Marks Disciples Convention," *Christian Century* 41/44 (30 October 1924): 1414, 1420–21. Cf. anonymous, "A Needed Committee," *Christian-Evangelist* 61/45 (6 November 1924): 6.

[53] Anonymous, "A Day-by-Day Story of the International Convention of the Disciples of Christ," *Christian-Evangelist* 62/42 (15 October 1925): 24.

[54] Ibid.

[55] Ibid. Cf. anonymous, "The Disciples Convention," *Christian Century* 42/43 (22 October 1925): 1314–15, 1322.

the evils which disturb the brotherhood" in eight pages each month.[56] The evils in question included "fostering denominationalism," "cultivating ecclesiasticism," "attempting to identify the brotherhood with a corporation," and "any and all departures from the New Testament as the supreme rule of the church."[57] In its inaugural edition, the *Spotlight* focused on the "UCMS Debacle in the Philippines." Elmore published pages of documents he alleged proved that the UCMS and its foreign secretary Stephen Corey had betrayed its contributors by secretly countenancing open membership.[58] The *Spotlight* also published, courtesy of J. Frank Norris, an undelivered address by William Jennings Bryan attacking evolution.[59] Finally, Elmore distributed a 31-page pamphlet titled "Should the United Christian Missionary Society Be Dissolved?"[60] There was no doubt what Elmore thought the answer should be.

Ironically, the Committee on Recommendations was divided about whether the Peace Committee report's demand to stop the practice of open membership amounted to an imposition of a creed. By a margin of six votes, the committee presented the peace report to the convention, recommending that the report be accepted with the exception of its statements on open membership.[61] The committee's recommendation of the peace report received vigorous debate extending over two days. Ultimately, the convention accepted the peace report as a whole and rejected the committee's recommendations.[62]

While the acceptance of the peace report helped quell strict restorationists, the convention's vote sent shock waves through the leadership of the UCMS and among modernist Disciples. The editor of the

---

[56] Anonymous, "A New Adjunct to the Standard Journalism," *Christian Standard* 60/45 (8 August 1925):1–2. The advertisement for the *Spotlight* appeared on the back cover of *Christian Standard* 60/45 (8 August 1925). Cf. Corey, *Fifty Years*, 96–101.

[57] Advertisement for *Spotlight*, in *Christian Standard*.

[58] Anonymous, "Disloyalty in the Philippines," *Spotlight* 1/1 (September 1925): 1–2; A. G. Saunders, "The Letter Suppressed by S. J. Corey," *Spotlight* 1/1 (September 1925): 3–4.

[59] William Jennings Bryan, "Shall the Religion of Materialism Be Taught in the Public Schools?" *Spotlight* 1/1 (September 1925): 5–8.

[60] R. E. Elmore, "Should the United Christian Missionary Society Be Dissolved?" (N.p.: n.p., n.d.).

[61] Anonymous, "Day-by-Day Story," 21.

[62] Ibid., 24.

Christian Century bemoaned what he perceived to be the improper ecclesiological models that allowed the acceptance of the peace report:

> The church has been victim of two vicious analogies with reference to the kingdom of God...The first is a governmental analogy: that the kingdom of God is primarily a government, with an absolute monarch, a perfect constitution of unmistakable clarity and not subject to either amendment or interpretation, and a code of laws embodied by the New testament.... The second is the economic analogy borrowed from the current practice of the business world. The church is a corporation carrying on a big business, and it is plain business sense that its operations should be controlled by those who furnish the capital.[63]

Ultimately, liberal Disciples feared that both visions of the church allowed "reactionaries" to control autocratically the agencies of the church by means of "sectarian, mechanistic" creeds and money.[64] In early December, fifty progressive Disciples met in Columbus, Ohio, to consider the "peace resolution." The members voted to inform the UCMS board of managers of "their humiliation because of the approval of the Convention of what amounts to a creedal enactment."[65] They further argued that the peace resolution would undermine the credibility of foreign missionaries and participants in ecumenical movements.

The UCMS board of managers worried about the practical implications and likely divisiveness the peace report would cause at home and abroad. In December 1925, the board of managers met in St. Louis, Missouri, in order to interpret the Oklahoma City convention's demands. Although the board did not explicitly reveal its theological underpinnings, a subsequent article by UCMS foreign secretary Stephen J. Corey on the issue of baptism in the mission fields suggests that the board's interpretation was not simply motivated by practical concerns. Corey stressed the "preeminence of the Spirit in baptism" over the form of baptism's administration:

---

[63] Anonymous, "The World Field—Our Farm," *Christian Century* 42/43 (22 October 1925): 1299–1300.

[64] Anonymous, "For the Freedom of the Disciples," *Christian Century* 42/50 (10 December 1925): 1538.

[65] Anonymous, "Propagandists for 'Open Membership,'" *Christian Standard* 61/38 (18 September 1926 supplement): 3.

In the mission fields, to neglect the spiritual intent of baptism, with all the dead-level non-Christian formalism around one, is fatal. It would be better to have no baptism, than to have an organized church through which a spiritual ordinance was made less than useless and meaningless. Such a conception of baptism is further removed from believer's baptism than is infant baptism, because it has to do with the self-determining adults.... [The missionary's] greatest interest is to get beyond initiatory things into the realm of life and character. He feels that baptism is nothing, unless it is a token of godliness and the Christ spirit. Fortunately, he is out of the realm of controversy and doctrinal discussion. He is face to face with a non-Christian civilization or paganism itself, and it is a question of God's people showing the fruits of Christianity in their lives, and not the ascendancy of a form no matter how sacred and scriptural it may be.[66]

Corey's article revealed his commitment that the church's mission consisted in the development of Christian character and civilization in foreign lands. This vision of the church mirrored closely that promoted by advocates of the New Theology. Nonetheless, this downplaying of liturgical forms and doctrinal commitments rubbed both ways. The board of managers not only called for tolerance from strict restorationists but clearly expected those who, as a matter of conscience, held to open membership to relinquish the practice. After all, the practice of open membership was not simply a harmless form of administration but a divisive one. Specifically, the board argued that the peace report's phrase "committed to the belief in" open membership did not intend "to invade the right of private judgment, but only to apply to such an open agitation as would prove divisive."[67] The board sought to protect missionaries' individual liberty of conscience while ceasing divisive practices that might disrupt the business of the UCMS. In other words, "commitment" only encompassed willingness to comply with an administrative dictate of the UCMS. The UCMS board also called Disciples in the United States to be mindful that conditions in the mission field itself often required flexibility rather than strict conformity to American church models.

Such a compromise satisfied neither strict restorationists nor liberals. Strict restorationists, supporting a voluntary and local model of the church, believed the board's interpretation undermined the foundation of proper

[66] Stephen J. Corey, "Baptism on the Mission Fields," *World Call* 7/3 (March 1926): 31.

[67] N.a, "Statement of the Board of managers of the United Christian Missionary Society," *World Call* 7/1 (January 1926): 38.

fellowship—one Lord, one faith, and one baptism. Modernist Edward Scribner Ames insisted that the church must be open to change in order to meet the needs of its members and modern society. Therefore, he argued, the church must be inclusive, free thinking, experimental, and tolerant.[68] The *Christian Century*, while rejoicing at the moderating move of the board, worried that simple administrative rulings could not ultimately prevent strict restorationist intent to establish a Disciples creed. C. C. Morrison argued that such a clear nullification of the peace report's intent had certainly laid the groundwork for a future strict restorationist schism.[69]

Morrison's latter observation proved more prescient than his former one. Strict restorationists saw the board's move as an autocratic betrayal of the plain will of the Oklahoma City convention, not to mention a betrayal of the New Testament. A committee of the Christian Restoration Association met the following June and issued "a call to action to all who accept Christ alone as their creed, rejecting all authority that is in conflict with his word."[70] They decried the "interpretation" of the peace report as a surrender of the UCMS by its board "into the hands of the deadliest enemies of the faith."[71] They further accused progressives C. C. Morrison, Edward Scribner Ames, and Peter Ainslie of orchestrating an "open-membership raid on the coming Memphis convention."[72] Calling modernist advocates of open membership and the New Theology "parasites," the *Christian Standard* claimed that true Disciples were fighting a "species of civil war" with a movement attacking the "fundamentals held by all evangelical Christians." Therefore, the editor concluded, "exposing themselves as enemies at the gate, bent on the destruction of all we hold most dear, we no longer hold ourselves bound to treat them as honorable equals, but as traitors to a cause in which they cling only to its injury."[73]

---

[68] Ames, "Vital Church," 218–21.

[69] Editorial, "Disciples at the Crossroads," *Christian Century* 42/51 (17 December 1925): 1565–66.

[70] Anonymous, "A Call to Action," *Christian Standard* 60/33 (14 August 1926 supplement): 1. The Christian Restoration Association was formerly known as the Clarke Fund, an independent Disciples clearinghouse to support home missions. The name was changed in 1925.

[71] Anonymous, "A Call to Action".

[72] Anonymous, "Challenge of Modern Unbelief," *Christian Standard* 61/33 (14 August 1926 supplement): 2.

[73] Anonymous, "Our Parasites," *Christian Standard* 61/33 (14 August 1926): 8.

Despite attempts to rally the troops, strict restorationists' very ecclesiological principle of decentralization undermined any possibility of long-term success, and the 1926 Memphis convention proved a disaster. Before UCMS's annual business session, S. S. Lappin motioned that the convention dissolve the United Society into its originally independent parts.[74] The failure of Lappin's motion was only the first of several disappointments. Not only did the convention vote to accept the UCMS board of managers' interpretation of the peace report, but it also accepted the Commission to the Orient's report, which certified that no church in China, Japan, or the Philippines practiced open membership—a claim the *Touchstone* and the *Christian Standard* had vociferously denied.[75] A contributing editor for the *Christian-Evangelist* observed jubilantly that the Memphis convention showed that Disciples "have passed the day when any group, be they liberalists, fundamentalists, or any other group, can organize themselves into a bloc...with their minds closed to further light and their souls set on controlling the Convention's actions and have the faintest hope of succeeding."[76]

It was, perhaps, unfortunate that Z. T. Sweeney died before the convention; his moderating influence between strict and moderate restorationists Disciples might have succeeded a third time. Regardless, an exasperated P. H. Welshimer withdrew his own "peace resolution" from the convention floor. This resolution, penned by Russell Errett and presented by Welshimer, called the Executive Committee of the International Convention to appointment a twenty-four-member Commission on Brotherhood Comity and Associated Work. The resolution empowered the commission to canvass all Disciples agencies and investigate the most efficient and best use of extra-congregational organizations.[77] Welshimer's action was less an acknowledgment of a successful and peaceful convention

---

[74] Anonymous, "Business Sessions at Memphis," *Christian Standard* 61/50 (11 December 1926): 12.

[75] Anonymous, "As It Came to Pass at Memphis," *Christian-Evangelist* 63/47 (26 November 1926): 1491. The full text of the "Report of the Commission to the Orient" was published in *World Call* 7/8 (August 1926). A stenographic report of the meeting concerning the report was printed in the *Christian Standard* 63 (4 December 1926): 12–15, 18.

[76] Anonymous, "The Meaning of Memphis," *Christian-Evangelist* 63/48 (9 December 1926): 1550.

[77] Anonymous, "Resolutions the Memphis Convention Refused," *Christian Standard* 61/50 (11 December 1926): 6.

than a belief that his resolution was pointless. Edwin R. Errett expressed his frustration that the Memphis convention settled on a conception of the church that "calls for unity in organization, and in spite of diversity of belief on cardinal doctrines."[78]

Although the International Convention voted not to meet again until 1928, the strict restorationists, under the leadership of P. H. Welshimer and Mark Collis, created a Committee on Future Action to address their disappointments at Memphis. The committee planned a new convention at Indianapolis, Indiana, called the North American Christian Convention (NACC), which would meet that autumn to discuss among other issues the deity of Christ, the inspiration of the Scriptures, the church, and evangelism.[79] Optimistically, Mark Collis boldly declared that the Indianapolis convention "will mark the beginning of a new era in the kingdom of God."[80] However, little in this convention was new, except that "everyone was happy."[81]

The NACC modeled itself on the various restoration congresses advocated by the 1919 Louisville Restoration congress and run regionally since that time. These congresses provided a platform for like-minded Disciples to gather and hear traditional restorationist ideals and their present-day applications. Welshimer introduced the Indianapolis convention as an old-fashioned country meeting on a national scale to proclaim the fundamentals of the faith and to encourage the faithful to stand firm.[82] Typical of the addresses was that of Z. T. Sweeney's nephew, Edwin S. Sweeney of Charlottesville, Virginia. His sermon on the "Autonomy of the Local Church" warned his audience that the perils of centralization threatened the church as much today as it did in ancient times.[83] Such a reminder was hardly necessary for his audience and smacked more of preaching to the choir. The convention also hosted a symposium on "The

---

[78] Edwin R. Errett, "A Convention of Bad Faith," *Christian Standard* 61/48 (27 November 1926): 631.

[79] Anonymous, "A Grand Reunion to Honor the Plea," *Christian Standard* 62/9 (26 February 1927): 1.

[80] Mark Collis, "The Convention Proposed for This Fall," *Christian Standard* 62/12 (19 March 1927): 269.

[81] Edwin Errett, "A Happy Convention at Last," *Christian Standard* 62/44 (29 October 1927): 3–6.

[82] Ibid., 3.

[83] Edwin S. Sweeney, "Autonomy of the Local Church," *Christian Standard* 62/45 (5 November 1927): 4–5.

Way Out of Denominationalism" in which Disciples who had converted
from various denominations, including Congregationalism, Presbyterianism,
Roman Catholicism, Episcopalianism, and Methodism, explained why they
left their denominations in response to the restorationist plea.[84] Many
sermons showed clear connections with the broader fundamentalist
movement. C. C. Taylor's "The Menace of Modernism" railed against
destructive higher criticism and its effects upon young people in churches
and universities.[85] President of Kansas Bible College T. H. Johnson's
sermon on "The Office of the Holy Spirit" showed that Keswick
pneumatology could be fitted to serve a restorationist agenda. [86]

More than anything else the NACC represented a strict restorationist
movement worn down spiritually by constant conflict. The nature of the
non-delegated representation of the International Convention, while fully
democratic in the eyes of strict restorationists, required that the convention
expend an immense amount of time and energy to meet any perceived crisis
each year. S. S. Lappin admitted as much:

> The protest conventions and congresses that have gone before were
> necessary. Others may be held in days to come. We are a free people and
> must ever be. The older agencies now involved in the "International
> Convention" that proposes to court further disaster by attempting to become
> a delegate body, belong to all who have aided in accumulating their assets.
> Mismanagement invites correction. Publicity will hasten it, and may prove to
> be the only corrective.... Of greater import than any other consideration is
> the fact that continuous occupation with these abuses and wrangles has
> worked as a blight on the spiritual life that is at the bottom of all activity and
> that is the one and only hope of every enterprise. Our people need assemblies
> where fellowship can be cultivated apart from partisan squabbles and official
> domination.[87]

In fact, the convention resolved that "there should be no continuing
officiary or machinery whatsoever." [88] Even the committee formed to plan
the next convention did not retain a single member from the Committee on

---

[84] Anonymous, "North American Christian Convention Program," *Christian
Standard* 62/36 (3 September 1927): 24.
[85] C. C. Taylor, "The Menace of Modernism," *Christian Standard* 62/47 (19
November 1927): 3–5.
[86] T. H. Johnson, "Office of the Holy Spirit," 3–4.
[87] S. S. Lappin, "A Turn in the Road," *Christian Standard* 62/43 (22 October
1927): 8.
[88] Ibid., 1.

Future Action. In fact, the NACC did not meet with regularity until 1950, when its organizers made its sessions permanent. At that time, the *Christian Standard* and the *Restoration Herald* accused the NACC of exchanging the restorationist vision of its founders for an ecclesiasticism reminiscent of the International Convention.[89]

Welshimer declared that the organizers and participants of the NACC had no intention to divide the Disciples:

> Those who gathered at Indianapolis were Christians who have nothing more at heart than the Restoration movement. This talk of dividing the brotherhood because all are not in accord as missionary agencies is mere child's play. The only thing that will divide the brotherhood is departure by any group from the historic position which has given us a right to exist.... The Indianapolis Convention did not attempt to formulate a basis for union. That was done nineteen centuries ago, and we are quite content to accept the divine basis and pass it on to others.[90]

Nonetheless, the loose confederation of Disciples congregations that participated in the NACC supported their own institutions outside of centralized convention control. In an effort to subvert liberal control of education, they supported and founded new colleges and Bible institutes loyal to the basic principles of the New Testament faith, among them McGarvey Bible College and the Cincinnati Bible Seminary (1923), Manhattan Bible College (1927), and Atlanta Christian College (1928). The NACC also provided a venue for independent missionaries and missionary organizations to vie for the support of Disciples at the convention. They also offered the UCMS a place in the program; however, the organization declined.[91]

Most observers at the time and later historians argued that the creation of the NACC constituted a de facto schism in the Disciples.[92] Reporting on the 1928 Columbus convention, the *Christian Century* properly noted that a "deep peace brooded over Columbus" not of "denominational solidarity, but of one element—'faction' would be too acrimonious and divisive a word—meeting without the disturbing presence of the other."[93] Strict

---

[89] Corey, *Fifty Years*, 136–38.

[90] P. H. Welshimer, "Some Things That Were Not Done at Indianapolis," *Christian Standard* 62/45 (5 November 1927): 7.

[91] Ibid.

[92] Marsden, *Fundamentalism*, 178; Corey, *Fifty Years*, 127–56;

[93] Anonymous, "The Disciples Convention," *Christian Century* 45/18 (3 May 1928): 561–62.

restorationist ecclesiology made such a claim theologically absurd, and strict restorationists insisted that Disciples, as true undenominational Christians, looked at the International Convention and the UCMS as one of many possible fellowships and missionary enterprises local congregations had liberty to support or not. True to their word, they made no official requirement about supporting the UCMS; however, actual financial supporters must have few and far between. Nonetheless, they maintained their interest in the affairs of the International Convention, by attending and reporting on its proceedings.

The Des Moines international convention elected C. S. Medbury as its president in 1932. Medbury continued to promote compromise in the convention as he had a decade earlier. In a series of articles published in the *Christian Standard* he argued that "the International Convention of Disciples of Christ aims to be just what its name implies. It is not a convention of the United Christian Missionary Society, nor any missionary, educational, or benevolent group." Further, he extended the hand of fellowship to readers of the *Christian Standard* and offered that "amendments would be in order" to those with "better ideas ways, more fraternal, bigger spirited, or more efficient, than we have yet found."[94] Medbury's sudden death in April 1932 halted any serious attempts to institutionalize his compromises. However, the financial depression helped push the 1933 Pittsburgh international convention to separate the National Benevolent Association, the Board of Church Extension, and the Board of Ministerial Relief from the UCMS. The *Christian Standard* and its editor Edwin Errett expressed its delight over this development.[95]

Through a series of conflicts and compromises, the Disciples of Christ, for all intents and purposes, developed the structures and character of a denomination. While among Northern Baptists such compromises preserved the denominational structures, among the Disciples such structures and therefore any method to preserve them became serious bones of contention. Given the tradition of restorationism and the anti-denominationalism it adherents espoused, it is amazing not only that the International Convention and the UCMS survived the conflict but that they developed at all. Even the NACC found it difficult over time to withstand the denominational impulse. Not only were its sessions made permanent in

---

[94] Quoted in Corey, *Fifty Years*, 162.
[95] Ibid.,162–65.

1950, but its member congregations also formed the Christian Churches and Churches of Christ in 1968.[96]

---

[96] McAllister & Tucker, *Journey in Faith*, 446–47.

CHAPTER 9

Case Study: The Presbyterian Church
in the USA, 1922–1937

The fundamentalist and modernist attempts to influence the identity and vocation of the Presbyterian Church in the USA. (PCUSA) had slightly different dynamics than that of the Northern Baptists or the Disciples of Christ. Like their Baptist and Disciples coreligionists, three distinct parties existed within the PCUSA: liberals (or alternately "modernists"), fundamentalists, and strict "old school" confessionalists. On the one hand, liberals and many fundamentalists promoted an "inclusivist," or comprehensive, ecclesiology that emphasized commitment to the Presbyterian confessions of faith coupled with the liberty of individuals to interpret those confessions. Two Presbyterian reunions provided the backdrop for this view. Liberals noted that the reunion of the Old School and New School Presbyterians in 1870 assumed that "there are various methods of viewing, stating, explaining, and illustrating the doctrines of the Confession which do not impair the integrity of the system."[1] Inclusivists also invoked the confessional revision of 1903 that paved the way for the union of the Cumberland Presbyterian Church with the PCUSA in 1906. The 1903 revision not only allowed liberty of conscience on the issues surrounding election but implied that the confessionalism of the PCUSA was open to development. Strict confessionalists and some fundamentalists

---

[1] John T. Duffield, "The Revision of the Confession," *Independent* 52/2685 (17 May 1900): 1179. For a discussion of the reunion, see George M. Marsden, *The Evangelical Mind and the New School Presbyterian Experience: A Case Study of Thought and Theology in Nineteenth-Century America* (New Haven: Yale University Press, 1970) 212–29.

asserted a much more "exclusivist" ecclesiology.[2] They argued that the voluntary nature of the church required membership based upon common, traditional interpretations of the Presbyterian confessions. They argued that those not adhering to such interpretation should withdraw from the denomination.

Model 9.1
Presbyterian Church
in the U.S.A

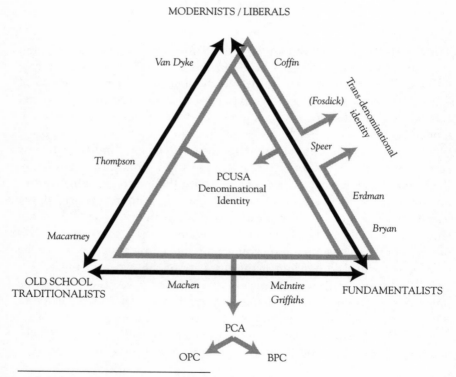

---

[2] Confessionalism, as distinct from fundamentalism or modernism, is convincingly used by D. G. Hart in his "J. Gresham Machen, Confessional Presbyterianism, and the History of Twentieth-Century Protestantism," in *Reforming the Center: American Protestantism, 1900 to the Present*, ed. Douglas Jacobsen and William Vance Trollinger (Grand Rapids: William B. Eerdmans Publishing Company, 1998) 129–49.

Other factors that shaped the conflict between 1922 and 1936 included a financial crisis (especially impacting Presbyterian missions) precipitated by the collapse of the Interchurch World Movement. Furthermore, the polity of the Presbyterian Church was different than either the Northern Baptist Convention or the Disciples of Christ. The elected delegate assemblies of the Presbyterian Church, whether presbyteries, synods, or the General Assembly, acted as legislative as well as judicial bodies. Therefore, the legislative and judicial decisions were binding on the church and made control of the General Assembly a significant achievement.

The so-called "Fosdick Case" resulting from Harry Emerson Fosdick's 1922 sermon "Shall the Fundamentalists Win?" precipitated the initial conflict in the PCUSA. In the fall of 1921, WCFA evangelist W. H. Griffith Thomas and the Bible Union of China rocked the PCUSA with controversy by claiming that modernism was rampant in the foreign field in China. Organized in 1920 by Griffith Thomas and Charles G. Trumbull, the Bible Union of China sought to ensure that only missionaries identifying themselves as loyal to the fundamentals of the faith participated in the mission enterprise.[3] After visiting China in 1921, Griffith Thomas addressed the Philadelphia Presbytery of the PCUSA, asserting that on a recent trip to China he had observed rampant apostasy among the Northern Presbyterian missionaries.[4] The traditionally conservative Philadelphia Presbytery became alarmed at the accusations and asked the board of foreign missions to investigate the situation. The board quickly responded that the allegations of doctrinal heterodoxy on the foreign field were groundless.[5] Two conservative Presbyterian premillennialists, Robert E. Speer (secretary of the mission board) and Charles R. Erdman, also came to the missionaries' defense and attempted to allay conservative fears of missionary infidelity.

Continuing accusations of heresy by members of the Bible Union of China against liberal missionaries instigated the famed liberal Baptist minister Harry Emerson Fosdick to preach in May 1922 a sermon titled

---

[3] William R. Hutchison, *The Modernist Impulse in American Protestantism* (Cambridge: Harvard University Press, 1976; reprint, Durham NC: Duke University Press, 1992) 158.

[4] For W. H. Griffith Thomas's published report, see his "Modernism in China," *Princeton Theological Review* 19/3 (October 1921): 630–71. Cf. Griffith, *Modernism in China* (Philadelphia: The Sunday School Times Company, n.d.).

[5] Anonymous, "Action of the Board of Foreign Missions with Reference to the Doctrinal Soundness of Missionaries," *Presbyterian Magazine* 27/12 (December 1921): 693.

"Shall the Fundamentalists Win?" at the First Presbyterian Church in New York, where he served as an associate minister. Having recently visited China, he worried over antiliberal tactics by members of the Bible Union of China. Fosdick asserted that fundamentalism comprised an aggressive conspiracy against liberals "to shut against them doors of the Christian fellowship."[6] He further chided fundamentalists for their intolerance and divisiveness. Right at the moment when the church had so much work to do in a world "with colossal problems, which must be solved with Christ's name and for Christ's sake, Fundamentalists propose to drive out from the Christian churches all consecrated souls who do not agree with their theory of inspiration. What immeasurable folly!"[7] The heart of Fosdick's appeal centered on the idea of ecclesiological tolerance, a concept he exemplified as a Baptist called to a Presbyterian pulpit. Further, Fosdick claimed that fundamentalist attempts to define "liberals" as being outside of the church out of the church added insult to injury, subverting the cause of Christ in a world that desperately needed his message of the fatherhood of God and the brotherhood of man.

Partially because of its press coverage and partly due to its content, Fosdick's sermon caused a national sensation. Because the sermon appeared just before the General Assembly in Des Moines, the issue of alleged missionary infidelity became a focal point of the assembly. Worried Presbyterians, however, had little luck convincing the majority of the commissioners that modernists had compromised the integrity of their missionary enterprise, and the General Assembly adopted the foreign missions board's defense of its missionaries.[8] Therefore, conservatives set their sights on Fosdick.

Following the Des Moines assembly, Philadelphia minister Clarence E. Macartney contributed a two-part rejoinder to Fosdick's sermon titled "Shall Unbelief Win?" Macartney was no fundamentalist; rather, he espoused Old School Presbyterianism in the Princeton Seminary tradition. With regard to Fosdick's accusation that there existed a fundamentalist conspiracy to displace liberals from the evangelical denominations,

---

[6] Harry Emerson Fosdick, *Shall the Fundamentalists Win? A Sermon Preached at the First Presbyterian Church, New York, May 21, 1922, Stenographically Reported by Margaret Renton* (New York: First Presbyterian Church, 1922) 6.

[7] Ibid., 14.

[8] Anonymous, "Assembly Votes Board Consolidation," *Continent* 53/22 (1 June 1922): 704.

Macartney admitted that he had neither heard of one nor been invited to join; nonetheless, he noted "that so long as the Presbyterian Church has not abandoned and repudiated its Confession of Faith, any of its pulpits holding and declaring the views of Dr. Fosdick occupies an anomalous place."[9] He further argued that Fosdick and other liberals need not fear "the processes of excision and ecclesiastical trial, because no such action could alter the fact that "they are already *out* of the church."[10] Although Macartney admitted that as an American Baptist Fosdick had the freedom to believe what he wanted, he argued that it did not follow that Fosdick had a right to preach what he wanted from a Presbyterian pulpit. In other words, as their published correspondence revealed, while the form of the debate centered on doctrine, the substantive issue of their controversy was ecclesiological. Writing to Fosdick, Macartney argued that "the Presbyterian Church in contrast with the Baptist Church, is a constitutional and creedal church, and wherever its polity and its doctrine are either neglected or assailed from those within its jurisdiction, it is the privilege, and the solemn duty, of its loyal ministers and members to make their protest."[11] The following October the Philadelphia Presbytery held a stormy three-hour session in which Macartney prevailed in sending an overture to the General Assembly protesting that Fosdick had denigrated Presbyterian doctrine while occupying a Presbyterian pulpit.[12]

The "Fosdick Case," as it eventually became known, provided the prelude of an unfolding ecclesiological debate within the PCUSA. Macartney's position, one representing strict Presbyterian confessionalists and many fundamentalists, focused upon a strict and literal interpretation of the Presbyterian confessions and the PCUSA's constitutional demand that Presbyterian ministers uphold and defend these confessions. The most vocal and articulate spokesperson of this position, J. Gresham Machen of Princeton Theological Seminary, defended this view even before Fosdick's sermon.[13] However, as the controversy escalated he published *Christianity*

---

[9] Clarence Edward Macartney, "Shall Unbelief Win? An Answer to Dr. Fosdick--Part II," *Presbyterian* 95/29 (20 July 1922): 10.

[10] Ibid. Emphasis in the original.

[11] Anonymous, "The Fosdick-Macartney Correspondence," *Continent* 53/51 (21 December 1922): 1642.

[12] Anonymous, "Presbyterians Move Against Dr. Fosdick," *New York Times*, 18 October 1922, 1

[13] See J. Gresham Machen's "Liberalism or Christianity," *Princeton Theological Review* 20/1 (January 1922): 115–16. Machen noted that *Christianity and Liberalism*

and Liberalism, arguing that the church was a voluntary institution of those who assented to a similar creed or essential beliefs. Not only did "liberals" within the PCUSA deny essential tenets of faith, Machen alleged, but the ideas to which they assented made them, for all intents and purposes, another religion: "What the liberal theologian has retained after abandoning to the enemy one doctrine after another is not Christianity at all, but a religion which is so entirely different than Christianity as to belong in a distinct category...Modern liberalism may be criticized on the ground that it is un-Christian."[14] Machen urged the "voluntary withdrawal of the liberal ministers from those confessional churches whose confessions they do not, in the plain historic sense, accept."[15] Other important allies of Machen and Macartney, including William Jennings Bryan, also held to this voluntary notion of church.[16]

Fosdick's position, articulated more fully by liberal Presbyterians, focused on the individual liberty to interpret the confessions, which they believed was granted by the constitution and the Presbyterian mergers of 1870 and 1906. In a letter to Clarence Macartney, Fosdick claimed that the Philadelphia minister had unfairly caricaturized his views and ignored the point of his now famous (perhaps infamous) sermon: "You have so largely neglected the real purpose of my sermon. It was a plea for tolerance."[17]

> There are many pleas for tolerance today, soft and sentimental, made upon the fallacious basis that there are no real differences of thinking between Christians. I did not wish to make a plea on so baseless an assumption. I therefore took pains to put over against each in brief and sketchy outline extreme conservative and extreme liberal positions, in order that I might say that even when people are as far apart as these two positions represent, we must still strive to keep them within the fellowship of the family of Christ, loyal to him and devoted to his work until fuller truth comes to light."[18]

The editor of the *Continent*, Nolan R. Best, agreed with Fosdick's assessment. He noted that those attacking Fosdick did so not because of the

---

was an expansion of this address. See Machen, *Christianity and Liberalism* (Grand Rapids: William B. Eerdmans Publishing Company, 1923; reprint, 1981) vi.

[14] Machen, *Christianity and Liberalism*, 7–8.

[15] Ibid., 167.

[16] William Jennings Bryan, "The Fundamentals," *Forum* 70/1 (July 1923): 1671–72.

[17] Anonymous, "Fosdick-Macartney Correspondence."

[18] Ibid.

sermon's content but upon their understanding that church fellowship demanded doctrinal standardization. Best claimed that historic Presbyterianism did not ask its ministers to "profess a phrase-by-phrase acceptance of the Westminster Confession but only to acknowledge a general assent to the 'system of doctrine' which it 'contains.'" [19] However, in the eyes of many Presbyterian conservatives, whether strict confessionalists or fundamentalists, liberal arguments for tolerance and liberty hardly seemed compelling.

No less than nine presbyteries joined the Philadelphia Presbytery in an overture to the General Assembly demanding that the First Presbyterian Church of New York City and Dr. Fosdick conform to the dictates of Presbyterian polity and doctrine. The Committee on Bills and Overtures presented the General Assembly with a 21–1 majority report, which argued that the Fosdick case should be sent to the Presbytery of New York for its review and assessment. The one-person minority report, penned and signed by A. Gordon MacLennan, minister of Bethany Presbyterian Church in Philadelphia, directed the Presbytery of New York "to take such action (either through its present committee or by appointment of a special commission) as will require the preaching and teaching in the First Presbyterian Church of New York to conform to the system of doctrines taught in the Confession of Faith." Furthermore, the minority report reaffirmed the General Assembly's commitment to the 1910 doctrinal deliverance, which demanded assent to five essential points of doctrine.[20] Calling the majority report "a pusillanimous document—a whitewash," Macartney, along with William Jennings Bryan, led the defense of MacLennan's report. After several hours of debate, the assembly adopted the minority report by a vote of 439 to 359.[21] Conservatives were elated. Macartney triumphantly proclaimed, "This is only the first skirmish in a battle which will shake the Protestant church."[22] Indeed, he was correct.

---

[19] Editorial, "The Freedom of Gospel Power," *Continent* 53/45 (9 November 1922): 1397.

[20] Anonymous, "Philadelphia Overture is Affirmed," *Continent* 54/22 (31 May 1923): 708. The five doctrines affirmed by the 1910 deliverance included the inspiration of the Scriptures, the virgin birth, the necessity of Christ's sacrifice for reconciliation with God, the resurrection and ascension of Christ, and supernatural miracles.

[21] Ibid. Bryan's assessment of the adoption of the minority report can be found in "The Fundamentals," 1665–80.

[22] T. C. Horton, "The Fall of Fosdick," *King's Business* 14/8 (August 1923): 796.

The following day, sixty-six ministers protested the General Assembly's adoption of the report. The protesters argued that the assembly judged First Presbyterian and Fosdick without a proper hearing and imposed an additional creedal statement beyond that required by the church's constitution.[23] An editorial in the *Continent* complained that the General Assembly had overstepped its authority and legislated a confession of faith without the necessary two-thirds approval of the presbyteries. Without such approval, the editorial continued, "a mere resolution of the General Assembly is positively not church law, no matter what it deals with. And certainly it is not law when it deals with doctrine."[24] Henry Sloane Coffin, pastor of Madison Avenue Presbyterian Church in New York City, dared conservatives to remove him from his pulpit, declaring that he believed none of the 1923 General Assembly's five "essential" doctrines were, in fact, essential. "While I will not voluntarily withdraw from the Presbyterian ministry and leave the Church to those who misconstrue its standards and repudiate its Protestant heritage, I wish to make my own position clear."[25]

Modernist Presbyterians' view of the church was different than that of confessionalists and many fundamentalists. Coffin spoke for many liberal Presbyterians in his day and was self-acknowledged liberal leader in the PCUSA. He pled for the same type of tolerance as Fosdick, his colleague at Union Theological Seminary in New York. Behind Coffin's plea for a tolerant and comprehensive church lay an ecclesiology inherited from the New Theology and social Christianity he advocated. Jesus, he claimed, "was primarily interested in the religious experience that lay back of government, worship and creed; and he gave Himself to develop it, apparently trusting a vigorous life with God to find forms of its own."[26] The Holy Spirit, according to Coffin, guided the church to institute the kingdom of God on earth in each new age:

> The same Spirit who lived and ruled in the Church of the first days has been breathed on us, through the long line of apostolic-spirited men and women who reach back to Jesus, and lives and rules in us. We must keep the

[23] Anonymous, "Assail Fosdick Ban as Assembly Ends," *New York Times*, 25 May 1923, 10.

[24] Anonymous, "The Extent of Assembly's Power," *Continent* 54/21 (21 June 1923): 799.

[25] Ibid.

[26] Henry Sloane Coffin, *Some Christian Convictions: A Practical Restatement in Terms of Present-day Thinking* (New Haven: Yale University Press, 1915) 185.

THE PRSEBYTERIAN CHURCH IN THE USA

unity of the Spirit with the believers of the past, and with all who are Spirit-led in the world today; and we must remember that "where the Spirit of the Lord is, there is liberty." We are not bound by the precedents of by-gone centuries in our organization; we are free to take from the past what is of worth to us, and we are free to let the rest go. Is not the Spirit of God as able to take materials at hand in our own age, and to use them for the government, the worship, the creed, the methods of the living Church of Christ?[27]

He argued, therefore, that the church's unity lay in its experience of Christ through the Spirit and its unity of mission. However, as an organism, the church ideally existed with "variety in unity."[28] Indeed, he stated that "dogmatists, be they radical or conservatives, who insist on a particular interpretation of Christianity" are among those that thwart the church from accomplishing its divinely ordained mission. Christians, therefore, must make their own communion as inclusive as possible to insure that no person possessing the Spirit of Christ find him or herself excluded.[29]

Presbyterian liberals typically affirmed the ecclesiology represented by Coffin, and this ecclesiology shaped the way they perceived the unfolding conflict sparked by the Fosdick case. Just before and after the 1923 General Assembly modernists protested the "exclusivist" vision of the church promoted by Machen, Macartney, and Bryan. Nolan R. Best could hardly contain his outrage as he reviewed Machen's *Christianity and Liberalism.* He not only thought Machen's claims about liberalism "unmitigated falsity," but he found the statement that liberals were not even Christians especially obnoxious.[30] The Rev. Dr. Henry Van Dyke, poet and author at Princeton University, denounced what he perceived to be "the literalism of the Scribes and the Pharisees" at work within the Philadelphia Presbytery (a clear allusion to Macartney and Machen). "If it [the spirit of the Philadelphia Presbytery] is to be divisive and exclusive, a beginning of theological word battles and heresy trials, if it is to set up new tests of orthodoxy unknown to our standards and to the Bible and attempt their rigid enforcement by expulsion or ecclesiastical boycott, why then I should be in hearty disaccord

---

[27] Ibid., 194–95.
[28] Ibid., 198.
[29] Ibid., 198–99.
[30] Nolan R. Best, "Professor Machen's 'Christianity and Liberalism,'" *Continent* 54/21 (24 May 1923): 679–80.

with such a spirit as highly injurious to the Church."[31] Further, Van Dyke resigned his pew at First Presbyterian Church of Princeton when Machen filled its pulpit in January 1924. He publicly declared that he had too few Sundays free from evangelical work to waste them "listening to such a dismal, bilious travesty of the gospel. We want to hear about Christ and the Son of God and the Son of Man, not about Fundamentalists and Modernists, the only subject your stated supply seems to have anything to say and on which most of what he says is untrue and malicious."[32] In both the cases of Best and Van Dyke the voluntary ecclesiology of the strict confessionalists coupled with Presbyterian polity appeared as an explosive combination that, if left unchecked, would destroy the proper variety of the Spirit-led church. The 1923 doctrinal deliverance, liberals prophesied, would eventually lead to heresy trials or schism.

In January 1924, 150 Presbyterian clergymen signed the "Affirmation Designed to Safeguard the Unity and Liberty of the Presbyterian Church in the United States of America," which protested what they perceived to be attempts by the 1923 General Assembly "to divide the church and abridge its freedom."[33] A group of Presbyterian ministers met immediately following the assembly and appointed a committee of ten to pen the document.[34] The "Auburn Affirmation," as the document became known, argued that the PCUSA historically did not require its ministers' "assent to the very words of the Confession, or to all of its teachings, or to interpretation of the Confession by individuals or church courts."[35] The document noted that the reunion of the Old School and New School Presbyterians in 1870 specifically safeguarded against the idea that only one interpretation of the confession could be tolerated. Further, its authors noted that the more recent reunion of the PCUSA with the Cumberland Presbyterian Church in 1906 also required that theological differences be accepted as genuinely and

---

[31] Anonymous, "Van Dyke Quits Pew in Anger," *New York Times*, 4 January 1924, 4.

[32] Ibid., 1.

[33] Anonymous, "Ministers Issue Unity and Liberty Affirmation," *Continent* 55/2 (10 January 1924): 40. Cf. Charles E. Quirk, "Origins of the Auburn Affirmation," *Journal of Presbyterian History* 53/2 (Summer 1975): 120–42.

[34] Ibid. The leaders met 19 June 1923 and appointed the committee consisting of M. S. Howland as chairman, R. H. Nichols as secretary, P. S. Bird as treasurer, R. B. Beattie, James E. Clarke, J. J. Lawrence, Alexander MacColl, W. P. Merrill, W. L. Sawtelle, and G. B. Stewart.

[35] Ibid.

loyally Presbyterian. The ministers also addressed the authority of the General Assembly, which, they argued, could not make binding statements regarding doctrines without the constitutionally mandated approval of two-thirds of the presbyteries. Therefore, they claimed not only that the 1923 doctrinal deliverance was unconstitutional, but also that the General Assembly had overstepped its bounds by declaring against First Presbyterian Church and Fosdick without a proper hearing beginning at the level of the presbytery.[36]

Very soon after the publication of the Auburn Affirmation, the New York Presbytery's Special Committee investigating the Fosdick case reported its findings. While chiding Fosdick for the provocative nature of his sermon, the committee said that it found no instances of doctrinal infidelity or breach of public trust. The committee also acknowledged that, while it could take no binding action on a Baptist minister, the presbytery rightfully expected that Fosdick would voluntarily accept the same responsibilities and obligations of any other Presbyterian minister.[37] The New York Presbytery accepted the committee's report by a vote of 111 to 28.[38] Not satisfied with his presbytery's decision in the Fosdick case, W. D. Buchanan and fifteen other dissenters filed a complaint with the General Assembly that the presbytery had failed to uphold the assembly's 1923 mandate.[39]

The Auburn Affirmation and New York Presbytery's decision on the Fosdick case became a storm center of controversy as the 1924 Grand Rapids General Assembly approached. Machen attacked the Auburn Affirmation as "a deplorable attempt to obscure the issue." "The plain fact," he continued, "is that two mutually exclusive religions are being proclaimed in the pulpits of Presbyterian Church."[40] The editor of the *Presbyterian* offered that "affirmationists" were "free to withdraw, and conscience and

---

[36] Ibid., 59.

[37] Anonymous, "New York Committee Reports on Fosdick Case," *Continent* 55/4 (24 January 1924): 118. Cf. anonymous, "A Presbyterian Bill of Rights," *Literary Digest* 80/5 (2 February 1924): 32–33.

[38] Anonymous, "Fosdick Vindicated by Presbytery but Opponents Appeal," *New York Times*, 5 February 1924, 5.

[39] Anonymous, "Vote Exonerating Fosdick Taken to Church Assembly" *Washington Post*, 17 February 1924, 1.

[40] Anonymous, "Moderns Agnostic, Says Dr. Machen," *New York Times*, 10 January 1924, 4.

decency instruct him to do so."[41] The *Presbyterian* also argued that the lack of proper action on the Fosdick case showed that the New York Presbytery had sanctioned preaching and teaching that "contravenes the Confession of Faith and evangelical and historic Christianity."[42] Confessionalists and many fundamentalists perceived the 1924 General Assembly as an important crossroad that would decide the fate of American Presbyterianism, and they attempted to marshal support for their cause.

Liberal Presbyterians saw the 1924 General Assembly as equally momentous. The *Continent* claimed that the Auburn Affirmation and Fosdick's personal doctrinal declaration (included with the presbytery's verdict on his case) proved the orthodoxy and broad unity of the Presbyterian Church. The publication further claimed that only "where contumacious mischief and hopeless bigotry control men's spirits to the exclusion of brotherly love" could one continue "talking about dividing the church."[43] Nolan Best continued to advance the argument that the issues at stake in the Fosdick case, as suggested by the Auburn Affirmation, were constitutional ones. He defended the right of the "affirmationists" to plead their case on behalf of Fosdick and First Presbyterian:

> Even though one, two, or many men should suffer unjustly, there remains the right of every other person, standing free of the incidence of such particular judgments to continue to plead and press for a juster interpretation. This is, indeed, disputed. It is said that the word of the General Assembly is the verdict of the supreme court of the church and nothing can override it; whoever thinks the verdict is wrong has no further liberty except to depart. But that saying forgets something. The Assembly is truly the church's supreme court. But there is always one power which can reverse even a supreme court. That is the same supreme court.[44]

Perhaps preparing for short-term defeat, Best admonished his liberal coreligionists that "it is always in order to ask any Assembly to speak better than Assemblies of other years have spoken. And absolutely no disloyalty attached to such requests."[45] The *Presbyterian Advance* agreed, stating that the Auburn Affirmation "ought to convince the whole church that there is

---

[41] Quoted in anonymous, "Presbyterian Fears of a Split," *Literary Digest* 80/7 (16 February 1924): 34.

[42] Ibid.

[43] Anonymous, "Presbyterian Fears."

[44] Anonymous, "The Constitutional Question," *Continent* 55/18 (1 May 1924): 549.

[45] Ibid.

no reasonable ground for the allegations of those who would promote division."[46] Finally, three weeks before the General Assembly in Grand Rapids, the committee reissued the Auburn Affirmation in pamphlet form, complete with an additional 1,124 additional signatories and documents (including statements on the church by Old School Princetonian Charles Hodge) supporting their interpretation of the constitution.[47] The battle lines in Grand Rapids had been drawn.

The controversy, however, cannot be simply understood as fundamentalists and confessionalists versus liberals. As previously suggested, the pneumatology and eschatology of fundamentalists led them to focus on the Bible as the church's most important and divinely inspired authority. Therefore, many fundamentalists felt a natural affinity with the doctrinal emphasis of the confessionalists that included the brilliant Princetonian defense of the inerrancy of the Scriptures. Their dispensationalism also left them with a denominational ambivalence that made schism a viable option if the PCUSA could not excise its liberals. Not all self-avowed fundamentalists felt comfortable with a fundamentalist-confessionalist coalition. The two most politically powerful premillennialists and self-avowed fundamentalists within the General Assembly, Charles Erdman and Robert Speer, hoped to avoid denominational schism. Speer and Erdman were generally theologically conservative but "inclusivist" in their ecclesiology, which flowed naturally from the Keswick Holiness movement. While neither signed the Auburn Affirmation, Erdman and Speer believed that the constitution of the PCUSA allowed for a measure of theological liberty.

Erdman's inclusiveness was pragmatic. He, like other soul-saving evangelicals, believed that the church must preach the gospel to eliminate social ills and obviate the dilemma of democracy: "There can be no abiding morality aside from the influences and sanctions of the church," and "without morality, neither society nor state can continue to exist."[48] He further believed that a church in turmoil would be ineffectual in addressing social chaos.[49] This practical side of Erdman meant that he was less concerned with uniform doctrine than with unified mission. Many liberals,

---

[46] Ibid., 35.

[47] *An Affirmation Designed to Safeguard the Unity and Liberty of the Presbyterian Church in the United States of America* (Auburn NY: The Jacobs Press, 1 May 1924).

[48] Quoted in Bradley J. Longfield, *The Presbyterian Controversy: Fundamentalists, Modernists, and Moderates.* (New York: Oxford University Press, 1991) 146.

[49] Ibid., 147.

albeit for a number of different reasons, shared Erdman's vision of a church unified primarily by mission. Erdman was no doctrinal liberal, but he entertained the notion that there could be a range of opinion with the church. He also did not abide the idea that the church could abandon any of its constitutional principles. For these reasons, Erdman was nominated by liberals as moderator during the 1924 General Assembly. A perplexed editor of the *Christian Century* wondered "by what violence of the dictionary Dr. Erdman came to be looked upon as a liberal candidate?"[50] However, liberal Presbyterians understood well that a theologically conservative yet inclusivist candidate was their only hope to maintain influence within their denomination.

The health of the Presbyterian foreign missions board motivated Robert E. Speer first and foremost. Throughout his career he argued that "evangelization is the primary duty of the Church."[51] Further, part of the great witness of the church was its unity, which presaged the final unity of all humanity under God.[52] To this end, Speer became an ardent supporter of ecumenical enterprises such as the Interchurch World Movement and the Federal Council of Churches. He also insisted upon the most "inclusive" ecclesiology possible within the Presbyterian Church to carry out effectively and efficiently this missionary duty of the church. "Whatever disunity in the Christian Church compromises or weakens her testimony to the unity of humanity is unallowable. Whatever diversity of the Christian Church enriches and does not destroy her testimony to human unity is not only allowable but desirable."[53] Speer, therefore, naturally perceived any controversy surrounding the Presbyterian foreign missionary enterprise as a threat to the very nature of the church and its task. When Griffith Thomas attempted to impeach the character of Presbyterian missionaries in China, Speer used his influence as a secretary of the foreign missions board to ensure that the responsibility of determining missionary suitability passed

---

[50] Anonymous, "Presbyterianism Goes Fundamentalist," *Christian Century* 41/23 (5 June 1924): 732.

[51] Robert E. Speer, *Missionary Principles and Practice* (New York: Fleming H. Revell Company, 1902) 483.

[52] Robert E. Speer, *The Gospel and the New World* (New York: Fleming H. Revell Company, 1919) 21.

[53] Ibid., 22.

from the board to individual presbyteries.[54] Therefore, conservative presbyteries, such as that of Philadelphia, could, in effect, enforce doctrinal tests of faith and send missionaries sympathetic with soul-saving evangelism while liberal presbyteries, such as that of New York, could avoid doctrinal tests and send missionaries sympathetic with social gospel programs.

Even with such compromises, the expanding controversy meant that the foreign missions board was vulnerable to action by presbyteries and the General Assembly. The board's looming financial crisis exacerbated these concerns. In November of 1923 Speer warned that the board would close the year with a $1,200,000 in debt; the following year rising costs forced the board to cut its budget by 20 percent.[55] The board attempted to deflect insinuations of its doctrinal complicity with unorthodox missionaries because of its liberal membership and location in the liberal presbytery of New York. It implored its constituency "to remember that withholding or diverting gifts penalizes not members of the Board but the devoted missionaries and their work."[56] Speer also asked his fellow Presbyterians to "disregard every suggestion of unfaithfulness" and take up "the great task the Lord has laid upon us."[57] His worry over the viability of the foreign missions board did not incline him to countenance the attacks made by conservatives against the very agency that carried out the church's most important task. Because the foreign missions board remained in a state of financial crisis throughout the decade, many fundamentalists like Speer became uncomfortable with the unfolding denominational conflicts promoted by confessionalists.[58]

The 1924 Grand Rapids General Assembly did little to diffuse uncertainty among Northern Presbyterians. Clarence Macartney defeated

---

[54] Lefferts Loetscher, *The Broadening Church: A Study of Theological Issues in the Presbyterian Church since 1869* (Philadelphia: University of Pennsylvania Press, 1954) 106.

[55] Anonymous, "Warns of Crisis in Mission Field," *New York Times*, 13 November 1923, 8; anonymous, "Halt Talks to Pray for Mission Funds," *New York Times*, 15 February 1924, 7.

[56] Anonymous, "The Action of the Foreign Board," *Presbyterian Magazine* 30/1 (January 1924): 8.

[57] Robert E. Speer, "Where We Stand Today," *Presbyterian Magazine* 30/1 (January 1924): 12.

[58] For example, the missions and benevolence boards of the PCUSA carried $1,240,000 in debt in 1925. See anonymous, "Presbyterians Face Financial Crisis," *Christian Century* 42/29 (16 July 1925): 934.

Charles Erdman as moderator by only eighteen votes, hardly a resounding mandate. During the report of the board of education, Macartney helped create a circus-like atmosphere by ruling it acceptable to attack the theological orthodoxy of individual professors from the floor.[59] More excitement arose when the Standing Judicial Committee ruled that the New York Presbytery had acted in good faith on the Fosdick case. The committee, however, suggested that the presbytery should inquire whether Fosdick should be willing to become a Presbyterian to "remove much of the cause of irritation" associated with his special status as Baptist preacher in a PCUSA pulpit. Dissatisfied with this ruling, fundamentalist Mark A. Matthews, pastor of the First Presbyterian Church in Seattle, Washington, moved that the General Assembly become a court and review the entire Fosdick case. The assembly defeated the motion to review by a 504–311 vote.[60] The conservative coalition ultimately managed to remove liberal W. P. Merrill from the foreign missions board. However, the attacks against Fosdick and Merrill came at great cost because they allowed liberals to paint conservative tactics as unsavory.[61] The *Christian Century*, for example, railed against the 1924 General Assembly:

> Nobody, of course, questions the "right" of the Presbyterian denomination to take the action last May which resulted in Dr. Fosdick's resignation.... But this defense of what Dr. Fosdick neatly calls the "closed shop" on the ground of the denomination's "right" to control its own pulpit is wide of the mark. The question is, Does the Presbyterian church have any Christian right *to be that sort of church?* The issue does not strike at the church's right but at the church's character. It is only when the question is put this way that one can feel how unchristian a church the Presbyterian Church is, how engaged it is in fostering unbotherliness and misunderstanding, in setting up false standards by which to judge its leaders, in busying itself with interest and consideration which only eclipse the real interest of Christ's true kingdom.[62]

The conservative coalition had won the battle; however, the victories of the 1924 General Assembly would prove Pyrrhic and short-lived.

---

[59] Anonymous, "Presbyterianism Goes Fundamentalist," 733.

[60] Anonymous, "Fosdick Admonished to Enter Church or Forsake His Pulpit," *Washington Post*, 29 May 1924, 5.

[61] Anonymous, "Assembly Balks at Full Divisionist Plan," *Continent* 55/23 (5 June 1924): 755.

[62] Anonymous, "Dr. Fosdick's Punishment," *Christian Century* 41/42 (16 October 1924): 1326. Emphasis in the original.

Machen and Macartney believed that the best offensive was a good defense and articulation of their position. Macartney used his position as moderator to argue his case around the nation. He contended that liberal Christianity (which he alternately called non-doctrinal, non-factual, and/or pseudo-Christianity) was bankrupt because it lacked the power to regenerate souls, call individuals to repent, or grant assurances of salvation.[63] Macartney reminded his coreligionists that the Presbyterian Church stood at a crossroads between truth and error. The voluntary nature of the church provided the crux of his argument against liberal claims for freedom of thought:

> The Form of Government of the church declares that in perfect consistency with the principle of freedom and private judgment, Christian people have a right to associate themselves in groups or churches and to declare what the terms of admission to that church shall be, and what the qualifications of its ministers. The Presbyterian Church does not seize and press men into its ministry. On the contrary, it bids them search their hearts, and carefully examines them as to their acceptance of the doctrines which the church declares all her ministers must hold.[64]

Further, Macartney admonished irenic conservatives that "any one who at this time shrinks from defending the doctrine and government of his church, lest he should become a target for ridicule, criticism and abuse, is not worthy of the great and glorious name, Presbyterian."[65] Machen agreed. Because he demanded strict interpretation of Presbyterian doctrine, Machen became the object of relentless liberal attacks against denominational intolerance. In response he argued that his detractors misunderstood the nature of the church. Machen claimed that they missed the essential distinction between liberty within voluntary organizations (like the church) and involuntary organizations (such as the state). He responded that it is not intolerant for voluntary organizations to create and hold to their own standards of admission, while a too-centralized federal or state government ought to be resisted.[66] In other words, Machen believed that liberty within a

---

[63] Clarence E. Macartney, "The Moderator's Message," *Presbyterian* 95/2 (8 January 1925): 10.

[64] Clarence E. Macartney, "The Presbyterian Church at the Cross Roads" *Presbyterian* 95 (16 February 1925): 6.

[65] Ibid., 7.

[66] J. Gresham Machen, "Does Fundamentalism Obstruct Social Progress?—The Negative" *Survey-Graphic* 52/7 (1 July 1924): 392. This also explains why Machen

voluntary organization must be circumscribed by the very polity and ideals on which the organization was founded.

Erdman's alliance with liberals made his uneasy relationships with Macartney and especially Machen tenser. The conservatives perceived Erdman's fraternizing with liberals as treachery and labeled him a turncoat and "indifferentist." When Erdman replaced Machen in the pulpit of First Presbyterian in Princeton, Henry Van Dyke publicly announced his return to the church. The announcement, noticed even by the *New York Times*, was less a statement about Van Dyke's confidence in Erdman than his disdain of Machen.[67] Even so, the *Presbyterian* rhetorically questioned, "Does the return of such a pronounced and avowed modernist as Dr. Van Dyke to the old church, under the new pastor, mean that he is anticipating more liberal preaching under the new regime?"[68] Erdman took offense. Defending his orthodoxy, Erdman repudiated the *Presbyterian*'s "insinuations as unfounded unwarranted, unkind, and unchristian."[69] He further claimed that the only division between himself and others at Princeton concerned spirit and method. Although he never mentioned Machen by name, Erdman appeared to accuse his Princeton colleague of "unkindness, suspicion, bitterness and intolerance."[70] The gloves had come off, and Machen responded in kind:

> There is a division between Dr. Erdman and myself, a very serious doctrinal difference indeed. It concerns the question not of this doctrine or that, but of the importance which is to be attributed to doctrine as such. Dr. Erdman's answer to this basal question has been, so far as it can be determined by his public actions, the answer of doctrinal indifferentism.... Dr. Erdman does not indeed reject the doctrine of our church, but he is perfectly willing to make common cause with those who do reject it, and he is perfectly willing on many occasions to keep it in the background.[71]

---

consistently could hold to strict confessionalism within the church and general libertarianism in terms of government intrusions (like the Volsted Act).

[67] Anonymous, "Fundamentalist Gone, Dr. Van Dyke Returns," *New York Times*, 13 December 1924, 3.

[68] Quoted in Longfield, *Presbyterian Controversy*, 131.

[69] Anonymous, "Dr. Erdman Speaks in Self-defense," *Presbyterian Advance* 32/3 (22 January 1925): 24. The letter was also eventually published in the 5 February 1925 edition (95/6) of the *Presbyterian*.

[70] Ibid.

[71] Anonymous, "Dr. Machen Replies to Dr. Erdman," *Presbyterian* 95/6 (5 February 1925): 20–21.

Machen used as evidence for his claim Erdman's support for the 1920 Plan of Organic Union and his willingness to run for moderator in 1924 against Macartney. He further contrasted himself with Erdman by noting that he could not refrain from preaching the gospel, a gospel "identical" with proper Christian doctrine, lest he be "guilty of sheer unfaithfulness to Christ."[72] If Erdman's ecclesiastical collusion with liberals seemed a treachery to many conservatives, it was outright infidelity in Machen's eyes.

Erdman and Machen's personal animosities for one another only highlighted their differences in ecclesiology. When the Princeton faculty led by Machen narrowly voted to remove Erdman as student advisor, a post he had held for eighteen years, Erdman continued to argue that the difference between he and the likes of Machen and Macartney were "spirit and method":[73]

> The alleged grounds [of my removal], as I understand them, were that I have not been sufficiently polemic in my attitude toward rationalism. I hold no brief for rationalism or Modernism, as it has been popularly known.... However, Dr. Macartney and Dr. Machen represent a party which is attempting to fight against rationalism in an unconstitutional method. An example of this was their unsuccessful attempt at the last general Assembly to introduce the "Philadelphia overture" which would compel every member of the Church to re-sign the confession of faith upon taking a new office.... For my part I have always attempted to be conciliatory, because I believed it to be the most Christian. I believe that we should bring every case of heterodoxy into the Church court and decide it in a constitutional manner, and not by discussion outside of the court. All this trouble can be obviated if we act in a kindly, Christian spirit and with confidence in one another.[74]

Beneath insinuations that Macartney and Machen lacked Christian charity, Erdman clearly showed that the issues at stake were deeper than personality and broader than Princeton Seminary. Macartney, preaching at Princeton only two days after Erdman lost his position as student advisor, declared that the church's greatest threat were "those who say they believe in the facts of the gospel but who have not the courage to defend them before the world." He added, however, that "Today, we are confronted with a strange indifference to the facts of the gospel. On the ground of these facts

---

[72] Ibid, 21.

[73] Anonymous, "Dr. Erdman Deposed by Fundamentalists," *New York Times*, 6 April 1925, 1.

[74] Ibid.

only can the church live."[75] Macartney warned that without proper doctrine unequivocally preached and taught, the church would degenerate to nothing more than a humanitarian organization.

Machen and Macartney unsuccessfully campaigned to keep Erdman from becoming moderator of the General Assembly at the 1925 assembly in Columbus, Ohio. Despite an attempt by Machen and his allies to prevent Erdman from even becoming a commissioner, the New Brunswick Presbytery not only elected to send him to Columbus but unanimously elected him as moderator of the presbytery.[76] In his acceptance speech as moderator of the presbytery, he made clear his vision concerning the church's disputes: "It is my earnest hope that by loyal and unswerving allegiance to all the standards, both doctrinal and administrative, we may together keep our beloved Church in the paths of peace and spiritual power."[77] This speech revealed the foundation of Erdman's candidacy for moderator of the General Assembly: "old fashion orthodoxy and Christian spirit and constitutional procedure."[78] A committee of eight, including Machen, lost no time attempting to undermine Erdman's candidacy.[79] The committee dispatched press releases making clear that Erdman was a favorite candidate of church liberals, while positing that the conservative coalition preferred either Lapsey A. McAfee or Frederick N. McMillan.[80] Erdman's supporters shot back that the confessionalists in the church "did not want peace" and intended, through a "surgical operation," to excommunicate 1,500 ministers and any wayward presbyteries.[81] Divisions within the ranks of the conservative coalition, however, surfaced when William Jennings Bryan endorsed the retiring President of Ohio State

---

[75] Anonymous, "Modernists Chided by Dr. Macartney," *New York Times*, 8 April 1925, 23.

[76] Anonymous, "Dr. Erdman Winner in Church Dispute," *New York Times*, 15 April 1925, 18.

[77] Ibid.

[78] Anonymous, "Dr. Erdman's Statement," *Presbyterian Banner* 112/45 (7 May 1925): 5.

[79] Anonymous, "Friends See Plot against Erdman," *New York Times*, 26 April 1925, 9. The other committee members were John F. Carson, Albert D. Ganz, Frank E. Simmons, Maitland Alexander, A. Gordon MacLennan, Ford Cottman, and Walter D. Buchanan.

[80] Ibid.

[81] Anonymous, "Says Bryan Victory Mean Church Split," *New York Times*, 16 May 1925, 3. This was a clear allusion to the Auburn Affirmation and the Presbytery of New York.

THE PRSEBYTERIAN CHURCH IN THE USA

University, W. O. Thompson. Although Thompson refused to run, this was a bad portent for the coalition's candidate Lapsey A. McAfee.

The General Assembly elected Erdman over McAfee by a margin of fifty votes on the second ballot. Upon the announcement of Erdman's victory, many of the commissioners rose to their feet and sang the doxology.[82] However, when the judicial committee upheld the complaint against the Presbytery of New York for licensing Henry P. Van Dusen and Cedric A. Lehman because they could neither confirm not deny their belief in the virgin birth of Christ, the ruling crushed liberal optimism. Henry Sloane Coffin officially protested the decision of the judiciary committee as unconstitutional; nonetheless, the General Assembly upheld the committee's ruling.[83] Liberals prepared to withdraw from the denomination. Erdman personally visited their caucus meeting and coaxed them to support a special commission studying church unrest; they agreed.[84] The "peace" commission of fifteen was broadly representative. It included liberals such as Edgar W. Work of New York City and Edward D. Duffield of Newark; Lapsey McAfee and Mark Mathews represented the conservatives. Other members included former moderator Henry C. Swearingen and three future moderators, W. O. Thompson (1926), Robert E. Speer (1927), and Hugh T. Kerr (1930).[85]

During his tenure as moderator, Erdman worked tirelessly to promote the peace and unity on which his campaign rested. This was no easy feat. The denomination already faced a financial crisis and the missions budget from the previous year had a deficit of over $5,000,000.[86] In December a group of ninety-five ministers calling themselves the Committee on Protestant Liberties petitioned the "Peace Commission." The committee alleged that the General Assembly used "Tammany methods" to demand that presbyteries conform to its dictates concerning the standards of

---

[82] Anonymous, "Dr. Erdman, Peace Candidate, Chosen by Presbyterians," *New York Times*, 22 May 1925, 1.

[83] The entire ruling and protest is printed in anonymous, "The One Hundred and Thirty-Seventh General Assembly," *Presbyterian Magazine* 31/7 (July 1925): 358–59.

[84] Loetscher, *Broadening Church*, 128–29.

[85] The other seven committee members were Harry C. Rogers, Cheeseman A. Herrick, John H. Dewitt, Nelson H. Loomis, Nathan C. Moore, Alfred H. Barr, John M. T. Finney.

[86] Anonymous, "Presbyterians Face Financial Crisis," *Christian Century* 42/29 (16 July 1925): 934.

ordination to the ministry.[87] The petition further threatened that, if such practices persisted, several presbyteries would sever their connection with the General Assembly.[88] Coffin, who signed the petition, made clear his willingness, if need be, to consider schism as a matter of principle. His essay "Why I am a Presbyterian" might have more accurately been titled "Why I am a Presbyterian for the Moment." In the essay Coffin railed against "the narrowness and crass stupidity" of some ecclesiastic assemblies and certain "retrograde leaders" in his Presbyterian church. He also claimed that he remained a Presbyterian despite the tendency of many of his coreligionists to place "literalist constructions" on ministerial vows and promote an ecclesiology that made the Presbyterian Church nothing more than "a denomination which is held together by agreement in theological opinions."[89] Coffin warned, however, that "should this thoroughly unprotestant view prevail, the Church will inevitably be broken into two sections, as it has unhappily been several times in the past."[90]

More worrisome, perhaps, the New York Presbytery adopted a report from its committee to investigate implementation of the General Assembly's ruling in the Lehman and Van Dusen cases. The committee argued that it had "tenable constitutional grounds" to reject the ruling of the assembly. It further argued that it could not undo its licensing of Lehman and Van Dusen despite their failure to affirm positively their belief in the virgin birth because the General Assembly could not make doctrinal changes without approval of two-thirds of the presbyteries. While the committee admitted that the two could be individually tried in the church court, it acknowledged that "no action by the presbytery is possible."[91] Fundamentalist Walter D. Buchanan of Broadway Church immediately filed a complaint against the presbytery with the General Assembly, hoping the issue would be overturned on the national level.

---

[87] Anonymous, "Modernists Score Church Board Acts," *New York Times*, 3 December 1925, 11; anonymous, "Seek to Please All in Church Dispute," *New York Times*, 4 December 1925, 12; anonymous, "Ask Meaning of Presbyterian Creed," *Christian Century* 42/53 (31 December 1925): 1647.

[88] Loetscher, *Broadening Church*, 130–33.

[89] Henry Sloane Coffin, "Why I am a Presbyterian," in *Twelve Modern Apostles and Their Creeds*, ed. Gilbert K. Chesterton, Charles L. Slattery, and Henry Sloane Coffin (New York: Duffield and Company, 1926) 62, 64.

[90] Ibid., 64–65.

[91] Anonymous, "Presbytery Backs Unorthodox Acts," *New York Times*, 12 January 1926, 8.

Erdman continued to make his inclusivist vision of the church public. He agreed with virtually all evangelicals that the church had a social mission especially to the nation. Using his pulpit as moderator, he proclaimed in his "monthly letter" that "religion and patriotism are closely related." Because morality was the perquisite for national stability and strength, Erdman concluded, it was the duty for loyal and patriotic Presbyterians to support their national missions board. Like Speer, he saw the board's financial difficulties not only as an embarrassment, but also a crisis for the church as a whole. "This is our Board. It is not an organization outside of the Church; it is not an independent society, functioning within the Church; it is the Church at work, and accomplishing its first great task of evangelizing the homeland."[92] Erdman, having served as chairman of the Board of National Missions under Macartney, had a heart for this ministry; however, his appeal revealed an organic understanding of the church in which any part impacted the health, effectiveness, and spiritual vitality of the whole. Erdman never relinquished the premillennialist or Keswick Holiness heritage of his father. He believed that the church constituted the union of its individual members; nonetheless, he maintained that it was not an organization but an organism "composed of living souls united by faith to a living Lord." This ecclesiology, according to Erdman, meant that nothing "can be of such vital consequence to the church as the nurture of its spiritual life and the proper expression of this life through the activities of its members."[93] It also meant that mean-spiritedness, intolerance, and disunity weakened and undermined the church's witness and mission.[94] Erdman, however, did not intend to implicate his confessionalist adversaries as the sole cause of disunity in the church. If spiritual maturity provided the necessary element of a healthy church, "spiritual childishness" could be found among liberals as well. He clearly believed that "a temper making for strife and competition and separation" undermined the church's mission. However, he equally rejected "instability of conviction or uncertainty as to what and why one believes, or inability to withstand the currents of doubt and the assaults of unbelief."[95]

---

[92] Charles R. Erdman, "The Moderator's Monthly Letter," *Presbyterian Magazine* 31/11 (November 1925): 540.

[93] Charles R. Erdman, *The Spirit of Christ: Devotional Studies in the Doctrine of the Holy Spirit* (New York: George H. Doran Company, 1926) 90–91.

[94] Ibid., 91–92. Cf. Erdman, "The Moderator's Monthly Letter: An Ideal Church," *Presbyterian Magazine* 32/5 (May 1926): 211.

[95] Erdman, *Spirit of Christ*, 98–99.

While church unity did not consist simply of unanimity of belief or worship, it certainly did not consist of any and all beliefs.[96]

The following year the General Assembly enthusiastically affirmed the report made by the peace commission, much to the dismay of Macartney and his coalition. Having met with representatives from conservative and liberal parties in the church, the special commission understood its mandate to promote the purity and peace of the church in a constitutional manner.[97] While noting that external religious and cultural forces had exacerbated the dispute, the commission's report spent twice as much ink examining internal causes. These causes included historical divisions between Old and New School theology, difference as to the content of constitutional and administrative authority, the inaction of presbyteries against theological extremists (liberal and conservative), and public campaigns of slander.[98] The commission attempted to navigate a middle course between the two ecclesiological visions that emphasized common beliefs like conservatives and liberty of interpretation like liberals. As the commission put it, "Foremost among the forces making for unity is a common faith expressed in our confessional symbols, but intimately related to this, and defining the way in which the faith is to be held among the brethren in the Presbyterian Church, is the constitutional principle of toleration. This principle has been obscured in the recent controversies which have agitated the Church, and this obscurity underlies many of the causes of the unrest in the preceding section."[99] To rousing applause the commission reiterated the Presbyterian Form of Government chapter 1, section 5, which allowed for liberty in interpretation and demanded mutual forbearance of reasonable difference. Most important, the commission crafted a constitutional compromise that simultaneously affirmed the five-point doctrinal deliverance as true Presbyterian doctrine yet rescinded the mandate by the General Assembly to enforce it. The fourth section of the report, concerning the powers of the General Assembly, defended this approach historically. The commission concluded that the assembly had the right to make doctrinal deliverances (paragraph 2.1); however, they were neither irrevocable nor binding (paragraphs 2 and 3) because no executive or judicial body or the General

---

[96] Ibid., 93.

[97] Anonymous, "Report of the Special Commission of 1925," *Presbyterian Advance* 33/15 (10 June 1926 suppl.): 1.

[98] Ibid., 2–4.

[99] Ibid., 4.

Assembly itself had the authority to make constitutional amendments without a joint action in the presbyteries (paragraph 2.3).[100] Furthermore, because the General Assembly could err, as argued by the Westminster Confession itself, the assembly was also not bound by precedent (paragraph 3).[101]

The General Assembly passed out written copies of the report to all commissioners and held over discussion of the report until the following Monday. Liberals had made it clear that the report, if adopted, satisfied their concerns. Coffin, in fact, called the report "magnificent!"[102] When Monday arrived the General Assembly waited with bated breath to see if the report would be adopted. M. L. Thomas of Los Angeles, California, moved to strike out section 5.3 regarding public campaigns of slander, arguing that it unfairly targeted one group in the church. Lapsey A. McAfee's denial of this charge helped ensure the almost unanimous defeat of Thomas's motion.[103]

Before a motion to vote on the whole report could be seconded, Clarence Macartney took the floor and moved to remove the crucial compromises found in section 4.3 of the report, which he believed would allow the New York Presbytery to "flaunt its defiance."[104] Macartney lamented that the commission took such pains to study the documents of the church only to find "such words as Liberty, Toleration, and not the admonitions not to depart from the faith."[105] The drama heightened when Macartney's brother A. J. Macartney took the platform and implored his brother in the name of their deceased mother's memory to accept the report. Adding to Macartney's humiliation, his brother publicly "defended" him to the commissioners, announcing that "brother Clarence is all right. The trouble with him is that he isn't married. If that old bachelor would get married he would do more for the peace and harmony of the Presbyterian Church and would not have time to worry about the church's theology."[106] John W. Kennedy perhaps represented the general sentiment of impatience

---

[100] Ibid., 7.

[101] Ibid.

[102] Anonymous, "Presbyterian Split Averted by Report of 15," *New York Tribune*, 29 May 1926, 5.

[103] Anonymous, "Second Week of the General Assembly," *Presbyterian Advance* 33/15 (10 June 1926) 9.

[104] Ishbel Ross, "Presbyterians Adopt Peace Finding Report," *New York Herald*, 1 June 1926, 4. Cf. anonymous, "Second Week," 9, 16.

[105] Anonymous, "Second Week," 16.

[106] Ross, "Presbyterians Adopt Peace Finding Report," 4.

that pervaded the hall when he shouted, "Let's quit all this technical stuff. Half of us don't know what we're talking about, and let us get back to work without a controversy. Leave it to the big guns to settle things and we preachers will go on quietly with our work." Mark Matthews, at the request of commission chairman Henry Sweringen, defended the document, although he hastened to remind liberals that "when we say tolerance we don't expect you to take liberties with it."[107] With Matthews's tentative imprimatur the conservative coalition's attack all but crumbled. Macartney's motion failed by a wide margin, and subsequently the report was adopted almost unanimously. Adding insult to injury for the conservative coalition, the General Assembly unceremoniously adopted the judicial committee's dismissal of Buchanan's complaint that the Presbytery of New York stood in "rebellion" because of its action concerning Lehman and Van Dusen.[108]

Despite the special peace commission's remarkable political maneuvering, Macartney and Machen's shrinking coalition remained dissatisfied. After the General Assembly reorganized Princeton Seminary in 1929, Machen and his followers founded Westminster Theological Seminary in nearby Philadelphia, Pennsylvania.[109] In 1933, Machen, H. McAllister Griffiths, and a group of confessionalists and fundamentalists attacked the board of foreign missions for tolerating the alleged heresy of missionary and author Pearl S. Buck. Writing in *Harper's Monthly Magazine*, Buck labeled traditional rationales of missions as "superstition."[110] She

---

[107] Ibid. In a 1924 sermon preceding the Young People's Life Investment rally, Matthews, like Erdman and Speer, emphasized the importance of the church's chief mission, evangelizing the world before the Second Advent of Christ. Further, his premillennialism did not seem to sour his optimism in the ultimate success of the church on earth. While Matthews took quite seriously the need to protect individuals from the damning effect of rationalism, he seemed convinced that rationalists had more bark than bite. This may explain his willingness to compromise. See Paul Rader, "The Position, Power, and Prayer of the Church" (1924) Daniel Paul Rader ephemera, collection 38, box 1, folder 29, Billy Graham Center archives, Wheaton IL.

[108] Anonymous, "Presbytery Here Wins Vindication," *New York Times*, 2 June 1926, 1. For the complete verdict see anonymous, "Presbytery of New Sustained," *Presbyterian Advance* 33/16 (17 June 1926): 16–17.

[109] Ronald T. Clutter makes the point that ecclesiology, at least in part, lead to the reorganization of Princeton Seminary. See "The Reorganization of Princeton Seminary," *Grace Theological Journal* 7/2 (Fall 1986): 188–97.

[110] Pearl S. Buck, "Is There a Case for Foreign Missions?" *Harper's Monthly Magazine* 166/2 (January 1933): 149.

further promoted a "creedless faith." Such faith had vitality, according to Buck, because of its connection to the ethics and life of Jesus rather than the inherent superiority of Christian dogma to the tenants of other religions.[111] When the national foreign missions board defended Buck, Machen set up an independent Presbyterian foreign board and acted as its president.[112] The 1934 Cleveland General Assembly ruled against participation in the newly formed Independent Presbyterian Board:

> The organization of any Independent Board or Agency for Presbyterian Foreign Missions, which does not receive the sanction of the General Assembly, and which attempts to carry on any administrative functions involving the missionary work of the Presbyterian Church in the United States of America, constitutes a rebellious defiance of lawful authority. Any Presbyterian ministers or laymen who have a part in such an organization, and any church, presbytery, or synod which supports such an organization, place themselves in the position of schismatics, and subject to that censure which not only the Presbyterian Church but any form of constitutional government must for the maintenance of its very existence inevitably exercise.[113]

Ironically, the Independent Board insisted that, because it had no affiliation with the PCUSA and did not require particular ecclesiastical connection of its missionaries, the ruling of the General Assembly did not apply to its supporters. Therefore, Machen, Griffiths, Wheaton College president J. Oliver Buswell, and Carl McIntire of Collingswood, New Jersey, among others, refused to relinquish their membership with the board.[114] They received unwelcome support from Coffin, who argued that "we have to be tolerant to the intolerant."[115]

The Independent Board proved equally controversial within the conservative coalition itself. After the General Assembly, Joseph A. Schofield resigned from the Independent Board, stating that, while he

---

[111] Ibid., 151.
[112] Anonymous, "Pearl Buck's Foes Lose Mission Fight," *New York Times*, 28 May 1933, 7. Cf. anonymous, "145th Assembly Meets; New Mission Board Announced," *Christianity Today* 4/2 (June 1933): 4, 8–14.
[113] *Minutes of the General Assembly of the Presbyterian Church in the U.S.A.* (Philadelphia: Office of the General Assembly, 1934) 98.
[114] Anonymous, "Man Versus the Machine: The 146th General Assembly," *Christianity Today* 5/2 (July 1934): 43.
[115] Henry Sloane Coffin, "That 'New' Foreign Board," *Presbyterian Tribune* 50/6 (1 November 1934): 6.

believed the General Assembly's ruling unconstitutional, the board_caused more harm than good. In his published letter of resignation he claimed that membership in the Independent Board necessarily involved the "abandonment of any effort to preserve the vast assets of the official Board for the purpose for which they were given." The Independent Board not only proved divisive, but according to Schofield its existence subverted the debate "from questions of doctrine" to "questions of polity."[116] Samuel Craig, chief editor of the conservative *Christianity Today*, had a falling out with managing editor H. McAllister Griffiths over participation in the Independent Board. Griffiths promptly resigned from *Christianity Today* and began his own periodical, the *Presbyterian Guardian*.[117] Warren W. Ward, moderator of the Philadelphia Presbytery and a Westminster Seminary trustee, asserted that the seminary was "committing suicide" by continued association with the Independent Board.[118] Ward's assertions, coupled with the subsequent resignations from the board of F. Paul McConkey of Detroit, Michigan, and Alexander Alison of Bridgeport, Connecticut, signaled growing division among Machen's supporters concerning the Independent Board.[119] By January 1936, the dispute had escalated into personal attacks against Craig, who also served as a Westminster Seminary trustee. Machen, as chairman of the trustees, demanded that the Independent Board express their disapproval of Craig and *Christianity Today* or resign from Westminster. Machen miscalculated the board's response. Almost half of the board, including Craig, Maitland Alexander, Clarence Macartney, and John H. McComb, resigned. Oswald T. Allis also quit his position as professor of the Old Testament.[120]

In 1935, Machen, McIntire, Griffiths, and four others were officially suspended from the ministry. The following year, a small contingent of Machen's followers (including some fundamentalists) withdrew from the

---

[116] Anonymous, "The Rev. Joseph A. Schofield's Letter of Resignation," *Presbyterian* 105/30 (25 July 1935): 5–6.

[117] Anonymous, "An Executive Quits 'Christianity Today,'" *New York Times*, 2 August 1935 15; anonymous, "Editor is Assailed in Machen Dispute," *New York Times*, 28 October 1935, 34.

[118] Anonymous, "Warns on School of Presbyterians" *New York Times*, 4 December 1935, 28.

[119] Anonymous, "2 Westminster Trustees Quit," *Philadelphia Evening Bulletin*, 31 October 1935, D6.

[120] Anonymous, "13 Trustees Quit Machen Seminary," *New York Times*, 8 January 1936, 17.

PCUSA and founded the Presbyterian Church of America, later renamed the Orthodox Presbyterian Church (OPC). However, the ecclesiological weakness of Machen's coalition soon manifested itself in another schism. Although there existed certain similarities between Machen's understanding of the church and that espoused by the fundamentalists, Machen clearly stood in a different camp. He intended to create a doctrinally pure Presbyterian church in the Old School tradition. His "old school" convictions did not reconcile easily with the Arminianism and premillennial eschatology typically affirmed by fundamentalists. These differences proved ecclesiologically significant.

The failure of Machen's appeal lay in its inherent contradiction between his "voluntary" ecclesiology in theory and in practice. If the church were a purely voluntary institution of those who simply agreed on theological principles, as Machen suggested, then it was theoretically unclear why he willingly joined forces with premillennialists, revivalists, and Keswickers. Upon the election of J. Oliver Buswell as moderator, Machen declared, "your election has shown that reports that the Presbyterian Church of America rejects premillennialism are untrue and that the church not only tolerates but welcomes its adherents."[121] Machen's assurances notwithstanding, fundamentalists demanded that the confession of the PCA constitutionally "safeguard" dispensational doctrines.[122] After all, fundamentalists had just participated with the confessionalists in a failed experiment to create a church based upon the exclusion of doctrinal dissenters. Despite fundamentalist concerns, a committee headed by Ned B. Stonehouse refused to change the Confession of Faith except to remove the 1903 declaratory statement that paved the way for the PCUSA's merger with the Cumberland Presbyterian Church. In the end, dispensationalists remained with Machen as a matter simply of great respect rather than doctrinal consistency. His sudden death in January 1937 made another schism inevitable, and that same year fundamentalists under the leadership of Carl McIntire and H. McAllister Griffiths organized the Bible Presbyterian Church.[123] Although the 1936 schisms tied the PCUSA in

[121] Anonymous, "Heads New Groups of Presbyterians," New York Times, 13 November 1936, 8.

[122] Anonymous, "Fundamentalists Adopt Old Creed," New York Times, 14 November 1936, 21.

[123] For a lengthy discussion of the Princetonian ecclesiology exemplified by Machen in comparison with more fundamentalist versions, see especially chapter five

several lawsuits over property, the denomination by and large remained intact by establishing and maintaining the "inclusivist" ecclesiology of a fundamentalist-modernist coalition that allowed regional Presbyterians, whether liberal, fundamentalist, or confessionalist, to enforce their own interpretations for the standards of ministry and missions. In the words of one *Christian Century* editor, the PCUSA discovered "the magic by which to progress by dissention."[124]

---

in Ki Hong Kim, "Presbyterian Conflict in the Early Twentieth Century: Ecclesiology in the Princeton Tradition and the Emergence of Presbyterian Fundamentalism," unpublished Ph. D. dissertation, Drew University, 1983.

[124] "The Presbyterians—Progress by Dissention," *Christian Century* 41/24 (12 June 1924): 753.

CONCLUSION

The Church's one foundation
Is Jesus Christ her Lord;
She is his new creation
By water and the word.
From heav'n he came and sought her
To be his holy bride;
With his own blood he bought,
And her life he died.

Tho' with a scornful wonder
Men see her sore opprest,
By schisms rent asunder,
By heresies distressed,
Yet saints their watch are keeping,
Their cry goes up, "How long?"
And soon the night of weeping
Shall be the morn of song.

—Samuel John Stone, hymn

CHAPTER 10

Yet Saints Their Watch Are Keeping

The disputes between fundamentalists, modernists, and traditionalists did not last forever. Indeed, like the waiting saints of Samuel Stone's hymn, evangelicals in the Northern establishment increasingly cried, "How long?" Critics of the day often revealed their fatigue and ambivalence of the controversies' effects on establishment denominations. Stewart G. Cole, professor at Crozer Theological Seminary, reflected that "though the disagreeable features of the controversy have been restrained, there is no evidence that the church has recovered either spiritual poise or clarity of vision."[1] In his opinion, the only hope for either movement was to "mutually share their values in the divine adventure."[2] George A. Coe predicted that fundamentalism, lacking comprehensive organizational structures, would be unable to resist theological changes; the uncreative and imitative characteristics of theological liberalism promised a slow demise of its movement as well.[3] He hopefully noted, however, that there always existed the possibility "of a remaking of Protestantism within itself."[4] By 1935, even Harry Emerson Fosdick declared that modernism had run its course and he was necessarily moving beyond it. He warned that "unless the church can go deeper and reach higher than [modernism] it will fail indeed."[5]

---

[1] Stewart G. Cole, *The History of Fundamentalism* (New York: Richard R. Smith, Inc, 1931) 337.

[2] Ibid.

[3] George A. Coe, "What's Coming in Religion? The Main Stream and the Eddies," *Christian Century* 47/52 (31 December 1930): 1620–21.

[4] Ibid., 1621.

[5] Harry Emerson Fosdick, "Beyond Modernism," *Christian Century* 52/49 (4 December 1935): 1550.

Yet not all evangelicals within the Northern Protestant establishment lacked appreciation for the role that modernists and fundamentalists played in their denominations. Methodist missionary E. Stanley Jones declared (prematurely perhaps) an end to denominational hostilities at a 1929 meeting of the Greater New York Federation of Churches. He reminded his audience, however, that "in every nation you have the conservatives and the radicals, and it is so in religion. The conservative needs the radical and the radical needs the conservative, and I think the Lord needs them both."[6] James Snowden, editor of the *Presbyterian Banner*, equally appreciated the influence of both movements within denominations: "Fundamentalism and modernism are both principles and processes and not results. They are both true principles and necessary processes and can no more be stopped than can the activity and growth of the human mind. They are complementary aspects of conservatism and liberalism, of the stabilized root and the growing branches and unfolding blossoms and ripening fruit, and neither ought to be suppressed, much less misrepresented and vilified, but they should mutually support each other."[7] Indeed, in many ways the various parties within the denominations of the Northern establishment had, through compromise, begun a process of healing and mutual support. In relative peace they awaited the next necessary movements to revitalize their denominations.

In charting the ecclesiology of evangelicals in the Northern Protestant establishment, I have sought to do two things. First, I explored the "oxymoron" of evangelical ecclesiology, marked by denominational ambivalence. Evangelicals, by and large, clung tenaciously to their denominational affiliations while forging trans-denominational alliances between or outside of those institutions. Second, I wished to examine the ecclesiological effect of the so-called fundamentalist-modernist controversies on the denominations of Protestant establishment. To this end I challenged the two-party thesis and models of denominational declension of American Protestantism as explanations for the significance of these controversies. Instead I promoted a multi-party model of contention and noted that inter-party compromise led to denominational persistence.

---

[6] Anonymous, "Fundamentalist Row Ended, Says Preacher," *New York Times*, 26 March 1929, 32.

[7] James H. Snowden, "Fundamentalism and Modernism," *Presbyterian Banner* 120/52 (28 June 1934): 9.

Bruce Hindmarsh's description of the "oxymoron" of evangelical ecclesiology, while apt, makes such ecclesiology sound more mysterious than perhaps it is. Insofar as evangelicals, whether liberal or conservative, wanted to *be* the church, they needed to bring their ecclesiological visions into *being*. Edward Schillebeeckx rightfully reminds us that "belief in God...is only possible in the forms of the human condition." Therefore, the ways evangelicals shaped their ecclesiology depended upon many different factors: the historical milieu in which they lived, practical attempts to engage American culture, pneumatology, and eschatology. Ideas and experiments, however, cannot engage in a mission, change a nation, or convert the world; people do these things. Therefore, evangelicals, manifesting their serious sense of calling and purpose, labored to shape those individuals and institutions that could and should carry out the church's mission. Schillebeeckx, however, further argues that "it is almost impossible to hand down living belief in God without some alienation from the institution. ...Precisely for that reason an institutional religion also always comes under the criticism of the power and freedom of the original religious experience. However, no one can live all day with the high tension of a religious experience. So religion makes the power of the religious experience as it were 'bearable,' all through life."[8] Evangelicals, all of whom especially valued the importance of their religious experience, were driven by their sense of mission and divine purpose. They also took solace in institutions that allowed them the share the burden of their task. However, when those institutions did not live up to the high calling of religious experience, they typically criticized and attempted to change them.

It is also important to remember that implementation of ecclesiology by evangelicals took place in particular denominations. While there were similarities, the conflicts and compromises within the Northern Baptist Convention, the Disciples of Christ, and the Presbyterian Church in the U.S.A. were shaped by the specific histories, personalities, polities, and traditions as much as they were exacerbated and invigorated by the evangelical movements of fundamentalism and modernism. To this end, I presented a nonlinear, multiparty model of conflict and compromise in these three establishment denominations. Fundamentalists and modernists were neither opposites nor alone in their conflicts and compromises. Furthermore, the commitment of the majority of Northern establishment

---

[8] Edward Schillebeeckx, *Church: The Human Story of God* (New York: Crossroad Publishing Company, 1993) 59.

evangelicals, both liberal and conservative, to seek ecclesiological compromise amid serious contention suggests that the death of denominationalism has been greatly exaggerated.

Writing about the characteristics of the Protestant establishment between 1900 and 1960, William Hutchison observed that "[w]hat was at stake, for most Protestant leaders, was an established status that they were sure could and must be maintained despite the numbers. In short, the issue was hegemony. Seen from that perspective, the remarkable characteristic of the Protestant establishment, up to the 1960s and perhaps afterward as well, was not decline but persistence."[9] In the late nineteenth century, evangelicals sought to maintain the cultural center of American life. Their different strategies represented the diverse ideas about the church in the Protestant establishment. While the leaders of these trans-denominational networks often argued that their rivals' tactics were ineffective or even damaging, the denominational tent remained broad enough to tolerate more than one ecclesiological vision, even in the midst of crisis. Ironically, the creation of an institutionally viable establishment by means of denominational centralization and interdenominational cooperation challenged its comprehensiveness and threatened its unity.

Given these circumstances, it is less surprising that conflict arose than compromise prevailed. Inertia was certainly on the side of denominational persistence. H. Richard Niebuhr suggested as early as 1926 that social factors (i.e., class, race, and culture) rather than intellectual ones (creed, tradition, and theology) explained why churches held together.[10] Three years later he argued that the strength of denominational structures had overcome the strife of the 1920s:

> In more fluid times, with less powerful ecclesiastical organizations in command, the parties of rural Fundamentalism and of bourgeois Modernism might well have produced denominations which would have handed down for many decades in creeds and traditions, the temporary, local differences of opinion found in post-war America. The advantage of strong ecclesiastical organization, in preserving compulsory unity until inner harmony can be

---

[9] William R. Hutchison, "Preface: From Protestant to Pluralist America," in *Between the Times: The Trail of the Protestant Establishment, 1900–1960,* ed. William R. Hutchison (New York: Cambridge University Press, 1989) viii.

[10] H. Richard Niebuhr, "What Holds Churches Together?" *Christian Century* 43/11 (18 March 1926): 346–48.

re-established, have come to light in this instance as they came much more patently to light in the medieval world.[11]

Niebuhr's analysis of the origins of fundamentalism and modernism has rightly been questioned; however, his need to explain why establishment denominations could withstand the social sources that ought to have torn them apart is telling. Indeed, strong ecclesiastical organization helped establishment denominations weather the storm of conflict. However, the strength of the evangelical commitment to American culture and world evangelism made the denominational structures, in which they and their forebears had invested time, money, sweat, and prayer, too important not to preserve.

Ecclesiologically speaking, this suggests that the controversies of the 1920s and 1930s were not a social or theological inevitability. In the establishment many rival ecclesial communities, with different understandings about the true nature of Christian community, coexisted for decades before the controversy. Evangelicals in these denominations also sought or created trans-denominational fellowship outside of their denominational affiliations. However, in a pluralistic and voluntary American society, those in the evangelical establishment of the early twentieth century felt that they were forced to choose between remaining broadly evangelical or viably established. The choice of the latter helped precipitate the controversy in the 1920s and 1930s. In other words, the conflicts and compromises within the Protestant establishment, rather than suggesting the decline of establishment denominations, reflected growing pains created by evangelical attempts to change the ecclesiology of their denominations to fulfill their mission to American culture.

Of course, ecclesiology in establishment churches did not remain static after the conflicts and compromises of the 1920s and 1930s. The Second World War, the Jewish Holocaust, the civil rights movement, the advance of international communism, the counter-culture, and the Vietnam War continued to challenge Protestants who perceived themselves to have an important mission to American culture. The Christian Realist movement, espoused in the United States by Henry P. Van Dusen, Reinhold and H. Richard Niebuhr, Samuel McCrea Cavert, and Georgia Harkness, challenged establishment denominations again to reexamine their ecclesiology. We should not, therefore, be surprised at H. Richard

---

[11] H. Richard Niebuhr, *Social Sources of Denominationalism* (New York: Henry Holt and Company, 1929) 186.

Niebuhr's attacks on fundamentalism and modernism. Heather A. Warren has noted that the Christian Realist movement (like fundamentalism and modernism before it, I might add) felt the need to construct a new ecclesiology to meet the needs of a new day. In Niebuhr's view, therefore, fundamentalism was hopelessly antiquated and modernism sinfully bourgeois. Christian Realists attempted to shape their denominations to be more internationalist while forging ecumenical alliances in the United States and Europe.[12]

Joel A. Carpenter argued that, while some fundamentalists asserted that institutional purity provided the only acceptable option for faithful Christians, others in the movement actively supported nondenominational and parachurch ministries as well as schools with fundamentalist proclivities, thereby cultivating a religious subculture within their denominations.[13] While he argued that "fundamentalists contributed to the decline of mainline denominations by promoting dissatisfaction with those bodies' work," I am more inclined to see their transdenomination affiliations as breathing new life into their home churches.[14] The next generation of fundamentalists continued to challenge their denominations to be the church. It is, of course, fair and right to ask whether parachurch, or special-interest, religious organizations evidence the decline of denominations. But the recent phenomenon of evangelicals on the "Canterbury trail" or the "Roman road" and the spread of "charismatic" and "seeker" churches within the mainline should at least allow us to admit that the jury is still out on whether we can reasonable speak of the eclipse of denominationalism.

New players, such as Lutherans and Southern Baptists, also eventually tried on the establishment mantle while others, like Methodists, Presbyterians, and Congregationalists, reconfigured their membership through institutional mergers with their Southern or ethnic coreligionists. Not surprisingly, conflicts, compromises, and in some cases schism occurred as these denominations tried to shape their ecclesiology to engage American culture with the same commitments as establishment churches of the past. Regardless, establishment churches have depended upon trans-denominational movements (in many cases the distinct heirs of

---

[12] Heather A. Warren, *Theologians of a New World Order: Reinhold Niebuhr and the Christian Realists, 1920–1948* (New York: Oxford University Press, 1997) 130.

[13] Joel A. Carpenter, *Revive Us Again: The Reawakening of American Fundamentalism* (New York: Oxford U. Press, 1997) 33–88.

[14] Ibid., 32.

fundamentalism and modernism) to reinvigorate their institutions in a new generation. In fact, denominations are one of the very few places where evangelicals of various ecclesial visions are compelled to interact and challenge one another's claims of how to be the church in the world. Therefore, conflict and compromise continue within their boundaries. Trans-denominational movements are not simply irritants; they also revitalize and keep institutions fresh. For this reason, those in these denominations might, like St. Paul, gracefully abide this thorn in the flesh.

BIBLIOGRAPHY OF CITED WORKS

Archival Collections

Mel Trotter papers, collection 47, Billy Graham Center archives, Wheaton IL.
Daniel Paul Rader ephemera, collection 38, Billy Graham Center archives, Wheaton IL.
History of the Interchurch World Movement is a collection of IWM documents compiled in ten parts around 1924 after the movement finally shut down all operations. These documents were microfilmed by the William Adams Brown Ecumenical Library, Union Seminary NY.

Pamphlets

An Affirmation Designed to Safeguard the Unity and Liberty of the Presbyterian Church in the United States of America. Auburn NY: The Jacobs Press, 1 May 1924.
The Baptist Bible Union of North America. *Information Concerning the Baptist Bible Union of North America with By-Laws and Aims*. No place or date of publication [1925].
The Church Takes a Leaf from Successful Business. New York: Interchurch World Movement, 1920. Pamphlet #50–5734, Wisconsin Historical Society, Madison WI.
Elmore, R. E. *Should the United Christian Missionary Society Be Dissolved?* No place or date of publication.
Executive Committee of the Baptist Bible Union of North America, *A Call to Arms*. No place or date of publication [1924].
Fosdick, Harry Emerson. *Shall the Fundamentalists Win? A Sermon Preached at the First Presbyterian Church, New York, May 21, 1922, Stenographically Reported by Margaret Renton*. New York: First Presbyterian Church, 1922.
Gray, James M. *The Deadline of Doctrine around the Church: A Reply to Dr. Harry Emerson Fosdick's Sermon Entitled "Shall the Fundamentalists Win?"* Chicago: Moody Bible Institute, no date.
Griffith Thomas, W. H. *Modernism in China*. Philadelphia: The Sunday School Times Company, no date.

Haldeman, I. M. *Professor Shailer Mathews' Burlesque on the Second Coming of Our Lord Jesus Christ.* New York: First Baptist Church, no date.

————. *Why I Am Opposed to the Interchurch World Movement.* New York: I. M. Haldeman, no date.

Institutional Churches—A Vision. New York: Open or Institutional Church League, no date.

Massee, J. C. *How to Be a Soul-Winner.* Evangelistic Series, number 555. Philadelphia: American Baptist Publication Society, no date.

Mathews, Shailer. *Will Christ Come Again?* Chicago: American Institute of Sacred Literature, 1917.

Officers, Constitution, and Platform of the Open or Institutional Church League. New York: 83 Bible House, no date.

The Open and Institutional Church League: Our Work. New York: Open or Institutional Church League, no date.

Temple College Catalogue. Philadelphia: Temple College, 1896. Conwellana-Templana collection, Temple University, Philadelphia PA.

Conference Proceedings and Essay Collections

1922 Year Book of Organizations of Disciples of Christ. St. Louis: United Christian Missionary Society, 1923.

Annual of the Northern Baptist Convention 1921 Containing the Proceeding of the Fourteenth Meeting Held at Des Moines, Iowa June 22 to 28, 1921. New York: American Baptist Publication Office, 1921.

Annual of the Northern Baptist Convention 1922 Containing the Proceeding of the Fifteenth Meeting Held at Indianapolis, Indiana June 14 to 20, 1922. New York: American Baptist Publication Office, 1922.

Annual of the Northern Baptist Convention 1924 Containing the Proceeding of the Seventeenth Meeting Held at Milwaukee, Wisconsin May 28 to June 3, 1924. New York: American Baptist Publication Office, 1924.

Annual of the Northern Baptist Convention 1925 Containing the Proceeding of the Eighteenth Meeting Held at Seattle, Washington June 30 to July 5, 1925. New York: American Baptist Publication Office, 1925.

Annual of the Northern Baptist Convention 1926 Containing the Proceeding of the Nineteenth Meeting Held at Washington, D. C. May 25–30, 1926. New York: American Baptist Publication Office, 1926.

Baptist Doctrines: Addresses at the North American Pre-Convention Conference, Des Moines, Iowa, June 21, 1921. No place: J. C. Massee, 1921.

Baptist Fundamentals Being Addresses Delivered at the Pre-Convention Conference at Buffalo, June 21 and 22, 1920. Philadelphia: Judson Press, 1920.

Christianity in a New World. Philadelphia: Judson Press, 1921.

The Coming and Kingdom of Christ: A Stenographic Report of the Prophetic Bible Conference Held at Moody Bible Institute of Chicago, February 24–27, 1914. Chicago: The Bible Institute Colportage Association, 1914.

Congregational Churches of the United States, *Reports of Commissions and Mission Boards Moderator's Add, Council Sermon, Minutes, Roll of Delegates, Constitution and By-laws, Etc.* New York: Office of the National Council, 1921.

The Fundamentals: A Testimony to the Truth. 12 volumes. Chicago: Testimony Publishing Company, n.d.

Garrison, J. H., editor. *Our First Congress Consisting of Addresses on Religious and Theological Questions, During the First Congress of Disciples of Christ Held in St. Louis, April 25–27, 1899*. St. Louis: Christian Publishing Company, 1900.

God Hath Spoken: Twenty-five Addresses Delivered at the World Conference of Christian Fundamentals. Philadelphia: Bible Conference Committee, 1919.

Light on Prophecy, a Coordinated, Constructive Teaching Being the Proceedings and Addresses at the Philadelphia Prophetic Conference, May 28–30, 1918. New York: Christian Herald, 1918.

Minutes of the General Assembly of the Presbyterian Church in the U.S.A. Philadelphia: Office of the General Assembly, 1920.

Minutes of the General Assembly of the Presbyterian Church in the U.S.A. Philadelphia: Office of the General Assembly, 1934.

National Perils and Opportunities: The Discussion of the General Christian Conference Held in Washington, D. C. December 7th, 8th, and 9th, 1887 under the Auspices and Direction of the Evangelical Alliance for the United States. New York: The Baker & Taylor Co., 1887.

The Open and Institutional Church League Preliminary Conference Held in Madison Avenue Presbyterian Church, New York City, March 27, 1894. Boston: Everett Press Company, 1894.

Report of the Sixteenth Annual Conference of the Brotherhood of the Kingdom Held at Marlborough-on-Hudson, New York, August 9th to 12th, 1910. Kingston NY: R. W. Anderson & Son, 1910.

Book Articles and Periodicals

Abbott, Lyman. "The Mission of the Christian Church." *Outlook* 70/5 (12 April 1902): 911–15.

Ainslie, Peter. "The Message of the Disciples of Christ." *World Call* 1/3 (March 1919): 23–24

———. "The Rapproachement of the Churches." *Christian Century* 44/38 (22 September 1927): 1099–1101.

Ames, Edward Scribner. "A Vital Church." *Christian Century* 43/7 (18 February 1926): 218–21.

Atterbury, Anson P. "The Church Settlement." *Open Church* 1/3 (October 1897): 161–73

Baird, George B. "Church Membership in China." *Christian Century* 36/44 (28 October 1920): 13–14.

Barton, Bruce. "Nobody Is Interested in Religion." *American Magazine* 110/3(September 1930): 69, 156, 158.

Batten, Samuel Zane. "The Church as the Maker of Conscience." *American Journal of Sociology* 7/5 (March 1902): 611–28.

Beard, Gerald H. "Church Work for Men." *Open Church* 2/3 (July 1898): 324–26.

Beecher, Willis J. "The Logical Methods of Professor Kuenen." *Presbyterian Review* 3/4 (October 1882): 701–31.

Best, Nolan R. "Professor Machen's 'Christianity and Liberalism.'" *Continent* 54/21 (24 May 1923): 679–80.

Bok, Edward. "The Young Man and the Church." *Outlook* 76/16 (16 April 1904): 934–38.

Book, W. H. "New Testament Meetings instead of Modern Emotional or Mechanical Revivals." *Christian Standard* 53/11 (15 December 1917): 332–33.

Briggs, Charles A. "Critical Theories of the Sacred Scriptures in Relation to Their Inspiration: I. The Right, Duty, and Limits of Biblical Criticism." *Presbyterian Review* 2/3 (July 1881): 550–79.

———. "A Critical Study of Higher Criticism with Special Reference to the Pentateuch." *Presbyterian Review* 4/1 (January 1883): 69–130.

———. "Response to the Charges and Specifications Submitted to the Presbytery in New York." *Andover Review* 16/96 (December 1891): 623–39.

Brown, John T. "Three Years a Member of the Executive Committee (U.C.M.S.) and Why I Resigned: Third in a Series." *Christian Standard* 59/9 (1 December 1923): 5–6.

Brown, William Adams, "Millennium," in *A Dictionary of the Bible Dealing with its Language, Literature, and Contents including Biblical Theology. Vol. III: KIR-PLEIADES*, edited by James Hastings et al. (New York: Charles Scribner's Sons, 1900) 370–73.

Bryan, William Jennings. "The Bible the Word of God." *Christian Standard* 56/43 (23 July 1921): 2453–54.

———. "The Fundamentals." *Forum* 70/1 (July 1923): 1665–80.

———. "Shall the Religion of Materialism Be Taught in the Public Schools?" *Spotlight* 1/1 (September 1925): 5–8.

Buck, Pearl S. "Is There a Case for Foreign Missions?" *Harper's Monthly Magazine* 166/2 (January 1933): 143–55

Burr, Everett D. "The Methods of an Open and Institutional Church." *Open Church* 1/2 (April 1897): 97–99.

Bushnell, Horace. "The Kingdom of Heaven as a Grain of Mustard Seed," *New Englander* 2/8 (October 1844): 600–619.

Campbell, James M. "The Place of the Doctrine of the Holy Spirit in the Preaching of To-day." *Homiletic Review* 46/4 (October 1902): 297–305.

Case, Shirley Jackson. "Modern Belief About Jesus." *Biblical World* 37/1 (January 1911): 7–18.

———. "The Premillennial Menace." *Biblical World* 52/1 (January 1918): 16–23.

Coe, George A. "What's Coming in Religion? The Main Stream and the Eddies." *Christian Century* 47/52 (31 December 1930): 1619–22.

Coffin, Henry Sloane. "Why I am a Presbyterian." In *Twelve Modern Apostles and Their Creeds*, edited by Gilbert K. Chesterton, Charles L. Slattery, and Henry Sloane Coffin (New York: Duffield and Company, 1926) 53–71.

———. "That 'New' Foreign Board." *Presbyterian Tribune* 50/6 (1 November 1934): 6.

Collis, Mark. "The Crisis in Missions." *Christian Standard* 57/11 (10 December 1921): 3–4, 6.

———. "The Convention Proposed for This Fall." *Christian Standard* 62/12 (19 March 1927): 269.

Cook, J. "The Holy Spirit as the Administrator of the Church," *Our Day* 15/90 (December 1895): 288–94.

Corey, Stephen J. "Baptism on the Mission Fields." *World Call* 7/3 (March 1926): 31–34.

Crane, Caroline Bartlett. "The Story of an Institutional Church in a Small City." *Charities and the Commons* 14/6 (May 1905): 723–31.

Croker, Richard. "Tammany Hall and Democracy." *Atlantic Monthly* 165/423 (February 1892): 225–30.

Curtiss, Samuel I. "Delitzsch on the Origin and Composition of the Pentateuch." *Presbyterian Review* 3/3 (July 1882): 553–88.

Davis, James E. "Kansas City to Have Institutional Church." *Christian Standard* 53/18 (9 February 1918): 607.

Dennett, Tyler. "The Interchurch World Movement." *World's Work* 39/6 (April 1920): 569–77.

Dixon, A. C. "The Greatest Need of the Greater New York." *Homiletic Review* 38/6 (December 1899): 519–20.

Duffield, John T. "The Revision of the Confession." *Independent* 52/2685 (17 May 1900): 1179–82.

Ellis, William T. "New Era of Church Work: Ruggles St. Baptist Church, Boston." *Open Church* 2/1 (January 1898): 205–13.

Elmore, R. E. "An Intimate Review of the China Situation." *Christian Standard* 57/1 (1 October 1921): 3–5, 22–33.

Erdman, Charles R. "Premillennialism Defended Against Assailants." *Christian Workers Magazine* 16/12 (August 1916): 914–17.

———. "Dr. Erdman Speaks in Self-defense." *Presbyterian Advance* 32/1 (22 January 1925): 24

———. "The Moderator's Monthly Letter: An Ideal Church." *Presbyterian Magazine* 32/5 (May 1926): 211.

Errett, Edwin R., "The Designation Hoax." *Christian Standard* 57/34 (20 May 1922): 5–6.

———. "The Colorado Springs Convention." *Christian Standard* 58/51 (22 September 1923): 3–4, 9.

———. "The Fundamentalists' Rally." *Christian Standard* 58/38 (9 June 1923): 3–4.

———. "A Convention of Bad Faith." *Christian Standard* 61/48 (27 November 1926): 3–4, 8.

———. "A Happy Convention at Last." *Christian Standard* 62/44 (29 October 1927): 3–6.

Errett, Russell. "The 'Standard' vs. the 'General Convention.'" *Christian Standard* 52/2 (9 September 1916): 1686.

Faber, William Frederic. "The Real Question: Why We Have a Church?" *Andover Review* 9/50 (February 1888): 113–27.

Fairchild, E. M. "The Function of the Church." *American Journal of Sociology* 2/2 (September 1896): 220–33.

Fosdick, Harry Emerson. "What Christian Liberals Are Driving At?" *Ladies Home Journal* 42/1 (January 1925): 18, 128, 131.

———. "Beyond Modernism." *Christian Century* 52/49 (4 December 1935): 1549–52.

Garrett, Frank. "China Missionary Hurt by Convention Demand." *Christian Century* 37/1 (6 January 1921): 20.

Geistweit, W. H. "'The Church' and 'Church Unity': What Does My Denomination Mean by This Phrase?" *Watchman-Examiner* 9/7 (17 February 1921): 204.

Gladden, Washington. "The Church." *Chautauquan* 29/2 (May 1899): 125–30.

Gordon, A. J. "The Ministry of Women." *Homiletic Review* 7/12 (December 1894): 910–21.

Graves, Charles. "Are the Churches Declining?" *World's Work* 4/1 (May 1902): 2076–80.

Gray, James M. "The Proposed World Church Union—Is It of God or Man?" *Christian Worker's Magazine* 19/9 (May 1919): 632–36.

Griffith Thomas, W. H. "The Victorious Life I." *Bibliotheca Sacra* 76/303 (July 1919): 267–72.

———. "The Victorious Life II." *Bibliotheca Sacra* 76/304 (October 1919): 455–67.

———. "Modernism in China." *Princeton Theological Review* 19/3 (October 1921): 630–71.

———. "The Bible as an Authority." *Christian Standard* 57/42 (15 July 1922): 8.

Green, William Henry. "Professor W. Robertson Smith on the Pentateuch." *Presbyterian Review* 3/1 (January 1882): 108–56.

Hartt, Mary Brownson. "Westminster House." *Open Church* 2/3 (July 1898): 309–16.

Hayden, M. P. "Interchurch World Movement." *Christian Standard* 55/25 (20 March 1920): 7.

Helt, W. C. "The Liberalistic Shibboleth—'The Fatherhood of God and the Brotherhood of Man.'" *Homiletic Review* 35/1 (January 1898): 41–43.

Henkle, Rae D. "A Plain Statement Concerning the Interchurch World Movement." *Christian Evangelist* 57/25 (10 June 1920): 576–77, 592.

Hodge, Archibald A., and Benjamin B. Warfield. "Inspiration." *Presbyterian Review* 2/2 (April 1881): 225–60.

Horton, T. C. "The Fall of Fosdick." *The King's Business* 14/8 (August 1923): 793–96.

Hunt, T. W. "The Grace of Soul-Winning." *Homiletic Review* 42/5 (November 1901): 411–17.

Jaekel, Blair. "The Inasmuch Mission." *World's Work* 25/2 (December 1912): 205–13.

Johnson, T. H. "The Office of the Holy Spirit." *Christian Standard* 62/49 (3 December 1927): 3–4.

Lappin, S. S. "The Interchurch World Movement." *Christian Standard* 55/25 (20 March 1920): 3–4.

———. "A Turn in the Road." *Christian Standard* 62/43 (22 October 1927): 7–8.

Laws, Curtis Lee. "The Interchurch World Movement." *Watchman-Examiner* 8/3 (15 January 1920): 73–75.

———. "Convention Side Lights." *Watchman-Examiner* 8/27 (1 July 1920): 834–35.

———. "Pre-Convention Days at Des Moines." *Watchman-Examiner* 9/26 (30 June 1921): 809–13.

Leonard, Adna W. "Essentialist." *Northwestern Christian Advocate* 77/16 (21 April 1927): 372.

Macartney, Clarence Edward. "The Fall of the Colossus." *Christian Standard* 56/23 (5 March 1921): 1977–78.

———. "The Moderator's Message." *The Presbyterian* 95/2 (8 January 1925): 10.

———. "Shall Unbelief Win? An Answer to Dr. Fosdick—Part II." *Presbyterian* 92/29 (20 July 1922): 8–10.

———. "The Presbyterian Church at the Cross Roads." *Presbyterian* 95 (16 February 1925): 6–7.

McConnell, Francis J. "The Methodist Church and Fundamentalism." *Homiletic Review* 87/2 (February 1924): 94–96.

Machen, J. Gresham. "Liberalism or Christianity." *Princeton Theological Review* 20/1 (January 1922): 93–117.

———. "Does Fundamentalism Obstruct Social Progress?—The Negative." *Survey-Graphic* 52/7 (1 July 1924): 391–92, 426–27.

———. "Dr. Machen Replies to Dr. Erdman." *Presbyterian* 95/6 (5 February 1925): 20–21.

Magruder, J. W. "The Open Church and the Closed Church." *Methodist Review* 14/5 (September 1898): 769–76.

Manning, William T. "A Message to the Diocese: The Present Situation in the Church." *Churchman* 129/7 (16 February 1924): 16–17, 28–31.

Martin, W. S. "The Plymouth Brethren." *Christian Standard* 58/48 (1 September 1923): 4.

Massee, J. C. "The Churches and the Schools." *Watchman-Examiner* 9/4 (17 March 1921): 335–37.

Mathews, Shailer. "Fundamentalism and Modernism." *American Review* 2/1 (January-February 1924): 1–9.

Minton, Henry Collin. "The Holy Spirit in Christian Experience." *Homiletic Review* 42/1 (July 1901): 31–36.

Moehlmann, Conrad Henry. "The Apocalyptic Mind." *Biblical World* 54/1 (January 1920): 58–69.

Moody, Dwight L. "How to Develop and Make Pastoral Evangelism General." *Homiletic Review* 35/5 (May 1898): 407–409.

Mott, John R. "Growth of the Interchurch Movement." *Missionary Review of the World* 43/3 (March 1920): 177–78.

Nicholson, Meredith. "Should Smith Go to Church?" *Atlantic Monthly* 109/6 (June 1912): 721–33.

Niebuhr, H. Richard. "What Holds Churches Together?" *Christian Century* 43/11 (18 March 1926): 346–48.

North, Frank Mason. "Above That Which Is Written." *Open Church* 2/1 (January 1898): 256–57.

Ockenga, H. J. "Methodists among the Princeton Secession." *Essentialist* 5/6 (November 1929): 131–34.

Packard, Edward N. "Can We Know What Jesus Would Do?" *Independent* 52/2671 (8 February 1900): 393–94.

Parks, Leighton. "Intellectual Integrity." *Churchman* 129/1 (5 January 1924): 10–17.

Patton, Francis L. "The Dogmatic Aspects of Pentateuchal Criticism." *Presbyterian Review* 4/2 (April 1883): 341–410.

Phares, W. W. "The Dead Horse." *World Call* 3/5 (May 1921): 7.

Pierson, A. T. "The Problem of City Evangelization." *Missionary Review of the World* Second Series 12/6 (June 1899): 408–15.

———. "Dwight L. Moody, the Evangelist." *Missionary Review of the World* 13/2 (February 1900): 81–92.

Powell, Elmer William. "What Is a Baptist Church?" *Christian Century* 43/14 (8 April 1926): 446–47.

Powell, Lyman P. "Can the Churches Work Together?" *American Review of Reviews* 61/5 (May 1920): 517–30.

Rauschenbusch, Walter. "The Stake of the Church in the Social Movement." *American Journal of Sociology* 3/1 (July 1897): 18–30.

Richard, Charles H. "Some Needed Factors in the New Evangelism." *Bibliotheca Sacra* 62/246 (April 1905): 354–69.

Riis, Jacob. "Religion by Human Touch." *World's Work* 1/5 (March 1901): 495–505.

Riley, William B. "The Peril to Christian Education." *Christian Standard* 57/52 (22 October 1921): 3–4, 6–7.

———. "Shall the Northern Baptists Come to Peace by Compromise?" *Watchman-Examiner* 10/2 (18 May 1922): 623–24.

———. "What Is Fundamentalism?" *Bible Champion* 33/8 (August 1927): 409–16.

Sanford, E. B. "The Relation of the Church to the Kingdom of God." *Open Church* 3/1 (March 1899): 30–31.

Saunders, A. G. "The Letter Suppressed by S. J. Corey." *Spotlight* 1/1 (September 1925): 3–4.

Schofield, Joseph A. "The Rev. Joseph A. Schofield's Letter of Resignation." *Presbyterian* 105/30 (25 July 1935), 5–6.

Scudder, John L. "The People's Palace of Jersey City." *Charities Review* 1/2 (December 1891): 90–92.

Sharp, C. J. "Campaign for New Testament Evangelism." *Christian Standard* 53/11 (15 December 1917): 331–36, 402–404.

Sidwell, Irl R. "The Church: The New Testament Missionary Society." *Christian Standard* 62/43 (22 October 1927): 8.

Singiser, F. King. "The New World Movement: What It Is and What It Is Not." *Watchman-Examiner* 8/9 (26 February 1920): 285.

Sloan, Harold Paul. "The Law of the Church Not Fulfilled by the New Course of Study." *Methodist Review* 37/5 (September 1921): 792–99.

———. "Fundamentalism: Organized and Unorganized." *Christian Advocate* 98/44 (1 November 1923): 1336–37.

———. "The Value of the General Conference of 1924 for Faith," *Christian Advocate* 99/26 (26 June 1924): 806–807.

———. "Faith's Story in the General Conference of 1928." *Essentialist* 4/3–4 (June-July 1928): 49–61.

Smith, Henry Preserved. "The Critical Theories of Julius Wellhausen." *Presbyterian Review* 3/2 (April 1882): 357–88.

Snowden, James H. "The One Hundred and Thirty-first General Assembly of the Presbyterian Church in the U.S.A." *Union Seminary Review* 30/4 (July 1919): 311–12.

———. "Fundamentalism and Modernism." *Presbyterian Banner* 120/52 (28 June 1934): 7–9.

Soares, Theodore Gerald. "Baptist Polity in the New Order." *Review and Expositor* 17/3 (July 1920): 307, 311–13.

Speer, Robert E. "Where We Stand Today." *Presbyterian Magazine* 30/1 (January 1924): 12–13.

Stead, William T. "The Civic Church." *Review of Reviews* 8/4 (November 1893): 438–45.

Stelzle, Charles. "Reaching the Street-Boy." *Outlook* 72/11 (15 November 1902): 649–52.

Straton, John Roach. "Shall the Funnymonkeyists Win? An Answer to Dr. Fosdick's Sermon 'Shall the Fundamentalists Win?'" *Religious Searchlight* 1/7 (1 October 1922): 1–8.

Stuckenberg, J. H. W. "Questions: How Can I Win Men to the Church…?" *Homiletic Review* 42/6 (December 1901): 557–58.

Sweeney, Edwin S. "Autonomy of the Local Church." *Christian Standard* 62/45 (5 November 1927): 4–5.

Taylor, C. C. "The Menace of Modernism." *Christian Standard* 62/47 (19 November 1927): 3–5.

Taylor, Graham. "The Social Function of the Church." *American Journal of Sociology* 5/3 (November 1899): 305–21.

Thompson, Charles L. "Symposium on the Institutional Church." *Homiletic Review* 35/6 (December 1896): 560–64.

Tucker, Commander Booth. "The Winter Relief and Christmas Dinners of the Salvation Army." *Social Service* 6/6 (December 1902): 119–21.

Van Kirk, Robert Woods. "Organic Church Union and Structural Baptist Beliefs." *Watchman-Examiner* 7/43 (23 October 1919): 1479–80.
Vosburgh, George B. "The Mission of the Church." *Watchman* 76/44 (31 October 1895): 10–11.

Warfield, B. B. "True Church Unity: What It Is?" *Homiletic Review* 20/6 (December 1890): 483–89.

Welshimer, P. H. "New Testament Evangelism." *Christian Standard* 53/18 (2 February 1918): 3–4.

———. "Canton (O.) Church Withdraws Financial Support from U.C.M.S." *Christian Standard* 57/10 (3 December 1921), 1–2

———. "The Canton Church and the United Society." *Christian Standard* 57/53 (30 September 1922), 8.

———. "Some Things that Were Not Done at Indianapolis." *Christian Standard* 62/45 (5 November 1927): 7.

Wilkinson, William C. "Dwight L. Moody as Preacher." *Homiletic Review* 36/2 (August 1898): 110–19.

———. "Dwight L. Moody as a Man of Affairs." *Homiletic Review* 36/3 (September 1898): 201–208.

Willett, Herbert L. "Activities and Menace of Millennialism: A Study of the Dangers Implicit in the Millenarian Propaganda." *Christian Century* 35/33 (29 August 1918): 6–8.

Williams, Mosley. "The New Era of Church Work in Philadelphia." *Open Church* 1/2 (April 1897): 53–75.

Wilson, Rufus Rockwell. "The Institutional Church and Its Work." *Outlook* 54/9 (29 August 1896): 384–87.

Winslow, Florence E. "The Settlement Work of Grace Church." *Charities Review* 8/8 (October 1892): 418–25.

Books

Abbott, Lyman. *Christianity and Social Problems*. Boston: Houghton, Mifflin and
        Company, 1897.

Blackstone, William E. *Jesus Is Coming!* Chicago: Fleming H. Revell Company, 1908.

Beattys, Harry H. *Smith and the Church*. New York: Frederick A. Stokes Company,
        1915.

Bilhorn, P. P. *Soul Winning Songs for Soul Winners*. Chicago: P. P. Bilhorn Publisher,
        1896.

Booth, William. *In Darkest England and the Way Out*. London: International Head
        Quarters of the Salvation Army, 1890.

Bowne, Borden P. *The Christian Life: A Study*. Cincinnati: Curts and Jennings, 1899.

Briggs, Charles A. *Whither? A Theological Question for the Times*. New York: Charles
        Scribner's Sons, 1890.

Brookes, James H. *Israel and the Church: The Terms Distinguished as Found in the Word
        of God*. Chicago: The Bible Institute Colportage Association, no date.

Brooks, Phillips. *The Best Methods of Promoting the Spiritual Life*. New York: Thomas
        Whittaker, 1897.

Brown, William Adams. *The Essence of Christianity: A Study in the History of a
        Definition*. New York: Charles Scribner's Sons, 1906.

Broughton, Len G. *The Soul-Winning Church*. Chicago: Fleming H. Revell
        Company, 1905.

Burns, James. *Revivals: Laws and Leaders*. New York: Hodder and Stoughten, 1909.

Burr, Agnes Rush. *Russell H. Conwell: Founder of the Institutional Church in America*.
        Philadelphia: John C. Winston Company, 1905.

Bushnell, Horace. *Christian Nurture*. New Haven CT: Yale University Press, 1960.

————. *Views of Christian Nurture*. Hartford: Edwin Hunt, 1847.

————. *God in Christ*. Hartford: Brown and Parsons, 1849.

————. *The Character of Jesus: Forbidding His Possible Classification with Men*. New
        York: The Chautauqua Press, 1888.

————. *The Spirit in Man: Sermons and Selections*. Centenary edition. New York:
        Charles Scribner's Sons, 1910.

Campbell, James M. *The Indwelling Christ*. Chicago: Fleming H. Revell Company,
        1895.

————. *The Second Coming of Christ: A Message for the Times*. New York: Methodist
        Book Concern, 1919.

Caroll, H. K. *The Religious Forces of the United States: Enumerated, Classified, and
        Described*. Revised edition. New York: Charles Scribner's Sons, 1912.

Case, Shirley Jackson. *The Millennial Hope: A Phase of War-Time Thinking*. Chicago:
        University of Chicago Press, 1918.

————. *Jesus: A New Biography*. Chicago: University of Chicago Press, 1927.

Chafer, Lewis Sperry. *He That Is Spiritual*. Chicago: Fleming H. Revell Company, 1918; reprinted Chicago: Moody Press, 1943.

Chapman, J. Wilbur. *Received Ye the Holy Ghost?* Chicago: Fleming H. Revell Company, 1894.

————. *Revivals and Missions*. New York: Lentilhon & Company, 1900.

————. *Present-Day Evangelism*. Chicago: Fleming H. Revell Company, 1913.

Clarke, William Newton. *An Outline of Christian Theology*. Second edition. New York: Charles Scribner's Sons, 1898.

Coe, George A. *The Religion of a Mature Mind*. New York: Fleming H. Revell Company, 1902.

————. *Education in Religion and Morals*. New York: Fleming H. Revell Company, 1904.

Coffin, Henry Sloane. *Some Christian Convictions: A Practical Restatement in Terms of Present-Day Thinking*. New Haven: Yale University Press, 1915.

Cole, Stewart G. *The History of Fundamentalism*. New York: Richard R. Smith, Inc., 1931.

Conrad, Arcturus Z. *A Complete Account of the Great Boston Revival under the Leadership of J. Wilbur Chapman and Charles M. Alexander*. Boston: The King's Business Publishing Company, 1909.

Corey, Stephen J. *Fifty Years of Attack and Controversy: The Consequences Among Disciples of Christ*. St. Louis: Christian Board of Publication, 1953.

Crane, Stephen. *Maggie: A Girl of the Streets and Other Short Fiction*. New York: Bantam Classics, 1986.

Cumming, James Elder. *Through the Eternal Spirit: A Biblical Study on the Holy Ghost*. Chicago: Fleming H. Revell Company, 1896.

Darby, John Nelson. *The Collected Writings of J. N. Darby*. 34 volumes. Edited by William Kelly. Kensington-on-Thames: Stow Hill Bible and Tract Depot, 1957.

————. *The Letters of J. N. D. Volume 3, 1879–1882*. Sunbury PA: Believer's Bookshelf, 1971.

Dixon, A. C. *Heaven on Earth*. Greenville SC: The Gospel Hour Inc., no date.

Dixon, Jr., Thomas. *The Failure of Protestantism in New York and Its Causes*. New York: The Strauss and Rehn Publishing Co., 1896.

Doe, Walter P., editor. *Revivals: How to Promote Them*. Second edition. New York: E. B. Treat, 1895.

Dreiser, Theodore. *Sister Carrie*. New York: Bantam Books, 1982.

Eckman, George P. *When Christ Comes Again*. New York: Abingdon Press, 1917.

Ely, Richard T. *The Social Aspects of Christianity and Other Essays*. New York: Thomas Y. Crowell & Company, 1889.

Erdman, William J. *The Holy Spirit and Christian Experience*. New York: Gospel Publishing House, 1909.

Erdman, Charles R. *The Spirit of Christ: Devotional Studies in the Doctrine of the Holy Spirit.* New York: George H. Doran Company, 1926.

Finney, Charles G. *Lectures on Revivals of Religion.* Chicago: Fleming H. Revell Company, no date.

Fisher, George Park. *The Nature and Method of Revelation.* New York: Charles Scribner's Sons, 1890.

Fosdick, Harry Emerson. *Christianity and Progress.* New York: Fleming H. Revell Company, 1922.

———. *The Meaning of Faith.* New York: Association Press, 1927.

Gaebelein, Arno Clemens. *Half a Century: The Autobiography of a Servant.* New York: Publication Office of "Our Hope," 1930.

Gladden, Washington. *The Christian Pastor and the Working Church.* New York: Charles Scribner's Sons, 1914.

———. *How Much Is Left of the Old Doctrines? A Book for the People.* Boston: Houghton, Mifflin and Company, 1899.

———. *Recollections.* Boston: Houghton, Mifflin and Company, 1909.

———. *Ruling Ideas of the Present Age.* Boston: Houghton, Mifflin and Company, 1896.

———. *Social Facts and Forces.* New York: G. P. Putnam's Sons, 1897.

Gordon, A. J. *The Ministry of the Spirit.* Chicago: Fleming H. Revell Company, 1894.

Gordon, George A. *The New Epoch for Faith.* Boston: Houghton, Mifflin and Company, 1901.

Von Harnack, Adolf. *What Is Christianity?* Philadelphia: Fortress Press, 1986.

Hodges, George and John Reichert, *The Administration of an Institutional Church: A Detailed Account of the Operation of St. George's Parish in the City of New York.* New York: Harper & Brothers Publishers, 1906.

Huntington, William Reed. *The Church-Idea: An Essay Towards Unity.* Harrisburg PA: Morehouse Publishing, 1870, 2002.

———. *The Peace of the Church.* New York: Charles Scribner's Sons, 1893.

Judson, Edward. *The Institutional Church: A Primer in Pastoral Theology.* New York: Lentilhon & Company, 1899.

King, Henry Churchill. *Theology and the Social Consciousness.* New York: Macmillan Company, 1902.

Lawrence, William. *Fifty Years.* Boston: Houghton, Mifflin and Company, 1923.

Lewis, Edwin. *Jesus Christ and the Human Quest.* New York: Abingdon Press, 1924.

Mabie, Henry C. *Method in Soul-Winning: On Home and Foreign Fields.* Chicago: Fleming H. Revell Company, 1906.

Machen, J. Gresham. *Christianity and Liberalism.* Grand Rapids: William B. Eerdmans Publishing Company, 1923.

Mains, George Preston. *Premillennialism: Non-Scriptural, Non-Historic, Non-Scientific, Non-Philosophical.* New York: Abingdon Press, 1920.

Massee, J. C. *The Second Coming*. Philadelphia: Philadelphia School of the Bible, 1919.

Mathews, Shailer. *The Faith of Modernism*. New York: Macmillan Company, 1924.

Modern Eloquence: American Historical Masterpieces. 11 volumes. New York: Modern Eloquence Corporation, 1928.

Niebuhr, Reinhold. *Moral Man, Immoral Society*. New York: Charles Scribner's Sons, 1960.

Moody, Dwight L. *Secret Power, or Success in Christian Life and Work*. Chicago: Fleming H. Revell Company, 1881.

Morgan, G. Campbell. *The Spirit of God*. Chicago: Fleming H. Revell Company, 1900.

Munger, Theodore T. *The Freedom of Faith*. Eleventh edition. Boston: Houghton, Mifflin and Company, 1885.

Munhall, L. W. *The Lord's Return and Kindred Truth*. Philadelphia: E. & R. Munhall, 1888.

————. *Breakers! Methodism Adrift*. New York: Charles C. Cook, 1913.

Murray, Andrew. *The Master's Indwelling*. Chicago: Fleming H. Revell Company, 1896.

Myers, Cortland. *Why Men Do Not Go to Church*. New York: Funk and Wagnalls Company, 1899.

Niebuhr, H. Richard. *Social Sources of Denominationalism*. New York: Henry Holt and Company, 1929.

Parkhurst, Charles H. *Our Fight With Tammany*. New York: Charles Scribner's Sons, 1895; reprinted New York: Arno Press and the New York Times, 1970.

————. *The Pulpit and the Pew*. New Haven: Yale University Press, 1913.

Leighton Parks, *What Is Modernism?* New York: Charles Scribner's Sons, 1924.

Pell, Edward Leigh. *Dwight L. Moody: His Life, His Work, His Words*. Richmond VA: B. F. Johnson Publishing Co., 1900.

Pierson, A. T. *The Acts of the Holy Spirit: Being an Examination of the Active Mission and Ministry of the Spirit of God in the Acts of the Apostles*. Chicago: Fleming H. Revell Company, 1898.

————. *The Keswick Movement in Precept and Practise*. New York: Funk & Wagnalls Company, 1907.

Rainsford, William. *A Preacher's Story of His Work*. New York: The Outlook Company, 1904.

————. *The Story of a Varied Life: An Autobiography*. New York: Doubleday, Page & Company, 1922.

Rall, Harris Franklin. *Modern Premillennialism and the Christian Hope*. New York: Abingdon Press, 1920.

Rauschenbusch, Walter. *Prayers of the Social Awakening*. Boston: The Pilgrim's Press, 1909, 1910.

————. *Christianity and the Social Crisis*. New York: Macmillan Company, 1907, 1913.

————. *A Theology for the Social Gospel*. Nashville: Abingdon Press, 1917, 1945.

Religious Bodies 1916: Part 1, Summary and General Tables. Washington: Government Printing Office, 1919.

Riley, William B. *The Perennial Revival: A Plea for Evangelism*. Chicago: Winona Publishing Co., 1904.

————. *The Menace of Modernism*. New York: Christian Alliance Publishing Co., 1917.

————. *The Interchurch or the Kingdom by Violence*. Minneapolis: W. B. Riley, no date.

————. *Pastoral Problems*. New York: Fleming H. Revell Company, 1936.

Scofield, C. I. *Rightly Dividing the Word of Truth*. Neptune NJ: Loizeaux Brothers, 1896.

————. *Plain Papers on the Doctrine of the Holy Spirit*. Chicago: Fleming H. Revell Company, 1899; reprinted Grand Rapids: Baker Book House, 1969.

————, editor. *The King James Study Bible: Reference Edition*. Uhrichsville OH: Barbour Publishing, Inc., no date. [1907].

Sheldon, Charles M. *In His Steps*. Springdale PA: Whitaker House, 1979.

Sloan, Harold Paul. *Historic Christianity and the New Theology*. Louisville: Pentecostal Publishing Company, 1922.

Simpson, A. B. *The Fourfold Gospel*. Camp Hill PA: Christian Publications, 1984.

Smith, Robert Pearsall. *Holiness Through Faith: Light on the Way of Holiness*. New York: Anson D. F. Randolph & Co., 1870; reprinted in *The Devotional Writings of Robert Pearsall Smith and Hannah Whitall Smith*. Edited by Donald Dayton. New York: Garland Publishing, Inc., 1984.

Smith, Hannah Whitall. *The Christian's Secret of a Happy Life*. Boston: The Christian Witness Co., 1885; reprinted in *The Devotional Writings of Robert Pearsall Smith and Hannah Whitall Smith*. Edited by Donald Dayton. New York: Garland Publishing, Inc., 1984.

Smyth, Newman. *Passing Protestantism and Coming Catholicism*. New York: Charles Scribner's Sons, 1908.

Approaches Toward Church Unity. Edited by Newman Smyth and Williston Walker. New Haven: Yale University Press, 1919.

Snowden, James H. *Is the World Growing Better?* New York: Macmillan Company, 1919.

————. *The Coming of the Lord: Will It Be Premillennial?* Second revised edition. New York: Macmillan Company, 1919.

Speer, Robert E. *Missionary Principles and Practice*. New York: Fleming H. Revell Company, 1902.

————. *The Gospel and the New World*. New York: Fleming H. Revell Company, 1919.

Strong, Josiah. *Our Country: Its Possible Future and Its Present Crisis.* New York: The Baker & Taylor Co., 1891.

———. *The New Era or the Coming Kingdom.* New York: The Baker & Taylor Co., 1893.

———. *The Challenge of the City.* New York: The Young People's Missionary Movement of the United States and Canada, 1907.

———. *The New World Life.* New York: Doubleday, Page & Company, 1913.

———. *The New World-Religion.* Garden City NJ: Doubleday, Page & Company, 1915.

Sunday, William Ashley. *The Second Coming.* Sturgis MI: Journal Publishing Company, 1913.

de Tocqueville, Alexis. *Democracy in America.* Translated by George Lawrence. New York: Harper Perennial, 1969.

Torrey, R. A. *The Baptism of the Holy Spirit* Chicago: Fleming H. Revell Company, 1895.

———. *How to Study the Bible.* New edition. New Kensington PA: Whitaker House, 1985.

———. *How to Bring Men to Christ.* Chicago: Fleming H. Revell Company, 1910.

———. *Why God Used D. L. Moody.* Chicago: Moody Press, 1923.

———, editor. *How to Promote and Conduct a Successful Revival with Suggestive Outlines.* Louisville: Charles T. Dearing, 1901.

———, editor. *Individual Soul Winning: Its Obligation and Its Methods.* Philadelphia: Sunday School Times Company, 1906.

Trumbull, Charles Gallaudet. *The Life Story of C. I. Scofield.* New York: Oxford University Press, 1920.

Turner, Frederick Jackson. *The Frontier in American History.* Tucson: University of Arizona Press, 1986.

Warfield, B. B. *Perfectionism.* Two volumes. New York: Oxford University Press, 1931; reprinted Grand Rapids: Baker Book House, 1981.

Waters, N. McGee. *A Young Man's Religion and His Father's Faith.* Thomas Y. Crowell & Co. Publishers, 1905.

Wesley, John. *The Works of John Wesley.* Volume 11. London: Wesleyan Methodist Book Room, 1872; reprinted Peabody MA: Hendrickson Publishers, 1991.

West, Nathaniel. *The Thousand Years in Both Testaments.* Chicago: Fleming H. Revell Company, 1889.

Secondary Unpublished Manuscripts

Calderwood, Robert Charles. "The Fundamentalist Movement in the Methodist Episcopal Church." M.A. dissertation, University of Chicago, 1927.

Delnay, Robert George. "A History of the Baptist Bible Union." Th.D. dissertation, Dallas Theological Seminary, 1963.

Kim, Ki Hong. "Presbyterian Conflict in the Early Twentieth Century: Ecclesiology in the Princeton Tradition and the Emergence of Presbyterian Fundamentalism." Ph.D. dissertation, Drew University, 1983.

Secondary Articles and Book Chapters

Butler, Jonathan, "Protestant Success in the New American City, 1870–1920," in *New Directions in American Religious History*, edited by Harry S. Stout and D. G. Hart (New York: Oxford University Press, 1997) 296–333.

Clutter, Ronald T. "The Reorganization of Princeton Seminary." *Grace Theological Journal* 7/2 (Fall 1986): 179–201.

Cunningham, Floyd T. "Harold Sloan and Methodist Essentialism." *Asbury Theological Journal* 42/1 (Spring 1987): 65–76.

Gleason, Randall. "B. B. Warfield and Lewis S. Chafer on Sanctification." *Journal of the Evangelical Theological Society* 40/2 (June 1997): 241–56.

Handy, Robert. "American Baptist Polity: What's Happening and Why." *Baptist History and Heritage* 14/3 (July 1979): 12–21.

Harrell, David Edwin, "Bipolar Protestantism: The Straight and Narrow Ways," in *Re-forming the Center: American Protestantism, 1900 to the Present*, edited by Douglas Jacobsen and William Vance Trollinger (Grand Rapids: William B. Eerdmans Publishing Company, 1998): 15–30.

Hart, D. G. "J. Gresham Machen, Confessional Presbyterianism, and the History of Twentieth-Century Protestantism," in *Re-forming the Center: American Protestantism, 1900 to the Present*, edited by Douglas Jacobsen and William Vance Trollinger (Grand Rapids: William B. Eerdmans Publishing Company, 1998): 129–49.

Hiebert, Paul G. "Conversion, Culture, and Categories." *Gospel in Context* 1/4 (October 1978): 24–29.

Hughes, Richard T., "Are Restorationists Evangelicals?" in *The Variety of American Evangelicalism*, edited by Donald W. Dayton and Robert K. Johnston (Knoxville: University of Tennessee Press, 1991), 109–134.

Hughes, Richard T., "Why Restorationists Don't Fit the Evangelical Mold; Why Churches of Christ Increasingly Do," in *Re-forming the Center: American Protestantism, 1900 to the Present*, edited by Douglas Jacobsen and William Vance Trollinger (Grand Rapids: William B. Eerdmans Publishing Company, 1998): 194–213.

Jansen, Hugh M. "A Threatened Heresy Trial in the Twenties." *Anglican Theological Review* 49/1 (January 1967): 17–44.

Kragenbrink, Kevin R. "The Modernist/Fundamentalist Controversy and the Emergence of the Independent Christian Churches of Christ." *Restorationist Quarterly* 42/1 (first quarter 2000): 3–17.

Komonchak, Joseph A. "Ecclesiology and Social Theory: a Methodological Essay." *The Thomist* 45/2 (April 1981): 262–83.

Lankford, John. "Methodism 'Over the Top': The Joint Centenary Movement, 1917–1925." *Methodist History* 2/1 (October 1963): 27–37.

Muller, Dorthea R. "Josiah Strong and the Social Gospel: A Christian's Response to the City." *Journal of Presbyterian History* 39 (Summer 1961): 50–175.

Osburn, Ronald E. "The Irony of the Twentieth-Century Christian Church (Disciples of Christ): Making It to the Mainline Just at the Time of Its Disestablishment." *Mid-Stream* 28/4 (July 1989): 293–312.

Quirk, Charles E. "Origins of the Auburn Affirmation." *Journal of Presbyterian History* 53/2 (Summer 1975): 120–42.

Ripley, John W. "The Strange Story of Charles M. Sheldon's *In His Steps.*" *Kansas Historical Quarterly* 34/3 (autumn 1968): 241–65.

Rogers, Max Gray, "Charles Augustus Briggs: Heresy at Union," in *American Religious Heretics: Formal and Informal Trials*, edited by George H. Shriver (Nashville: Abingdon Press, 1966): 89–147.

Robert, Dana L., "Arthur Tappan Pierson, 1837–1911: Evangelizing the World in This Generation," in *Missions Legacies, American Society of Missions Series 19* (Marynoll NY: Orbis, 1994): 28–36.

Russell, C. Allyn. "William Bell Riley: Architect of Fundamentalism." *Minnesota History* 43/1 (Spring 1972): 14–30.

Toulouse, Mark., "Practical Concern and Theological Neglect: The UCMS and the Open Membership Controversy," in *A Case Study of Mainstream Protestantism: The Disciples' Relation to American Culture, 1880–1989*, edited by D. Newell Williams (Grand Rapids: William B. Eerdmans Publishing Company, 1991): 194–235.

Stephens, Bruce M. "Changing Conceptions of the Holy Spirit in American Protestant Theology from Jonathan Edwards to Charles G. Finney." *St. Luke's Journal of Theology* 33/3 (June 1990): 209–23.

Wacker, Grant. "The Holy Spirit and the Spirit of the Age in American Protestantism." *Journal of American History* 72/1 (June 1985): 45–62.

Secondary Books

Addison, James Thayer. *The Episcopal Church in the United States, 1789–1931.* New York: Charles Scribner's Son's, 1951.

Ahlstrom, Sydney. *A Religious History of the American People.* New Haven: Yale University Press, 1972.

Albanese, Catherine. *America: Religions and Religion*. Second edition. Belmont CA: Wadsworth Publishing Company, 1992.

Albright, Raymond W. *A History of the Protestant Episcopal Church*. New York: Macmillan Company, 1964.

Anstice, Henry. *The History of St. George's Church in the City of New York, 1752–1811–1911*. New York: Harper & Brothers Publishers, 1911.

Bainbridge, William Sims. *The Sociology of Religious Movements*. New York: Routledge, 1997.

Bebbington, David. *Evangelicalism in Modern Britain: A History from the 1730s to the 1980s*. Grand Rapids: Baker Book House, 1989.

Bederman, Gail. *Manliness and Civilization: A Cultural History of Gender and Race in the United States, 1880–1917*. Chicago: University of Chicago Press, 1995.

Bloom, Harold. *The American Religion: The Emergence of the Post-Christian Nation*. New York: Simon & Schuster, 1992.

Boyer, Paul. *Urban Masses and Moral Order in America, 1820–1920*. Cambridge: Harvard University Press, 1978, 1997.

Brereton, Virginia Lieson. *Training God's Army: The American Bible School, 1880–1940*. Bloomington: Indiana University Press, 1990.

Carpenter, Joel A. *Revive Us Again: The Reawakening of American Fundamentalism*. New York: Oxford University Press, 1997.

Cherry, Conrad. *Hurrying Toward Zion: Universities, Divinity Schools, and American Protestantism*. Bloomington: Indiana University Press, 1995.

Crutchfield, Larry V. *The Origins of Dispensationalism: The Darby Factor*. Lanham MD: University Press of America, 1992.

Curtis, Susan. *A Consuming Faith: The Social Gospel and Modern American Culture*. Baltimore: Johns Hopkins University Press, 1991.

Dayton, Donald. *Discovering an Evangelical Heritage*. New York: Harper & Row Publishers, 1976.

The Variety of American Evangelicalism, edited by Donald W. Dayton and Robert K. Johnston (Knoxville: University of Tennessee Press, 1991) 113.

DeGroot, Alfred Thomas. *The Ground of Divisions among the Disciples of Christ*. Chicago: privately printed, 1940.

Ernst, Eldon G. *Moment of Truth for American Protestantism: Interchurch Campaigns Following World War One*. Missoula MT: American Academy of Religion & Scholars Press, 1974.

Finke, Roger and Rodney Stark, *The Churching of America, 1776–1990: Winners and Losers in Our Religious Economy*. New Brunswick NJ: Rutgers University Press, 1994.

Five Views on Sanctification. Grand Rapids: Academie Books, 1987.

Furet, François. *In the Workshop of History* (*L'Atelier de l'historie*). Translated by Jonathan Mandelbaum. Chicago: University of Chicago Press, 1984.

Guelzo, Allen C. *For the Union of Evangelical Christendom: The Irony of Reformed Episcopalians.* University Park: University of Pennsylvania Press, 1994.

Gustafson, James M. *Treasure in Earthen Vessels: The Church as a Human Community.* New York: Harper & Row Publishers, 1961.

Haight, Roger. *Christian Community in History: Historical Ecclesiology.* Volume 1. New York: Continuum Press, 2004.

Handy, Robert T. *The Social Gospel in America, 1870–1920.* New York: Oxford University Press, 1966.

———. *A Christian America: Protestant Hopes and Historical Realities.* Second edition. New York: Oxford University Press, 1984.

———. *Undermined Establishment: Church-State Relations in America, 1880–1920.* Princeton: Princeton University Press, 1991.

Hatch, Nathan O. *The Democratization of American Christianity.* New Haven: Yale University Press, 1989.

Hawkins, Mike. *Social Darwinism in European and American Thought: Nature as Model and Nature as Threat.* New York: Cambridge University Press, 1997.

Henry, Carl F. H. *The Pacific Garden Mission: A Doorway to Heaven.* Grand Rapids: Zondervan Publishing House, 1942.

Hofstadter, Richard. *Social Darwinism in American Thought, 1860–1915.* Philadelphia: University of Pennsylvania Press, 1944.

Hopkins, C. Howard. *The Rise of the Social Gospel in American Protestantism, 1865–1915.* New Haven: Yale University Press, 1940.

Hunter, James Davison. *Culture Wars: The Struggle to Define America.* New York: Basic Books, 1991.

Hutchison, John A. *We Are Not Divided: A Critical and Historical Study of the Federal Council of Churches of Christ in America.* New York: Round Table Press, Inc., 1941.

Hutchison, William R. *The Modernist Impulse in American Protestantism.* Cambridge: Harvard University Press, 1976; reprint, Durham NC: Duke University Press, 1992.

———, editor. *Between the Times: The Travail of the Protestant Establishment in America, 1900–1960.* New York: Cambridge University Press, 1989.

Ironside, H. A. *A Historical Sketch of the Brethren Movement: An Account of Its Inception, Progress, Principles and Failures, and Its Lessons for Present Day Believers.* Grand Rapids: Zondervan Publishing House, 1942.

Re-forming the Center: American Protestantism, 1900 to the Present. Edited by Douglas Jacobsen and William Vance Trollinger. Grand Rapids: William B. Eerdmans Publishing Company, 1998.

Jordan, Philip D. *The Evangelical Alliance for the United States of America, 1847–1900: Ecumenism, Identity and the Religion of the Republic.* New York: The Edwin Mellen Press, 1982.

Kirby, James et. al. *The Methodists.* Westport CT: Greenwood Press, 1996.

Lindbeck, George A. *The Nature of Doctrine: Religion and Theology in a Postliberal Age.* Philadelphia: Westminster Press, 1984.

Livingstone, David N. *Darwin's Forgotten Defenders: The Encounter Between Evangelical Theology and Evolutionary Thought.* Grand Rapids: William B. Eerdmans Publishing Company, 1987.

Loetscher, Lefferts A. *The Broadening Church: A Study of the Theological Issues in the Presbyterian Church since 1869.* Philadelphia: University of Pennsylvania Press, 1954.

Longfield, Bradley J. *The Presbyterian Controversy: Fundamentalists, Modernists, and Moderates.* New York: Oxford University Press, 1991.

McAllister, Lester G., and William E. Tucker. *Journey in Faith: A History of the Christian Church (Disciples of Christ).* St. Louis: Chalice Press, 1975.

McBeth, H. Leon. *The Baptist Heritage: Four Centuries of Baptist Witness.* Nashville: Broadman Press, 1987.

McKinley, Edward H. *Marching to Glory: The History of the Salvation Army in the United States, 1880–1992.* Revised and expanded second edition. Grand Rapids: William B. Eerdmans Publishing Company, 1995.

McLoughlin, William G. *Modern Revivalism: Charles Grandison Finney to Billy Graham.* New York: The Ronald Press Company, 1959.

Magnuson, Norris. *Salvation in the Slums: Evangelical Social Work, 1865–1920.* Paperback edition. Grand Rapids: Baker Book House, 1990.

Marsden, George. *The Evangelical Mind and the New School Presbyterian Experience: A Case Study of Thought and Theology in Nineteenth Century America.* New Haven: Yale University Press, 1970.

———. *Fundamentalism and American Culture: the Shaping of Twentieth-Century Evangelicalism, 1870–1925.* New York: Oxford University Press, 1980.

Marty, Martin E. *Righteous Empire: The Protestant Experience in America.* New York: The Dial Press, 1970.

———. *Modern American Religion Volume 1: The Irony of It All, 1893–1919.* Chicago: University of Chicago Press, 1986.

———. *Modern American Religion Volume 2: The Noise of Conflict, 1919–1941.* Chicago: University of Chicago Press, 1991.

May, Henry. *The End of American Innocence: A Study of the First Years of Our Time, 1912–1917.* New York: Columbia University Press, 1992.

Meeks, Wayne A. *The First Urban Christians: The Social World of the Apostle Paul.* New Haven: Yale University Press, 1983.

Miller, Timothy. *Following In His Steps: A Biography of Charles M. Sheldon.* Knoxville: University of Tennessee Press, 1987.

Moberg, David O. *The Great Reversal: Evangelism and Social Concern.* Revised edition. Philadelphia: J. B. Lippincott Co., 1977.

Moltmann, Jürgen. *The Crucified God: The Cross of Christ as the Foundation and Criticism of Christian Theology.* New York: Harper & Row Publishers, 1974.

Moore, R. Laurence. *Religious Outsiders and the Making of Americans*. New York: Oxford University Press, 1986.

Morgan, Edmund. *Visible Saints: The History of a Puritan Idea*. Ithaca NY: Cornell University Press, 1963.

Moulton, Elizabeth. *St. George's Church, New York*. New York: The Rector, Church Wardens, and Vestrymen of St. George's Church, 1964.

Noll, Mark A. *A History of Christianity in the United States and Canada*. Grand Rapids: William B. Eerdmans Publishing Company, 1992.

Pahl, Jon. *Paradox Lost: Free Will and Political Liberty in American Culture, 1630–1760*. Baltimore: Johns Hopkins Press, 1992.

Ryrie, Charles Caldwell. *Dispensationalism Today*. Chicago: Moody Press, 1965.

Sandeen, Ernest R. *The Roots of Fundamentalism: British and American Millenarianism 1800–1930*. Chicago: University of Chicago Press, 1970.

Schillebeeckx, Edward. *Church: The Human Story of God*. New York: Crossroad Publishing Company, 1993.

Schlesinger, Arthur Meier. *The Rise of the City, 1878–1898*. Chicago: Quadrangle Books, Inc., 1961.

Schmidt, Jean Miller. *Souls or the Social Order: The Two-Party System in American Protestantism*. Brooklyn: Carlson Publishing, Inc., 1991.

Smith, Gary Scott. *The Search for Social Salvation: Social Christianity and America, 1880–1925*. Lanham MD: Lexington Books, 2000.

Smith, Timothy L. *Called Unto Holiness: The Story of the Nazarenes, the Formative Years*. Kansas City MO: Nazarene Publishing House, 1962.

———. *Revivalism and Social Reform*. Baltimore: Johns Hopkins University Press, 1980.

Smylie, James H. *A Brief History of the Presbyterians*. Louisville: Geneva Press, 1996.

Stackhouse, Jr., John G., editor. *Evangelical Ecclesiology: Reality or Illusion?* Grand Rapids: Baker Academic, 2003.

Stewart, William Rhinelander. *Grace Church and Old New York*. New York: E. P. Dutton & Company, 1924.

Szasz, Ferenc Morton. *The Divided Mind of Protestant America, 1880–1930*. University: University of Alabama Press, 1982.

Troeltsch, Ernst. *The Social Teachings of Christian Churches*. Volume 1. Translated by Olive Wyon. Chicago: University of Chicago Press, 1981.

Trollinger, William Vance. *God's Empire: William Bell Riley and Midwestern Fundamentalism*. Madison: University of Wisconsin Press, 1990.

United States Bureau of the Census. *Historical Statistics of the United States, Colonial Times to 1970*. Washington: US Deptartment of Commerce, 1975.

Warren, Heather A. *Theologians of a New World Order: Reinhold Niebuhr and the Christian Realists, 1920–1948*. New York: Oxford University Press, 1997.

Webber, Robert E. *The Younger Evangelicals: Facing the Challenges of the New World*. Grand Rapids: Baker Books, 2002.

Weber, Max. *The Protestant Ethic and the Spirit of Capitalism.* Translated by Talcott Parsons. New York: Charles Scribner's Sons, 1958.

———. *Basic Concepts in Sociology.* Translated by H. P. Secher. London: Peter Owen, 1962.

Weber, Timothy P. *Living in the Shadow of the Second Coming: American Premillennialism, 1875–1925.* New York: Oxford University Press, 1979.

Wiebe, Robert H. *The Search for Order, 1877–1920.* American Century series. New York: Wang and Hill, 1968.

Williams, D. Newell, editor. *A Case Study of Mainstream Protestantism: The Disciples' Relation to American Culture, 1880–1989.* Grand Rapids: William B. Eerdmans Publishing Company, 1991.

Wilson, Madele and A. B. Simpson, *Henry Wilson: One of God's Best.* New York: Alliance Press Company, 1908.

Wuthnow, Robert. *Restructuring of American Religion: Society and Faith since World War II.* Princeton: Princeton University Press, 1988.

———. *After Heaven: Spirituality in America since the Late 1950s.* Berkley: University of California Press, 1998.

Zarfas, Fred C. *Mel Trotter: A Biography.* Grand Rapids: Zondervan Publishing House, 1950.

INDEX

Abbott, A. L., 206
Abbott, Lyman (1835-1922), 17, 46, 47
Africa Inland Mission, 88
Ahlstrom, Sydney, 149-150
Ainslie, Peter (1867-1934), 225-226, 232
Albanese, Catherine, 148
Alexander, Charles M. (1867-1920), 57, 137.
Alexander, Maitland (1867-1940), 266
Allis, Oswald T. (1880-1973), 266
Ames, Edward Scribner (1870-1958), 213, 226, 227, 232
Amillennialism, 112
Anderson, Frederick L. (1862-1938), 191
Armstrong, H. A., 118
Atlanta Christian College, 236
Atterbury, Anson Phelps (1854-1931), 51
Auburn Affirmation, 248-251
Augustine of Hippo (354-430), 111-112

Bainbridge, William Sims, 5
Baker, Gordon H., 208-209
Baptist Bible Union, 199-201, 207-209; conflict with Baptist Fundamentals Conference, 201
Baptists, see Northern Baptist Convention
Barnes, Lemuel Call (1854-1938), 206
Batten, Samuel Zane (1859-1925), 108
Beattys, Harry H. (b. 1860), 45

Bebbington, David, 88
Beecher, Henry Ward (1813-1887), 33fn.11, 71
Belden, F. O., 205
Berkley Temple (Boston), 37-39
Best, Nolan R. (b. 1871), 244-245, 247, 248, 250
Bethany College (PA), 40, 54
Bethany Presbyterian Church (Philadelphia), 39-40, 245
Bible Schools, 89
Bible, see Scripture
Bible League of North America, 177, 179
Bible Presbyterian Church, 267
Bible Union of China, 241
Birney, W. N., 220
Blanchard, Charles (1848-1925), 159, 162
Bliss, Phillip Paul (1838-1876), 137
Book, Jr., W. H. (1898-1965), 219
Booth, Catherine Mumford (1829-1890), 60
Booth, William (1829-1912), 60-61, 89
Bowne, Borden Parker (1847-1910), 102, 103-105
Brent, Charles H. (1843-1934), 183
Briggs, Charles Augustus (1841-1913), 89-91, 109; on ecumenism, 109; on Holy Spirit, 90-91
Briney, J. B. (1839-1927), 226
Brookes, James Hall (1830-1897), 90, 113, 118-120; on the Church, 119
Brooks, Phillips (1835-1893), 98-99, 107
Brotherhood of the Kingdom, 139